BALL IN MY HANDS

BALL IN MY HANDS

Essays on Black Athletes, Race, and American Culture

DAVID K. WIGGINS

With a Foreword by Damion L. Thomas

SPORT AND POPULAR CULTURE
Brian M. Ingrassia, Series Editor

The University of Tennessee Press
Knoxville

Copyright © 2025 by The University of Tennessee Press / Knoxville.
All Rights Reserved. Manufactured in the United States of America.
FIRST EDITION.

Library of Congress Cataloging-in-Publication Data

Names: Wiggins, David Kenneth, 1951- author. | Thomas, Damion L., author of foreword.
Title: Ball in my hands : essays on Black athletes, race, and American culture / David K. Wiggins, with a foreword by Damion L. Thomas. Other titles: Essays on Black athletes, race, and American culture
Description: First edition. | Knoxville : The University of Tennessee Press, [2025] | Series: Sport and popular culture / Brian M. Ingrassia, series editor | Includes bibliographical references and index. |
Summary: "Intended for the Sport and Popular Culture series, this is a collection of previously published essays from scholar David Wiggins all centered around the history of black athletes. Essays include an exploration of black athletes during segregation, racism and Olympic athletes, and a look at contemporary black athletes, including the late Kobe Bryant. Wiggins includes a new introduction to the work and will be securing a foreword from Damion Thomas, curator for the Smithsonian's National Museum of African American History and Culture"
—Provided by publisher.
Identifiers: LCCNN 2025005758 (print) | LCCN 2025005759 (ebook) | ISBN 9781621909347 (paperback) | ISBN 9781621909361 (adobe pdf) | ISBN 9781621909354 (Kindle edition)
Subjects: LCSH: African Americans—Sports—History. | African American athletes—History. | Racism in sports—United States—History. | Public opinion—United States. | Stereotypes (Social psychology) in sports. | African Americans—Attitudes. | United States—Race relations—History. | Sports—Anthropological aspects—United States. | Sports—Sociological aspects—Case studies.
Classification: LCC GV583 .W544 2025 (print) | LCC GV583 (ebook) | DDC 796.089/96073—dc23/eng/20250212
LC record available at https://lccn.loc.gov/2025005758
LC ebook record available at https://lccn.loc.gov/2025005759

*To Finn, Palmer, and Daphne,
my three beautiful and spirited grandchildren
who give me hope for the future.*

CONTENTS

Foreword *Damion L. Thomas* — ix
Acknowledgments — xiii

Introduction — 1

1. Charles Holston Williams: Hamptonian Loyalist and Champion of Racial Uplift through Physical Education, Dance, Recreation, and Sport — 7

2. Creating Order in Black College Sport: The Lasting Legacy of the Colored Intercollegiate Athletic Association — 33
   With Chris Elzey

3. The Biggest "Classic" of Them All: The Howard and Lincoln Thanksgiving Day Football Games, 1919-1929 — 59

4. With All Deliberate Speed: High School Sport, Race, and *Brown v. Board of Education* — 85

5. Milt Campbell: Olympic Decathlon Champion "Famous for Not Being Famous" — 107

6. "Star Maker": George Powles, McClymonds High School, and the Youth of West Oakland — 129

7. Vince Matthews, Wayne Collett, and the Forgotten Disruption in Munich — 157

8. Symbols of Possibility: Arthur Ashe, Black Athletes, and the Writing of *A Hard Road to Glory* — 185

9. "The Struggle That Must Be": Harry Edwards, Sport, and the Fight for Racial Equality — 211

10. Kobe Bryant's Second Act: A Brief but Beautiful Post-Basketball Life — 237

11. "The Color of My Writing": Reflections on Studying the Interconnection among Race, Sport, and American Culture — 263

Index — 283

FOREWORD

I first became acquainted with David K. Wiggins's work in the spring of 1998: a pivotal time in my development as a scholar. As a History PhD student at the University of California, Los Angeles (UCLA), I had recently made the decision to write my dissertation about the role of sports in the Civil Rights Movement; however, when I shared my plan with my advisor, it was met with a lukewarm response. Despite its importance in US history throughout the twentieth century, sports had not been a major focus of intellectual engagement; for example, during my undergraduate years at UCLA in the early 1990s, there was not a single course taught on the historical, cultural, and social significance of sports on campus. As I look back, it is still a bit perplexing. At the time, UCLA had won more national championships than any other university and had a storied history of athletes and coaches using sports for social change, including Kareem Abdul-Jabbar (then known as Lew Alcindor), Arthur Ashe, Jackie Robinson, Florence Griffith Joyner, Jackie Joyner-Kersee, and John Wooden.

After meeting with my advisor, I was less excited by my decision but determined to move forward. I went to the library and checked out every book that I could find on sports. I left the library with forty books and decided to read them all, starting with those that had been most recently published. As it turns out, 1997 was a watershed year for pathbreaking sports history books. Over twenty-five years later, the following books still influence how I think, write, study, and talk about sports: *Jackie Robinson: A Biography* by Arnold Rampersad; *Darwin's Athletes: How Sport Has Damaged Black America and Preserved the Myth of Race* by John Hoberman; and *Glory Bound: Black Athletes in a White America* by David K. Wiggins. While I disagreed with the arguments in Hoberman's book, it was influential because it revealed how important it was to engage with this topic. Rampersad's and Wiggins's books provided me with a model for how to produce engaging yet accessible historical narratives that help contextualize sport within the contemporary moment.

For me, *Glory Bound*'s groundbreaking collection of eleven essays served as a superb introduction to sports history as a legitimate area of study. With essays focused on slavery, segregation, integration, and then-contemporary debates surrounding the alleged biological superiority of African American athletes, this work proved to be a crucial introduction to a vast array of topics one could explore. Moreover, Wiggins's skillful argumentation, research depth, and ability to connect sports to contemporary cultural controversies served as a model for me as I began my career.

I first met David—or Dave, as I grew to know him—in 2004 when I attended the North American Society for Sport History (NASSH) Conference in Asilomar, California. NASSH is a tight-knit group of scholars that universally respect and admire Dave's work and his collegial nature. I could not have known that Dave and I would develop such a close working relationship. When I was named the Museum Curator of Sports for the Smithsonian National Museum of African American History and Culture in 2014, I knew that I wanted Dave to serve on my scholarly advisory committee.

As I began to curate the exhibition, I knew that I did not want the gallery to be a hall of fame: a collection of stories just focused on sports-related statistics and victories. I also didn't want the gallery to be seen as the "toy department" of the museum: a place where visitors would come to avoid the museum's engagement with the unvarnished truths of American history. I wanted to create a gallery where athletes, games, and teams were entry points into larger conversations focused on the African American struggle for greater rights and freedoms. Hence, the gallery had to be deeply invested in the question posed by the Trinidadian scholar, C. L. R. James, who famously asked, "What do they know of cricket who only cricket know?" Through this question, James pointed out that those who are only interested in understanding sport through the lens of performance on the field failed to grasp the ways that sports shape our worldview, our sense of fairness and opportunity, as well as our perceptions of our own countries. Similarly, I have always believed that the sports gallery's role is not principally about telling sports history but rather telling African American history through the lens of sports. As I shaped this vision, Dave's insight, feedback, and guidance was incredibly helpful.

Now that the museum has been open for almost ten years, I have had the opportunity to reflect on this journey, a journey that began with checking out those forty books in 1998. For me, choosing to write the history of African Americans through the lens of sports has been incredibly rewarding and awe-inspiring. My hope for *Ball in My Hands: Essays on Black Athletes, Race, and American Culture* is that it will serve as an inspiration, guide, and benchmark for a new generation of scholars similarly to how *Glory Bound: Black Athletes in a White America* has been those things for me.

DAMION L. THOMAS
National Museum of African American History and Culture

ACKNOWLEDGMENTS

I would like to thank several people who have contributed in various ways to this project. Chris Elzey, a good friend and former colleague at George Mason University, provided suggestions and cogent comments on earlier drafts of many of the chapters in this book and is co-author with me on one of them. This book would not have been possible without his assistance and expertise. Damion L. Thomas, Curator of Sports at the Smithsonian's National Museum of African American History and Culture (NMAAHC) in Washington, DC, was kind enough to write the foreward to this book and has done as much as anyone I know, through his own writings and position at the NMAAHC, to make public the history of the African American experience in sport. I would also like to express my appreciation to Thomas Wells, Associate Director of the The University of Tennessee Press, and Brian M. Ingrassia, associate professor of history at West Texas A&M University and editor of the Press's Sport and Popular Culture series, for their enthusiastic endorsement of this book and support of sport history more generally. Lastly, I would like to thank my wife Brenda for her unwavering support and reminding me of the joys of living on the central coast of California and watching the sun dip into the Pacific each day.

INTRODUCTION

In 1997 I published eleven of my essays in a book titled *Glory Bound: Black Athletes in a White America*. Ten of the essays were previously published as either articles or book chapters and one was original to the collection. The essays range far and wide in terms of topics and time periods, beginning with a piece on the play of slave children in the early nineteenth century and ending with an assessment of the writing life of Edwin Bancroft Henderson, noted physical educator, civil rights activist, and chronicler of African American athletes. In between these two pieces are essays on such topics as sportswriter Wendell Smith and his campaign to include Blacks in Organized Baseball, Muhammad Ali's relationship to the Nation of Islam, the revolt of Black athletes on predominantly White university campuses during the late 1960s and early 1970s, and history of the debate over supposed Black athletic superiority.

Importantly, the book was published during a period in which African American athletes were receiving increased popular interest as well as scholarly attention. The previous decade and a half were particularly noteworthy for the number of quality books published on African Americans in sport. Spurred by the growth of sport history as an academic disciplinary area of study, including the founding of organizations and teaching of university courses devoted to the subject as well as a fascination with Black life and history more generally, a plethora of outstanding biographies of African American athletes, monographs on Negro League Baseball, and one survey text on the Black athletic experience in sport, highlighted the works published during the 1980s and early 1990s.[1]

The same year that *Glory Bound* appeared also saw the publication of John Hoberman's, *Darwin's Athletes: How Sport Has Damaged Black America and Preserved the Myth of Race* (1997) and Arnold Rampersad's, *Jackie Robinson: A Biography* (1997).[2] Decidedly different books, Rampersad's biography of Robinson was highly praised for its research and intimate details of the life of modern organized baseball's first Black player, while Hoberman's monograph was positively reviewed by some for its conceptualization of the African American experience in sport and harshly condemned by others, particularly many Black academicians, for its contention that the undue emphasis placed on sport by African Americans had done irreparable damage to their community.³ Be that as it may, the Hoberman and Rampersad monographs garnered enormous publicity and may have drawn some attention away from and even diminished sales of *Glory Bound,* yet the book received very positive reviews and has been frequently read and cited. In *History: Reviews of New Books,* Phil Vaughn wrote that *Glory Bound* "will stand on its own merits because it is the only work that covers the subject in such an incisive and coherent manner. . . . The book should appeal to anyone interested in American social, intellectual, and sports history."⁴ Rob Ruck wrote in the *Journal of American History,* that "*Glory Bound* will serve as a training manual for students in sport history, especially those focusing on the complex relationship of race to sport."⁵

This volume, with the subtitle, "*Ball in my Hands*" from Kobe Bryant's 2015 Academy Award-winning poem "Dear Basketball," consists of, as in *Glory Bound* some twenty-seven years ago, eleven essays I previously published as either articles in scholarly journals or book chapters from notable anthologies. One of the essential differences between this volume and *Glory Bound* is that it covers the African American experience in sport from the early twentieth century onward. Unlike *Glory Bound,* this volume does not delve into the pattern of sport among African Americans during the nineteenth century. Another essential difference between this volume and *Glory Bound* is that it includes essays emanating from a broader range of publications. While Glory Bound includes five essays alone from the *Journal of Sport History* along with two book chapters, one original essay, and three essays from three different scholarly journals, "Ball in my Hands" consists of two book chapters and nine essays from six different scholarly journals, including two each from *The International Journal of the History of Sport, Journal of Sport History,* and *The Journal of African American History.*

Yet another important difference between this volume and *Glory Bound* is that it includes essays covering in greater depth the experiences of African Americans at the interscholastic level of competition. I view this as a particularly important addition to the scholarly literature since much of the work on African American athletes has been completed on their involvement in college and professional sport. Last, but certainly not least, an essential difference between this volume and *Glory Bound* is that there is much more information provided on those separate or "parallel" sports teams, leagues, and organizations that were established in the African American community behind the walls of segregation during the first half of the twentieth century. Although Negro League Baseball was the most famous of these institutions, vibrant and culturally significant athletic programs were also established at historically Black colleges and universities (HBCUs) as well as outside the confines of college campuses in such sports as tennis, golf, basketball, football, and bowling. These programs were significant because they provided African Americans an opportunity to satisfy their competitive impulses but were perhaps most important in that they fostered a sense of racial pride, contributed to community building, and illustrated business acumen and organizational skills and self-reliance.

The first essay in the volume examines the career of Charles Holston Williams, a longtime physical educator, coach, and athletic administrator at Hampton Institute (now Hampton University) who believed strongly, like so many at HBCUs, in the power of sport to develop character and serve as a form of racial uplift. The last essay in the collection is largely an autobiographical account in which I reflect on my experiences as a White scholar who spent his entire thirty-eight years in academia, including ten years at Kansas State University and twenty-eight years at George Mason University, analyzing and writing about the African American experience in sport. Sandwiched between these two essays are nine others ranging from a piece on Olympic decathlon gold medalist Milt Campbell and biography of activist scholar Harry Edwards to an assessment of the Howard University and Lincoln University Thanksgiving Day football classic and analysis of Kobe Bryant's short-lived but remarkable post-basketball career.

Each of the essays in the volume hold out special meaning to me and I am proud to have written them. There is not one essay I would change in any substantive way, satisfied to let each of them stand on their own without apology. Notwithstanding that fact, I am someone who re-reads and critically assesses everything I have written. I am not an academician who finishes a project and never looks back to reexamine writing style, analyses and interpretations that have been made, and types of sources that have been utilized. I also take very seriously the external evaluations of essays and book manuscripts I have submitted for publication. This approach has proved effective for me over the years, providing needed context for upcoming projects that hopefully show improvement and are more sophisticated than those that have come before. Although not always the easiest thing to do, the key for me as a writer is not to take criticism too personally, recognize the enormous value of external reviews, and tirelessly forge ahead by figuratively peeling off, as I have noted previously, each layer of the onion to get at the core of the interconnection among race, sport, and American culture. In large part, experience, which I now attach far more importance to since entering my Autumn years, has taught me that there is no substitute for taking seriously the opinions of others, even if they are diametrically opposed to my own, and heeding the advice of those from different backgrounds. I believe my experience, however, has also provided me a level of discernment as well as confidence that has allowed for more nuance, style, and refinement in my work.

If asked my favorite essay in the volume, I would probably choose the last one in which I muse about being a White academician focused on studying race and sport. Writing the essay, which I chose to subtitle "The Color of my Writing," forced me to think deeply about how race had impacted my life and what led me to concentrate almost exclusively on investigating the experiences of African Americans in sport. With the obvious advantage of hindsight, it became clear to me growing up that I had lived a privileged existence and did not have to experience the everyday slights and racially discriminatory practices lodged against African Americans. I did not have to confront racial epithets, have someone question my character and work ethic merely because of the color of my skin, and did not have to worry about where I would get my next haircut or whether I would be pulled over in my car by police for no apparent reason. With the obvious advantage of hindsight, it also became clear to me, for reasons I am still not exactly sure, that from a very early age I was always very aware of the negative consequences of racial discrimination and matters of inequality more generally and that at some point in time while pursuing my advanced degrees realized that if we want to thoroughly understand the history of American sport it is imperative race be included in the analysis and that the analysis be undertaken by serious scholars of all races and backgrounds. If this approach is not taken, how else are we to comprehend such concepts as the socialization into sport, fairness in sport, and mobility in sport as well as how sport is intertwined with education, politics, religion, business, and other societal institutions?

Tellingly, while "The Color of my Writing," is not my most frequently cited work, I have probably had more people express to me their appreciation for the piece than anything I have ever written. I assume it has much to do with the autobiographical nature of the essay, a genre that seemingly resonates so deeply with so many people. With that said, my hope is that readers of this volume will gain a better grasp of the many barriers that African Americans had to overcome to participate in sport at the highest levels of competition. At the same time, I also hope that readers of this volume will come away with more of an appreciation of what sport has meant to those African American athletes who have graced this country's playing fields and the legion of both Black and White fans who have had the privilege of observing and rooting for them over the years. I hope, moreover, that readers of this volume will be encouraged to conduct their own investigations into the topic while at once being motivated to explore in greater depth the excellent scholarship of my many academic colleagues who have added immeasurably to our understanding of the African American experience in sport through their articles, many book chapters, anthologies, and monographs during the last couple of decades. There is now a much larger number of serious scholars who are examining the experiences of African Americans in sport and the interconnection between race, sport, and American culture than there were when I first began my academic career over four decades ago. Thankfully, I am just one of many academicians who recognize the importance of a topic that promises to become even more crucial because of the continual funneling of large numbers of African Americans into selected sports and persistent divisiveness in the United States and around the world resulting from inequality, racism, and discriminatory practices.[6]

Notes

1. See for example: Jules Tygiel, *Baseball's Great Experiment: Jackie Robinson and His Legacy* (New York: Oxford University Press, 1983); Janet Bruce, *The Kansas City Monarchs: Champions of Black Baseball* (Lawrence: University Press of Kansas, 1985); Randy Roberts, *Papa Jack: Jack Johnson and the Era of White Hopes* (New York: Free Press, 1983); Chris Mead, *Champion: Joe Louis, Black Hero in White America* (New York: Scribner's, 1985); William J. Baker, *Jesse Owens: An American Life* (New York: Free Press, 1986); Rob Ruck, *Sandlot Seasons: Sport in Black Pittsburgh* (Urbana: University of Illinois Press, 1987); Donn Rogosin, *Invisible Men: Life in Baseball's Negro Leagues* (New York: Athenaeum, 1987); Joseph T. Moore, *Pride Against Prejudice: The Biography of Larry Doby* (Westport, CT: Greenwood, 1988); Andrew Ritchie, *Major Taylor: The Extraordinary Career of a Champion Bicycle Racer* (San Francisco: Bicycle Books, 1988); Arthur Ashe, *A Hard Road to Glory: A History of the African American Athlete* (New York: Warner Books, 1988); and David W. Zang, *Fleet Walker's Divided Heart: The Life of Baseball's First Black Major Leaguer* (Lincoln: University of Nebraska Press, 1995).

2. *Darwin's Athletes* was published by Houghton Mifflin and *Jackie Robinson* by Knopf.

3. Ten years after the publication of Hoberman's book Jeffrey Sammons, now professor emeritus of history at New York University, organized a gathering of

African American scholars at his home institution to discuss the merits and ramifications of *Darwin's Athletes*. The participants were generally highly critical of the book for its lack of historical context and broad generalizations, among other things. See Ronald Roach, "Black Scholars on Sport: Controversial Book Brings Black Intellectuals Together to Discuss Whether African Americans Are Preoccupied with Sports-John Hoberman," "Darwin's Athletes: How Sport Has Damaged Black America and Preserved the Myth of Race," *Diverse Issues in Higher Education*, July 12, 2007, np, https://www.diverseeducation.com/sports/article/15084580/.

4. Phil H. Vaughn, Review of Glory Bound: Black Athletes in a White America, *History: Reviews of New Books* 26:2 (1998), 64, https://DOI:1080/03612759.1998.10527973

5. Rob Ruck, Review of *Glory Bound: Black Athletes in a White America*, *Journal of American History*, 84:4 (March 1998), 1473, https://DOI.org/10.2307/2568104

6. The last couple of decades has seen some terrific work completed on the African American experience in sport. Some of the most notable of these works are Damion L. Thomas, *Globetrotting: African American Athletes and Cold War Politics* (Urbana, IL: University of Illinois Press, 2012); Jennifer H. Lansbury, *A Spectacular Leap: Black Women Athletes in Twentieth-Century America* (Fayetteville, AR: The University of Arkansas Press, 2014); Donald Spivey, *If You Were Only White: The Life of Leroy Satchel Paige* (Columbia, MO: University of Missouri Press, 2012); Rita Liberti and Maureen M. Smith, *(Re) Presenting Wilma Rudolph* (Syracuse, NY: Syracuse University Press, 2015); Jaime Schultz, *Moments of Impact: Injury, Racialized Memory, and Reconciliation in College* Football (Lincoln, NE: University of Nebraska Press, 2016); Louis Moore, *I Fight for a Living: Boxing and the Battle for Black Manhood, 1880–1915* (Urbana, IL: University of Illinois Press, 2017); Louis Moore, *We Will Win the Day: The Civil Rights Movement, the Black Athlete, and the Quest for Equality* (Lexington, KY: University of Kentucky Press, 2021); Derrick E. White, *Blood, Sweat, and Tears: Jake Gaither, Florida A&M, and the History of Black College Football* (Chapel Hill: University of North Carolina Press, 2019); Cat M. Ariail, *Passing the Baton: Black Women Track Stars and American Identity* (Urbana, IL: University of Illinois Press, 2020); Howard Bryant, *The Heritage: Black Athletes, A Divided America, and the Politics of Patriotism* (Boston: Beacon Press, 2018); Randy Roberts and Johnny Smith, *Blood Brothers: The Fatal Friendship Between Muhammad Ali and Malcolm X* (New York: Basic Books, 2016); and Jason Winders, *George Dixon: The Short Life of Boxing's First Black World Champion, 1870–1908* (Fayetteville, AR: The University of Arkansas Press, 2021).

CHARLES HOLSTON WILLIAMS

Hamptonian Loyalist and Champion of
Racial Uplift through Physical Education,
Dance, Recreation, and Sport

Charles Holston Williams was an extraordinarily gifted man whose entire life was devoted to the promotion of physical education, dance, recreation, and sport during the first half of the twentieth century and the years immediately following. Highly intelligent, modest, hard-working, entrepreneurial, loyal, and committed to improving the conditions and advancing the causes of African Americans, Williams was a faculty member for over forty years at Hampton Institute, the famous HBCU (Historically Black Colleges and Universities) founded in 1868 by Samuel Armstrong Chapman with the assistance of the American Missionary Association.

He set up a model physical education and athletic program at Hampton Institute based on the latest pedagogical principles regarding dance, recreation, and sport. In 1912, just two years after taking his full-time position at Hampton Institute, Williams became one of the founding members of the Colored (now Central) Intercollegiate Athletic Association (CIAA), the oldest sports organization among HBCUs. In 1934 he established the Hampton Institute Creative Dance Group, the first national touring group of dancers consisting of college students.

He supplemented his involvement with the CIAA and Creative Dance Group with a prolific writing life and a plethora of service and professional contributions both on the Hampton campus and beyond. Despite his many and varied accomplishments, relatively little has been written about Williams and what has been published deals primarily with his dance group.[1]

This essay attempts to rectify this gap in the literature by addressing all facets of Williams's life and career. A more robust analysis reveals the fact that Williams's basic ethos as a highly educated African American was to serve the Black community and contribute to racial uplift by embodying respectability in all aspects of his life. Like many other Blacks of his social class and educational background who lived amid the rigid racial segregation of the first half of the twentieth century, Williams believed that education, achievements, and marks of propriety could help refute notions of Black inferiority while at once improving the economic and moral conditions of African Americans. Central to his brand of racial uplift was an emphasis on and recognition of the importance of physical education, dance, recreation, and sport. Involvement in these popular movement forms were important marks of personal distinction that could contribute, among other things, to the development of positive Black identities and more integral role for Blacks in American society. Williams's efforts at racial uplift came with inevitable struggles as he constantly, like other African Americans, had to balance group loyalty, democratic principles, and integrationist ambitions. Ultimately, however, Williams fight for racial uplift was extraordinarily impactful, largely resulting from his intimate involvement in a very diverse number of human movement forms, some of them characterized by heightened masculinity and the others with a more aesthetic dimension.[2]

FROM KENTUCKY TO HAMPTON INSTITUTE

Charles Holston Williams was born on January 25, 1886, in Kentucky. According to both the passenger list of the *SS Noordam* which carried him back to New York following World War I and his World War II draft registration card that were found in the National Archives, Williams's place of birth was Camp Nelson, the historic grounds where thousands of slaves who had joined Union forces during the Civil War were stationed and then released following the bitter and deadly conflict.[3] He may have been a descendant of slaves stationed at Camp Nelson, although there is no one with his surname buried at the Camp Nelson cemetery and nowhere in the historical record does he mention his parents. The failure to mention his parents is not surprising since Williams never divulged much, at least in the written records, about his family and personal life. He kept copious notes and corresponded frequently with colleagues, friends and business associates, but no letters apparently exist between him and his wife (Alma) of many years and the two had no children of their own. The closest Williams comes to talking about family matters are letters he wrote to relatives he was helping to support financially in some way. As well-known as he would become and perhaps largely because of it, Williams always remained reluctant to divulge personal information and sensitive to taking up others' time with his private concerns.

The lack of information about Williams's birth parents is also true for his preadolescent years. No information exists as to how he spent his childhood and about those significant others who might have shaped his identity and nurtured him during his earliest years. We do know, however, that at the age of eighteen Williams enrolled in 1904 at Berea College, the small liberal arts institution in Kentucky founded in 1855 by Reverend John G. Fee who fashioned the school after Oberlin College in Ohio, which had been integrally involved in the anti-slavery movement and always open to students irrespective of race. Exactly why he chose Berea is unknown, but we do know why he left. After only one year at the institution, Williams was forced to leave because of the passage of the Day Law which forbade Black and White students in the state from attending the same institution.[4]

After being forced to leave Berea, Williams chose to enroll in Hampton Institute, the prestigious Virginia HBCU known largely for its education of both African American and Native American students. Williams excelled as an all-around athlete at the institution and in 1909 graduated with a degree in painting. The following year, he was hired as Physical Director (by 1930 holding the title Director of Athletics and Chairman of the Department of Physical Education), a position he would hold, with the exception of two years serving in World War I and one year and several summers in graduate school, for the next forty-one years. Although a degree in painting would not portend it, Williams's love of sport and human movement and experience as an athlete augured well for a successful career in physical education and athletics. He also pursued a path sometimes taken by other African Americans during this period who aspired to be professionals in the field. With no degree programs available in the field at HBCUs at the time, he eventually matriculated at two predominantly White institutions known for their training of physical culture specialists where he could gain access to prominent faculty and programs that would provide him the requisite skills and knowledge necessary to be an effective teacher, coach, and administrator.[5]

In 1910, the same year he was hired as Physical Director at Hampton Institute, Williams took a full schedule of physical education courses at the YMCA Training School at Springfield College and spent the summer taking additional classes at the Harvard Summer School of Physical Education. He followed this up with additional course work in the summers of 1911 and 1912 at the Harvard Summer School of Physical Education, studying during the 1922–1923 school year at Harvard's School of Education, and in the summer of 1924 taking courses back at the YMCA Training School. How he was able to juggle these courses while also fulfilling his responsibilities at Hampton Institute is impossible to know based on the available evidence. What we do know is that Williams graduated from Springfield College with a Bachelor of Physical Education (BPE) degree in the summer of 1924 and an MA degree in 1930 from Harvard's School of Education. He also received a diploma from the Harvard Summer School of Physical Education and used the credits he earned there and those from Harvard's School of Education toward his BPE degree at Springfield College in 1924.[6]

The decision to attend the YMCA Training School and Harvard University seemed to be perfect choices for a man with William's interests and proclivities. The YMCA Training School, where Williams spent much of his time and probably most closely identified, figuratively fit him like a glove with its emphasis on the strenuous life and making men out of boys. The school, with its famous inverted triangle of mind-body-spirit forever imprinted on the American consciousness, bridged sport and religion and bodily development in what has been termed the Muscular Christianity movement. As would eventually become clear, everything Williams did throughout his long career was underpinned by these values in his efforts to educate Black youth and to lift the race and engender Black pride.[7]

The transcripts from his time at Springfield College make clear that Williams was a solid B+/A- student who took a variety of theory and methods courses in physical education. Among the courses he completed were play administration, histology, personal hygiene, anthropometry, chemistry, psychology of physical education, history of the human body, physiology, and gymnastics and field sports. He was fortunate to have instructors who were well-known specialists in various aspects of physical education, including Frank N. Seeley who specialized in histology, psychology, and personal evangelism; James H. McCurdy who taught physiology of exercise, bibliographical methods and for a year served as editor of the *American Physical Education Review*; George B. Affleck who specialized in hygiene, anthropometry, gymnastics, and swimming; and George E. Dawson who taught psychology of physical education and mental hygiene and for a number of years served as Director of the Psychology Laboratory for the Springfield Public Schools.[8]

Evidence of Williams's insatiable appetite for learning and interest in gaining as much knowledge as possible about physical education, sport, dance, and recreation is made clear following the completion of his formal education at Springfield College and Harvard. He continued to seek new methodologies for teaching sport and dance skills, searched out the most recently published books in the field, took additional academic coursework, and participated in coaching schools and clinics. For instance, he returned to Springfield College in the summers of 1933 and 1934 to take a class in tennis coaching, physical education seminar, and two dance courses; visited the Bennington Summer School of Dance in 1937 and 1938 to observe classes and watch performances; spent part of the summer in 1938 studying in New York City with dancers and choreographers Doris Humphrey and Hanya Holm; attended Clair Bee's Long Island University Coaching School in the summer of 1939; and in 1941 took a class in Education at West Virginia State College.[9] Lifelong learning for Williams also involved nurturing and maintaining relationships with teachers from his undergraduate and graduate school days. While his race prohibited him from teaching at White institutions, he obviously felt comfortable in seeking the advice and counsel of his former teachers and they seemed perfectly happy and willing to provide it. "I have just completed a very successful work in physical education at our summer school," wrote Williams in a 1931 letter to Clarence Van Wyck, longtime secretary to Dudley Sargent and later assistant athletic director at Harvard. "For many years I have had the opportunity to look in on the Harvard Summer School and to get some idea of the work. This year I will not get a chance to visit Cambridge. Because of that fact I would like for you to send me the copies of the work which you have been giving in the various courses."[10]

Williams put the knowledge he had gained at Springfield College and Harvard and insights he had gleaned from other physical education programs to good use at Hampton Institute. Although physical education and organized athletics had existed far before his arrival at Hampton Institute, Williams put his own individual stamp on the programs. He implemented policies and enacted changes in both the women's and men's physical training programs at the school, even though the women's program would always officially be led by their own teachers and administrators. He played a significant role in Hampton Institute's decision in 1916 to make physical training mandatory for nearly all students at the institution irrespective of grade level and area of study. He was largely responsible for the creation of Hampton Institute's four-year undergraduate professional preparation program in physical education in 1924. In 1931 Williams was the driving force behind the consolidation of the men's and women's physical activity programs at the school, a rare administrative structure in higher education at the time in which he was appointed director and Mary C. Baker, a White woman with a BS degree in Education, being selected as the first leader of the women's division. In addition to these initiatives, Williams organized summer physical education and coaching schools as well as conferences on health and physical education. As was customary for Williams, these initiatives often involved the participation of some of the most well-known academics from predominantly White universities. His efforts at advancing the cause of the race frequently meant nurturing relationships and eliciting the expertise and support of prominent Whites. For example, for a summer conference in 1946 on health and physical education at Hampton Institute, Williams brought in as consultants such prestigious individuals from predominantly White institutions as Seward C. Staley, Director of Physical Education at the University of Illinois; Frances A. Hellebrandt, Director of the Baruch Center of Physical Medicine at the Medical College of Virginia; Helen Luffman, Director of Physical Education at Russell Sage College; and John Bunn, Director of Athletics at Springfield College.[11]

The physical training program for women at Hampton Institute by the time of Williams's appointment as Physical Director in 1910 included a variety of games and sports and eventually instruction in posture and dance. Women at the school were also required to engage in recreational activities on their own at least two afternoons each week and participated, like their counterparts at predominantly White institutions that stressed the non-competitive nature of sport, in intramural contests in field hockey, croquet, baseball, basketball, and volleyball. A program long guided by White teachers and adhering to what historian Martha Verbrugge described as being "white middle-class femininity, unsullied by masculine athleticism," these activities would eventually be under the control of the Girls Athletic Association and by 1918 Hampton Institute began sponsoring a yearly May Day festival and an interclass intramural Field day that emphasized sport for recreational purposes.[12] By the late 1930s, with Williams's blessing and support but less than progressive attitude regarding the capabilities of women, Hampton Institute joined with Howard University and Virginia State College and organized a series of Women's Sports Days that were extramural in nature, but were more cooperative and recreational than competitive. These events would eventually be held under the auspices of the Women's Sports Day Association (WSDA), an organization that included the above-mentioned institutions along with Bennett College and several other HBCUs. The WSDA organized sports days throughout the 1940s and 1950s and provided girls "an opportunity," in the words of Williams, "to see other institutions, to study and compare life and programs, to get acquainted, and to develop real friendships among the girls from other schools."[13]

Notwithstanding his conservative position regarding the participation of women in highly competitive sport, Williams's belief in the importance of pedagogically based organized physical activity for women can be gleaned from his defense of the women's four-year undergraduate professional preparation program at Hampton Institute. Responding to a 1940 report by Hampton Institute's President Arthur Howe indicating the small number of students that had graduated from the program during the previous four years (eleven students between 1936 and 1939) and questioning whether the program should continue to exist, Williams provided a passionate defense of why women at the school should continue to be able to major in physical education. He noted, among other things, that women in the South had few opportunities to prepare for careers in physical education and the result was that men in the region typically taught physical education to women and coached them almost exclusively in basketball "played by boy's rules, with the emphasis being on winning." The implication here, of course, is that more women trained in physical education would mean more of them teaching and coaching women in a variety of sports that emphasized sportsmanship and character development. In addition, Williams, sounding like Clark Hetherington, R. Tait McKenzie, and other prominent academics who stressed the total education of children through what was termed the "New Physical Education," defended the physical education major for women at Hampton Institute based on the use of leisure time, hygienic concerns and lifetime skills. "Great emphasis is being placed today upon Education for Life," wrote Williams. "This means, among other things, the proper use of leisure time which will increase according to educational experts. The social progress in the future will need more and more women trained in health and physical education who will understand hygienic home conditions, and who through the schools, community centers and parent teacher's associations can help develop a richer and more wholesome life for the youth of the race."[14]

Like women at the school, the male students at Hampton Institute were provided a physical training program under Williams that stressed health, physical fitness, and, increasingly over time, the educational value of play and games. Prior to his appointment as Physical Director in 1910, the men at Hampton Institute were provided no regular physical training but took part in some calisthenics in connection with their military drills. Almost immediately upon assuming his position as Physical Director, Williams implemented a program under the title Military Drill and Physical Training that required all men at the institution to take a physical examination and various strength tests in the hopes of "arousing their interest in taking exercise."[15] As part of the program, all men took classwork consisting of calisthenics, marching, exercises with Indian clubs, wands, and dumbbells, apparatus work and indoor games as well as participation in intramurals where competitions were held in basketball, football, baseball, and track and field. In 1913 rowing was added to the intramural competitions and would become, according to Williams, the most popular of the sports, with the exception of football (perhaps not surprising since the school's waterfront campus is located near the mouth of the Chesapeake Bay). At some point, probably at about the same time rowing was added to the intramural contests, the men at Hampton Institute, like their women counterparts, were required to participate in recreation on their own time and in gymnasium exhibitions "consisting of regular gymnastics, apparatus, drills, games, and folk dances."[16]

In addition to altering and improving the physical education and intramural programs, Williams also added needed organizational structure and increased the visibility and prestige of the men's intercollegiate athletic program at Hampton Institute. The school was relatively slow to get started in highly organized sport, students evidently playing baseball against local hotel teams in the 1880s and some dormitories playing football against one another in the 1890s. The school's first formal athletic contest was a football game in 1903 against Armstrong Training School of Washington, DC. From 1906 through 1912, the school played five to eight football games each season, with the exception of 1909 when the team made a southern tour competing in a game each day for a week.[17]

The most significant turning point for men's intercollegiate athletics at Hampton Institute took place when the school brought Williams on board in 1910. With the support of the school's second president Hollis Burke Frissell—who apparently noted at some point during his some fifteen-year tenure that "If football is making Hampton better known to the young people who should know about the school, then our boys must have time to play, and they must play the game in the right way,"—Williams vastly improved and added needed organizational structure and increased the visibility and prestige of the men's intercollegiate athletic program at Hampton Institute.[18] He directed the program, coached a number of sports, and increased contests in everything ranging from football and wrestling to baseball and tennis. He also contributed to the growth and recognition of Black high school sports by creating Hampton Institute's famous high school and college track meet in 1922 and the National Interscholastic Basketball Tournament (NIBT) in 1929. He oversaw, moreover, the expansion of the athletic facilities at Hampton Institute, including most notably Armstrong Field.[19]

Williams maintained a strict devotion to the amateur ideal and educational value of sport throughout the entire time he directed the men's intercollegiate athletic program at Hampton Institute. It was not easy to do so. He continually faced pressure from some members of the university community and the Hampton Alumni Association to subsidize the school's athletes and to lower academic standards in an attempt to capture more championships. Evidence of Williams's commitment to preserving the integrity and high scholarly standards in the school's athletic program is made clear in a January 10, 1941, letter he wrote to Malcolm Maclean, who served as Hampton Institute's President from 1940 to 1942. He reminded Maclean that Hampton Institute was serious about the academic success of its student athletes, establishing higher eligibility standards than other members of the Colored Intercollegiate Athletic Association (CIAA). He also told Maclean that he was adamantly opposed to subsidizing athletes, recommending that jobs on campus be given to athletes "as well as to students with abilities in other lines" and providing "scholarship aid to athletes exactly as it is given to all other students."[20]

THE COLORED INTERCOLLEGIATE ATHLETIC ASSOCIATION AND HAMPTON INSTITUTE CREATIVE DANCE GROUP

Two of Williams's most significant contributions were his co-founding of the CIAA and creation of the Hampton Institute Creative Dance Group. He had perhaps his greatest influence in expanding the sporting opportunities for African Americans through his co-founding and leadership positions in the CIAA. In 1912, Williams, along with representatives from Howard University, Shaw University, Virginia Union University, and Lincoln University, met at Hampton Institute and created the CIAA to "govern athletic competition" among member institutions. Troubled by the ills plaguing Black college sport while also believing in the power of sport to combat the believe in Black inferiority and improve race relations, Williams and his co-founders drafted a "Constitution and By-Laws" that stipulated the rules that players and institutions were expected to follow. They also published, beginning in 1923, what they titled the *CIAA Bulletin*. Published and distributed by Hampton Institute, the *Bulletin* included, among other things, details regarding the two-day annual meeting of the CIAA from the previous year, listing of scores and team champions, in-depth articles on various sport-related subjects, recording of certified officials in each sport, images of tournament champions in each sport, yearly financial statements, and a "In Memoriam" section that recognized the passing of players, coaches, administrators, and other officials who had contributed positively to the organization. Perhaps most importantly, Williams and his co-founders sponsored competitions and championships for men in such sports as football, basketball, baseball, boxing, track and field, wrestling, and tennis. Of all the activities they sponsored, nothing eventually brought the organization more notoriety than its postseason basketball tournament that began in 1946. Still in existence, the tournament over the years has showcased great players and coaches and has always been, in many ways, as much a reunion/homecoming as an athletic event.[21]

The success of the CIAA was largely attributable to the leadership of its founders and, among those founders, perhaps no one was more important than Williams. By virtue of his talent and length and quality of his service, Williams was the guiding force behind the CIAA and had an especially lasting impact on the association. He held every major office in the organization at some point, serving for many years as its secretary-treasurer and at least one stint as president. His financial and business acumen were essential in insuring that the organization remained economically solvent and continued to offer quality sports programs through the turbulent years of the Great Depression and World War I and II. He was integrally involved in seemingly every conversation that CIAA officials had regarding rule changes, eligibility questions, scheduling issues, selection of championship teams, aid to athletes, and the like. He was the editor of the *CIAA Bulletin*, charted the early history of the organization, and publicized its major events to a larger audience through the Black press. Recognizing the value of nurturing a close relationship with the Black press, Williams regularly wrote about upcoming athletic contests and detailed the results of games between association schools in Black weeklies—oftentimes, of course, with special reference to Hampton Institute. His most frequently written articles were published in the *Chicago Defender*, perhaps largely a result of his close friendship with the newspaper's founder and publisher Robert S. Abbott who was a graduate of Hampton Institute. The legacy of Williams lives on in the CIAA as the association bestows the C. H. Williams All-Sports Award each year to the member institution that has achieved the most success athletically.[22]

Twenty-two years after the creation of the CIAA, Williams founded the Hampton Institute Creative Dance Group. Always a lover of dance, Williams could not have found himself at a better institution to organize such a group. Hampton Institute founder Samuel Chapman Armstrong, while stressing the importance of labor, industry, and manual training, ultimately determined that it was through at least one aspect of art and culture that the school could attract attention and much-needed philanthropy. In 1870 Armstrong had established the Hampton Singers, a touring group that helped market the school and caught the attention of donors by "Singing Up." Although not without controversy, particularly during the 1920s when students on campus revolted against the singing of demeaning "Plantation Songs" which ran counter to the emphasis on Black pride reflected in the "New Negro Movement," the success of the group was not lost on Williams who believed dance could have the same impact on the institution while at once contributing to the discipline and moral development of his students and larger emphasis on racial uplift.[23]

A key event for Williams, and the entire Hampton Institute community for that matter, took place on February 21, 1925, when the Denishawn Dance Company performed in the school's Ogden Hall. Led by dance pioneers Ruth St. Denis and Ted Shawn, the company, which had made several tours across the United States during the three years prior to their performance in Ogden Hall through arrangements made by well-known impresario and booking agent Daniel Mayer, mesmerized the audience. Perhaps most importantly, the occasion provided an opportunity for Williams to meet Shawn, a man whose work he had always admired from afar and yearned to establish a professional connection based on their mutual love for dance. Although difficult to determine the exact extent of their relationship, Shawn would be a source of inspiration and provide a wealth of knowledge regarding dance that greatly influenced Williams before and after he founded the Hampton Institute Creative Dance Group in 1934.[24]

Williams was largely motivated to attend the YMCA Training School in the summer of 1933 because he knew he would have access to the teachings of Shawn who was in his second year of appointment at the school. He spent the summer of 1934 taking courses at the YMCA Training School and attending Shawn's retreat and dance school called Jacob's Pillow outside of Lee, Massachusetts. As to Shawn's attitude and treatment of Williams, the evidence is not clear, but Shawn regularly booked Black dancers in concert programs at Jacob's Pillow despite his racist and misogynistic views and connection to the Eugenics movement. Among these performers were such dance luminaries as Alvin Ailey, Pearl Primus, Geoffrey Holder, and Doris Humphrey.[25]

The founding of the Hampton Institute Creative Dance Group was undergirded by William's contention that Blacks had a "native capacity" to dance and "a remarkable sense of rhythm." In what would be termed today biological determinism, a concept largely debunked, at least by those in the humanities and social sciences, Williams was merely reflecting the views of Black intellectuals during the decade of the 1920s who believed that African Americans could improve their position in the United States by asserting that their success in artistic activities resulted from innate racial gifts and that these skills were "nearest the heart of his African ancestor."[26]

Williams's use of the phrase "heart of the African ancestor" is no coincidence. He was fascinated with the life and customs of native Africans, and it was reflected in the dances he choreographed for his group. Wanting to ensure Hampton Institute students were cognizant of their rich African heritage, Williams choreographed, eventually with the chief assistance of Charlotte E. Moton, the daughter of Robert R. Moton who succeeded Booker T. Washington as head of Tuskegee Institute, dances developed from folk materials and infused them with work songs from earlier generations, Negro spirituals, and older African dances. Williams, Moton, and others that worked with the Hampton Institute Creative Dance Group certainly had to walk a fine line in the dances they developed, careful to design movement forms that were dignified and reflected "intelligent proficiency" rather than resembling "cheap theatrical exhibitions" that undermined the self-respect and moral progress of the performers. Since male students were also members of the group, Williams and his colleagues had to be cautious in developing dances that neither confirmed the historical image of the Black male as savages and hypersexualized or substantiating the belief that men who engaged in aesthetic movement forms were overly effete or homosexuals. It is for these reasons that Williams choreographed dances for men in his group that were performed in isolation and emphasized power and athleticism and muscularity.[27]

The Hampton Institute Creative Dance Group became well-known not long after its founding because of its talent level and many tours it took throughout both the North and South. Williams had many influential contacts throughout the eastern part of the United States, and he capitalized on them by scheduling performances on both the campuses of HBCUs and predominantly White universities and in other venues in major cities. Just three years after the troup's founding, Williams detailed the many places where the group had already performed in front of both White and African American audiences. The group gave annual performances on the Hampton Institute campus, appeared at major venues throughout Virginia, North Carolina, and in the deep South, and traveled to the north where they danced in front of large crowds, including such cities as Philadelphia, Montclair, New Jersey, and New York City. Unfortunately, World War II put a temporary end to the performances of the Hampton Institute Creative Dance Group as many of its members were off fighting in the great conflict. The group resumed its tours in 1946, with popular performances being given in both the north and the south. By the late 1940s, however, the group had committed to fewer tours, largely because of William's preoccupation with his many other duties on campus as well as business interests. The group is still in existence but operating under the name Terpsichorean Dance Company.[28]

A WRITING LIFE AMID ALL THE OTHER DUTIES

Williams was a very busy man, but amid all his duties he found time to write and to publish various books and essays. The first book he published was *Sidelights on Negro Soldiers* (1923), a detailed analysis of the experiences and living conditions of Black soldiers during World War I. He was the ideal person to write such a book (reprinted in 1970 as *Negro Soldiers in WWI: The Human Side*) since he observed first hand over an extended period of time the treatment of Black soldiers in his two years (1917–1919) as Assistant Secretary of the Army YMCA at Camp Sherman in Chillicothe, Ohio, and as Field Secretary for the Committee on Welfare of Negro Troops. He followed up this work with *Cotton Needs Pickin: Characteristic Negro Folk Dances* (1928), a book that describes in detail creative dance forms in African American culture.[29]

Williams was not reluctant to promote his own works. He seemingly bought into the old maxim that the best marketers of books are the authors themselves. The economic benefits of doing so were certainly a motivating factor. A classic example of this was the assertiveness Williams exhibited in seeing that *Negro Soldiers in WWI: The Human Side* (1970) was adequately promoted and received the attention it deserved. Prior to its publication, Williams made clear to John Hopper, Editor-in Chief of AMS Press, that the Hampton Institute Public Relations Department stood ready to distribute hundreds of flyers advertising the book if AMS Press would help defray some of the costs. Williams pointed out to Hopper that this was the arrangement made by the Hampton Institute Public Relations Department with Weybright and Tally which was set to publish Hampton Institute's President Jerome Holland's book *Black Opportunity*. Following the publication of *Negro Soldiers in WWI*, Williams wrote to Hopper again with several suggestions intended to increase sales of the book, including lowering the price, providing an attractive jacket cover, distributing the book more widely throughout the country, and focusing much of the marketing on military installations.[30]

Not unexpectedly, the bulk of Williams's articles were published in the *Southern Workman*. Launched as Hampton Institute's official publication by Samuel Chapman Armstrong in 1872 and consisting of sixty-eight issues until ceasing operation in 1939, the *Southern Workman* disseminated information on a broad range of topics dealing with African American and Native American life through articles, commentaries, and editorials. Many of the most prominent African American intellectuals published in the journal. Booker T. Washington published over a dozen letters and essays in the journal, some of which would ultimately appear in his autobiography *Up from Slavery* (1901). Monroe N. Work, the highly respected sociologist who directed Tuskegee Institute's Department of Records and Research, was a regular contributor to the *Southern Workman*. Other noted African American intellectuals who published in the journal included such people as sociologist E. Franklin Frazier, historian Rayford W. Logan, writer and activist Anna Julia Cooper, poet and playwright Paul Laurence Dunbar, and author and civil rights activist W.E.B. DuBois.[31]

Williams published at least five featured articles in the *Southern Workman*.[32] These writings, combined with his two books, columns in the *Chicago*

Defender and articles in the *CIAA Bulletin*, provide deeper insights into his thinking, particularly as it relates to his beliefs regarding how organized physical activity, recreation, sport, and dance contributed to moral development and racial uplift. Detailing two of Williams's five articles in the *Southern Workman* provides sufficient insights into his beliefs about these matters. In the January 1917 issue of the journal, Williams published "Recreation in the Lives of Young People." Based on an address he delivered before the Negro Organization Society of Virginia, Williams laid out why it was important for African American children to engage in recreation. Obviously knowledgeable of the scholarly literature on contemporary play theories and recreation, Williams argued that it was imperative that African American youth have access to organized play and supervised recreation. Similar to his contention that African Americans possessed a natural love for and native ability to dance, the essay was undergirded by Williams belief that "it is a racial characteristic to 'love a good time.'"[33] Unfortunately, Williams wrote, there were very high levels of juvenile delinquency among African Americans and a large percentage were confined to jails and prisons— principally a result of the lack of proper recreation. Too many African American children were "left on the streets to play during the day and became contaminated by the worst influences." Meanwhile, their parents, with few constructive ways to satisfy "their love of pleasure," were enticed by the "vice district" and attracted to cheaper forms of amusement such as "vaudeville shows" and "the lowest type of theatre."[34]

To Williams, the best way to attack this problem was by providing healthy and rational recreation for African American youth. "As a people," noted Williams, "we have too long neglected the place of normal play in our lives." It is imperative that African American youth are furnished opportunities to participate in wholesome recreation since it "is one of the fundamental elements in life; it is the renewing of life." There was no better way to instill "within them the value of cooperation, loyalty, fair play, and square dealing." In William's view, recreation, which for him was an umbrella term that also included everything from sport and exercise to gymnastics, had "one great purpose, and that is to direct the energies and pleasures of young people so they will bring back to them what Mr. Roosevelt [President Teddy Roosevelt] calls their 'lost heritage,' and give them an opportunity to develop the type of citizenship needed in the progress of this nation."[35]

Some twenty years later Williams turned to a different topic in the pages of the *Southern Workman* and that was the highly controversial 1936

Olympic Games in Berlin. In an article titled "Negro Athletes in the Eleventh Olympiad," Williams provides profiles of those African American athletes who participated in an Olympic Games fraught with enormous political and racial symbolism. Although devoting some space to those who have largely been lost from historical memory because of their failure to medal in the Games often referred to as the "Nazi Olympics," Williams focuses, not unexpectedly, on those African American athletes who were triumphant in the track and field events in Berlin. He devoted, of course, a great deal of space to Jesse Owens, the great Ohio State University track and field star who realized worldwide acclaim by capturing gold medals in the 100-meters, 200-meters, long jump, and 400-meter relay. He also recounts the triumphs of the other great track and field performers who medaled in various events. These included the University of Oregon's Mack Robinson, Marquette University's Ralph Metcalfe, University of California Berkeley's Archie Williams, University of California Los Angeles's Jimmy LuValle, University of Pittsburgh's John Woodruff, Compton Junior College's Cornelius Johnson, Ohio State University's David Albritton, and University of North Dakota's Fritz Pollard, Jr. To Williams, the great performances of these athletes were particularly important because they could be used in the larger civil rights struggle and served, as Arthur Ashe and some other Black chroniclers would later claim, as symbols of possibility. These triumphs were made that much more impactful and racially significant because they were achieved by honorable and clean-living Black men whose character was above reproach. The victories of these athletes, combined with "their tact and diplomacy, their 'impeccable manners and unimpeachable demeanor' wrote Williams, "all contributed toward making them ambassadors of good will and racial understanding. Their achievements in the games showed to an unsuspecting world great racial talents and possibilities."[36] Given his views, one would assume that Williams was terribly troubled by the revolts of Black athletes in the late 1960s and early 1970s, but he was silent on the matter in his correspondence which was admittedly becoming less frequent because of his advanced age.

Williams certainly had reason to be proud of his publications, but like every writer he had his disappointments and not everything he wrote found its way into print. The sources make clear, for example, that Williams had every intention from very early in his professional career to write a monograph on the African American experience in sport. At least as early as 1923 Williams was reaching out to people seeking information about African American athletes and making clear his desire to write about their struggles and various accomplishments. In some of the correspondence he mentions seeking information for a thesis he was completing at Harvard on the Black athlete, while in others he simply notes searching out details on the accomplishments of black athletes in various sports and at all levels of competition for a study he was completing. "I am working for my master's degree at Harvard," wrote Williams in a March 13, 1928, letter to former Negro League player and historian Sol White. "In looking up the records of Negroes in various sports, it was my feeling that baseball, and the records of some of the Negro players deserved a place in such a thesis ... any information which you find you can give me and which will not interfere with your study, will be most gratefully received and appreciated."[37] "For more than five years I have been trying to gather material for the history of the Negro athlete," Williams noted in a January 31, 1930, letter to longtime Alabama State University coach and administrator George H. Lockhart. "I am endeavoring to secure information with reference to Negro athletes who have distinguished themselves in northern and western universities."[38]

Unfortunately, as sometimes happens in the world of academia, another individual ended up writing the book that Williams had planned for so long to do himself. In 1939, Edwin Bancroft Henderson, noted physical educator and civil rights activist from Falls Church, Virginia, and an acquaintance of Williams who also believed that success in sport served as an important symbol of possibility and could break down racial barriers, published, at the request of Carter G. Woodson, the "Father of Black History," *The Negro in Sports*. The publication of the book must have been terribly disheartening to Williams after he had spent so much time gathering information on the Black athletic experience and after he contacted the A. S. Barnes Company in 1934 to determine their interest in such a project. But you would never know it based on his correspondence with Henderson immediately before and following the release of The *Negro in Sports*.[39] He wrote Henderson after learning that the book would soon be published, "As you know, I have been working on that subject [Black athletes] for several years. What is most interesting, I had just finished talking with my secretary this morning about plans to complete this study, when I received your letter stating that your task was near completion."[40] After receiving a complimentary copy of the book, Williams wrote six months later to Henderson: "I want to congratulate you in doing what I believe a splendid job, and certainly one well worth doing. I believe the gathering of this material and putting it in book form as you have done will prove a source of inspiration to many of our youngsters."[41]

Although failing to publish a book on the experiences of African American athletes, Williams continued to disseminate information on the subject thru different mediums and formats. Henderson upstaged him regarding publishing the first book on the African American experience in sport, but Williams was determined to make known to the larger public the accomplishments of Black athletes. One classic example of this was his involvement as an advisory committee member with the *Freedom's People* radio show broadcast by NBC in 1941 and 1942. Sponsored by the US Office of Education in cooperation with the Julius Rosenwald Fund and Southern Education Foundation, the show was created because of the federal governments increasing concern about racial unrest in the United States.[42] Along with other members of an advisory board made up of prominent White and Black Americans, Williams was responsible for providing input on a show that was broadcast weekly and covered "contributions from Negroes" in such fields as education, science, theater, music, and sports. It is difficult to assess his exact contributions, but he did provide insightful suggestions regarding the broadcasts on sports. The two-year show certainly aligned with Williams's overall philosophy, making clear the centrality of African Americans to the United States and engendering racial pride through the examination of Black history and culture. In a November 6, 1941, letter to Ambrose Caliver, Senior Specialist in the Education of Negroes in the Federal Security Agency who was largely responsible for the content of the broadcast, Williams wrote: "We find in athletics and sports more democratic practices than in any other American institution today. For that reason, I believe your script should emphasize the social value of sports and athletics to Negro people."[43]

NOT HAVING "TO MOVE BY BELLS"

Shortly after his retirement from Hampton Institute in 1951, legendary Black New York City playwright Andrew M. Burris sent Williams a letter congratulating him on how "honorably" and "so well" he had served his "alma mater."[44] Williams responded to Burris nearly three months later in a manner that would accurately assess much of his post-retirement career. "My retirement from Hampton did not mean resting for me," Williams told Burris. "I am about as busy as ever though not under so much pressure and I don't have to move by bells."[45] In retirement, Williams did not stand idly by. He continued to assume leadership positions and be involved in multiple projects and causes.

Much of Williams's time following his official retirement continued to be devoted to Hampton Institute. Although no longer directing the physical education and athletic programs, Williams worked on behalf of and tirelessly promoted the university as if retirement never occurred. Always the ultimate university citizen, Williams spent much of his time assisting the Hampton Institute Alumni Association (HIAA) and serving on the university's Board of Trustees. Retirement certainly provided Williams more time to focus on the work of the HIAA and he relished the opportunity. He used his business skills and took advantage of the large number of alumni he had befriended during his more than forty-five years at Hampton Institute to bring more money into the university coffers.[46] He also took advantage of the close connections he had established with individuals from the world of entertainment in his efforts to generate additional alumni funding that, in turn, could be used for building construction and a host of other projects and initiatives.

Williams's influence was made all that much greater by the fact he was for several years Chairman of the HIAA Fund Raising Committee. His leadership qualities and the high regard for him in the university community were evidenced by the fact that he headed up several strategic plans designed to increase alumni giving. One of those plans was what was termed the $50,000 Scholarship Fund, an initiative that ran during the latter stages of the 1950s. As part of that plan, the HIAA, with Williams almost certainly playing a big role, arranged eight benefit concerts by singer Dorothy Maynor, a 1933 graduate of Hampton Institute who established the Harlem School of the Arts. The concerts would net more than $4,000 and leave the HIAA just $5,000 short of its goal of $50,000.[47]

Williams complemented his work on the HIAA with membership on the university's Board of Trustees from 1954 to 1969. Like his work on the HIAA, Williams assumed a leading role on the board of trustees during a period that would witness much debate at Hampton Institute regarding infrastructure, curriculum, and leadership. One of his most significant contributions to the board of trustees was through his membership on a Special Committee on Curriculum constituted at some time in the mid-1950s under the presidency of Alonzo G. Morón.[48] Joined on the committee by four others, including former University of North Carolina President Frank P. Graham as Chairman, Williams was a driving force among the five members, providing much-needed historical context regarding curriculum offerings at Hampton Institute and farsighted philosophical rationales as to the direction the institution should take concerning academic courses and program offerings. He was instrumental in suggesting changes and ultimately improving the institution's struggling Home Economics program that had experienced falling enrollments. He was also instrumental in pushing the institution to think more creatively about other curricular offerings and to ensure African American students were prepared to compete in a rapidly changing world. One important suggestion Williams made was to "enlarge and Modernize its [Hampton's] Engineering Programs," a suggestion that would ultimately become true.[49]

Williams also spent his supposed retirement years in other capacities not directly connected to Hampton Institute. He served, for instance, as President of the Peoples Building and Loan Association in the city of Hampton and worked closely with a local group to secure more money for the United Negro College Fund.[50] Most importantly, Williams became President and General Manager of the Bay Shore Resort, an all-Black resort in Buckroe Beach, Virginia just outside of Hampton. Originally founded in 1898, Bay Shore was in the mold of other great all-Black resorts such as Highland Beach outside of Annapolis, Maryland, American Beach north of Jacksonville, Florida, and Freeman Beach in Wilmington, North Carolina. Williams served as President and General Manager of Bay Shore Resort for over 20 years, guiding it with great adeptness through good times and bad. With his educational background, variety of interests, and financial acuity, he was the perfect man to oversee a popular resort that hosted many prominent Black dignitaries and groups as well as Black families and ordinary citizens over the years. Williams was paid handsomely for managing Bay Shore, making more than $5,000 in salary each year between 1951 and 1967. This salary only added to Williams's hefty financial portfolio. In his 1968 Financial Statement, Williams listed $166,100.00 as his approximate assets, $1,451,328 in today's dollars.[51]

The Bay Shore Resort finally closed in 1974, more than seven and a half decades after first opening its doors to Black citizens who were forced to vacation and seek amusements in segregated settings in the South during the era of Jim Crow. Ironically, just like so many other separate Black institutions, it was integration that was largely responsible for its demise. With more resorts welcoming Black citizens, the Bay Shore Resort gradually lost the patronage that would have allowed it to stay open and thrive. Williams valiantly tried to save the Bay Shore Resort, ultimately determining that the best way to do that was by selling it and ideally to an African American or group of African Americans. "There are some white people who really want Bay Shore and are willing to pay for it," wrote Williams in 1960. "However, we would like for Negroes to get Bay Shore." Unfortunately, no one ever stepped up with a legitimate offer for the Black resort.⁵²

Williams must have been saddened by the closing of a resort he had poured his heart and soul into for so many years, but also heartened by the increased opportunities available to African Americans resulting from recent civil rights legislation. We will never be completely sure about his feelings about these matters, partly because he was sometimes, as noted previously, reticent about expressing his emotions and innermost thoughts about personal matters. We do know, however, what people thought of him and his many accomplishments. He was a remarkable force in the separate Black sporting culture that developed in the first half of the twentieth century, certainly one of the most important individuals in school sports because of his coaching and plethora of leadership positions in prestigious athletic organizations. He also marked himself off from virtually all his contemporaries by administrating model physical education and highly competitive athletic programs while at once leading a dance troupe that garnered enormous regional and national acclaim and is still in existence to this very day. Fortunately, prior to his death in 1978 in Charleston, West Virginia at the age of 92, Williams had been bestowed with a plethora of honors because of his many achievements, including having a building on the campus named in his honor and being elected to the Hampton Institute, CIAA, and Virginia Sports Halls of Fame. Williams had also been the recipient of many letters from former students and colleagues on the Hampton Institute campus and elsewhere expressing their appreciation for his numerous accomplishments. One of those written shortly after his retirement was particularly poignant and representative of how people felt about the loyal Hamptonian and champion of racial uplift. "We do hope you will continue to be active in the field" wrote prominent Tuskegee Institute coach and administrator Cleve Abbott, "and that you will always be available for consultation and inspiration which is so necessary in work in the field of Health, Physical Education and Athletics with our young men and women. You can look back upon your long career at Hampton Institute and rejoice in the fact that your sound teachings have developed thousands of strong men and women and that forever you will live in their memories."⁵³

Notes

1. For two exceptions, see John O. Perpener, *African-American Concert Dance: The Harlem Renaissance and Beyond* (Urbana: University of Illinois Press, 2005), Ch. 4 and

Mary Ann Laverty, *Finding A Way Out: Charles H. Williams and the Hampton Institute Creative Dance Group* (Saarbrucken: Lap Lambert Academic Publishing, 2012).

2. Williams's efforts at racial uplift mirror those of other Black educators in the South who adopted a similar strategy in their struggle to erase discriminatory practices and increase equal opportunities for all African Americans. See, for example: Leroy Davis, *A Clashing of the Soul: John Hope and the Dilemma of African American Leadership and Black Higher Education in the Early Twentieth Century* (Athens, Ga: University of Georgia Press, 1998); Gerald L. Smith, *A Black Educator in the Segregated South: Kentucky's Rufus B. Atwood* (Lexington, KY: University Press of Kentucky, 1994); Charles M. Payne and Adam Green, *Time Longer than Rope: A Century of African American Activism, 1850–1950* (New York: New York University Press, 2003); John Egerton, *Speak Now Against the Day: The Generation Before the Civil Rights Movement in the South* (Chapel Hill: The University of North Carolina Press, 1995); Jelani Manu-Gowan Favors, *Shelter in a Time of Storm: How Black Colleges Fostered Generations of Leadership and Activism* (Chapel Hill: The University of North Carolina Press, 2019); Antonio F. Holland, *Nathan B. Young and the Struggle Over Black Higher Education* (Columbia: University of Missouri Press, 2006); Bobby L. Lovett, *America's Historically Black Colleges and Universities: A Narrative History, 1837–2009* (Macon, GA: Mercer University Press, 2015); and Melissa E. Wooten, *In the Face of Inequality: How Black Colleges Adapt* (Albany, NY: State University of New York Press, 2015).

3. US Department of Labor, List of United States Citizens arriving in New York City on the SS *Noordam*, 21 August 1919 and World War II Draft Card, National Archives, College Park, Maryland.

4. For the Day Law, see Lowell H. Harrison and James C. Klotter, *A New History of Kentucky* (Lexington: University Press of Kentucky, 1997).

5. Information on African Americans who pursued physical education degrees at predominantly White universities during this time can be gleaned from David K. Wiggins and Brenda P. Wiggins, "Striving to be in the Profession and of it: The African American Experience in Physical Education and Kinesiology," *Research Quarterly for Exercise and Sport* 82.2 (June 2011): 320–333.

6. Biographical information on Charles Holston Williams, Springfield College Archives. Retrieved by Jeffrey L. Monseau, College Archivist, Springfield College, 25 October 2018.

7. See Clifford Putney, *Muscular Christianity: Manhood and Sports in Protestant America, 1880–1920* (Cambridge: Harvard University Press, 2003); Nina Mjagkij and Margaret Spratt, eds. *Men and Women Adrift: The YMCA and the YWCA in the City* (New York: New York University Press, 1997).

8. Transcripts of Charles Holston Williams, Springfield College Archives. Retrieved by Jeffrey L. Monseau, College Archivist, Springfield College, 25 October 2018. Information on the faculty at Springfield College faculty can be found in the yearly catalogs published by the school.

9. Williams's diploma from the Clair Bee Coaching School indicates he took

sixty-three hours of Theoretical and Applied Instruction and 3 ½ semester hours in Applied Athletics. See "Correspondence and Letters" in the Charles H. Williams Papers (hereafter referred to as CHW Papers), Hampton University Archives (hereafter referred to as HUA).

10. Charles H. Williams to Clarence Van Wyck, 30 July 1931, "Correspondence and Letters," CHW Papers, HUA.

11. See Participants in the Conference on Health and Physical Education, 12, 13, and 14 July 1946, CHW Papers, HUA.

12. Martha H. Verbrugge, *Active Bodies: A History of Women's Physical Education in Twentieth-Century America* (New York: Oxford University Press, 2012), 127.

13. Quoted in Martha H. Verbrugge, Active Bodies, 131. Fortunately, the last number of years has seen an increasing number of excellent works dealing with the involvement of women in physical education and sport at HBCUs. Besides Verbrugge's Active Bodies, see for example Susan K. Cahn, *Coming on Strong: Gender and Sexuality in Women's Sport* (New York: Free Press, 1993), especially chapter 5; Jennifer H. Lansbury, *A Spectacular Leap: Black Women Athletes in Twentieth-Century America* (Fayetteville: The University of Arkansas Press, 2014); Rita Liberti, "We Were Ladies, We Just Played Basketball Like Boys: A Study of Women's Basketball at Historically Black Colleges and Universities in North Carolina, 1925-1945 (unpublished doctoral dissertation, University of Iowa, 1998) and "'We Were Ladies, We Just Played Like Boys:' African American Womanhood and Competitive Basketball at Bennett College, 1928-1942" *Journal of Sport History* 26 (Fall 1999): 567-584 (reprinted at least three times in various anthologies).

14. Charles H. Williams to Arthur Howe, "Correspondence and Letters," CHW Papers, HUA.

15. Charles H. Williams, "The History of Physical Education and Athletics at Hampton Institute" (n.d.), "Correspondence and Letters," CHW Papers, HUA.

16. Ibid.

17. Ibid.

18. Ibid.

19. For Williams and the National Interscholastic Basketball Tournament, See Robert Pruter, "The National Interscholastic Basketball Tournament: The Crown Jewel of African American High School Sports During the Era of Segregation," in *Separate Games: African American Sport Behind the Walls of Segregation*, eds. David K. Wiggins and Ryan A. Swanson (Fayetteville: The University of Arkansas Press, 2016), 75-92.

20. Charles H. Williams to Malcolm S. MacLean, 10 January 1941, "Correspondence and Letters," CHW Papers, HUA. The long-standing debate about scholarships and amateurism has not just been evident in Black college sport, but also in athletics among predominantly White universities as well. See, for example: Ronald A. Smith, *Sports and Freedom: The Rise of Big-Time College Athletics* (New York: Oxford University Press, 1990); John R. Thelin, *Games Colleges Play: Scandal and Reform in Intercollegiate Athletics* (Baltimore: Johns Hopkins University Press, 1996); John Sayle

Watterson, *College Football: History, Spectacle, Controversary* (Baltimore: Johns Hopkins University Press, 2002); Michael Oriard, *King Football: Sport and Spectacle in the Golden Age of Radio and Newsreels, Movies and Magazines, the Weekly and the Daily Press* (Chapel Hill, NC: The University of North Carolina Press, 2004); and ibid., *Bowled Over: Big-Time College Football from the Sixties to the BCS* (Chapel Hill, NC: The University of North Carolina Press, 2009).

21. See David K. Wiggins and Chris Elzey, "Creating Order in Black College Sport: The Lasting Legacy of the Colored Intercollegiate Athletic Association," in *Separate Games: African American Sport Behind the Walls of Segregation*, eds. David K. Wiggins and Ryan A. Swanson (Fayetteville: The University of Arkansas Press, 2016), 145–164.

22. For insights into the administrative structure and programs currently offered by the CIAA, please consult https://theciaa.com. Information on Cleve Abbott can be gleaned in Metz T. P. Lochard, "Phylon Profile, XII: Robert S. Abbott-Race Leader," *Phylon* 8.2 (1947): 124–132. For examples of Williams's pieces in the Chicago Defender, see "Hampton Hands Howard Its Worst Defeat," 15 December 1915; "Hampton Gains Great Victory Over Shaw," 31 January 1920; "High Standard in Athletics is Set By Colleges," 2 April 1921; "Lincoln Awarded Championship; Intercollegiate Body Names All-Star Elevens; Howard Quits," 27 December 1924; "CIAA Takes Drastic Action Against Forfeited Grid Games;" 17 December 1927; "Hampton and Lincoln Will Play on Nov. 2," 6 July 1929; "Hampton Opens Football Season on Oct. 5 At Home Against Howard University," 14 September 1929; and "Hampton Plays Lincoln U in Yank Stadium," 13 September 1930.

23. The phrase "Singing Up" was used specifically in the *Southern Workman* to describe the northern tour of Hampton singers in 1872–1875 to generate money for the building of the school's Virginia Hall. See the *Southern Workman*, Vol. 41, December 1912, p. 682. For information on revolts at Black colleges during the decade of the 1920s, see Raymond Wolters, *The New Negro on Campus: Black College Rebellions of the 1920s* (Princeton: Princeton University Press, 1975); James E. Alford, Jr. "For Alma Mater: Fighting for Change at Historically Black Colleges and Universities," unpublished doctoral dissertation, Columbia University, 2013.

24. John O. Perpener, *African-American Concert Dance: The Harlem Renaissance and Beyond*, 84; Martha H. Verbrugge, *Active Bodies*, 131. See also Mary Ann Laverty, *Finding a Way Out: Charles H. Williams and the Hampton Institute Creative Dance Group*.

25. Charles H. Williams to Harwood B. Catlin, 12 June 1934, "Correspondence and Letters," CHW Papers, HUA. For information on Shawn, see Patricia Vertinsky's insightful "'This Dancing Business is More Hazardous than any "He-Man" Sport': Ted Shawn and His Men Dancers," *Sociology of Sport Journal* 35.2 (June 2018): 168–177.

26. Charles H. Williams, "The Hampton Institute Creative Dance Group," 4 (October 1937), 97–98.

27. Quoted in Martha H. Verbrugge, *Active Bodies*, 131.

28. For information on the Terpsichorean Dance Company, see Libars.hampton.edu/edhd/hper_terps.cfm.

29. Charles H. Williams, *Sidelights on Negro Soldiers* (Boston: B.J. Brimmer Co.1923); Charles H. Williams, *Negro Soldiers in WW I: The Human Side* (New York: AMS Press, 1970); Charles H. Williams, *Cotton Needs Pickin: Characteristic Negro Folk Dances* (Norfolk: Guide Publishing Co., 1928).

30. Charles H. Williams to John Hopper, "Correspondence and Letters," 28 August 1969, 19 November 1970, CHW Papers, HUA.

31. See James D. Anderson, *The Education of Blacks in the South, 1860–1935* (Chapel Hill: The University of North Carolina Press, 1988); Donald Spivey, *Schooling for the New Slavery: Black Industrial Education, 1868–1915* (Westport, Conn: Greenwood Press, 1978).

32. See Charles H. Williams, "Recreation in the Lives of Young People," *Southern Workman* 46 (February 1917): 95–100; Charles H. Williams, "Twenty Years Work of the CIAA," *Southern Workman* 61 (February 1932): 65–76; Charles H. Williams, "Negro Athletes in the Tenth Olympiad," *Southern Workman*, 61 (November 1932): 449–460; Charles H. Williams, "'Darkest Africa at 'A Century of Progress,'" *Southern Workman* 62 (November 1933): 429–437; and Charles H. Williams, "Negro Athletes in the Eleventh Olympiad," *Southern Workman* 66 (February 1937); 45–59.

33. Charles H. Williams, "Recreation in the Lives of Young People," 96.

34. Ibid.

35. Charles H. Williams, "Recreation in the Lives of Young People," 97.

36. Charles H. Williams, "Negro Athletes in the Eleventh Olympiad," 58–59.

37. Charles H. Williams to Sol White, 13 March 1928. See also Charles H. Williams to Sol White, 6 March 1928, "Correspondence and Letters," CHW Papers, HUA. What topic Williams ultimately decided to write on for his master's thesis is not known. There is no indication in his papers at Hampton Institute what topic he chose, and his thesis could not be located at the Harvard University Archives. This is apparently not surprising as indicated by correspondence from the reference staff at the Harvard University Archives to the author: "Unfortunately, after a thorough review of our collections, we have been unable to locate a thesis by Charles Holston Williams. This is not particularly unusual, as the Archives has traditionally only kept undergraduate and doctoral theses." Letter from reference staff to David K. Wiggins, 22 October 2018.

38. Charles H. Williams to George H. Lockhart, 31 January 1930, CHW Papers, HUA.

39. Like Williams, Henderson was a trained physical educator, race man, and prolific author who fought his entire adult life to secure equality for Blacks in sport and the larger American society. He became famous for introducing basketball to African American children in Washington, DC, and has garnered much attention for writing *The Negro in Sports*. Perhaps the essential differences between the two men were that Henderson was more directly involved in civil rights organizations while Williams's prominent position in a university, and a well-known one at that, provided space in which he could be more impactful in both interscholastic and intercollegiate sport at the regional and national levels. More Information on Henderson can be gleaned

from David K. Wiggins, "Edwin Bancroft Henderson, African American Athletes, and the Writing of Sport History" in *Glory Bound: Black Athletes in a White America*, David K. Wiggins (Syracuse: Syracuse University Press, 1997), 222–241 and David K. Wiggins, "Edwin Bancroft Henderson: Physical Educator, Civil Rights Activist, and Chronicler of African American Athletes," *Research Quarterly for Exercise and Sport* 70.2 (June 1999): 91–112.

40. Charles H. Williams to Edwin B. Henderson, 8 June 1939, "Correspondence and Letters," CHW Papers, HUA.

41. Charles H. Williams to Edwin B. Henderson, 12 December 1939, "Correspondence and Letters," CHW Papers, HUA.

42. Insights into the Freedom's People radio show can be gathered through Barbara Dianne Savage, *Broadcasting Freedom: Radio, War, and the Politics of Race, 1938–1948* (Chapel Hill: The University of North Carolina Press, 1999).

43. Charles H. Williams to Ambrose Caliver, 6 November 1941, "Correspondence and Letters," CHW Papers, HUA.

44. Andrew M. Burris to Charles H. Williams, 29 August 1951, "Correspondence and Letters," CHW Papers, HUA.

45. Charles H. Williams to Andrew M. Burris, 15 November 1952, "Correspondence and Letters," CHW Papers, HUA.

46. See, for instance, Charles H. Williams to Alumnus, 1 October 1957, "Correspondence and Letters," CHW Papers, HUA.

47. Charles H. Williams to Walter H. Aiken, 13 January 1960, "Correspondence and Letters," CHW Papers, HUA.

48. Charles H. Williams, "To Members of the Special Committee on Curriculum, Hampton Board of Trustees, 1956," "Correspondence and Letters," CHW Papers.

49. Ibid.

50. See, for instance, Charles H. Williams to William S. Hart, 3 May 1956; "Remarks by Chas. H. Williams" Dedication of People's Building and Loan Association New Building, "Correspondence and Letters," CHW Papers, HUA.

51. "Financial Statement of Charles H. Williams, 12 May 1968," "Correspondence and Letters," CHW Papers, HUA. As a result of his position at the Bay Shore Resort, Williams ultimately became Vice President of the Nationwide Hotel Association. It was an association that included as members owners and operators of Black motels, hotels, and tourist's home. It put out a directory like the more famous Green Book that made suggestions regarding safe lodging and other travel accommodations for African American tourists. See Dykes A. Brookins to Charles H. Williams, 5 March 1956.

52. Charles H. Williams to Gideon E. Smith, 23 January 1960, Correspondence and Letters, CHW Papers, HUA.

53. Cleve L. Abbott to Charles H. Williams, 10 July 1952, "Correspondence and Letters," CHW Papers, HUA.

CREATING ORDER IN BLACK COLLEGE SPORT

The Lasting Legacy of the Colored Intercollegiate Athletic Association

With Chris Elzey

Black college sport realized significant growth during the twentieth century. Black institutions of different sizes and reputations, including Howard University and Hampton Institute in the upper south and Tuskegee Institute and Morehouse College in the lower south, expanded their athletic programs, resulting in more competitions in a greater number of sports. But increased emphasis on intercollegiate athletics also had a downside. Accompanying the growth were many problems, such as a greater number of injuries, inadequate coaching, poor officiating, inappropriate fan behavior, player eligibility concerns, and game scheduling issues.[1]

The problems associated with burgeoning sports programs at Black colleges caused serious concerns among faculty and administrators. The aftermath of the football crisis of 1905, in which dozens of players were either seriously injured or killed, eventually led to the establishment of the National Collegiate Athletic Association (NCAA) in 1906 after several prominent individuals suggested the creation of a national organization to oversee Black college sport. In 1906, Samuel H. Archer, football coach, dean, vice president, and later fifth president of Morehouse College, penned an essay titled "Football in Our Colleges" in *The Voice of the Negro*. In the piece, Archer declared a "pressing need" for an "Intercollegiate Athletic Association" to govern sport among Black colleges. Claiming that "most of the charges made against the game (football) are general and might well apply to any of the sports that appeal to young and vigorous manhood," the future Morehouse president advocated for a national organization with a "constitution and printed rules" that would promote "every kind of outdoor sport, prevent the establishment of uncertain precedents, create a wholesome athletic enthusiasm, and maintain a uniform rule in all the colleges concerning professionalism and eligibility of players."[2]

Archer's colleague at Morehouse College, and later secretary of the Colored Men's Department of the International Committee of the YMCA, as well as president of the University of Arkansas Pine Bluff, John Brown Watson, also argued for a national organization to oversee Black college sport. In a 1907 essay entitled "Football in Southern Negro Colleges," Watson wrote "an institution in demand now is an Intercollegiate Athletic Association affecting all the colleges of the whole South." Such a group was needed. "With intercollegiate organization," Watson noted, "many evils connected with the choice of officials and the playing of games could be done away with and the whole matter of college athletics given a higher tone."[3]

Although a separate national organization to govern Black college sport never materialized, several regional Black athletic associations did come into existence during the second decade of the twentieth century. One of the first regional associations was the CIAA. In 1912, Ernest J. Marshall, professor of chemistry and football coach at Howard University in Washington, DC, convened a meeting of representatives from several well-known Black colleges at Hampton Institute to discuss the creation of an organization to govern sports at their respective schools. Attending the meeting from Shaw University in Raleigh, North Carolina, were W. E. Atkins, H. P. Hargrave, and C. R. Frazier. From Virginia Union University in Richmond came J. W. Pierce and J. W. Barco. George Johnson, a professor at Lincoln University in Oxford, Pennsylvania, also attended. Acting as the conclave's de facto hosts were Hampton's Charles H. Williams and Allen Washington.[4]

United in their belief that a governing body was needed to bring order to Black college sport, the men established the CIAA, the first Black athletic conference in the United States. Over two days of intense discussion and debate, they drafted a "Constitution and By-Laws," which each member institution—Hampton Institute, Howard University, Shaw University, Virginia Union University, and Lincoln University—pledged to follow. The five schools became the original members of the CIAA.

The educators meeting at Hampton in 1912 were all prominent men who, like many middle-class Black Americans, believed in the principle of racial uplift. Experiencing various forms of racial hostility, forced to live in a segregated society, and suffering the indignities of Jim Crow laws, the founders of the CIAA emphasized through sport positive images of highly educated and assimilated African Americans who carried themselves with unimpeachable character. To the founders, the new athletic organization would represent the very best sport could offer—characterized by strict adherence to rules, sportsmanship, fiscal transparency, and impeccable organizational structure. In this way, they believed, the CIAA would provide optimal conditions for athletic competition and, by extension, combat deeply entrenched stereotypes of Black inferiority and moral degradation. Providing high quality sports programs and achieving respectability, however, would be difficult. In an era that denied African Americans equal rights and freedom of opportunity while condoning racialist thinking irrespective of educational attainment, cultural background, and social status, the CIAA, like other Black institutions at the time, was engaged in a constant battle to prove its worth, conquer social marginalization, and gain recognition in a society that viewed African Americans as being inferior to Whites.[5]

Highly detailed and written in unambiguous language, the "Constitution and By-Laws" provides insights into the new organization's priorities and the issues confronting Black college sports more generally. Perhaps nothing generated more concern than player eligibility. Like officials at predominantly White schools, the founding members of the CIAA wanted to eliminate "tramp athletes," physically gifted players who were known to extend their college football career beyond four years by transferring from one institution to another with little regard for academics.[6] To rein in tramp athletes, the CIAA stipulated that no student would be eligible for athletics until satisfying the "entrance requirements of the department in which he is enrolled, has completed a full year's work equivalent to that required of candidates for a degree, and is taking during his year of competition a full year's work in the institution."[7]

In addition, the CIAA proclaimed itself to be the national governing body of Black college sport, specifying that "no student shall participate in inter-collegiate athletics more than four years in the aggregate in" nineteen Black colleges and universities, "and [in] many other institutions hereafter approved eligible for membership in the association."[8] But after other Black athletic associations were established—the Southeastern Intercollegiate Athletic Conference (SIAC) in 1913, South Atlantic Intercollegiate Athletic Association in 1916, and Southwestern Athletic Conference (SAC) in 1920, for example-and after the CIAA joined the NCAA in 1921, the regulations were modified and the association officially ceased to speak for Black college sport as a whole.[9]

The rules set by the CIAA were rigidly enforced. Claiming itself to be "the pioneering organization for the purpose of raising the standard of athletics in the negro schools and colleges," and recognizing the importance of exhibiting skills of self-organization and business acumen in a racially segregated America, the CIAA sharply punished member schools for violating the association's written policies.[10]

Howard University and Lincoln University, two of the most prestigious HBCUs in the United States, were among the first to be punished by the young organization for rules violations. In 1923, a student named Robert Miller played football for Virginia Union. The following year, Miller transferred to Dunbar High School in Washington, DC, and then to Howard University, where he also played football. Virginia Normal and Industrial Institute (later Virginia State), Lincoln University, and Hampton Institute all protested, arguing that Miller should have been declared ineligible for the 1924 season because he had violated CIAA guidelines that specified students who transferred from high school to college were required to sit out a year before returning to competition. Howard University officials, in a telegram sent by Edward P. Davis, president of the university's Board of Athletic Control, responded by withdrawing the school from the CIAA, noting that "we regret that we are forced to this step by the impossibility of reconciling collegiate and high school standards in the association and hope that our pleasant relations with the member institutions may continue."[11] The CIAA accepted the university's decision, claiming "that the association feels that it is incumbent upon it to say to Howard that it has done its duty in attempting to carry on the spirit and letter of our association, and in furtherance of that policy cannot in justice to our ideals of true sportsmanship arrange athletic contests under conditions which destroy the integrity of the association."[12]

Having withdrawn from the CIAA, Howard was forbidden to play other conference teams. Even though Lincoln University was one of the three schools to have protested Miller's eligibility, it went ahead and played Howard in the annual Thanksgiving Day football game that year anyway—also a clear violation of CIAA rules. As a result, Lincoln was dropped from the conference in 1925. By not showing favoritism to such prestigious institutions as Howard and Lincoln, the CIAA was able to garner much respect, ultimately giving the conference more power, and thus greater control. After much discussion with athletic leaders of both institutions, and after both schools instituted changes to their academic policies, the CIAA reinstated Howard in 1929, and Lincoln in 1932.[13]

Another incident occurred in 1941. On March 7, Virginia Union played the Harlem Globetrotters in a basketball exhibition in Richmond, Virginia. It was not unusual for CIAA schools to play such exhibitions, but Virginia Union had violated conference rules by not seeking permission from the association to compete against a professional team. In what it claimed was an effort to keep its players "from being contaminated or from losing their proper amateur standing," Virginia Union had instead obtained permission from the Virginia Association of the Amateur Athletic Union (AAU), having agreed that proceeds from the game were to be donated to a building fund at the school.[14]

The CIAA, however, was not persuaded. According to J. L. Whitehead, then secretary-treasurer for the CIAA, the AAU's sanctioning of the game had not invalidated the regulations of the league. Consequently, the CIAA, on recommendation from its eligibility committee, suspended Virginia Union for the remainder of the academic year, though the association was quick to point out "that the amateur status of the union's 1941 basketball team was not affected because the University, and not the players, had violated the CIAA code." A message, though, had been sent. Meting out harsh punishments bolstered the association's efforts to upgrade the integrity of its sports programs, while ensuring that all athletes were treated fairly and given the best opportunity to realize a positive educational experience in the classroom.[15]

The CIAA scrupulously applied attention to all aspects of college sport. No matter the task—the proper scheduling of games; the maintenance of records; fostering good sportsmanship; generating appropriate publicity and media coverage; and improving the quality of coaching, officiating, and administrative leadership—the association strived to be the very best.

Such meticulousness was displayed in the *CIAA Bulletin*. First published in 1923 and printed and distributed by Hampton Institute, the *Bulletin* was a detailed account of the organization's yearly activities. Each issue typically consisted of the names of delegates and minutes from the previous year's two-day CIAA meeting; essays on a variety of sport-related topics; comprehensive financial statements; lists of certified officials for each sport; a chronicling and cataloging of scores and team champions; and photographs of tournament participants and victorious squads in each sport.[16]

The 1924 *Bulletin* illustrates the seriousness with which the association conducted its business. Only the second *Bulletin* ever published, the issue listed the delegates of the previous year's meeting held at the Virginia Theological Seminary and College and the names of officers, including William H. Rogers of Virginia Normal and Industrial Institute (president); Louis L. Watson of Howard University (first vice president); and Charles H. Williams of Hampton University (secretary-treasurer).[17] In the issue, Charles H. Williams penned a brief introduction, reinstating the purpose of the CIAA and noted that three schools—Virginia Seminary, Virginia Normal and Industrial Institute, and St. Paul—had recently become CIAA members. William A. Rogers provided a "review of the season of 1923 in athletics" for each sport, noted the various accomplishments of the association and offered recommendations to improve the organization.[18] The issue also listed detailed minutes of the annual meeting and the organization's financial statement, which revealed that the CIAA had paid dues of $25 to the NCAA, contributed $75 to the United States Olympic Fund, and spent $89.65 to publish the *Bulletin*, leaving the association a balance of $147.90.[19]

In addition, the 1924 issue featured seven essays. Topics ranged from the impact of Greek societies on sports to interscholastic basketball and issues of athletic eligibility. J. H. Lawrence, Director of Athletics at Virginia Theological Seminary and College, contributed a piece. Edwin B. Henderson, Director of Physical Education for the segregated public schools in Washington, DC, wrote an essay entitled, "How Can Schools Co-operate with Officials to Develop Greater Efficiency."[20]

Perhaps no piece was as thought provoking as Henderson's. An educator and civil rights activist who wrote the first books on the history of African American participation in sport, Henderson made the obvious but unspoken observation that for many years "the leading qualifications for an official was that he be a white man."[21] Henderson pointed out that while more African Americans were hired as officials, they still received less money than did their White counterparts. He ended by expressing his philosophy of college athletics and sport more generally. "Even if presidents cry out for victories" Henderson wrote, "no matter the cost, our profession cannot hope to be considered for its real worth and value in education unless we teach the presidents themselves, if need be, the real virtue in well-played games with victories and defeats as secondary matters."[22]

Subsequent issues of the *Bulletin* were similar. Essays addressing the organizational structure of the association, issues of amateurism, and improvements to the quality of play for all participants were published. After 1924, however, the *Bulletin* added several important sections, including summations of one-day coaches and officials conferences, reports of presentations by members of the Black press, testimonials from former CIAA athletes, and a section called "In memoriams" for athletes and others who had been affiliated with the organization.[23] The 1933 *Bulletin*, for example, gave an account of the first "CIAA Coaches Officials Conference at Hampton" held the previous year. Attended by sixty officials, coaches, and journalists from the *Norfolk Journal and Guide* and *Baltimore Afro-American*, the conference—which included keynote addresses and question-and-answer sessions—was designed to ensure optimal officiating and that CIAA football coaches understood the rules of the game. Over time, other conferences would be held for basketball. The football and basketball conferences eventually broadened participation by inviting team captains from league schools, as well as high school coaches.[24]

Unsurprisingly, Black journalists attended the coaches and officials conferences. Members of the Black press were frequent participants at CIAA meetings and regularly wrote columns about the association. Moreover, prominent journalists often gave presentations at the meetings, which were then published in the *Bulletin*. The relationship between the Black press and the CIAA was mutually beneficial. Black newspapers provided extensive coverage to the association, disseminating news about sporting events and programs that were usually not covered by the mainstream press, while the Black press enhanced its credibility and, in turn, increased readership and the price of advertising space by covering a principled organization.[25]

The *Bulletin* was strengthened by the inclusion of published testimonials from league players. Seeking to garner positive public relations while making clear the association's view of sport, CIAA officials asked selected players to discuss their athletic careers and what the league had meant to them. In the 1936 issue, Otis E. Thorpe, quarterback at Morgan College in Baltimore, extolled the virtues of athletics and, by extension, the association. To Thorpe, sports inculcated values necessary for good citizenship. "After four years of development along the lines of sportsmanship, team play, SELF-CONTROL and SELF-CONFIDENCE," Thorpe wrote, "the athlete finds himself better fitted to become a citizen. Respect for the officials of the game and the rules of the game, one will carry over and will have due regard for the governing body and the laws they enact."[26] In the 1938 *Bulletin*, Junius L. T. Jeffries, a sprinter from Hampton Institute, discussed the goodwill and friendships established through athletic competition. "There is created a spirit of goodwill and fair play among men in competition," noted Jeffries. "The personal contacts made with men we have met for the first time, although we are trying to beat one another, are of inestimable value in our attempt to play life's game fairly."[27]

The "In Memoriams" published in the *Bulletin* paid respects to athletes, administrators, and other key figures who had contributed to the success of the association. An especially poignant memoriam recalled the life of John Borican, the outstanding track star from Virginia State who died unexpectedly in December 1942 from a mysterious case of pernicious anemia. Written by CIAA President George G. Singleton, the memoriam noted that Borican's sudden death "caused deep grief in the hearts of his many admirers throughout the sports world in general and among the coaches, former competitors and present and future track luminaries of the Colored Intercollegiate Athletic Association in particular." Borican, who was just twenty-nine when he died, was remembered not only for his AAU titles in the pentathlon, decathlon, and 800 meters, but also for his famous victory in 1939 over the legendary Glenn Cunningham in the 1000-yard run. In addition, Borican's brief yet highly successful post-athletic career as a portrait artist and illustrator was recalled. At the time of his death, Borican was a PhD student in the arts program at Columbia University.[28]

The *Bulletin* was only superseded in quality by the association's leadership, organizational structure, and various sports programs. CIAA leadership consisted of a president, three vice presidents, a secretary-treasurer, and an assistant secretary-treasurer—all elected yearly. The men who held each office occupied important professional and administrative positions at their respective institutions. Ernest Marshall, for example, one of the founders of the CIAA and its president from 1912 to 1915, was a professor of chemistry at Howard University. William A. Rogers, president of the CIAA from 1920 to 1924, was secretary of Virginia State University, and chaired the school's athletic committee for twenty years. Walter G. Alexander, president of the CIAA between 1925 and 1928, graduated from Lincoln University in 1899 and would go on to become a medical doctor in Orange, New Jersey. H.C. Perrin, president of the CIAA from 1939 to 1941, was a professor at Shaw University; and George C. Singleton, President of the CIAA from 1943 to 1945, was a professor and director of the Department of Business at Virginia State University.[29]

Under the guidance of such men, the CIAA would expand. In 1920, Virginia State University became a member, followed by St. Paul's College three years later. North Carolina A&T College joined the association in 1924, Johnson C. Smith University in 1926, and North Carolina Central University and Bluefield State College in 1928. By 1945, five other schools—Morgan State University, Livingston College, St. Augustine's College, Delaware State University, and Winston & Salem State University—had signed on. Boasting sixteen teams, the league was divided into three regional districts: northern, central and southern. In 1950, the association changed its name to the CIAA.[30]

In addition to enduring player eligibility issues and rules violations by member institutions, the CIAA was forced to weather circumstances beyond its control, namely the Great Depression and two World Wars. Fortunately, the conference emerged from the crises relatively unscathed. But it had been tested. The Depression, for instance, demanded that the CIAA be extra vigilant in safeguarding its money. In 1931, Charles H. Williams, then secretary-treasurer, deposited association funds in the "Farmers and Merchants Bank, Lawrenceville, VA and in another bank in another city of his selection" because, in his view, it "was the prudent and safe procedure to follow until conditions get back to normalcy."[31] The following year, CIAA President James T. Taylor of North Carolina Central University suggested that to help save money, the number of football officials be reduced. Having fewer officials, Taylor wrote, "is in keeping with the general trend in wages and salary. Most of our institutions are finding it rather hard to finance athletics and it would seem only fair that the 'hen' that lays the golden egg should be given due consideration."[32]

Far more problematic were World War I and II. As a result of the United States' entry into World War I in 1917, the CIAA, for the only time in its history, held no annual meeting and canceled the football season. World War II would test the CIAA even more. Since many CIAA athletes were entering the military, teams became depleted. Transportation was also an issue. During the war years, the cost of traveling increased, making it more difficult for schools to complete their schedules. The smaller and less financially endowed institutions were hit the hardest. St. Paul's College, for example, canceled its 1942 football season. Smaller schools, such as Shaw University and St. Augustine's College, were forced to withdraw from some contests after receiving permission from the association to do so.[33]

Despite the difficulties caused by World War II, the CIAA maintained the quality of its sports programs. There was a tradeoff, however, the association relaxing many of its academic policies. For instance, it took the unprecedented move—albeit for one year—of altering its eligibility requirements to ensure that member schools could field teams. It even gave permission to St. Augustine's College and Shaw University to organize a "joint football team," because of the shortage of players. In addition, member schools were allowed to play opponents more than once, and teams were encouraged to play opponents within their districts, thereby adhering to the wishes of the Office of Defense Transportation.[34]

World War II also led the CIAA to enlarge program offerings. Exhibiting patriotism, the association felt compelled to expand both its physical education and intramural programs "so as to reach more students and thus to make the maximum contribution to the nation's war job."[35] The CIAA's contribution to the war effort reflected its belief that sports developed healthy bodies, courage, respect for authority, and other traits essential for success on the battlefield. Perhaps Virginia State's George G. Singleton best expressed such a view in his presidential address at the 1943 convention. Recalling Abraham Lincoln's famous Gettysburg Address, Singleton spoke of the importance of the CIAA, and the valuable role it played in developing upstanding young men. "One score and eleven years ago," Singleton said, "our founders brought forth upon this continent a new association converged in sportsmanship and dedicated to the proposition that clean athletic activities are essential to the physical, moral, mental, scholastic and cultural development of the negro youth of the land. Now we are engaged in a great war threatening that association to its very foundation and testing whether that association or any association so concerned and so dedicated can long endure."[36]

The CIAA, of course, did. Helping the association survive was football. Like many predominantly White institutions, CIAA schools embraced the gridiron game because it toughened young men, built character, made money, generated alumni support and contributed to institutional spirit and loyalty. The CIAA featured several outstanding players and teams. At first, a committee determined the yearly champion. Eventually, though, the Dickinson rating system was used. Several rivalries, which drew national attention and thus generated additional publicity for the CIAA, defined league competition.[37]

Arguably the most intensely followed rivalry was the one between Lincoln and Howard Universities, especially between 1919 and 1929, the so-called Golden Age of sports. Each year, on Thanksgiving Day, the two most northern and prestigious institutions in the conference squared off against each other on the gridiron. Alternating yearly between Philadelphia and Washington, DC, the game, otherwise known as "The Classic," drew huge crowds. Specially chartered trains would bring a multitude of fans from across the country—many of whom were members of the Black upper-class—to the host city. In addition to watching the game, Classic goers attended dances, receptions, parties, and pep rallies sponsored by the two institutions. To African Americans, The Classic was just as significant as Harvard vs. Yale and other football rivalries in White college sport.[38]

The CIAA offered other sports, including baseball, boxing and wrestling. But track and field, tennis, and basketball proved to be more popular among CIAA institutions. The first formally recognized CIAA track meet was held in 1922 at Hampton Institute. Organized under the direction of Charles H. Williams and held at Hampton's new Armstrong Field, the meet included athletes from every CIAA institution. There was also a high school division. Athletes representing Huntington High School in Newport News, Virginia; Booker T. Washington High School in Norfolk, Virginia; and Dunbar High School and Armstrong Tech High School in Washington, DC, competed. The inaugural meet was a huge success. For the next seven years, the league held its track meet at Hampton. In 1930, it was switched to Howard University. In the years that ensued, the meet was held at various locations.[39]

The CIAA track meet would grow in importance and stature, requiring greater oversight and organizational structure. The meet at Morgan State College in 1942 is a prime example. Hundreds of athletes—college as well as high school—competed in events that ranged from the 100-yard dash to the mile run to the shot put and javelin. Howard P. Drew, the one-time record holder in the sprints who starred at the University of Southern California, served as the meet's formal starter. Jesse Owens, the famous Ohio State track star and Olympic hero, was featured in an exhibition of the 100-yard dash and broad jump. A special one-mile relay race was held among several military service teams. Honorary referees for the meet included such local dignitaries as Edward S. Lewis, executive secretary of the Urban League in Baltimore; Carl J. Murphy, editor of the *Baltimore Afro-American*; Dr. David E. Weglein, Baltimore superintendent of schools; Dr. D. O. W. Holmes, Morgan State College president; Howard W. Jackson, mayor of Baltimore; and Maryland Governor Herbert R. O'Connor.[40]

In 1924, the CIAA expanded its sports program by holding its first tennis tournament. Four schools—Howard University, Hampton Institute, St. Paul's College, and Virginia Normal Institute—took part. Howard was victorious, capturing both the singles and doubles titles. Later, the winner of the CIAA singles title competed against Black champions from the Southern Intercollegiate Conference, the Southern Athletic Conference, and the Mid-Western Athletic Association at the annual American Tennis Association (ATA) tournament. The winner was given the Williams Cup. The Williams Cup tournament revealed the cooperation shown not only among Black athletic conferences but also between the ATA and HBCUs. Founded in 1916 by more than a dozen Black tennis clubs, the ATA staged several early national championships at HBCUs because the tennis courts on campuses were in good condition and because players would not encounter discriminatory policies regarding lodging. University administrators, for their part, recognized the benefits—financial as well as political—of hosting the ATA tournament. Large numbers of African Americans would be on campus sharing in the excitement of tennis matches and attending tournament parties and other social events.[41]

The CIAA held no tennis competition for women. While women from CIAA schools may have played in other tennis tournaments, there is no evidence that they competed in CIAA events. In 1928, Charles H. Williams noted that the CIAA had made provisions for women's participation, "but this innovation has met with little success."[42] In fact, there were no CIAA competitions for women in any sport, and only a few participated in events sponsored by other HBCUs and by Black athletic organizations. Such nonparticipation reflected the biases of the CIAA and the United States more generally. Reinforcing such views was the attitude of the African American community itself. Some influential Black organizations opposed highly organized sport for women, encouraging instead the playing of intramural games, which, the thinking went, were less likely to inflict physiological damage, cause emotional harm, and violate acceptable notions of Black femininity and womanhood. One such organization was the National Association of College Women (NACW), a prestigious group founded in 1910 by Mary Church Terrell.[43] As historian Rita Liberti notes, the NACW in 1929 and 1940 declared its opposition to highly organized college athletics for women, "urging the substitution of intramural contests and intercollegiate non-competitive play activities."[44]

Despite such opposition, there were many African American women who played organized sport. Lucy Diggs Slowe, the first dean of women at Howard University and one of the original founders of Alpha Kappa Sorority, for instance, captured the women's single title in 1917 at the first ATA national tournament in Baltimore. Ironically, Slowe, who won the championship nine years after graduating from Howard University and five years before becoming dean at the university, was the first president of the NACW.[45] Tuskegee Institute, competing in the SIAC, had the best women's track team in the country for decades. Coached by Cleve Abbott, then Christine Petty and finally Nell Jackson, Tuskegee captured multiple AAU national championships in the 1930s and 1940s.[46] Bennett College, a coeducational institution founded in 1873 in Greensboro, North Carolina, by the Methodist Episcopal Church, featured some of the top Black women's basketball teams during the Depression years. Showcasing tremendously skilled players, such as the great Ruth Glover, Bennett competed against such powerhouse clubs as the Philadelphia Tribunes—and more than held their own.[47]

No women played organized basketball in the CIAA. (It would not be until 1975 that the association held a postseason women's tournament.) Only men did. And it was hugely popular. Howard University, Hampton Institute, Virginia Union, North Carolina College and Morgan College especially embraced the sport, though the number of conference games played each year was modest by today's standards. For example, Howard University announced a 12-game schedule for the 1933–34 season. Twelve years later, St. Augustine's College played a scant six conference games. Most CIAA institutions, however, listed as many as twenty contests per season. North Carolina College's overall schedule for 1941–42 totaled thirty games. But in each of the next three seasons, the most games the school played was twenty-three, in 1942–43. Just as it did to other universities, World War II forced the college to curtail its sport schedules.[48]

CIAA schools did not just play basketball against other association teams. On occasion, they also played athletic clubs and predominantly White institutions. In 1938, CIAA titleholder Morgan College traveled to New York to play Long Island University (LIU), a perennial power coached by the legendary Clair Bee. That same year, Virginia Union also played LIU in the Big Apple, but lost, 57–40. In late March 1939, Virginia Union, champions of the CIAA, again took on Bee's squad, in Harlem—LIU had just won the coveted National Invitation Tournament (NIT)—and this time prevailed. The victory, however, was fleeting. Several days after the game, Tristram Walker Metcalfe, the head of LIU, announced that the team Virginian Union had defeated consisted of only seniors, and therefore did not represent LIU's actual varsity squad. The following year, Virginia Union returned to Harlem and played Brooklyn College. The Panthers, whom the *New York Times* described as "speedy," routed the Brooklynites, 54–38.[49]

In 1946 the CIAA held its first postseason basketball tournament. Organized by association members Talmadge Hill, John B. McLendon, John Burr, and Harry Jefferson—all except Hill were head basketball coaches—the tournament grew to become arguably the most significant athletic event among association schools and HBCUs more generally. William M. Bell, president of the CIAA in the 1940s, would later call the tournament "the greatest indoor attraction in the United States which is sponsored by predominantly Black institutions of higher education."[50]

Not that other Black conferences had shied away from organizing postseason basketball tournaments. In 1934, for instance, the SIAC began sponsoring an annual conference tournament, and seven years later, the inaugural National Invitational Intercollegiate Basketball Tournament (NIIBT) gathered six HBCUs in Cincinnati to determine the unofficial Black college champion. But the SIAC tournament never achieved the kind of fame that the CIAA's did, and the NIIBT was a fiscal train wreck—so few people attended games. *Baltimore Afro-American* columnist Art Carter wrote, "The fans stayed away as if the scene of the tournament . . . was a leper colony." When Kentucky State College President R. B. Atwood tried to organize a Black college national basketball tournament the following year, there were no takers. Officials of Black athletic conferences claimed that the ongoing war effort made participation impossible. The troubles associated with the NIIBT may have also helped convince them.[51]

At first CIAA officials were lukewarm to the idea of staging a postseason tournament. The matter had been raised as early as 1937. In the years that ensued, the idea would again be debated at least twice, and each time it was rejected. Opponents fretted over the cost and questioned why a tournament was needed. Would it be the only factor determining the league champion? If so, what about the games played during the regular season? Would they not count for anything?[52]

But tournament supporters pressed on. Their hard work eventually paid off. In December 1945, at the annual CIAA gathering in Washington, DC, representatives agreed to organize a tournament—after initially deciding not to. Part of the reason why officials changed their mind was because of money. CIAA coffers were almost bare. At the end of 1944, the association had only $165.75 in the bank. Making things worse, several schools were having difficulties paying dues. A basketball tournament, officials argued, would provide a much-needed infusion of cash. Delegates also believed that a tournament would promote the conference while showcasing the league's best players and teams. Morgan College's Talmadge Hill was appointed tournament committee chairman. Joining Hill were John Burr of Howard University, John B. McLendon of North Carolina College, and Harry R. "Big Jeff" Jefferson of Virginia State.[53]

By early 1946, a host city and venue had been selected. Turner's Arena, at 14th and W Streets, NW, in Washington, DC, sat two blocks away from the city's famous U Street, a.k.a. Black Broadway. A former auto service shop, Turner's could seat roughly 2,000 spectators for basketball—not a huge number, but big enough, particularly for such an unknown commodity as the CIAA tournament. Turner's was well-known among Black Washingtonians. Many Black events—sporting and otherwise—had been held in the arena. The Washington Bears, for example, a popular all-Black professional basketball team that captured the World Professional Basketball Tournament in 1943, played their home games at Turner's. Black boxers, including future World Light Heavyweight titleholder Archie Moore, also fought there. Among the African American entertainers who performed in Turner's were Duke Ellington, Ella Fitzgerald, Jimmie Lunceford, and Paul Robeson.[54]

The inaugural CIAA basketball tournament began on Thursday afternoon, March 7. Of sixteen league teams, half were invited to participate. Because league schools had played a different number of conference games, officials used the Dickinson system to determine which teams would take part. Lincoln University received the top seed, followed by Virginia Union, Morgan College and West Virginia State University. Seeded fifth through eighth, respectively, were North Carolina College, J.C. Smith University, Virginia State and Winston-Salem State University.[55]

From the outset, the tournament yielded the unexpected: North Carolina College, coached by John B. McLendon, bested higher-rated West Virginia State, 60–56, and then beat the number-one seed, Lincoln University. Meanwhile, the other half of the bracket unfolded according to the rankings. On Thursday evening, Virginia Union eked by Virginia State, and the next night, overpowered Morgan College, 42–37. The championship game was set. It would be the fast-breaking North Carolina College Eagles versus the Panthers of Virginia Union.[56]

The league could not have hoped for a more exciting final. *Norfolk Journal and Guide* columnist Lem Graves, Jr., called it "my all-time sports 'thrill-of-a-lifetime.'" Spectators attending the sold-out game that Saturday afternoon were left feeling as if they had just finished riding the Cyclone at Coney Island. Virginia Union started quickly, building a 7-point margin in the first half. McLendon's team, however, battled back, and by halftime, it was 23-all. For much of the second half, the score was close, but in the final minutes of the game, Virginia Union moved in front, 46–40. Once again, the undersized Eagles rallied, scoring three straight baskets, including one, incredibly, as time ran out. Each team tallied a bucket in the first overtime, and then added eight points apiece in the second. In the third extra period, the Panthers failed to score, and the Eagles went on to win, 64–56. Players and fans alike were exhausted. "North Carolina College Surprises to Win CIAA Tourney in Hectic Tilt with Union," the *Baltimore Afro-American* headlined. Approximately 75 percent of the sports page in the *Norfolk Journal and Guide* was devoted to tournament write-ups.[57]

The inaugural tournament surpassed almost every expectation. Fans came away enthused. Newspapermen applauded the high level of play. Many coaches were pleased. CIAA authorities gladly welcomed the money generated by the three-day affair, which, altogether, had earned almost $934—more than five times the amount the association had had in reserves fifteen months earlier.[58]

But not everyone was satisfied. Lincoln University's basketball coach Manny Rivero, whose team finished the regular season atop the CIAA, strongly opposed the decision to crown tournament winner North Carolina College conference champion. Rivero minced no words, labeling CIAA President John H. Burr, who also served on the tournament committee, "weak-kneed." Rivero had a point. Back in December, when league representatives first gave the go-ahead for a tournament, it was determined that the team with the highest rating based on the Dickinson system—which Lincoln was, at the end of the 1945–46 season—would be named CIAA champions. In the intervening months, however, a poll taken by the league indicated that a majority of association members believed the decision should be reversed. Some officials feared that without having the conference title up for grabs, the tournament would be a flop. Nine months later, at the 1946 meeting in Institute, West Virginia, the issue was finally resolved. Delegates ruled that the poll could not override the preceding year's vote. Consequently, Lincoln was named CIAA champions, while North Carolina College claimed the tournament title.[59]

The Black press gave wide coverage to the basketball squabble. The Negro Newspaper Publishers Association reported the story, and Sam Lacy, the acclaimed sports journalist for the *Baltimore Afro-American*, wrote lengthy pieces detailing the issue. Several Black papers, including the *Atlanta Daily World* and *Norfolk Journal and Guide*, also covered the wrangle. Because of the reporting, readers not only gained further insights into how the CIAA operated, they also learned, once again, that the conference took matters seriously. Such a view bolstered the image of the association.[60]

In 1947 and 1948, Turner's again hosted the CIAA tournament. Like the inaugural competition, both tournaments—Virginia State won in 1947; West Virginia State prevailed in 1948—played to large crowds. Higher earnings reflected the tournament's growth. In 1947, the association banked $1,566. The next year, the sum totaled $1,300. One reason for greater interest was because of the electrifying finish in 1946. In addition, Black newspapers promoted the tournaments, and Howard University played several home games at Turner's. Sponsors, too, got the word out, and supported the tournament financially. The Black-run North Carolina Mutual Life Insurance Company sponsored a trophy, as did the Southern Aid Society, The Afro-American Newspapers, Inc., and The Guide Publishing Company, publisher of the *Norfolk Journal and Guide*. The 1947 and 1948 tournament programs contained dozens of ads, the majority of which were placed by establishments along U Street, including You and Me Luncheonette; Three Score Drug Store; Club Bengasi, the self-proclaimed "Mecca of Cafe Society"; and The Hotel Dunbar, where four of the eight tournament teams stayed.[61]

Pragmatic in their approach, organizers believed the tournament could result in lasting changes in sport. In the 1947 tournament program, CIAA President John H. Burr wrote: "The 1946 Basketball Tournament set the stage for the realization of one of the more ambitious projects of the CIAA; the recognition of our association, and its inclusion into the NCAA regional and national basketball tournaments. We are hoping that this recognition will come with the 1947 tournament." Several days after the 1948 tournament, Lin Holloway, columnist for the *Norfolk Journal and Guide*, admitted that while basketball played by White institutions was "plaudit-evoking," it "was no better than that seen at Turner's for three days last week and on numerous sepia college basketball courts during the past few years." The comparison, Holloway added, "presents the question whether Negro basketball as such can long endure, or whether the factions advocating separation of races in sports events will continue to prevent Negro athletes from taking their rightful places in the national scope of sports."[62]

In 1949, the tournament was moved two miles across town to the much larger Uline Arena. Completed in 1941, the venue was named after its 74-year-old owner, Michael Uline, Washington's ice magnate. For years, Uline's squint-eyed views of race relations dictated that African Americans be barred from those arena events he deemed inappropriate for Black viewership: rodeos, ice shows, basketball games, hockey matches, anything considered middlebrow. Events Blacks could attend were baser, cruder—such as boxing and wrestling. The arrangement reflected negative assumptions about African Americans.[63]

For much of the 1940s, Black Washingtonians chafed under the discrimination. Outraged, they held demonstrations and boycotted arena events. But Uline was unmoved. In January 1948, under the leadership of Edwin B. Henderson, who in addition to his involvement with the CIAA, chaired the Citizen's Committee Against Segregation in Recreation (CASR), in Washington, D.C., Black protesters forced Uline's hand. For years, the District's Golden Gloves Boxing Tournament had been the sole province of White boxers. However, in 1947, Black fighters at last were granted the opportunity to take part. Organizers, understandably, envisioned a large African American turnout. Instead, the opposite happened. Heeding Henderson's advice to continue boycotting events at the arena, Black residents stayed away. When the tournament's promoter, upset over the lack of Black fans, announced that he was considering moving the event in 1948, Uline promptly eliminated the race-based restrictions.

The 1949 tournament at Uline outdrew the three that preceded it—which was no great surprise. The tournament's popularity was growing, and Uline was capable of squeezing in more than 7,000 people, dwarfing the measly 2,000 capacity of Turner's. By moving the tournament to Uline, the CIAA hoped to reap greater profits. Sadly, it was not to be. While revenues climbed, expenditures did as well. The result was that the association realized a modest $300 increase in profits from the previous year. If the 1949 tournament raised doubts about holding the competition at Uline, the tournament in 1950 confirmed them. That year, the association was able to bank only $147. Both tournaments, however, had displayed exciting basketball. In 1949, West Virginia State beat Virginia State, 60–53, to take the tournament. The next year, after downing West Virginia State, 74–70, North Carolina College was crowned champion. The 1949 West Virginia State squad featured Earl Lloyd, a 6'5" forward who, along with Chuck Cooper and Nat "Sweetwater" Clifton, broke the color line in the National Basketball Association (NBA), in 1950. Lloyd played for the Washington Capitols, whose home venue was Uline Arena. That same year, the Capitols inked Harold Hunter, a lightning-quick guard on the 1950 West Virginia State team and MVP of the CIAA tournament. Unlike Lloyd, Hunter never played in the NBA.[64]

West Virginia State was not just known for producing talented players and winning CIAA championships. In 1949, it did something few schools in the East, let alone HBCUs: it traveled to the West Coast to play several games. Jimmy Booker of the *New York Amsterdam News* hailed the West Virginia school as "being the first Negro college basketball team to make an extended tour of the Pacific coast." In an age before jetliners, the great distances separating eastern and western clubs made intersectional matchups difficult to arrange. As an HBCU, however, West Virginia State faced an additional obstacle: the Jim Crow idea that Blacks and Whites should never compete together or against each other in sports.[65]

The man most responsible for State's western trip was "Frank Walsh, impresario of San Francisco's Cow Palace"—the Bay Area's then-preeminent sports arena, which also staged livestock exhibits—"who is more generally known as 'Mr. Bow Tie,'" as one *United Press* journalist put it. According to Herman Hill—the famous *Pittsburg Courier* editor who, along with other Black sportswriters, persuaded the Los Angeles Rams in 1946 to hire two African American players, Kenny Washington and Woody Strode, thereby puncturing the National Football League's color barrier—Walsh had approached Hill several months earlier and inquired about the possibility of having the Yellow Jackets play a handful of teams out west. Hill presumably assisted Walsh and before long, the trip was announced. Walsh, it appears, had been drawn to State because of its exceptional record—in 1947–48, it was 23–0—and because, in the words of Hill, "[Walsh] had also learned how [top-notch Black] teams had been stymied in their efforts to show in Madison Square Garden in open competition. He said he was determined to wipe out this injustice."[66]

On the evening of February 5, West Virginia State players departed for the West Coast. In his memoir *Moonfixer: The Basketball Journey of Earl Lloyd*, Earl Lloyd remembered, "[A]bout two thousand people . . . showed up to see us off." Traveling by train, the Yellow Jackets—whose group included ten players, a manager, and head coach Mark Cardwell—arrived in California four days later. The tour intrigued Black and White West Virginians. In a letter to the university a day before the team left, West Virginia governor Okey L. Patterson stated in part: "All West Virginians, I know, are very proud indeed of the West Virginia State team. . . . All power and success to you on your western trip." In the West, commentators called State the "national Negro intercollegiate champion" and "the best Negro college team in the country," and underscored the school's unbeaten streak of thirty-two games (including the twenty-three victories from the season before).[67]

On the trip, State played four games. On October 11, at the Cow Palace, St. Mary's College defeated the travel-weary visitors, 66–52, snapping the Yellow Jackets' undefeated streak. The following evening, however, the Jackets garnered a 57–44 win over Santa Clara University. Two days later, in Los Angeles, State lost to Loyola University, 65–58. Profits from the game went to West View Hospital, a facility that Herman Hill described as being "interracial, non-sectarian, [and] non-profit." On February 16, Cardwell's team lost again, this time to the University of Nevada. The game was played in Reno.[68]

Despite a disappointing 1–3 record for the trip, the Jackets remained upbeat. In his memoir, Earl Lloyd wrote, "[We] came back [from the trip] feeling good about ourselves." Sam Lacy of the *Baltimore Afro-American* quoted Cardwell as saying, "I am happy about the whole experience, everyone was swell and many of the [opposing] players expressed satisfaction over the fact they won't have to meet the likes of our Wilson, Clark, Lloyd, and the others again." In a development that would have pleased the CIAA founders, State's exemplary behavior drew praise. "[The Yellow Jackets] were good losers and graceful winners," Herman Hill wrote, following the games in San Francisco. "Their sportsmanship and conduct was highly commendable." Cardwell's players left such a favorable mark that they were invited back the following year. Their record for that trip was 3–3, including a win over a squad of San Quentin inmates. According to West Virginia sports historian Bob Barnett, "The governor of California was so impressed with the State team that he arranged for the Yellow Jackets to play against the San Quentin State Prison basketball team."[69]

In 1951, State finished second at the CIAA basketball tournament. It would be the last CIAA tournament held at Uline Arena. Association officials concluded that the profit margin was too small and moved the tournament to an on-campus site. Morgan State University in Baltimore hosted the 1952 competition. But Morgan State's Hurt Gymnasium was hardly any bigger than Turner's. In November 1952, the CIAA transferred the tournament once more—this time to North Carolina College in Durham. Fans came in droves. Playing games at the college's McDougald Gymnasium, which could hold 5,000 spectators, the CIAA made more than $4,600. Profits rose to $6,349 in 1956, and then to $8,786, two years later. In 1960, the newly constructed War Memorial Coliseum in Greensboro, North Carolina, hosted the event (War Memorial's capacity was 7,100). From 1961 to 1963, the tournament was held on the campus of Winston-Salem State University in North Carolina. The next year, it was moved back to War Memorial.[70]

In all, the success of the CIAA basketball tournament matched that of the association as a whole. Unlike many other separate Black sports organizations that were unable to survive integration, the most notable being the Negro Baseball Leagues, the CIAA still exists, and thrives. Now named the Central Intercollegiate Athletic Association—the change took place in 1950 after members determined that "colored" was no longer de rigueur—the CIAA consists of twelve public and private institutions ranging in size from 750 to 7,000 students, with schools located largely in North Carolina, Maryland, and Virginia. Backed by such companies as Toyota, Nationwide Insurance, Coca-Cola, and Russell Athletic, the CIAA holds annual championships in sports ranging from football and baseball to men's and women's basketball to men's and women's tennis. The reasons for the association's continued success are many, but certainly a major factor is due to the founders, who, with great foresight and acuity, crafted a durable "Constitution and By-Laws," while implementing high quality sports programs that outlasted racial and domestic crises, as well as two World Wars.

The CIAA is now more than 100 years old, and still going strong. The founders' efforts at racial uplift have obviously been realized. Affirmation of this reality has come from many sources, including none other than President John F. Kennedy who in 1962, just a year before his assassination and two years before the passage of the historic Civil Rights Act, cabled CIAA President Leroy T. Walker—who had been John McLendon's assistant in 1946, when North Carolina College won the inaugural CIAA basketball tournament, and who would go on to become the first African American to coach an American Olympic track and field team, in 1976 in Montreal—congratulating him on the fiftieth anniversary of the association. "The long record of service and progress of your conference, "wrote Kennedy, "is well-known and respected in athletic and academic circles. It deserves the esteem for its continued pursuit of the highest standards, both on the field and in the classroom." The CIAA founders would have indeed been proud.[71]

Notes

1. Ocania Chalk, *Black College Sport* (New York; Dodd, Mead, 1976); Patrick B. Miller, "Slouching Towards New Expediency: College Football and the Color Line during the Depression Decade," *American Studies* 40 (Fall 1999): 5–30; ibid., "To Bring the Race Along Rapidly: Sport, Student Culture, and Educational Mission at Historically Black Colleges During the Interwar Years," *History of Education Quarterly* 35 (summer 1995), 111–133; Raymond Schmidt, *Shaping College Football: The Transformation of an American Sport, 1919–1930* (Syracuse NY: Syracuse University Press, 2007).

2. S. H. Archer, "Football in our Colleges," *Voice of the Negro* 3 (1906): 202.

3. J.B. Watson, "Football in Southern Negro Colleges," *Voice* 4 (1907): 169.

4. Earl Henry Duval, Jr. "An Historical Analysis of the Central Intercollegiate Athletic Association and Its Influence on the Development of Black Intercollegiate Athletics: 1912–1984," unpublished doctoral dissertation, Kent State University, 1985; Charles H. Williams, "Twenty Year's Work of the CIAA" *The Southern Workman* 61 (1932): 65–76.

5. For an excellent work on African Americans and racial uplift, see Kevin K. Gaines, *Uplifting the Race: Black Leadership, Politics, and Culture in the Twentieth Century* (Chapel Hill, NC: The University of North Carolina Press), 1996. Also see Miller, "To Bring the Race Along Rapidly:" 111–133.

6. Colored Intercollegiate Athletics Association, "Constitution and By-laws," 1912, n.p.

7. Ibid.

8. Ibid.

9. See http://www.Theside.com/sports2010/2/2gen_0202103837.aspx., and http://en.wikipedia.org/wiki/southernwestern_athletic_conference, accessed February 8, 2014.

10. Charles H. Williams, "Twenty Years' Work of the CIAA," 69.

11. *CIAA Bulletin*, 1925, 11.

12. Ibid.

13. Ibid. See also: "Putting Lincoln out Unfair" *Chicago Defender,* April 4, 1925, 10; "Gideon Smith gives us some light on the CIAA controversy," *Chicago Defender*, April 18, 1925, 9; Duval, Jr. "An Historical Analysis of the Central Intercollegiate Athletic Association and its Influence on the Development of Black Intercollegiate Athletics: 1912–1984;" Miller, "'To Bring the Race Along Rapidly:' Sport, Student Culture, and Educational Mission at Historically Black Colleges During the Interwar Years," 111–33.

14. *CIAA Bulletin*, 1942, 16.

15. Ibid.

16. Full collections of the *CIAA Bulletin* are located at Virginia State University in Petersburg, Virginia, and Virginia Union University in Richmond, Virginia.

17. Like many other professional organizations, leaders in the CIAA often held multiple offices over their lifetime.

18. *CIAA Bulletin*, 1924, 5.

19. Ibid., 30.

20. Ibid. Essays ranged from two to five pages in length.

21. *CIAA Bulletin*, 18.

22. Ibid., 22.

23. The CIAA occasionally extended invitations to well-known individuals from the world of physical education and sport to speak at their annual meetings. For example, in 1944 Jay B. Nash, the famous physical educator from New York University, spoke at the association's annual meeting on "Athletic Competition in Physical Fitness for Post-War America." See *CIAA Bulletin*, 1945, 14–15.

24. An important group that had a close connection with the CIAA was the Eastern Board of Officials (EBO). Founded in 1906 by Edwin B. Henderson, a well-known educator, civil rights activist, and historian of African American athletes, the EBO is still in existence and reorganized as the oldest predominately Black sports officiating group in the United States. See David K. Wiggins, "Edwin Bancroft Henderson: Physical Educator, Civil Rights Activist and Chronicler of African American Athletes," *Research Quarterly for Exercise and Sport* 70 (June 1999): 91–112; and www.eboinc.org/history-of-the-board.

25. For information on the Black press, see Frederick G. Detweiler, *The Negro Press in the United States* (Chicago: University of Chicago Press 1922); Roland E. Wolseley, *The Black Press U.S.A.* (Ames, Iowa: Iowa State University Press, 1974).

26. *CIAA Bulletin*, 1936, 15.

27. Ibid., 1938, 31.

28. Ibid., 1943, 25–27.

29. Earl Henry Duval, Jr. "An Historical Analysis of the Central Intercollegiate Athletic Association and its Influence on the Development of Black Intercollegiate Athletics: 1912–1984," and Charles H. Williams "Twenty Years' Work of the CIAA."

30. CIAA official website of the Central Intercollegiate Athletic Association, http://www.theciaa.com/information/about_ciaa/index, accessed February 14, 2014; Earl Henry Duval, Jr. "An Historical Analysis of the Central Intercollegiate Athletic Association and its Influence on the Development of Black Intercollegiate Athletics: 1912–1984;" Charles H. Williams "Twenty Years' Work of the CIAA."

31. *CIAA Bulletin*, 1932, 15.

32. Ibid., 1933, 9.

33. Ibid., 1943, 12.

34. Ibid., 13.

35. Ibid., 1944, 11.

36. Ibid.

37. The Dickinson rating system was named after Frank G. Dickinson of St. Paul's College. Dickinson, at the request of John Whitehead, Assistant Secretary-Treasurer of the CIAA for 1920 and 1921, devised a ranking system that decided conference champions in both football and basketball. For details, see Duval, "An Historical Analysis of the Central Intercollegiate Athletic Association and its Influence on the Development of Black Intercollegiate Athletics: 1912–1984," 59–60.

38. See David K. Wiggins, "'The Biggest 'Classic' of Them All': The Howard University and Lincoln University Thanksgiving Day Football Games, 1919–1929" in *Rooting for the Home Team: Sport, Community, and Identity*, Daniel A. Nathan, ed. (Urbana: University of Illinois Press, 2013), 36–53, and Raymond Schmidt, *Shaping College Football: The Transformation of an American Sport, 1919–1930* (Syracuse New York: Syracuse University Press), 2007.

39. Charles H. Williams "Twenty Years' Work of the CIAA," 74; "Hampton opens new athletic field May 20, with track meet," *Chicago Defender*, March 25, 1922; "Track meet to open new field," *Christian Science Monitor*, May 10, 1922.

40. "Twenty-first CIAA track meet is on May 16," *Chicago Defender*, May 16, 1942.

41. Charles H. Williams, "Twenty Years' Work of the CIAA," 74–75; Sundiata Djata *Black's at the Net: Black Achievement in the History of Tennis*, Vol. I (Syracuse, New York: Syracuse University Press, 2006), and ibid., *Black's at the Net: Black Achievement in the History of Tennis*, Vol. II (Syracuse, New York: Syracuse University Press, 2008).

42. Charles H. Williams, "Twenty Years' Work of the CIAA," 75.

43. Paula Giddings, *When and Where I Enter: The Impact of Black Women on Race and Sex in America* (New York: Bantam Books, 1984) and Mary Church Terrell, *A Colored Woman in A White World* (New York: G.K. Hall, 1940).

44. Rita Liberti, "'We were ladies, we just played basketball like boys': African American Womanhood and Competitive Basketball at Bennett College 1928–1942." *Journal of Sport History* 26, (Fall 1999), 575.

45. Carroll L. L. Miller and Anne S. Pruitt-Logan, *Faithful to the Task at Hand: The Life of Lucy Diggs Slowe* (Albany, New York: State University of New York Press, 2012); Linda M. Perkins, "Lucy Diggs Slowe: Champion of the Self-determination of African American Women in Higher Education," *The Journal of Negro History* 81 (Winter—Autumn 1996): 89-104.

46. Susan K. Cahn, *Coming on Strong: Gender and Sexuality in Twentieth-Century Women's Sport* (New York: The Free Press, 1994) and Cindy Himes-Gissendanner, "African American Women and Competitive Sport, 1920–1960," in Susan Birrell and Cheryl L. Cole, eds. *Women Sport and Culture* (Champlain, IL: Human Kinetics, 1994), 81-92.

47. Rita Liberti, "'We were ladies, we just played basketball like boys': African American Womanhood and Competitive Basketball at Bennett College, 1928–1942," 567-584.

48. "Howard Five Lists 12-game Schedule," *Washington Post*, December 17, 1933 and "Lincoln Eyed as Favorite in CIAA Cage Tournament," *Baltimore Afro-American*, March 9, 1946, 18. For North Carolina College records, see John B. McLendon, The First CIAA Championship Basketball Tournament (Downers Grove, IL: Maxaid, 1988), 51.

49. See "L.I.U. meets Morgan Five on Saturday," *Chicago Defender*, March 26, 1938; "Long Island U all set for union," *Chicago Defender*, March 25, 1939; "Union Five Beats Long Island U.," *Chicago Defender*, April 1, 1939; "Union Did Not Defeat Long Island U. Varsity," *Chicago Defender* (national ed.), April 8, 1939, 8; "White college team to play VA Union," *Chicago Defender*, December 7, 1940; and "Brooklyn College Loses," *New York Times*, December 28, 1940, 23.

50. Bell quoted in L. Douglas Wilder Library, Virginia Union University, Archives-AR-0005, Athletics Department, Box 1/3, Folder: CIAA Basketball Tournament Programs 1971, 1973, 1977, 1978, Richmond, Virginia. For more on the CIAA tournament, see Pamela Grundy, *Learning to Win: Sports, Education, and Social Change in Twentieth-Century North Carolina* (Chapel Hill, NC: The University of North Carolina Press), 183-185 and Milton S. Katz, *Breaking Through: John B. McLendon, Basketball*

Legend and Civil Rights Pioneer (Fayetteville, AR: The University of Arkansas Press, 2007), 46–53.

51. "Cage Capers," *Baltimore Afro-American*, April 5, 1941, 20; "R.B. Atwood Abandons Cage Tourney Idea," *Norfolk Journal and Guide*, January 10, 1942, 19C.

52. Origins of tournament in "To Limit The Number of Cages Games," *Norfolk Journal and Guide*, February 13, 1937, 16; "CIAA Votes Tournament Plan on Experimental Basis," *Baltimore Afro-American*, December 21, 1940, 19; and John B. McLendon, *The First CIAA Championship Basketball Tournament* (Downers Grove, IL: Maxaid, 1988), 26–28. The Virginia Union Archives at the L. Douglas Wilder Library in Richmond, Virginia, has a copy of McLendon's work.

53. Figure in 1945 *CIAA Bulletin*, L. Douglas Wilder Library, Virginia Union University, Archives-AR-0005, Athletics Department, Box 1/3, Folder: Athletics Department, CIAA Bulletins, 1942–1947, Richmond, Virginia.

54. For information on singers and musicians who performed at Turner's, see "500 Hear Robeson on Peace Program," *Philadelphia Tribune*, September 26, 1940, 14; "Bands on Tour," *Chicago Defender*, September 13, 1941, 20; "Capitol Comments," *Atlanta Daily World*, March 21, 1943, 4; "'Dirty Gertie' is Mad; 'Send Me to Hades,'" *Baltimore Afro-American*, September 25, 1943, 10; and "Sports, Entertainment, Politics Were at Home at Turner's Arena," *Washington Post*, June 16, 1964, 4D.

55. McLendon, *The First CIAA Championship Basketball Tournament*, 32–34.

56. Ibid.

57. *Norfolk Journal and Guide*, March 16, 1946, 12 and *Baltimore Afro-American*, March 16, 1946, 18. For more on the game, see McLendon, *The First CIAA Championship Basketball Tournament*, 43–46, 49–50.

58. Figure in 1946–47 *CIAA Bulletin*, L. Douglas Wilder Library, Virginia Union University, Archives-AR-0005, Athletics Department, Box 1/3, Folder: Athletics Department, CIAA Bulletins, 1942–1947, Richmond, Virginia.

59. "Lincoln Coach Blasts CIAA Prexy Burr; Says 'Weak-Kneed' Policy Robbed Lions," *Baltimore Afro-American*, March 16, 1946, 18.

60. Ibid.; "Looking 'Em Over," *Baltimore Afro-American*, March 23, 1946, 18; "Lively Session Forecast for CIAA Meet This Week," *Baltimore Afro-American*, December 14, 1946, 14; "CIAA Officials Hold Successful Meeting at West Virginia State," *Atlanta Daily World*, December 20, 1946, 5; and "CIAA Gives Lincoln Cage Title; Suspends Two Officials," *Norfolk Journal and Guide*, December 21, 1946, 14.

61. Figures in 1954 *CIAA Bulletin*, L. Douglas Wilder Library, Virginia Union University, Archives-AR-0005, Athletics Department, Box 1/3, Folder: Athletics Department, CIAA Bulletin, 1949–1954, Richmond, Virginia. According to the article, the sums were recalculated because early tabulations had not subtracted the $500 advance the association gave tournament planners each year. The figures reflect the subtraction. CIAA programs in Moorland-Spingarn Research Center, Manuscript Division, Art Carter Papers, Box 170-24, Folder: 24, 25, Howard University, Washington, DC.

62. Burr quoted in 1947 program, Moorland-Spingarn Research Center, Manuscript Division, Art Carter Papers, Box 170–24, Folder: 24, Howard University, Washington, DC; *Norfolk Journal and Guide*, March 20, 1948, 21.

63. This and the next paragraph in David K. Wiggins, "Edwin Bancroft Henderson: Physical Educator, Civil Rights Activist, and Chronicler of African American Athletes," *Research Quarterly for Exercise and Sport* 70 (June 1999), 99–101 and Justine Christianson, "The Uline Arena/Washington Coliseum: The Rise and Fall of a Washington Institution," *Washington History* 16 (Spring/Summer 2004), 24–26.

64. Figures in *CIAA Bulletin* from 1949, 1950, and 1951, L. Douglas Wilder Library, Virginia Union University, Archives-AR-0005, Athletics Department, Box 1/3, Folder: Athletics Department, CIAA Bulletins, 1949–1954.

65. "Here's the Story of the Campaign to get Negro Five in Invitation Tourney," *New York Amsterdam News*, February 19, 1949.

66. "Colored West Virginia State Five to Meet Gaels, Broncos," *Bakersfield Californian*, February 11, 1949. Herman Hill, "Courageous Cage Promoter Who Booked W.Va. on Coast Praised," *Pittsburgh Courier*, January 29, 1949.

67. Lloyd quoted in Earl Lloyd and Sean Kirst, *Moonfixer: The Basketball Journey of Earl Lloyd* (Syracuse, NY: Syracuse University Press, 2010), 57. Patterson letter in "State Quentin Leaves Tonight for California," *Charleston Gazette*, February 5, 1949. Patterson's letter was also reprinted in the *Baltimore Afro-American*, February 12, 1949. "Dons Play Bradley," *San Francisco Examiner*, February 11, 1949, and "Nevada Cagers Meet Yellow Jackets of West Virginia Here Tonight," *Reno Evening Gazette*, February 16, 1949.

68. Herman Hill, "Courageous Cage Promoter Who Booked W.Va. on Coast Praised," *Pittsburgh Courier*, January 29, 1949. Newspapers in each of the three cities covered the games. For instance, see *San Francisco Chronicle*, February 12, 1949, and February 13, 1949; *Los Angeles Times*, February 15, 1949; and *Nevada State Journal*, February 17, 1949. The Black press also reported the scores. See *Norfolk Journal and Guide*, February 19, 1949; *Atlanta Daily World*, February 22, 1949; *Baltimore Afro-American*, February 26, 1949; and *Cleveland Call and Post*, February 26, 1949.

69. Lloyd and Kirst, Moonfixer,58. "From A to Z," *Baltimore Afro-American*, February 26, 1949. "West Virginia Cagers Win, Lose on Coast," *Pittsburgh Courier*, February 19, 1949. Bob Barnett, *Hillside Fields: A History of Sports in West Virginia* (Morgantown: West Virginia University Press, 2013), 162. In the book, Barnett also discusses the 1949 trip. See pages 159–60.

70. Figures in *CIAA Bulletin* from 1954, 1956, and 1958, L. Douglas Wilder Library, Virginia Union University, Archives-AR-0005, Athletics Department, Box 1/3, Folder: Athletics Department, CIAA Bulletins, 1949–1954, and Folder: Athletics Department, CIAA Bulletins, 1955–59, 1962.

71. Kennedy telegram in McLendon, *The First CIAA Championship Basketball Tournament*, 53.

3

THE BIGGEST "CLASSIC" OF THEM ALL

The Howard and Lincoln Thanksgiving Day
Football Games, 1919–1929

African Americans established many successful and important separate sports programs during the latter half of the nineteenth and first half of the twentieth centuries. Banned from most predominantly White organized sport during this period because of racial discrimination, African Americans organized their own teams and leagues behind segregated walls at the amateur and professional levels, in small rural communities and large urban settings, and among both men and women of different social and economic backgrounds. Some of the most important of these separate sports programs were those established at HBCUs. Since the latter stages of the nineteenth century, HBCUs have competed at a relatively high level in football, basketball, and a good number of other sports.[1]

The annual Thanksgiving Day football games played between well-known HBCUs drew a great deal of attention and much enthusiasm from African Americans. Arguably the most popular and significant of these games were those pitting Howard University and Lincoln University from 1919 to 1929. Described in 1922 by *Chicago Defender* sportswriter Frank Young as "the most important game in the country as far as we [African

Americans] are concerned," the Howard and Lincoln Thanksgiving Day matchups during the 1920s, a decade commonly termed the "golden age of American sport," garnered some attention in the White press, voluminous coverage in the Black press, and attracted great interest among upper-class African Americans in Philadelphia, Washington, DC, and other Black communities across the country.[2]

The Howard and Lincoln annual Thanksgiving Day football games, along with the accompanying social activities were, like the creation of Black All-American teams and naming of mythical national champions, a way for two of the most prestigious HBCUs to exhibit a much-needed sense of racial pride and self-determination while at once measuring themselves against the standards of predominantly White university sport and its attendant rituals. The "classic" was also important in that it enhanced the already elevated prestige of Howard and Lincoln, which, in turn, contributed to intangible strategic advantages for two institutions that were becoming more entrepreneurial and commercialized. The games and their accompanying social activities, moreover, played an important role in the identity of upper-class African Americans in Philadelphia, Washington, DC, and other locales. For many African Americans, the "classic" was both a salve and a symbol of status, bringing them together while cordoning them off according to their respective social station. And things were in flux. Social changes, resulting from the northern migration of southern Blacks during the early decades of the twentieth century, cast racial identity in a new light. With alternative modes of social advancement becoming possible in Black communities, and toleration of Whites toward upper-class African Americans being diminished because of the geographical expansion and more economically mobile pattern of the Black population following the great migration, the "classic" was more than just a test to determine athlete superiority. It was "a social competition between the black populous of Washington, D.C. and Philadelphia," and a highly visible way to help keep African Americans of like kind together.[3]

The first football game between Howard and Lincoln took place in 1894 on Howard's campus in Washington, DC. Characteristic of the sport in the late-nineteenth century, the game was a vicious and bloody affair. Lincoln's right tackle James Harper suffered a broken jaw after colliding with Howard's star halfback "Baby" Jones. This incident, along with several other unfortunate confrontations during Lincoln's 5–4 victory and following the game, including a Lincoln player having a pistol drawn on him by a White man on a Washington, DC, street, were so serious that the schools did not play each other again until 1904. The games played between 1904 and 1918 attracted relatively little fanfare. During this period, Lincoln won seven games, and Howard four; three games ended in 0–0 ties. No games were played between the two schools in 1906 and 1915.[4]

In 1919 the Howard and Lincoln Thanksgiving Day football game, which was played at National League Park in Philadelphia and ended in a 0–0 tie, was advertised and promoted as the "classic" and "greatest event of the season."[5] It would prove to be an apt descriptor as the game, which attracted a reported 10,000 mostly Black fans, the usual composition of the crowds for these contests, was transformed into a grand social affair that combined the traditional gridiron battle between the two institutions with elaborately organized dances, visitor receptions, dinner parties, musical productions, breakfast socials, and alumni gatherings held over a frenetic three- to five- day period.[6]

In 1920 Howard crushed Lincoln, 42–0, in front of what was described as "the largest crowd regardless of race, that ever attended a football game in the capital city."[7] The Lincoln Lions, coached in the game by former Harvard University star Clarence Matthews and Paul Robeson, the great athlete, actor, singer and civil rights activist, were completely outclassed by the Howard Bison at American League Park (renamed Griffith Stadium that year in honor of Washington Senators owner, Clark Griffith) in Washington. Matthews and Robeson were brought in as replacements for Fritz Pollard, the former Brown University All-American running back who had spent the last two years splitting time as head coach of Lincoln and playing professionally with the Akron Pros. Opting to stay in Ohio to play for his professional team rather than returning to coach the Lions effectively ended Pollard's controversial tenure at Lincoln. Officials of the school, who had become increasingly upset with Pollard's absence from practices and games, decided to part ways with him following the 1920 season.[8]

The "classic" produced a far different outcome in 1921, the Lions defeating the Bison, 13–7, at the National Baseball Park in Philadelphia. Approximately 10,000 rain-soaked spectators attended the game. Lincoln's victory was due in large part to the outstanding coaching of John A. Shelbourne, former Dartmouth star,[9] and to captain James Law, who played the "greatest game of his career." Law threw for one touchdown and made several other crucial plays in a game where all "the players were plastered with mud and their features rendered unrecognizable by the brown ooze."[10]

In 1922, at the American League Park in Washington, Lincoln squeaked by Howard, 13–12. The star of the game was Franz "Jazz" Byrd, the speedy and elusive running back considered by many to be the greatest player in Lincoln history. Among Byrd's many great plays at American League Park that day was a 70-yard run for a touchdown.[11] The 1922 game was the first "classic" to be covered by a rain insurance policy. A year later, Howard and Lincoln battled to a 6–6 tie in front of approximately 16,000 spectators in Philadelphia. In a game marred by a highly publicized but unsubstantiated ticket scandal in which receipts supposedly came up some $10,000 short, "Jazz" Byrd dazzled fans with an 80-yard kick-off return that set up his one-yard plunge for a touchdown three plays later. Howard matched the touchdown, but, like Lincoln, missed the extra point. The *Chicago Defender* reported that "the great and only Charles P. McClane, manager of the Royal (referred to as 'America's Finest Colored Photoplay House') and Olympic Theaters and President of the Universal Advertising Company in Philadelphia" planned to film the "full game in action and close-ups of the grandstand and box parties."[12]

In 1924, a reported crowd of 27,000 at the American League Park in Washington watched Lincoln humiliate Howard, 31–0, in perhaps the most ballyhooed of all the "classics." Lincoln was once again led by "Jazz" Byrd, dubbed by the Black press as the "black Grange of football," a reference to Red Grange of the University of Illinois, White college football's boy wonder.[13] Sportswriters were rarely at loss for words describing Byrd's exploits. "Like a drop of mercury, Howard men put their fingers on Byrd only to find out he had slipped to one side," wrote the *Baltimore Afro-American*, in its coverage of Lincoln's 1924 victory. "He sidestepped, dodged, skipped, jumped and twisted from the grasp of eleven men as if they never existed."[14]

The drubbing of Howard was the least of the great Black institution's worries. Prior to the 1924 contest, Lincoln threatened to cancel its game against Howard unless the Washington, DC, school kept one of its players, a Robert Miller, out of the game since Miller had not sat out a year stipulated by CIAA guidelines following his transfer from Virginia Union the previous season. Part of a national discussion regarding eligibility requirements, professionalism, and increasing number of "tramp athletes," Howard balked at keeping Miller out of the game, but eventually acquiesced to Lincoln's demand, all the while claiming it had done nothing wrong. The depth of Howard's anger over the Miller affair was so strong that its Board of Athletic Control, chaired by Dr. Edward P. Davis, unanimously voted to withdraw from the CIAA[15]

The 1925 game was held at Philadelphia's Shibe Park. In front of a reported 16,000 fans, Lincoln and Howard tied, 0–0. Despite its success, the "classic" was marred again by controversy. In a strange and ironic turn of events, Lincoln was expelled from the CIAA sometime before the contest having disobeyed the conference's wishes to cancel the "classic" because Howard was no longer a CIAA member.[16] Lincoln would be reinstated two years later, but not before incurring the wrath of other CIAA schools, because the Lions had refused to discontinue the series against Howard and thereby seemed to condone the use of ineligible players. Reluctant to sever ties with its archrival because of the money it would have lost, Lincoln in truth was convinced Howard played "tramp" athletes. Many "Lincoln alumni" noted that Howard "would have used Red Grange if he were black."[17]

In 1926, with approximately 10,000 spectators on hand in the new Howard University Stadium, the home team demolished the visitors, 32–0. The game's star was Howard quarterback Jack Coles, who repeatedly weaved his way through the Lincoln line for huge gains.[18] Much was made of the new stadium, with an elaborate dedication ceremony held prior to the game. With first-year President Mordecai Johnson presiding, the celebration began with a speech by Representative Martin B. Madden of Illinois, Chairman of the House Appropriations Committee. Madden's committee had approved the $301,000 needed for the building of the new Howard stadium and gymnasium—armory project. Madden used the occasion to talk about the "progress of the negro in America and the contribution of Howard University to his advancement." Following Madden at the podium was Dr. Emmett J. Scott, Howard's secretary-treasurer and business manager, who was presented a plaque "in appreciation of his efforts to give to Howard University a larger program of athletics, health, and recreational activities." Albert Cassell, university architect, spoke next, followed by football coach Louis Watson.[19]

An indication of the importance of the 1926 game was the elaborate program published to commemorate it. Although all the programs for the "classic" were detailed and lengthy, perhaps none included as many images, specific information about the two institutions, and number of advertisements as the one from 1926. With a cover depicting both a male and female student from Howard sitting in the grandstand cheering on their team, the 46-page program included photographs of President Johnson and Secretary-Treasurer Scott, listings of the various social activities accompanying the game, rosters and pictures of the coaches, support staffs and players representing the two institutions, and a wide assortment of ads from Nail and Parker Real Estate in New York City to the Pryor Press in Chicago to the Capital Awning Company in Washington, DC, to the law offices of Raymond Pace Alexander in Philadelphia. The program also included a layout and directions to the new stadium, the "songs and yells" for Howard, alma maters of both schools, and a historical assessment of the "classic."[20]

In 1927, Howard, with one of its strongest and deepest teams, defeated Lincoln, 20–0, at Philadelphia's Shibe Park in front of an announced 15,000 spectators. The game followed by almost two months a temporary strike by the Howard football team, which protested the decision of President Johnson to eliminate athletic scholarships and the customary free training table and living quarters provided to players during the football season. Extending some of the policies of his predecessor, Stanley Durkee, who was forced to resign after confrontations with professors and alumni over the direction of the university, Johnson strove to improve the academic reputation of the school while also de-emphasizing highly competitive athletics in favor of a more expansive exercise and physical activity program for the majority of students on campus.[21]

In 1928 Howard again beat Lincoln, 12–0, much to the pleasure of some 10,000 spectators at Howard Stadium. The Howard team received an added boost from the expertise of coach Charles West, the former Washington and Jefferson College football and track star who had taken over for Louis Watson after Watson failed to reach a contract extension with President Johnson—a falling-out perhaps caused by Watson's support of the players' strike from the year before. Like the previously mentioned Clarence Matthews, Paul Robeson, John Shelbourne, and a host of other outstanding African American athletes who competed at predominantly White institutions but who could not coach at those same institutions, West helped support himself by coaching the team while attending Howard's medical school.[22]

In 1929, the final year of the "classic," Howard and Lincoln played, just as they had ten years earlier, to a 0–0 tie. Approximately 10,000 spectators attended the game, which was held at Municipal Stadium in Philadelphia. The Howard faithful were disappointed in the performance of the Bison team, claiming that the football program particularly and the athletic program more generally had deteriorated significantly since the "classic" began a decade earlier. Ralph Matthews, writing in the *Baltimore Afro-American* in 1938, contended that the downfall of the Howard Football Program was partly attributable, ironically enough, to the new stadium built on campus in 1926. Obviously pining for the days when the game was played at the American League Park, Matthews wrote:

The circus-like bleachers, the absences of boxes, the lack of a foyer, where women could show off their new styles, where old grads could prove how successful they had become, the inability to move about and mingle with old friends and acquaintances, removed the most important elements from the classic. Without these opportunities it was just another football game. And who in the old days really paid any attention to the game?[23]

Much of the blame for the faltering football and athletic program at Howard was laid at the feet of President Johnson for abolishing athletic scholarships, limiting players' access to the training table, and reducing their board and lodging privileges.[24] For many observers, Johnson's handling of the school's athletic program was a result of his efforts to adhere to the recommendations provided in the famous 1929 report by the Carnegie Foundation for the Advancement of Teaching. Originally titled "American College Athletics," the report was a condemnation of the increasing commercialization of college sport and its attendant professionalism and corruption.[25] In truth, Johnson, who was no doubt influenced by the Carnegie Foundation report, was being criticized by football loving fans for trying to bring some sanity and more balance to the school's athletic program while at once elevating the academic integrity of the institution. B. S. Baskerville, a 1926 alumnus of Howard, summed up the feelings of many of the school's avid supporters of football when he wrote in the *New York Amsterdam News* of 1927 that:

> President Johnson alone is to be blamed for the miserable football team that represents Howard University this year. He cut out the training table a couple of years ago because he feared the survey being made by the Carnegie Foundation. Then he began to ballyhoo clean sportsmanship in order to justify his act. I believe, however, that he was sincere in what he did, but sincerity or no sincerity, the effect is just the same. The miserable showing of his mediocre team has created a spirit of sullen indifference among the students and of sour indignation among the alumni.[26]

As evident from the comments by Baskerville, the end of the "classic" was difficult to bear for the alumni and other followers of the Howard and Lincoln Thanksgiving Day Game. Ending the "classic" was hard to take because for the previous ten years it had been so important and meaningful to African Americans in Washington, Philadelphia, and much of the eastern portion of the United States. How did it come about? Who was responsible for the "classic" and what significance did it hold for African Americans?

The "father" of the Thanksgiving Day football "classic," according to former president and historian of Lincoln, Horace Mann Bond, was Dr. Charles A. Lewis, a 1905 graduate of Lincoln and medical doctor from Philadelphia by way of the University of Pennsylvania. A lifelong supporter of all things Lincoln who regularly traveled with the team and sat on the bench tending to injured players, Lewis realized the monetary and intangible strategic advantages that could potentially result from a more highly publicized and commercialized football contest between his beloved alma mater and Howard.[27] And the time was right for such a series of contests: northern Blacks were experiencing an increasing number of southern Blacks making their way north; a relatively higher standard of living was becoming a reality for many Blacks in northern cities; and a consumer culture and national obsession with sport, were in their early stages—and destined to become much larger.[28]

Emmett J. Scott was highly supportive of Lewis's idea and perhaps the man most actively involved in marketing "the classic" and its ultimate success. A native of Houston, and former editor of the city's Black newspaper, the *Texas Freeman*, Scott had been a close friend, adviser, and private secretary to Booker T. Washington and the man in charge of the "Tuskegee Machine," an elaborate system in which Washington controlled and manipulated African American leaders and the press.[29]

These experiences would bode well for Scott as he set about promoting the "classic." Encouraged by the success of the first designated "classic" between Howard and Lincoln in 1919, Scott took much of what he had learned while working for the *Texas Freeman* and while at Tuskegee to ensure that the following year's game in Washington, and subsequent contests between the two institutions, were just as successful and generated the same amount of attention and publicity from the African American community. Just as he strove to improve the academic programs and bring financial stability to Howard, Scott worked tirelessly, called in favors from old friends, and utilized his professional contacts in order to provide as much publicity as possible for the annual Thanksgiving Day football "classic" between his institution and Lincoln. He was successful in his efforts, making the public fully aware of the contest—with the notable assistance of Dr. Charles A. Lewis and Dr. W. G. Alexander, Lincoln's graduate manager of athletics—through public announcements and press releases and other media initiatives.[30] "Everyone present realized the tremendous possibilities of the game," wrote the *Chicago Defender* in 1929, recalling the first classic played ten years earlier. "It remained, however, for the business sagacity of Dr. Emmett J. Scott, secretary-treasurer of Howard University, to perfect the details whereby the occasion might be financially profitable to both institutions as well as occasions worthy to be recorded in the annals of our history."[31]

What Scott helped to create was a recurring athletic and social ritual that allowed Howard and Lincoln to exhibit important feelings of self-pride and determination while at the same time comparing themselves against the standards of White college sport. Like the East-West All-Star game in Black baseball that had its beginnings in 1933 and any number of other sporting events organized behind segregated walls, the Howard and Lincoln Thanksgiving Day football games between 1919 and 1929 attested to the strength and vibrancy of the two institutions and the African American community more generally, while also providing an opportunity to measure themselves against the more nationally known and famous football contests between predominantly White institutions. Tellingly, the comparisons made were not with just any predominantly White institutions, but typically with one or more of the Big Three universities: Harvard, Yale, and Princeton. Although beginning to be challenged for football superiority by other institutions across the country, Harvard, Yale, and Princeton still represented the very best in higher education and college football, and the Black press was quick to point out the relative merits of the "classic" and by extension the quality of Howard and Lincoln as institutions in comparison to the Big Three.[32] "Dr. Scott has perfected arrangements to such a degree," noted the *Chicago Defender* of 1928, "that the classic takes first place in the games of our schools and to our people it is the Yale-Harvard game of our group."[33] "The football classic of the year is the title justly ascribed to the annual game between Howard and Lincoln Universities," wrote the *Philadelphia Tribune* in 1928. "The importance attached to the game has been likened to the annual classics between Yale and Harvard, Cornell and Penn or Princeton and Yale."[34]

Such heady comparisons could be more readily achieved if the annual Thanksgiving Day Black "classic" was hyped, helping create a much-talked-about rivalry. Black weeklies heightened interest by filling a voluminous amount of column space that preceded each of the contests and then followed with additional coverage once the games had been played. Commentators particularly devoted much energy in detailing the rich history and traditions of the "classic." They made clear that each upcoming "classic" was going to be more spectacular, colorful, and exciting than the one preceding it. "Two years ago," wrote the *Chicago Defender* in 1921, "when the Lincoln management announced that the annual football game between the two ancient rivals, Howard and Lincoln, would be held in Philadelphia at the big National League Park, the pessimists began to shout, 'this will be nothing less than athletic suicide,' but the move was without a doubt the most popular venture ever attempted in this country. It was the greatest athletic and social success that has ever been witnessed."[35] "With only seven days intervening, much interest in the annual Turkey Day clash involving the Lincoln and Howard game is being exhibited in Philadelphia and adjacent regions," wrote the *Philadelphia Tribune* in 1928. "As a spectacle and a colorful event little doubt exists that this year's game will rival and perhaps excel in splendor and grandeur those of the past."[36]

Representatives from Howard and Lincoln welcomed the build-up because it added to an already burgeoning rivalry. A rivalry—especially an intense rivalry—these representatives understood, enhanced their respective institutional interests and ensured that the African American community would more closely identify with them and their various constituents. The intense rivalry between the two institutions was born out of the same requisite qualifications for all rivalries; namely, similarities, differences, and contrasts.[37] While Howard and Lincoln were two of the most prestigious HBCUs and both in the business of educating the African American community's "talented tenth" and fielding strong athletic teams, they had different histories, different geographical settings, different student enrollments, different philosophies, and different academic specializations. White Presbyterian minister John Miller Dickey founded Lincoln University, located in the small town of Oxford in Chester County, Pennsylvania, in 1854. During the 1920s it charged $110 in tuition, which was one of the highest of any HBCU in the country. It had a White president, sixteen White faculty, and an all-Black male enrollment that by 1927 had reached only 305. The university offered a four-year bachelor of arts degree in liberal arts, a three-year bachelor of sacred theology degree, and a three-year diploma in theology. A committee made up of faculty, alumni, and students administered all athletic activities.[38]

Howard University was founded in 1866 in Washington, DC, and named after General Oliver Otis Howard, a philanthropist and commissioner of the Freedmen's Bureau. Although a privately controlled institution, Howard since 1879 has received a subsidy from the federal government for both maintenance and capital outlay. It hired its first African American president, Mordecai Johnson, in 1926, employed 171 faculty members (the majority of whom were Black), and had a coed enrollment that by 1927 had reached 2,118 students representing thirty-six states and ten foreign countries. The athletic program was governed by a board of athletic control, consisting of faculty, alumni, the secretary-treasurer (Emmett J. Scott), and the director of physical education.[39]

The differences between the two institutions were symbolically displayed on the football field and through distinctive songs, colors, ceremonies, rituals, and logos each Thanksgiving Day during the 1920s. These activities did not simply mimic those that took place in White college sport and in the White sporting world more generally. Students, alumni, and other followers of the "classic" refashioned these activities, like so many other things during this era of the "new negro," in a style and manner that reflected the Black experience in Philadelphia and Washington, as well as that of Howard and Lincoln. A ritual of the Lincoln alumnus was to march en masse to the game, which was recorded in the *Chicago Defender* of 1922: "The Lincoln Alumni will hold a get together meeting tonight. Tomorrow morning, headed by a sixty-piece band, the alumni headed by Drs. Cannon and Alexander of New Jersey, Prof. Saunders of West Virginia, with their pet lion cub sent from Liberia by the United States minister, an alumnus of Lincoln, will head for the park from the Whitelaw hotel, bedecked in Lincoln's colors, singing their 'Alma Mater' as they go. All Lincoln adherents will follow in the line."[40]

An example of a representative song from the game was recorded in an undated issue of the *Lincoln News*:

> Howard has a quarterback,
> Who thinks he's mighty cute;
> But when he hits the Lincoln line,
> He'll do the loop the loop.
>
> He'll ramble off the tackle,
> Ramble around the end,
> Ramble through the center,
> Then ramble back again.
>
> Chorus:
> He'll ramble, ramble, ramble all around,
> Hey! In and out the town.
> Oh! ramble, ramble, ramble 'til ole Lincoln cuts him down.[41]

One of the most original and regular features of the "classic" were the "rabbles," a pregame, halftime or improvisational dance in which students climbed out of the stands and marched around the field carrying their own musical instruments and singing songs praising their own institutions and denigrating their opponents. The *Howard University Record* of 1921 reported on the "rabble" that took place at halftime of that year's game between Howard and Lincoln: "The ending of the first half was the cue for 'rabble' exhibitions. The rabbles of both schools pounced upon the field in spite of its mud-soaked conditions and the continuous rain. The 'blue and white' rabble headed by its band, executed a wild snake dance while the Lincoln horde did its serpentine dance."[42] One example of a rabble yell appeared in the 1926 game program. Titled "Nine Rahs Yell," the shout had the Howard faithful perform a call-and-response cheer:

Rah, Rah, Rah,
Rah, Rah, Rah,
Rah, Rah, Rah,
Team! Team! Team!
Leader—Who?
Rabble—Team!
Leader—Who?
Rabble—Team!
Leader—Who?
Rabble—Team! Team! Team![43]

Historian Patrick Miller, in his oft-cited essay, "To Bring the Race Along Rapidly: Sport, Student Culture, and Educational Mission at Historically Black Colleges During the Interwar Years," initially brought attention to the "rabbles," citing the above-mentioned quote from the 1921 *Howard University Record*.[44] Historian Michael Oriard elaborates further on the "rabbles" in *King Football*. Using the work of William Pierson on "African American Festive Style" and referencing accounts of the Howard and Lincoln games of the 1920s from the *Chicago Defender* and *Baltimore Afro-American*, Oriard makes the point that "rabbles" were representative of "Black Expressive Culture" in that they emphasized improvisation, spontaneity, and the close interplay between performers and spectators. The "rabbles," like various types of dances, funeral processions, and celebrations in the African American South (including different activities in the slave-quarter community, it should be added) can also be seen as a means to satirize the "more formal celebrations" of the ruling class in the country, in this case the "precision marching bands of the big-time football universities." Quoting Pierson, Oriard notes, moreover, "that the marching bands at historically Black institutions in the 1990s still retained a 'cake-walking heroic (and comedic) quality' very different from the style at say, the University of Michigan or Ohio State."⁴⁵

Additionally, the annual "classic" was just as much, in the words of sport historian Raymond Schmidt, "the centerpiece of a social competition between the Black populace of Washington, D.C. and Philadelphia" as it was a football rivalry between Howard and Lincoln.⁴⁶ Washington, DC, referred to by historian Willard B. Gatewood as the "capital of the colored aristocracy," was a segregated southern city with a Black population that had reached more than 132,000 by 1930.⁴⁷ Among this population was a relatively large and influential Black elite made up of civil servants, schoolteachers, college professors, lawyers, and doctors who had made their way to Washington, DC, to take advantage of the jobs available with the federal government and because of the superb educational opportunities provided by Howard. Though Seventh Street housed important business and entertainment establishments and was the center of social life for the Black masses, the U Street corridor harbored the very best in Washington's African American community. Sometimes referred to as the "Black Broadway" and with many famous African Americans living within its confines, the U Street corridor included, in addition to Howard University and Griffith Stadium, such landmarks as the Howard Theatre, M Street School, True Reformer Hall, Lincoln Theatre, Meridian Hill, Café De Luxe, and Freedmen's Hospital.⁴⁸

Philadelphia had a Black population of more than 219,000 by 1930, which ranked it third behind only New York City and Chicago. Unlike African Americans in Washington, who were largely confined to limited segregated areas, African Americans in Philadelphia lived in several large integrated districts in the north, south, and western parts of the city. Perhaps the most wealthy and prestigious integrated neighborhood in Philadelphia during the 1920s was located west of Fifty-Third Street and north of Market Street in an area now known as Haddington. Black Philadelphians, both alumni and those who were not, adopted Lincoln University as their own. Located some forty-five miles from Philadelphia, Lincoln became the hometown college team for the city.⁴⁹

Each year of the "classic," the Black upper crust in the host city vied for social supremacy by staging elaborate dances, parties, receptions and other affairs. Chartered trains would bring the very best of Black America to Washington and Philadelphia to watch the game and to participate in the many accompanying social activities. For upper-class Blacks in both cities, prestige was at stake as well as bragging rights and reputations. Those who arrived in Philadelphia or Washington to attend the "classic" were some of this country's most prominent African Americans. The game and social activities that complemented it attracted distinguished African Americans from the worlds of education, business, medicine, politics, entertainment, and a host of other professions. The society pages of all the major Black newspapers regularly listed, in addition to notable faculty and administrators from both institutions and local dignitaries, the elite African Americans from out of town who attended the "classic." Among the many prominent African Americans listed as having attended one or more of the Howard and Lincoln games were: William Henry Lewis, United States Assistant Attorney General; Walter White, civil rights activist and future leader of the National Association for the Advancement of Colored People (NAACP); authors James Weldon Johnson and Mary McLeod Bethune; Henry Binga Dismond, noted Harlem physician; Robert Abbott, founder of the *Chicago Defender*; and E. C. Brown, banker and owner of the largest Black realty corporation in New York City.[50]

William H. Jones, in his 1927 study *Recreation and Amusement Among Negroes in Washington, D.C.: A Sociological Analysis of the Negro in an Urban Environment*, wrote that the annual Thanksgiving football game between Howard and Lincoln "has given to the negro life of Washington a prestige among other cities and a magnetic influence over vicinal districts which no other field of negro life in the capital can approximate. Every day for approximately a week scores of important social affairs are held. These consist of breakfast, matinee and evening dances, poker games, bridge parties, slumming, cabaret parties, and numerous other entertainments."[51] "The visitor within our gates," noted the *Philadelphia Tribune* in 1929,

> will evidently go home wondering who was the person that invented the saying "Philadelphia is a slow town," for with the Chi Delta Mu dance on Wednesday night, the breakfast and dance given [by] Mrs. George Deane and Mrs. Hobson Reynolds on Thursday morning, the game, cocktail parties, followed by dinner and the Japelmas dance on Thursday night, not to mention the Frogs and innumerable "official dances," the matrons matinee dance on Friday afternoon, the second annual supper dance of the cosmopolitan club which distinguished itself last season by giving the finest affair of the year on Friday night, a matinee dance given by the Frogs on Saturday when Mrs. Lawrence Christmas and Mrs. Julian Abele will also give a dance in the afternoon for their friends and visitors followed by several parties on that night there will be, very little sleeping. For while dances are over at 2 o'clock, one immediately transports himself to somebody else's home or his own home where the merriment goes right on.[52]

Writing in the *Chicago Defender* in 1924, a busy Frank A. Young provided a detailed account of the variety of social affairs accompanying the "Classic" that year in Washington, DC. "[I] have a minute or two to get a tabulated list together before I beat it to the nearest telegraph station," Young penned. "Here it goes:"

LIST OF EVENTS
Wednesday evening, Nov. 26
5:30—Reception to the press, Howard university.
8:00—Grand reunion reception. Howard university dining hall.
8:00—Student demonstration, Lincoln Colonnade.
9:00—Chi Delta Mu Frat dance, Murray Casino.

Thursday morning, Nov. 27
Thanksgiving Day
9:00 to 11:30—Arrival of special trains from New York, Philadelphia, Baltimore, Atlantic City and the South.
9:00—Breakfast promenade, Lincoln Colonnade.
9:00—The Ambassadors' dance, Murray Casino.
11:00—Meeting of executive council, Howard university alumni.

Thursday afternoon
1:30—Awarding varsity letter "H" to veteran football players.
2:00—The football classic of the year—Howard university vs. Lincoln university.
4:00—Matinee dance, Murray Casino.

Thursday evening
Allied Collegiate Dance, Convention hall, with Ford Dabney's Zeigfeld Frolic \orchestra of New York. Grand reunion reception, Howard university (this event is backed by the committees representing both Howard and Lincoln universities and is the official event of the evening).

Friday morning, Nov. 28
10:00—Breakfast dance, Murray Casino.
Friday afternoon
3:00—Interfraternity dance, Armstrong high.
Friday evening
8:00—Alpha Phi Alpha reception, Murray Casino.
Omega Psi Phi fraternity dance, Lincoln Colonnade."[53]

The competition between Howard and Lincoln, as well as that between Washington and Philadelphia, should not blind us to the fact that the "classic" was more than just one large party. Like present-day golf outings for business executives, the time before, during, and after the games were opportunities for representatives from the two schools, members of the Black press, and other prominent African Americans to conduct business and establish connections that could prove beneficial to their professional success. In addition, the "classic" played a supportive role in both the coalescence of the campus communities at each institution and upper-class Blacks more generally during the early decades of the twentieth century, when many poorer southern Blacks migrated to northern cities. The annual Thanksgiving Day contests between Howard and Lincoln, while important in bringing additional moneys into institutional coffers, were particularly significant because they provided occasions for fostering school spirit and helped bind students, alumni, and to a much lesser extent faculty, closer together on both campuses. *The Howard University Record* of 1921 provided its assessment of the significance of the "classic" when it wrote that the game served not only "to dispel any doubt that may have previously existed as to the high place of football as the most popular sport among American college and university students, but also showed that such contests are the best means of indicating the true coefficient of college alumni loyalty. . . . On no other occasion probably do all unite with one mind, one heart and one voice. The whole college gives a striking instance of group psychology and thousands of students act as one man in urging their struggling heroes on to victory."[54]

The need to unite the campuses of each institution was perhaps never so important than during the decade of the 1920s. Although able to maintain their prestige and national reputations, Howard and Lincoln both experienced well-known internal dissension and turmoil during this crucial ten-year period. As Raymond Wolters writes in *The New Negro on Campus: Black College Rebellions of the 1920s* (1975), Lincoln experienced its share of internal dissension during the decade, particularly concerning its all-White faculty and administration. Influential and angry alumni, including the likes of Langston Hughes and Frances Grimke, made concerted efforts to ensure that African Americans were added to the faculty and the board of trustees and also fought to have more voice in all decisions pertaining to the operation of the university. The situation was so bad that on three separate occasions presidents-elect ultimately decided to turn down offers to lead the university when determining that life would be made miserable for them because of the disgruntlement of alumni who believed they had not been adequately consulted on the new hires.[55]

Life on the Howard campus was not much better and, in some cases, perhaps even worse. For much of the decade, White President Stanley Durkee faced bitter opposition from students, faculty, and alumni who questioned his leadership and the direction in which he was taking the university. Carter G. Woodson, the "father of black history," and Kelly Miller, the distinguished professor of sociology and dean of the College of Arts and Sciences, were just two of the Howard faculty who wrote scathing denouncements of Durkee and bitterly opposed his presidency. In 1925, 1,200 Howard students went on strike in protest over Durkee's decision to expel anyone who missed a minimum number of courses in ROTC. Two years later, the football team, as previously mentioned, went on strike after President Mordecai Johnson, who would serve the university in that capacity from 1926 until 1960, abolished the football training table and severely reduced the athletic budget. Students walked out of their classrooms to show support for the players, and the Thanksgiving Day game with Lincoln was canceled until Johnson persuaded the strikers to give him more time while he considered their demands.[56]

The annual Thanksgiving Day games between Howard and Lincoln were not only important for fostering school spirit and binding the campuses of each institution together, but also assisted in uniting upper-class African Americans during the social disruption brought about by the northern migration of southern African Americans during the post–World War I period. Upper-class African Americans were being challenged for their special place in society as the great migration came into existence and as alternative modes of social advancement became possible within the Black community. In addition, White America's toleration of upper-class African Americans rapidly diminished as the larger African American population became more geographically and economically mobile.[57]

The Howard and Lincoln Thanksgiving Day football "classic," while drifting toward tribal display and exclusivity and a social competition between upper-class African Americans of Washington, Philadelphia, and other parts of the East and Midwest, also helped to keep these same African Americans together. This is evident in the recurrent descriptions of the succession of parties, dances, and other social gatherings that accompanied the games. These descriptions make clear that the annual contests between the two famous institutions was largely about upper-class African Americans reaffirming their special place in society, distancing themselves from lower-class Blacks—whom they blamed for the rising tide of racism—and creating an occasion to join with those of similar values and mutuality of interest in sports and other social and cultural rituals. "The 1919 game between Howard and Lincoln was augmented," noted the *Philadelphia Tribune*, "by the presence of thousands of fashionable and ultrafashionable visitors from Washington, Baltimore, New York, Atlantic City, and other neighboring cities, the latter coming in several days ahead in order to secure the choicest hotel and private accommodations and to participate in the numerous festivities and social functions preceding the open football classic in the afternoon of turkey day."[58] "It will be the eighteenth meeting of the two elevens," wrote Frank A. Young of the *Chicago Defender* before the 1922 game in Washington. "Every incoming train brings its quota. The vanguard of the hosts who will watch tomorrow's struggle are busy renewing acquaintances. The 'Flapper Special' from New York City is due in early in the morning as is a special from Pittsburgh and one from Philadelphia and early morning trains will bring the balance who will help to make up the gayest throng that ever witnessed a football game anywhere and the largest that has ever witnessed a struggle between any two institutions representing our people."[59]

Unfortunately, by 1929 the "classic" had lost much of its luster, though many fans and university leaders continued to believe that the Thanksgiving Day game was still the highlight of Black football and would continue to garner national attention. In 1931, for instance, the *Lincoln News* announced, "Thanksgiving brings us down to that classic of Negro football, the Howard-Lincoln game. Other schools advertise their games as classics but this one is not only advertised, but is, the classic of classics."[60] Notwithstanding this pronouncement, the overwhelming evidence makes clear that by 1929 the games generated far less media coverage, experienced a decrease in attendance, and was devoid of much of the great gridiron talent that had marked the previous nine contests between the two institutions. The weakening financial condition of Howard and Lincoln's football programs specifically, and of their athletic programs more generally, contributed to this state of affairs. Though the two schools would continue to play each other regularly until Lincoln dropped football after the 1960 season, the Howard-Lincoln game would never be as popular or meaningful as it was during the 1920s. In its heyday, the "classic" was an athletic and social event that provided upper-class African Americans the opportunity to exhibit racial pride, measure themselves against the standards of White universities, and come together as a distinct group. In the process, African Americans reaffirmed their place in a country that had undergone unprecedented geographical and economic changes wrought by the northern migration of southern Blacks. To African Americans, the Howard and Lincoln Thanksgiving Day football "classic" during the second decade of the twentieth century was just as important as the annual games between Harvard and Yale and any number of other famous gridiron contests between predominantly White institutions. Maybe more so.

EPILOGUE

On September 10, 2011, Howard University and Morehouse College played each other in what was billed as the "First Annual AT&T Nation's Football Classic" at RFK Stadium. Rekindling a rivalry that had been scrapped some fifteen years earlier, the game was advertised in the *Washington Post* in much the same way the Black press advertised the Howard and Lincoln Thanksgiving Day games between 1919 and 1929.[61] The *Post* suggested that the game could potentially provide a financial boost to both institutions, would contribute to a sense of kinship and camaraderie among the students, friends, and faculty from both institutions, and furnish these same individuals an opportunity to watch outstanding football and enjoy the marching bands that "compete with a unique flair."[62] The game was supplemented with many parties, joint fundraiser dances, a student debate, and an assortment of other social gatherings. To some, the game between Howard University and Morehouse College was less about football and more about the accompanying social activities and the opportunity for alumni to "join students to backslap and trash-talk, holler and rally in maroon and white or blue and red on the campus of Howard University and the streets of Washington."[63]

There appear to be many similarities in the descriptions of the Howard University and Morehouse College AT&T Nation's Football Classic with that of the Thanksgiving Day football games between Howard and Lincoln during the 1919 to 1929 period. In truth, however, because of the strict racial segregation in this country during the 1920s, the Howard and Lincoln Thanksgiving Day "Classic" was decidedly different regarding organization and probably far more meaningful and culturally significant to the African American community. With only a very select number of African American athletes able to participate in predominantly White college sport during this period, the Howard and Lincoln Thanksgiving Day games included extraordinarily gifted athletes whose names today would undoubtedly dot the rosters of Division I football powers. But because they participated behind racially segregated walls, the Howard and Lincoln games received little coverage in the White press and no sponsorship from major corporations. Finally, with the hopes of highlighting their athletic accomplishments and by extension their sense of Black pride and ability for self-organization and independent business acumen, the Howard and Lincoln Thanksgiving Day Football "Classic" was particularly significant in that it was part of a burgeoning Black national sporting culture that would eventually include other well-known Thanksgiving Day games between other HBCUs and such events and organizations as the East-West All-Star game, Gold and Glory Sweepstakes, ATA, National Negro Bowling Association, and Interscholastic Athletic Association Basketball Tournament. This Black national sporting culture, which was fueled by a consumer culture that was a boon to the growth of sport more generally in the United States, brought African Americans from across the country a great deal of pleasure and sense of satisfaction and accomplishment that was not easy to come by during the era prior to integration.

Notes

I would like to thank Chris Elzey, Tom Jable, and Patrick Miller for providing cogent comments and suggestions on an earlier draft of this manuscript. I would also like to thank Pierre Rodgers for sharing copies of the *Philadelphia Tribune* that were secured from the Lincoln University Library.

1. For examples of works that deal with various aspects of sports behind segregated walls, see: Janet Bruce, *The Kansas City Monarchs: Champions of Black Baseball* (Lawrence, Kan.: University Press of Kansas, 1985); Susan Cahn, *Coming on Strong: Gender and Sexuality in Twentieth-Century Women's Sport* (New York: Free Press, 1994); Nelson George, *Elevating the Game: Black Men and Basketball* (New York: Harper Collins, 1992); Neil Lanctot, *Negro League Baseball: The Rise and Ruin of a Black Institution* (Philadelphia: University of Pennsylvania Press, 2004); Jennifer H. Lansbury, " 'The Tuskegee Flash' and 'The Slender Harlem Stroker': Black Women Athletes on the Margin," *Journal of Sport History* 28 (Summer 2001): 233–52; Pete McDaniel, *Uneven Lies: The Heroic Story of African-Americans in Golf* (Greenwich, Conn.: American Golfers, 2000); Patrick B. Miller, "To Bring the Race Along Rapidly: Sport, Student Culture, and Educational Mission at Historically Black Colleges During the Interwar Years," *History of Education Quarterly* 35 (Summer 1995): 111–23; Troy D. Paino, "Hoosiers in a Different Light: Forces of Change vs. the Power of Nostalgia," *Journal of Sport History* 26 (Spring 2001): 63–80; Rob Ruck, *Sandlot Seasons: Sport in Black Pittsburgh* (Urbana: University of Illinois Press, 1987); Robert Gregg, "Personal

Calvaries: Sports in Philadelphia's African American Communities, 1920–60," *Sport in Society* 6 (October 2003): 88–115.

2. *Chicago Defender*, December 2, 1922; William H. Jones, *Recreation and Amusement Among Negroes in Washington, D.C.: A Sociological Analysis of the Negro in an Urban Environment* (Washington, DC: Howard University Press, 1927).

3. Raymond Schmidt, *Shaping College Football: The Transformation of an American Sport, 1919–1930* (Syracuse: Syracuse University Press, 2007), 13.

4. See Horace Mann Bond, "The Story of Athletics at Lincoln University" unpublished chapter from Horace Mann Bond, *Education for Freedom: A History of Lincoln University, Pennsylvania* (Princeton, NJ: Princeton University Press, 1976), 3–26; "History of Athletics," *The Bison*, 1924, N.P.; *Baltimore Afro-American*, November 28, 1919; *Pittsburgh Courier*, November 19, 1924, December 1, 1923; *Chicago Defender*, November 23, 1929.

5. *Philadelphia Tribune*, October 18 and November 1, 1919. See also *Washington Post*, November 28, 1919.

6. There are few autobiographical accounts of the games and the accompanying social activities. One exception was U. S. Young, former Lincoln coach who wrote an account of the 1925 game in the *Baltimore Afro-American*. See *Baltimore Afro-American*, December 12, 1925. Another exception was the account of the 1925 game written by Tad Lancaster, captain of the Lincoln team, in the *Baltimore Afro-American* of December 12, 1925.

7. *Philadelphia Tribune*, December 4, 1920, *Chicago Defender*, December 4, 1920; *Washington Bee*, December 4, 1920.

8. Bond, "The Story of Athletics at Lincoln University," 28–29; *Philadelphia Tribune*, December 4, 1920, *Chicago Defender*, December 4, 1920, *Baltimore Afro-American*, December 10, 1920. The first ballpark located at the site of Griffith Stadium was called Boundary Field or National Park. Built in 1891, the ballpark was renamed the American League Park in 1901 when the Washington Nationals baseball team joined Ban Johnson's new American League. In 1911, the ballpark was destroyed by fire, but was rebuilt with a seating capacity of over 27,000 and was called American Baseball Park II. In 1920 the ballpark was once again renamed, this time to Griffith. See the essay by Ryan Swanson in this volume, Michael Benson, *Ballparks of North America: A Comprehensive Historical Reference to Baseball Grounds, Yards, Stadiums, 1845-present* (Jefferson, NC: McFarland and Co., Inc., Publishers, 1989), and http://www.ballparksofbaseball.com/past/GriffithStadium.htm.

9. Bond, "The Story of Athletics at Lincoln University," 29; *Chicago Defender*, November 19, 26, December 3, 1921; *Howard University Record* 16 (December 1921): 125–26; *Washington Post*, November 21, 25, 1921.

10. *Chicago Defender*, December 3, 1921; *Baltimore Afro-American*, November 25, 1921.

11. Bond, "The Story of Athletics at Lincoln University," 30–31; *Chicago Defender*, November 25 and December 2, 9, 1922; *New York Age*, December 9, 1922; *New York Amsterdam News*, December 6, 1922.

12. For descriptions of the game see: *Chicago Defender*, December 1, 1923; *Baltimore Afro-American*, November 16, 17, 30, 1923 and December 7, 14, 1923; *Pittsburgh Courier*, November 17, 1923; *Boston Daily Globe*, November 30, 1923; *Norfolk Journal and Guide*, December 8, 1923; *New York Times*, November 30, 1923. The Lincoln team of 1923 was extraordinary for both its athletic accomplishments and the professional success of its players in their post-college lives. Five players were named to the All-Central Intercollegiate Athletic Association team, six players were selected to either the first, second, or third teams on Fay Young's *Chicago Defender* All-American squad; and following graduation three players took their medical degrees, two took their PhDs, two took their law degrees, and another four took various types of master's degrees. Bond, "The Story of Athletics at Lincoln University," 30–31; *Chicago Defender*, November 17, 24, 1923; *Howard University Record* 18 (January 1924): 199–200, 202; *Philadelphia Tribune*, December 8, 1923.

13. Bond, "The Story of Athletics at Lincoln University," 21–37; *Howard University Record* 19 (January 1925): 114–16; *Pittsburgh Courier*, November 1, 24, 29 and December 6, 20, 1924; *Chicago Defender*, November 22, 29 and December 6, 1924; *Philadelphia Tribune*, November, 22, 27, 29 and December 6, 1924; *Washington Post*, November 28, 1924; *Norfolk Journal and Guide*, December 6, 1924; The Crisis 29 (February 1925): 171–72; *Howard Alumnus* 3 (January 15, 1925): 62.

14. *Baltimore Afro-American*, November 29, 1924; Chicago Defender, December 6, 1924.

15. *Chicago Defender*, December 29, 1924; *Pittsburgh Courier*, December 27, 1924. For a nice secondary account of the Miller affair, see Raymond Schmidt, *Shaping College Football: The Transformation of an American Sport*, 1919–1930 (Syracuse: Syracuse University Press, 2007), pp. 138–139.

16. Bond, "The Story of Athletics at Lincoln University," 37; *Chicago Defender*, December 5, 1925; *Pittsburgh Courier*, December 5, 1925; *Washington Post*, November 27, 1925.

17. *Pittsburgh Courier*, December 11, 1926. See also *Chicago Defender*, December 18, 1926; *Norfolk Journal and Guide*, December 18, 1926.

18. Bond, "The Story of Athletics at Lincoln University," 37–38; *The Crisis* 34 (March 1927): 7; *Chicago Defender*, November 20 and December 4, 1926; *Pittsburgh Courier*, December 4, 18, 20, 1926; *Philadelphia Tribune*, November 20, 27 and December 4, 1926; *Washington Post*, November 14, 26, 1926; *New York Times*, November 26, 1926. The 1920s witnessed the building of many new stadiums with expanded seating capacities at predominantly White universities across the country. Northwestern University and the University of Missouri also built new stadiums in 1926, with seating capacities of approximately 40,000 to 50,000. See Raymond Schmidt, *Shaping College Football: The Transformation of an American Sport*, 1919–1930, esp. chapter three.

19. *Washington Post*, November 26, 1926.

20. Howard University Archives (hereafter cited as HUA), Department of Athletics, Box 34, "Programs, 1926–1932," 5 of 6.

21. Bond, "The Story of Athletics at Lincoln University," 38; *Philadelphia Tribune*, November 24, 1927; *The Crisis* 35 (February 1928): 45; *Chicago Defender*, November 12 and December 3, 1927. For a nice analysis of the conflict between education and athletics during both the Durkee and Johnson years at Howard, see Patrick B. Miller, "To 'Bring the Race Along Rapidly:' Sport, Student Culture, and Educational Mission at Historically Black Colleges During the Interwar Years," 111–23.

22. *Philadelphia Tribune*, November 22, 29, 1928; *Chicago Defender*, November 24, 1928; *Washington Post*, November 29, 1928; *New York Times*, November 30, 1928; *Washington Afro-American*, May 26, 1934. West became the first African American to play quarterback in the Rose Bowl in 1922 when Washington and Jefferson fought to a 0–0 tie in Pasadena against the University of California, Berkeley. He also qualified for the 1924 Olympic track and field team but could not participate because of an injury. For specific information on West see: E. Lee North, *Battling the Indians, Panthers & Nittany Lions: Washington & Jefferson College's Century of Football, 1890–1990* (Canton, OH: Daring, 1991) and Allyson Gilmore, "Breaking Barriers: W&J Remembers Legendary Athlete Who Changed the Game for African-Americans in Collegiate Sports." http://www.washjeff.edu/breaking-barriers-wj-remembers-legendary-athlete-who-changed-game-African-Americans-collegiate-sports, accessed February 11, 2013.

23. HUA, Department of Athletics, Box 33, "News Items, 1938–1943" 4 of 5.

24. *Chicago Defender*, November 23 and December 7, 1929; *Philadelphia Tribune*, November 28 and December 5, 1929; *Baltimore Afro-American*, December 14, 1929.

25. For nice overviews of the Carnegie Foundation Report, see Raymond Schmidt, *Shaping College Football: The Transformation of an American Sport, 1919–1930*, 217–233 and Ronald A. Smith, *Pay for Play: A History of Big-Time College Athletic Reform* (Urbana: University of Illinois Press, 2011), 59–70.

26. *New York Amsterdam News*, November 27, 1929. See also *Baltimore Afro-American*, December 14, 1929; *Chicago Defender*, December 5, 12, 1936.

27. Bond, "The Story of Athletics at Lincoln University," 26–27. Finding financial data on the Howard and Lincoln games is difficult, but an "income and expenditures" statement from Howard in 1929 indicated that the school netted $4,256.83 from the "classic" that year. The total income from their four other away games that year was $4,800. See "Statement of Athletics: Incomes and Expenditures July 1, 1929 to December 31, 1929." Moorland-Spingarn Research Center.

28. The changing nature of sport and the rise of a consumer culture during the 1920s is nicely analyzed in Mark Dyreson, "The Emergence of Consumer Culture and the Transformation of Physical Culture: American Sport in the 1920s," *Journal of Sport History* 16 (Winter 1989): 261–81.

29. Bond, "The Story of Athletics at Lincoln University," 26–27. For background information on Scott, see: Maceo Crenshaw Dailey Jr., "Emmett Jay Scott: The Career of a Secondary Black Leader." Unpublished PhD dissertation, Howard University, 1983.

30. See Dailey, "Emmett Jay Scott"; Edgar Allan Toppin, "Emmett Jay Scott,"

105–6, in Henry Louis Gates Jr. and Evelyn Brooks Higginbotham, eds., *African American National Biography* (New York: Oxford University Press, 2008); Louis R. Harlan, *Booker T. Washington: The Making of a Black Leader, 1952–1901* (New York: Oxford University Press, 1972); Louis R. Harlan, *Booker T. Washington: The Wizard of Tuskegee* (New York: Oxford University Press, 1983); J.L. Nichols and William H. Crogman, *Progress of a Race of the Remarkable Advancement of the American Negro* (Naperville, IL: J.L. Nichols & Company, 1929), 429; W.N. Hartshorn (ed.) *An Era of Progress and Promise, 1863–1910* (Boston: The Priscilla Publishing Co., 1910), 414–415. Information on both Lewis and Alexander is limited. See, however, Bond "The Story of Athletics at Lincoln University," 26–28.

31. *Chicago Defender*, November 23, 1929.
32. See Schmidt, *Shaping College Football*, 135.
33. *Chicago Defender*, November 24, 1928.
34. *Philadelphia Tribune*, November 22, 1928. For information on Thanksgiving Day games among predominantly White universities in the late-nineteenth century, see Michael Oriard, *Reading Football: How the Popular Press Created an American Spectacle* (Chapel Hill, NC: The University of North Carolina Press, 1993), esp. 89–101.
35. *Chicago Defender*, November 19, 1921.
36. *Philadelphia Tribune*, November 22, 1928.
37. For information on the characteristics and requisite features of sport rivalries, see David K. Wiggins and R. Pierre Rodgers, eds., *Rivals: Legendary Matchups that Made Sports History* (Fayetteville: The University of Arkansas Press, 2010); Richard O. Davies, *Rivals! The Ten Greatest American Sports Rivalries of the 20th Century* (Malden, Mass.: John Wiley and Sons, 2010).
38. Bond, *Education for Freedom*; US Office of Education, *Survey of Negro Colleges and Universities*, Bulletin 1928, No. 7, US Government Printing Office, 1929.
39. Walter Dyson, *Howard University: The Capstone of Negro Education, A History: 1867–1940* (Washington, DC: Howard University Press, 1941); Rayford Logan, *Howard University: The First Hundred Years* (New York: New York University Press, 1969); Paul E. Logan, ed., *A Howard Reader: An Intellectual and Cultural Quilt of the African American Experience* (Boston: Houghton Mifflin, 1997); US Office of Education, *Survey of Negro Colleges and Universities*.
40. *Chicago Defender*, December 2, 1922.
41. *Lincoln News*, n.d.
42. *Howard University Record* 16 (December 1921): 126.
43. HUA, Department of Athletics, Box 34, "Programs, 1926–1932," 5 of 6.
44. Miller, "'To Bring the Race Along Rapidly,'" 119.
45. Michael Oriard, *King Football: Sport and Spectacle in the Golden Age of Radio and Newspapers, Movies and Magazines, the Weekly and the Daily Press* (Chapel Hill: The University of North Carolina Press, 2001), 321, 323.
46. Schmidt, *Shaping College Football*: 135.

47. Willard B. Gatewood, *Aristocrats of Color: The Black Elite* (Bloomington: Indiana University Press, 1990), especially chapters two and four.

48. Blair A. Ruble, *Washington's U Street: A Biography* (Baltimore, MD: The Johns Hopkins University Press, 2010).

49. Gatewood, *Aristocrats of Color*, 96–97; Charles Hardy, "Race and Opportunity: Black Philadelphia During the Era of the Great Migration," unpublished PhD dissertation, Temple University, 1989, 131, 178, 441, 445.

50. See *New York Amsterdam News*, December 6, 1922; *Philadelphia Tribune*, December 8, 1923; *Baltimore Afro-American*, December 6, 1924; *Chicago Defender*, December 5, 1925; *New York Amsterdam News*, December 1, 1926.

51. Jones, *Recreation and Amusement Among Negroes*, 73.

52. *Philadelphia Tribune*, November 21, 1929.

53. *Chicago Defender*, November 29, 1924.

54. *Howard University Record* 15 (January 1921): 133.

55. Raymond Wolters, *The New Negro on Campus: Black College Rebellions of the 1920s* (Princeton, NJ: Princeton University Press, 1975), 278–93.

56. *Washington Afro-American*, May 16, 30, 1925; May 8, 1926; Zora Neale Hurston, "The Hue and Cry about Howard University," in *A Howard Reader*, 138–46.

57. See Hardy, *Race and Opportunity*, 19, 22; Gatewood, *Aristocrats of Color*, 332–48.

58. *Philadelphia Tribune*, November 29, 1919.

59. *Chicago Defender*, December 2, 1922.

60. *Lincoln News*, November 1931.

61. *Washington Post*, September 9, 10, 2011.

62. Ibid., September 10, 2011.

63. Ibid., September 9, 2011.

WITH ALL DELIBERATE SPEED

High School Sport, Race, and *Brown v. Board of Education*

The landmark 1954 *Brown v. Board of Education of Topeka*, 347 US 483 decision, sandwiched between the changes resulting from World War II and civil rights legislation of the 1960s, marked a turning point in the history of race relations in the United States. By a unanimous decision the Supreme Court determined that state sanctioned segregation of public schools was a violation of the 14th Amendment and therefore unconstitutional. This decision marked the end of the legally approved "separate but equal" precedent established by the Supreme Court some sixty years earlier and served as a catalyst in the struggle for equal rights of all citizens in this country.[1] The question I address in this essay is what effects the *Brown v. Board of Education* decision has had on African American high school students regarding both their participation in sport and educational attainments.

To understand the effects of *Brown v. Board of Education* on interscholastic sport, it is important to examine first the participation patterns of African Americans in high school athletics prior to 1954 and what that participation meant to the African American community. A significant fact to remember is that prior to the historic decision in 1954 a select number of outstanding African American athletes outside the South would find their initial success in integrated high school sport and then continue that success in some of the most prestigious predominantly White colleges in the country. Some of these athletes would even realize international acclaim for their great athletic performances. Paul Robeson, the great singer, actor, athlete, and civil rights activist, was one of fewer than a dozen African Americans among the approximately 200 students at New Jersey's Somerville High School where he starred in football, basketball, baseball, and track and field. After Somerville, Robeson enrolled at Rutgers University where he was a two-time member of Walter Camp's all-American football teams in 1917 and 1918. Fritz Pollard starred in several sports at integrated Lane Technical High School in Chicago before eventually becoming a student at Brown University where he was selected to Walter Camp's all-American football team in 1916. Archie Williams, who captured the gold medal in the 400-meter run at the 1936 Olympic Games in Berlin, attended integrated University High School in Oakland prior to enrolling at San Mateo Junior College and then later at the University of California, Berkeley. Jimmy LuValle, who won three bronze medals in the 1936 Olympic Games in Berlin, graduated from integrated Polytechnic High School in Los Angeles before finding his way to the University of California at Los Angeles (UCLA). Jesse Owens, the hero of the 1936 Olympic Games in Berlin, starred at racially mixed East Technical High School in Cleveland before taking his talents to The Ohio State University. Woody Strode and Kenny Washington, the UCLA stars who reintegrated the National Football League (NFL) with the Los Angeles Rams in 1946, attended racially mixed high schools in Los Angeles— Strode attending Jefferson High School and Washington, Lincoln High School. Finally, Jackie Robinson starred in several sports at Pasadena's racially mixed John Muir Technical High School in the mid-1930s before moving on to UCLA.[2]

    The fact that these athletes attended integrated high schools did not guarantee them equitable treatment or shield them from the racial realities of Jim Crow America or ensure that they would receive a quality education and realize academic success. The academic performances of the above-mentioned African American athletes, and other African American athletes during the first half of the twentieth century for that matter, was a mixed bag. Although statistics are not available on graduation rates for this period, it is apparent that prior to 1954 some of these African American athletes floundered academically while others realized great success in the classroom at both the interscholastic and collegiate levels. For instance,

Pollard was a C- plus student at Lane Technical High School before becoming what his biographer John Carroll, referred to as a "tramp athlete" and making stops at Northwestern, Dartmouth, and Bates before finding his way to Brown. His academic performance at Brown did not match his success on the football field and he eventually dropped out of the university with several failing grades dotting his transcript. Jesse Owens was no better than Pollard academically, an average student at both East Technical High School and The Ohio State University who never did graduate from college.[3]

Paul Robeson and Jimmy LuValle were the antithesis of Fritz Pollard and Jesse Owens from an academic standpoint. Robeson graduated with honors from Somerville High School and at Rutgers was Phi Beta Kappa, a member of the Cap and Skull Honor Society, and class valedictorian. LuValle was an excellent student at Polytechnic High School and Phi Beta Kappa from UCLA. After completing his undergraduate education, LuValle returned to UCLA to take his master's degree in chemistry and physics and then later earned his PhD in chemistry from Cal Tech where he worked under the renowned Linus Pauling.[4]

Explaining with any degree of certainty the decidedly different levels of academic success among African American athletes from integrated public schools and colleges during the first half of the twentieth century is an almost impossible task considering the lack of reliable sources. One man, however, places part of the blame for Owens's academic failures at the doorstep of the educational institutions he attended. Delbert Oberteuffer, the well-known physical educator and philosopher of sport from The Ohio State University, wrote a detailed letter to the school's athletic director shortly after the 1936 Olympic Games in Berlin complaining that no one had taken a genuine interest in Owens's welfare as a student or his future. Using terms such as a "beautiful and remarkable animal" and "remarkable psychomotor genius" to describe Owens, Oberteuffer claimed that the university had "been interested largely in keeping him eligible but beyond that we have been more or less unconcerned." "It is time," noted Oberteuffer in regard to Owens, "when we as a faculty should do what we can to fan the spark of interest into the flame which it can become."[5]

Classroom performances aside, the integrated world in which these African American athletes operated often made the realities of racial discrimination that much more personal and poignant. These athletes often enjoyed a more privileged status and greater opportunities, but these were offset by the athletes' constant exposure to racially discriminatory practices because of their closer proximity to the White power structure. Fritz

Pollard, for instance, recounted in some detail the racial discrimination he experienced while attending Lane Technical High School in Chicago. He continually encountered opponents who utilized illegal tactics and rough play in efforts to injure him and put him out of games. Most appalling and hurtful to Pollard were incidents in which his own coaches and teammates were complicit in the acts of discrimination against him. He recalled with much pain how his own coach, R. F. Webster, kept him out of a game in 1910 versus St. John's Military Academy in Wisconsin because of that school's refusal to play against an African American. An even uglier event occurred when coach Webster intentionally gave Pollard the wrong departure time and left him at the train station rather than telling him directly that the school in southern Illinois scheduled to play Lane Tech was opposed to competing against him because of his color.[6]

Notwithstanding the treatment of Pollard, it is important not to paint here with too broad a brush. In fact, it is apparent that some African American athletes in integrated high schools of Iowa, Minnesota, and other states with relatively small Black populations became integral parts of their sports teams without seemingly experiencing racial discrimination from teammates, opposing players, or spectators. A classic example of this would be Theatrece Gibbs who starred in football at Dubuque High School in Iowa from 1931 to 1933 and went on to play at the University of Dubuque from 1934 to 1937. Although he is not on the school's website or in their Hall of Fame, Gibbs, along with his backfield mate Jay Berwanger who became the inaugural Heisman Trophy winner, led Dubuque High School to the Mississippi Valley Conference title in 1931. In 1933 Gibbs was elected by his teammates as captain, even though he and his brother Leo were the only African Americans on the squad. That year Gibbs was named by the *Des Moines Register* to its first team all-state high school football team.[7]

Conspicuous by their limited involvement in integrated high school sport in the north prior to *Brown vs. Board of Education* were African American female athletes. They were like their White counterparts in that they apparently found most of their success on playgrounds and in Catholic youth organizations, Young Men's Christian Associations (YMCA), Young Women's Christian Associations (YWCA), industrial leagues, and Amateur Athletic Union (AAU) sponsored programs rather than high school-sponsored sport. For instance, Tidye Pickett and Louise Stokes, who in 1936 became the first African American women to compete on a United States Olympic Team, began their athletic careers on northern playgrounds.[8]

In the South the sport participation patterns of African American women athletes were seemingly quite different. Although finding some success in competitions sponsored by the AAU and other youth sport organizations, African American women athletes in the South enjoyed a more vibrant and comprehensive sports program in both public and private high schools. Pamela Grundy makes clear in her award-winning *Learning to Win* how important basketball was to African American women at West Charlotte High School in North Carolina and other segregated institutions and that by 1950 thirty-two of the greatest Black women's teams from North and South Carolina competed in the prestigious interscholastic Twin States tournament.[9]

Basketball was an especially popular sport among women students at Washington, DC's National Training School for Women and Girls, a private institution founded by noted educator Nannie Helen Burroughs.[10] Black educators and the Black community generally were apparently far more receptive to women participating in highly competitive sport and it was reflected in the high school athletic programs scattered throughout the South. Susan Cahn, in her frequently cited *Coming on Strong*, noted that despite expensive travel costs and the limited number of Black high schools in the South, African American women competed in highly organized track and field competitions at the interscholastic level in that part of the country. Perhaps the most important of these competitions occurred at Tuskegee Institute, Hampton, and other historically Black colleges that often-sponsored junior track and field meets for local high school students.[11]

These segregated high school sport programs for African American women athletes would be the standard mode of participation for their male counterparts as well. Notwithstanding the careers of Fritz Pollard, Paul Robeson, Jackie Robinson, and those other athletes mentioned previously, the largest number of African American athletes during the first half of the twentieth century participated in sport in segregated Black high schools and often against only Black opponents. Legal segregation in the South and de facto segregation in the north, particularly following the large northern migration of southern Blacks, would result in the creation of separate Black public schools that placed a high premium on both academic and athletic success. Perhaps the most famous of these institutions was the M Street School in Washington, DC, which was founded by Congress in 1870 as the Preparatory High School for Negro youth. Having a brilliant administrative and instructional staff that was unable to assume positions at White institutions because of the era's rigid racial segregation, M Street School evolved over time into a prestigious institution that provided a broad liberal education for Black youth. Graduates of the school, many of whom would attend predominantly White colleges in the north or well-known historically Black institutions, regularly assumed leadership positions and fashioned distinguished careers in education, business, law, medicine, music, religion and the military.[12]

Included among this group was Edwin Bancroft Henderson, the great physical educator, historian of the Black athlete, and athletic administrator, who in 1906 joined forces with five other notable Black educators in Washington, DC. to organize the Interscholastic Athletic Association (ISAA). Made up of schools from Washington, DC; Indianapolis, Indiana; Wilmington, Delaware; and Baltimore, Maryland; the ISAA organized athletic contests in football, baseball, basketball, and track and field. In 1910 Henderson, at the request of Roscoe Bruce, head of Washington, DC's Black public school system, organized the Public Schools Athletic League (PSAL). Modeled after the White public school's athletic leagues located in eighteen cities across the United States, Washington, DC's Black PSAL sponsored a vast array of sports for children of various skill levels at both the grammar school and high school levels. The PSAL organized, among other things, a grammar school baseball tournament, intercity soccer league, high school cross country meets, and Saturday night basketball games and dances during the winter months at the city's famous True Reformer's Hall.[13]

The ISAA and PSAL in Washington, DC, would eventually be followed by additional high school sports organizations in other African American communities nationwide. In 1924, for example, fourteen schools formed the West Virginia Athletic Union, a truly groundbreaking organization in that it was the first African American statewide athletic association in the South. By 1930 other Black state high school athletic associations had been organized in Virginia, North Carolina, Kansas, Missouri, Illinois, Indiana, and Florida. Slower to establish Black high school athletic associations were many of those states in the Deep South. Mississippi did not have one until 1940, Arkansas waited until 1942, and Alabama finally followed suit when it established a Black high school athletic association in 1948.[14]

The most popular sport of these athletic associations was basketball. More so than baseball and probably more so than football, the sport was initially a tool to help build pride, draw attention to the overall educational mission of the Black community, and a way to give underprivileged but athletically gifted African American youth a chance at a college education. In essence, basketball, as conceived of by African Americans, was about developing race leaders and not promoting stars, about developing character and not promoting professional athletes, and about developing model citizens and not promoting the singular pursuit of professional sports contracts.[15]

Black state high school athletic associations showcased basketball in year-end tournaments. The Black press is replete with descriptions of these tournaments, which were a combination of great sporting events and grand social occasions. The state basketball tournaments involving Black high schools were like the Negro League all-star baseball games, Thanksgiving Day football contests between historically Black colleges, and any number of other sports' events behind segregated walls in that they afforded African Americans an opportunity to exhibit skills of self-organization and strengthen feelings of connectedness and community. These tournaments were more than just opportunities to exhibit great athletic skills, but a chance for the African American community to reinforce exclusive identities and maintain a much-needed sense of solidarity in a world that denied them freedom of choice and relegated them to second-class citizenship based on race.[16]

The West Virginia Athletic Union (WVAU) sponsored one of the most important of these tournaments. Held for the first time in 1925 at West Virginia State College, the WVAU Basketball Tournament evolved into an extremely significant sporting event that provided, in the words of sport historian Robert Barnett, an "annual reunion for hundreds of black students, athletes, coaches, and supporters. They came from small isolated black communities within a larger White world. They faced segregation and discrimination in every aspect of life, but that adversity itself tended to create unity and togetherness."[17]

The WVAU tournament and those sponsored by other Black state high school athletic associations would be complemented by a national interscholastic basketball tournament involving outstanding Black high school teams from across the country. The National Interscholastic Basketball Tournament was first held in 1930 at Hampton Institute in Virginia. Organized by Charles H. Williams, a noted physical educator and coach from Hampton Institute, the tournament enjoyed some initial success attracting such perennial powerhouses as Washington, DC's Armstrong Technical High School; Chicago, Illinois' Wendell Phillips; and Gary, Indiana's Roosevelt High School. In 1933, however, Hampton Institute ended its sponsorship of the tournament, citing the exorbitant costs associated with running such an event. Instead, the tournament was held in Gary, Indiana, in 1934 and 1935; at Roanoke, Virginia's Lucy Addison High School in

1936; and then back to Gary, Indiana, in 1937 and 1938. Beginning in 1939 the tournament shifted to various sites, including Roanoke, Virginia and both Durham and Fayetteville, North Carolina, until World War II put a temporary halt to the event in 1942.[18]

In 1945 Tennessee A&I President Walter Davis and the school's athletic director, Henry Arthur Keane, revived the tournament. Held first in Nashville and then later at Alabama State under the auspices of the newly formed organization titled the National High School Athletic Association, the tournament was highly successful and continued to exist in one form or another until 1964. It was apparent long before 1964, however, that times were changing. Gary, Indiana's Roosevelt High School and Indianapolis' Crispus Attucks High School, two of the most famous and powerful Black high school basketball programs in the country, did not even play in the tournament since they began participating in 1943 in the recently desegregated Indiana High School Athletic championships. The reason for the tournament's change in location from Tennessee A&I to Alabama State resulted from the move toward integration on the part of the Tennessee National High School Athletic Association in 1954.[19]

In large part, the changes in the National High School Athletic Association Tournament resulted from *Brown vs. Board of Education*. The famous 1954 Supreme Court decision set in motion both individual and collective challenges to racial segregation in interscholastic sport. These challenges would ultimately result in the desegregation of various sports in high schools throughout the South. The first public school system in the South to integrate its athletic program after *Brown vs. Board of Education* was the same public school system to establish the first separate athletic programs in the early years of the twentieth century. No sooner had the justices rendered their decision, the District of Columbia, a federal city that could not assume the tactics of many southern states who deliberately stalled on desegregation by questioning whether it was the responsibility of the federal or state governments, announced that it had abolished its segregated physical education and athletic programs and merged them into two departments that included both Black and White high schools. It also established an athletic conference made up of two seven-school leagues divided by geographical location rather than the racial composition of the schools.[20]

The integration of high school athletics in the District of Columbia was duplicated in nearby Baltimore, Maryland, and a few other selected areas. These earliest incidents of integration in interscholastic sport, combined with the previous decade's entry of Jackie Robinson into Major League Baseball and the subsequent integration of other selected professional sports, was evidence to some that America was finally living up to its professed principles of fair play and equality and it resulted in a spate of writings acknowledging the achievements of African American athletes.[21] At long last, full integration on America's playing fields seemed to be at hand.

Unfortunately, it would be several *years* before large numbers of other public high schools in the South would follow the leads of the District of Columbia and Baltimore. The reason for the delay resulted from opposition in much of the South to *Brown vs. Board of Education*; this opposition taking the form of White citizen's councils, the passage of pro-segregation legislation, the substituting of private education for public schools, and an assortment of less obvious measures.[22] Finally, however, as a consequence of further civil rights legislation, continuing battles over equality of opportunity, and burgeoning Black Power movement during the 1960s, African American athletes were among the increasing number of African Americans who found their way onto the campuses of predominantly White public schools in the South.

It was in the border states that African American athletes apparently found their first opportunities to play with and against White athletes. The state of Virginia is a good case in point. As early as 1963, only a year after John F. Kennedy sent federal troops to ensure the entry of James Meredith into the University of Mississippi, African American football players Eric Burden and Victor Hundley integrated the predominantly White Newport News and Ferguson High Schools in the Hampton Roads area of Virginia.[23] The most famous instance, of course, of racial integration in Virginia high school athletics took place in 1971 at T.C. Williams High School in the City of Alexandria. Largely a result that year of the *Swann vs. Charlotte-Mecklenburg Board of Education* Supreme Court decision, which permitted busing of students in efforts to achieve racial integration and enforce the long overdue mandates of *Brown vs. Board of Education*, all students in Alexandria, regardless of race, were placed in T.C. Williams High School. Immortalized in the 2000 movie *Remember the Titans*, the newly constituted school's football team would go undefeated and capture the Virginia State Championship.[24]

The opportunity to participate with and against White athletes was certainly welcomed by African American high school athletes and the Black community more generally. In what ways would their lives be the same or different, however, than they were prior to *Brown v. Board of Education*?

Perhaps the most important and significant point that needs to be made in answering this question is that the participation of African Americans at the interscholastic level of competition has often continued to be found in selected sports and in public schools where racial minorities are the majority. De facto segregation, the result of systematic efforts to undermine the spirit of *Brown v. Board of Education*, the nation's lack of commitment to integration and the more conservative nature of the Supreme Court, all forced many African Americans, both in the north and the south, to compete in underfunded and inferior public schools that stressed athletics, much to the detriment of academics. The result—an unequal system in which academic success of more financially secure, predominantly White public and private schools, rarely is realized.[25]

This sad fact has been the death knell for many African American male athletes' intent on competing in college athletics. While some of these athletes have been fortunate enough to satisfy the academic standards established by the NCAA, and earn scholarship money to participate in intercollegiate athletics, and graduate at a higher rate than the Black male population in the general student body, a large majority is left to recall their glory days in high school, unable to meet minimum academic requirements and dreaming of what might have been.[26] It is difficult to overestimate the frustration and disillusionment these athletes must feel, especially when one considers the extraordinary importance many African American families, particularly those from lower-income brackets, attach to professional sport and athletic pursuits more generally.

Many academicians, while usually coming at the problem slightly differently, have made clear the very high percentage of young and frequently poor African American male athletes who have devoted all their attention to the singular pursuit of a life in professional sport at the expense of preparing for more realistic career choices. In unpublished data from 2002 out of the University of Oklahoma, it was reported that on a scale of 1 to 5 with five being the most probable and one being the least probable, African Americans had mean scores of 4.52 while Whites had mean scores of 3.28 when asked if they expected to have a career in professional sport.[27] Steven Riess cited a study, which found that 70 percent of Black youth ages 13–18 expected to play in the NBA.[28] A recent study by the Center for the Study of Sport in Society determined that 66 percent of African American males believe their first jobs would be as professional athletes.[29] Conversely, Jay Coakley, professor of Sociology at the University of Colorado, Colorado Springs, points out in his *Sports and Society* that forty-one million African

Americans are "underrepresented in or absent from most sports at most levels of competition," including "most of the dozens of sports played at the international amateur level, and all but five of the dozens of professional sports in the United States."[30] Earl Smith, former professor of Sociology and Rubin Professor and Director of American Ethnic Studies at Wake Forest University, notes that the odds of an African American student athlete becoming a professional basketball player "are 20,000 to one" and becoming a professional football player the "odds are 10,000 to one."[31]

Where African American women athletes fit into these numbers is difficult to determine since they are seldom the focus of serious scholarly analysis. Because professional sport opportunities are so limited for them it is safe to assume that a majority of African American women athletes do not look beyond the college level regarding sport participation. We know, at least based on information provided by Donna Lopiano, Executive Director of the Women's Sports foundation, that African American women represent less than 5 percent of high school athletes.[32] We also know, according to sport and legal studies scholar Sarah Fields and other academicians, that only some 15 percent of African American women in the inner cities participate in sport below the college age level and those that do typically find themselves in basketball and track and field rather than the frequently titled country club sports such as tennis, soccer, crew, and lacrosse. This was the participation pattern among African American women prior to *Brown v. Board of Education* and will probably continue to be so because of economic conditions and denial of access to certain sports.[33]

Notwithstanding this data, it is the poignant stories of the struggles and disappointments of African American high school male athletes told by popular writers and documentarians that have garnered much of the attention from the American public. In his book, *The Ticket Out*, Michael Sokolove, a *New York Times Magazine* writer, skillfully tells the story of Darryl Strawberry and the all-Black 1979 baseball team at Los Angeles's Crenshaw High School. Sokolove recounts the unfulfilled promises of the players at the school some Los Angeles natives refer to as Fort Crenshaw. With the exception of the temporary fame enjoyed by Strawberry and Charles Brown as major league all-stars, the Crenshaw players were never able to overcome their inadequate high school education and the "realities of being poor, urban and black in America."[34]

In his 1994 book, *The Last Shot: City Streets, Basketball Dreams*, Darcy Frey monitors the lives and career aspirations of the three best basketball players at Coney Islands' Lincoln High School: Corey Johnson, Tchaka

Shipp, and Russell Thomas. The major problem confronted by all three is the academic requirements for a Division I scholarship. Johnson is never able to reach the minimum on the SAT Test and he ends up playing two years at a junior college. His dream of one day playing in the NBA never materialized. Unlike his teammate, Shipp makes the minimum score on the SAT, and accepts a scholarship to play for P. J. Carlesimo at Seton Hall. After languishing on the bench and suffering the abuse of Carlesimo, Shipp transfers to the University of California, Irvine, but an automobile accident ends his playing career. Thomas never scores the minimum on the SAT Test. Like Johnson, he played at a junior college. Sadly, he ends up homeless, separated from his wife and child following the close of his basketball career, and at the age of 26, is hit by a train and killed instantly. Some believe it was suicide.[35]

In the celebrated 1994 documentary "Hoop Dreams" director Steve James, over a five-year period, chronicles the lives of William Gates and Arthur Agee, two basketball players from St. Joseph's High School in Chicago who aspire to play professionally. At first, Gates and Agee seem to flourish at the private institution and realize a measure of success athletically and academically. Gates, in particular gets off to a fast start, becoming a starter on the varsity team and an honor roll student. Gradually, however, the fortunes of both boys begin to fade. Coach Gene Pingatore decides that Agee is not making sufficient progress as a player and, as a result, forces a disheartened Arthur to return to public school where he struggles academically. Gates also begins to have academic problems after suffering a serious knee injury and receiving, like Agee, little support from teachers, coaches, and his parents. Neither player ever makes it into the NBA. As recently as 2006, Gates was serving as a pastor in the neighborhood he grew up in and Agee was trying to launch a hoop dreams sportswear line after spending many years playing semi-pro basketball.[36]

The stories of African American male athletes at Crenshaw, Lincoln, St. Joseph, and other high schools across the country have caught the attention of prominent African Americans who have spoken out about the seductive power of sport and that athletic success is transitory and must be counterbalanced by a genuine commitment to education. In contrast to many prominent African Americans of the late-nineteenth and first half of the twentieth century who often expressed the view that the individual success of African American athletes was enormously important from a symbolic standpoint, helped break down the prevailing opinions of the Black man's inferiority, and had an uplifting effect on the entire Black community, prominent African Americans since the 1970s in particular have consistently warned against an overemphasis on sport and stressed the importance of preparing for life after the end of a playing career. The direct message conveyed in their comments is that young African American athletes were putting themselves at a severe disadvantage if they considered their body to be their only resume and focused all their attention on sport rather than more realistic career choices. Implicit in their comments is that however psychologically satisfying or however materially advantageous to a few, success of individual African American athletes is not a satisfactory solution to the problem of discrimination because political and economic dominance continues to remain in White hands. Implicit in their comments, moreover, is that sport, while a worthy activity and legitimate endeavor, is not by itself going to change America and substantially improve the lives of the majority of African Americans.[37]

For instance, Arthur Ashe, the celebrated tennis player and civil rights activist, observed in a 1977 *New York Times* open letter to Black parents, titled "Send Your Children to the Libraries" that the African American community "expends too much time, energy, and effort raising, praising, and teasing Black children as to the dubious glories of professional sport." "We have been," wrote Ashe, "on the same roads—sports and entertainment—too long. We need to pull over, fill up at the library and speed away to Congress and the Supreme Court, the unions and the business world."[38] Anthony Leroy Fisher, a graduate of Grambling College and vice-principal of Gaskill Junior High School in Niagara, NY, wrote in a 1978 *The Phi Delta Kappan* essay, "The Best Way Out of the Ghetto" that too many young Blacks are looking for the 'ghetto to glory' storybook ending, and no one comes out to tell them that they are betting their lives with odds greater than 1,000 to one against them." "The young black," noted Fisher, "thinking of a bright future had better spend time studying science and math after school [and] not practicing his sky hook."[39] Earl Graves, publisher of *Black Enterprise* magazine, wrote in a 1979 essay "The Right Kind of Excellence" that for every Black who has made his mark as an athlete there are dozens of others who have done so as businessmen, lawyers, physicians, and engineers. "To a teenager," wrote Graves, "that is not apt to be an instantly persuasive argument yet gradually he must come to see and be helped to see that this is the reality that counts."[40] Finally, in a 1991 essay in *Sports Illustrated* titled "Delusions of Grandeur," Henry Louis Gates, Jr., W. E. B. Du Bois Professor of the Humanities at Harvard University and President Obama's beer-drinking buddy, echoed the same concerns as his predecessors, believing that Black athletic success has served a hegemonic function. "Let me confess," wrote Gates, "that I love sports," but "the blind pursuit of attainment in sports is having a devastating effect on our people. Imbued with a belief that our principal avenue to fame and profit is through sport and seduced by a win-at-all cost system that corrupts even elementary school students, far too many black kids treat basketball courts and football fields as if they were classrooms in an alternative school system."[41]

The cautionary tales regarding the overemphasis on sport among African American youth is especially significant since White youth generally have a higher participation rate in sport than their Black counterparts. As noted previously, African American women represent less than 5 percent of high school athletes. The few African American women participating in interscholastic sport are overrepresented in basketball and track and field and underrepresented in tennis, soccer, lacrosse, and other sports, which richer White students tend to select. A similar pattern is evident among male high school athletes. African American male high school athletes are 2.5 times more likely to play football and 5.7 times more likely to participate in basketball than their White counterparts. On the other hand, White male high school athletes participate in greater numbers in all other sports than their Black counterparts.[42]

These numbers, while perhaps a surprise to many who take seriously the selected media portrayals of athletes and assume African Americans dominate sport, are most alarming in that participation in football and basketball seem less likely to be associated with academic achievement while participation in all other sports appear to have more positive correlations with success in the classroom. Sociologists Tamela and David Eitle contend that African American males are not only more likely to play football and basketball, but also more likely to be negatively impacted by participating in these sports. "Rather than sports serving simply as a drain on energies that could be spent maximizing academic achievement," argue the Eitles, "males may end up pursuing some sports because they lack the resources to perform well academically which only serves to disadvantage them further in achieving academic excellence."[43]

Regardless of the connections between sport participation and educational achievement, which is obviously complicated and multidimensional, the consolidation of power in a White elite during the post 1954 period has successfully convinced lower-class African Americans specifically and others lacking power that permanent social change is possible and that participation in sport and other forms of entertainment will result not only in ephemeral benefits but redistribution benefits as well. It is why the cautionary tales of Henry Louis Gates, Jr., and others fall on deaf ears among many economically disadvantaged African American families who are not often making a choice between professional athletics or education but rather a choice between professional athletics or being a blue-collar worker or something worse. Earl Smith made clear in personal correspondence with me and (based on the work of many others as well as with his colleague Angela Hattery) that high school athletes from lower economic classes typically, if they are able to overcome their inadequate schooling and satisfy NCAA guidelines or do not make the rare leap directly from interscholastic to professional sport, choose a college based on the athletic rather than educational reputation of the institution in which they are being recruited. Once enrolled, they frequently find themselves clustered in degree programs for which they have little interest and do not adequately prepare them for satisfying professional careers.[44] And even if they do graduate it does not mean that education has occurred, as evidenced by the famous case of Creighton University basketball player Kevin Ross who graduated without knowing how to read, and perhaps a less famous but equally disturbing case of former Oklahoma State University and Washington Redskins football star Dexter Manley who testified about his inabilities to read before a Congressional Subcommittee on Education, Arts, and Humanities of the Committee on Labor and Human Resources.[45] Importantly, these examples do not specifically take into consideration those athletes whose paths first took them to Rise Academy in Philadelphia, Genesis One Christian Academy in Mendenhall, Mississippi, Eldon Academy in Michigan, and other bogus private high schools first uncovered by *The New York Times*' Pete Thamel.[46]

Making choices is what Harry Edwards, the noted sociologist and activist from the University of California, Berkeley, was referring to in a little-known yet important 2000 interview he conducted with *Colorlines Magazine*. Claiming that the Black athletic pool had been so emaciated through the judicial process, disqualification and deaths that we are "currently witnessing the end of the golden age of the black athlete" which he says had stretched over a fifty year period from Jackie Robinson's entry into Major League Baseball in 1947 until 1997, Edwards went against much of what he had expressed for years by noting that sports are crucial to the survival of African American youth and should be emphasized as such. "There is still, a disproportionately high emphasis on sport achievement in black society," notes Edwards, "relative to other high-prestige occupational career aspirations. Given what is happening to young black people, who have essentially disconnected from virtually every institutional structure in society, sports may be our last hook and handle."[47]

Edwards's claim that the Black athletic pool has been emaciated is not easily countered considering the data. In 2006, for example, Michael Ross of MSNBC reported that African Americans are seven times more likely than Whites to go to prison or jail and according to statistics released by the US Centers for Disease Control and Prevention in 2008 the homicide rate among Black males ages 10 to 24 is more than double that of Hispanic and White males, even though African Americans are a minority population in the United States.[48] Edwards claim, however, that there was a "golden age of the black athlete" is debatable as is the notion that a disproportionately high emphasis on sport is going to save African American youth.[49] However one defines it, I do not recall reading about or living through a period that could be termed a "golden age of the black athlete" and if sport is our "last hook and handle" to save young Blacks it must be a version that resembles more closely the Progressive Era's athletic code of preparation for life or as Douglas Hartmann, a sociologist from the University of Minnesota, noted in a 2008 report to the LA84 Foundation, be deliberately designed with "positive, proactive educational intervention" in mind.[50]

What seems less debatable is that the increased integration in post-1954 America has, in the words of *New York Times* sportswriter Bill Rhoden in his book *Forty Million Dollar Slaves*, "weakened the collective resolve of African Americans and spawned a mentality of using blackness as a way to get a piece of the pie without necessarily feeling any reciprocal responsibility to sustain black institutions."[51] Gone are the National Interscholastic Basketball Tournament, the WVAU Basketball Tournament, and a host of other sport and non-sport related Black institutions that allowed African Americans to maintain the collective spirit necessary to withstand the second-class citizenship they faced. Gone also is the apparent disengagement, to use W. E. B. Du Bois famous phrase "the talented tenth," from the poor and underrepresented members of the African American community, a fact that has played an important role in the spiral of poverty in urban America that has never been seriously confronted.

This group, along with concerned Whites, could take the lead in designing strategies and tactics to help overcome the racial disparities in public education that *Brown v. Board of Education* was meant to rectify. This group, along with concerned Whites, might also do well to heed the advice of Louis

Harlan, my former professor at the University of Maryland, and realize that often "the wisdom of one era is the foolishness of another" and embark on a more aggressive and more deliberate campaign of action that challenges the continuing assumptions of White dominance rather than the reliance on an egalitarian creed as outlined in *Brown v. Board of Education* and other civil rights legislation. If not, I fear we will never overcome the premise of the story told by Malcolm X that the White man's ice is colder or successfully challenge Booker T. Washington's 1895 declaration that "in all things that are purely social we can be as separate as the fingers" or ever fully realize Martin Luther King's "dream that one day this nation will rise up and live out the true meaning of its creed."[52]

Notes

1. For general studies on the *Brown v. Board of Education* decision, see: Charles J. Ogletree, Jr. *All Deliberate Speed: Reflections on the First Half Century of Brown v. Board of Education* (New York: W. W. Norton & Company, 2004); Richard Kluger, *Simple Justice: The History of Brown v. Board of Education and Black America's Struggle for Equality* (New York: Vintage, 1975); Jack Bass, *Unlikely Heroes: The Dramatic Story of the Southern Judges of the Fifth Circuit Who Translated the Supreme Court's Brown Decision Into a Revolution for Equality* (New York: Simon & Schuster, 1981); James T. Patterson, *Brown v. Board of Education: A Civil Rights Milestone and Its Troubled Legacy* (New York: Oxford University Press, 2001). For a nicely detailed study on sport and the *Brown v. Board of Education* decision see Samuel R. Hodge, Louis Harrison, Jr., Joe W. Burden, Jr., and Adrienne D. Dixson, "Brown in Black and White—Then and Now: A Question of Educating or Sporting African American Males in America." *American Behavioral Scientist*, 51 (March 2008), 928–952.

2. For information on these athletes, see: Martin B. Duberman, *Paul Robeson* (New York: Knopf, 1988); John M. Carroll, *Fritz Pollard: Pioneer in Racial Advancement* (Urbana: University of Illinois Press, 1992); William J. Baker, *Jesse Owens: An American Life* (New York: The Free Press, 1986); Woody Strode and Sam Young, *Goal Dust: The Warm and Candid Memoirs of a Pioneer Black Athlete and Actor* (New York: Madison Books, 1990); Arnold Rampersad, *Jackie Robinson: A Biography* (New York: Knopf, 1997); Jules Tygiel, *Baseball's Great Experiment: Jackie Robinson and His Legacy* (New York: Oxford University Press, 1983); George A. Hodak, Jimmy LuValle Interview, June 17, 1988, Palo Alto, CA LA 84 Foundation, pp. 1–32; "Archie Williams, Olympic Gold Medal Winner, dies-obituary-brief article" http://findarticles.com/p/articles/mi_m1355/is_n11_v84/ai_14100782/, accessed June 14, 2010; Lewis H. Carlson and John J. Fogarty, *Tales of Gold: An Oral History of the Summer Olympic Games Told by America's Gold Medal Winners* (New York: Contemporary Books, 1987), p. 144–158.

3. John M. Carroll, *Fritz Pollard: Pioneer in Racial Advancement*, pp. 18, 25, 29, 47–48, 90, 116–117; William J. Baker, *Jesse Owens: An American Life*, pp, 11–12, 25–28, 37, 39–42, 53, 63, 66, 68, 121–122, 161, 237.

4. Martin B. Duberman, Paul Robeson, pp. 12–17, 19–30; George A. Hodak, Jimmy LuValle Interview, 1–32.

5. Cited in William J. Baker, *Jesse Owens: An American Life*, p. 122.

6. John M. Carroll, *Fritz Pollard: Pioneer in Racial Advancement*, p. 38.

7. John Nauright, "Race and Football in the Heartland during the 1930's," Unpublished Manuscript (In possession of the Author).

8. See Susan Cahn, *Coming on Strong: Gender and Sexuality in Twentieth Century Women's Sport* (New York: Free Press, 1994), pp. 119–139; Gwendolyn Captain "Enter Ladies and Gentlemen of Color: Gender, Sport, and the Ideal of African American Manhood and Womanhood During the Late Nineteenth and Early Twentieth Centuries." *Journal of Sport History*, 18 (Spring,1991), 81–102; Jennifer H. Lansbury, "The Tuskegee Flash and The Slender Harlem Stroker: Black Women Athletes on the Margin." *Journal of Sport History*, 28 (Summer, 2001), 233–252.

9. Pamela Grundy, *Learning to Win: Sports, Education, and Social Change in Twentieth Century North Carolina* (Chapel Hill: The University of North Carolina Press, 2001), p. 46.

10. Traki L. Taylor, "Womanhood Glorified: Nannie Helen Burroughs and the National Training School for Women and Girls, Inc., 1909–1961" *The Journal of African American History*, 87 (Autumn, 2002), 390–402.

11. Susan Cahn, *Coming on Strong: Gender and Sexuality in Twentieth-Century Women's Sport*, pp. 110–139.

12. Carter Woodson, Anna Julia Cooper, Kelly Miller, and Mary Church Terrell are examples of the types of quality faculty who taught at the school. Graduates of the school included Sterling Brown, Nannie Helen Burroughs, Charles Drew, Charles Hamilton Houston, and Robert Terrell, among others. For detailed information on M Street School see: Mary Church Terrell, "History of the High School for Negroes in Washington," *Journal of Negro History*, 2 (July, 1917), 252–266; Lillian G. Dabney, "The History of Schools for Negroes in the District of Columbia, 1807–1947" (PhD Dissertation, The Catholic University of America, 1949); Henry S. Robinson, "The M Street High School, 1891–1916" *Records of the Columbia Historical Society of Washington, D.C.*, 51 (1984), 199–143; Kenneth Robert Janken, *Rayford W. Logan and The Dilemma of the African-American Intellectual* (Amherst, MA: The University of Massachusetts Press, 1993), especially pp. 18–27.

13. Edwin B. Henderson and William A. Joiner, eds. *Official Handbook: Inter-Scholastic Athletic Association of Middle Atlantic States* (New York: American sports Publishing, 1910–1913), "Biography-Edwin B. Henderson", September 1971, Edwin Bancroft Henderson Papers, Moorland-Spingarn Research Center, Howard University.

14. Nelson George, *Elevating the Game: The History & Aesthetics of Black Men in Basketball* (New York: Simon & Schuster, 1992), p. 27.

15. Nelson George, *Elevating the Game: The History & Aesthetics of Black Men in Basketball*, pp. 27-33.

16. Nelson George, *Elevating the Game: The History & Aesthetics of Black Men in Basketball*, pp. 27-33.

17. C. Robert Barnett, "The Finals: West Virginia's Black Basketball Tournament, 1925-1957" Goldenseal, 9 (Summer, 1983), 30.

18. Nelson George, *Elevating the Game: The History & Aesthetics of Black Men in Basketball*, 26, 28-29, 32. See also Gerald R. Gems, "Blocked Shot: The Development of Basketball in the African-American Community of Chicago," *Journal of Sport History*, 22 (Summer, 1995); 13-148; Troy D. Paino, "Hoosiers in a Different Light: Forces of Change Versus the Power of Nostalgia" *Journal of Sport History*, 28 (Spring, 2001), 63-80.

19. Nelson George, *Elevating the Game: The History & Aesthetics of Black Men in Basketball*, pp. 82-85. For another view of African American involvement in basketball, see: Reuben A. Buford May, *Living Through the Hoop: High School Basketball, Race, and the American Dream* (New York: New York University Press, 2008).

20. Wendell A. Parriss, "Integration of Athletics in the District of Columbia Public High Schools," *The Negro History Bulletin*, 19 (October 1955), 14-15.

21. Included among these works are: Sterling Brown, "Athletics and the Arts; Sports: They Set the Pace in 1947," *Opportunity*, 26 (Spring, 1948), 83; Edwin B. Henderson, *The Negro in Sports* (Washington, DC: Associated Publishers, 1949); Rufus Clement, "Racial Integration in the Field of Sports," *Journal of Negro Education*, 23 (1954), 222-230; Charles A. Bucher, "Sports Are Color-Blind," *Journal of Health, Physical Education, and Recreation*, 28 (December, 1957), 21-22.

22. Charles J. Ogletree, Jr. *All Deliberate Speed: Reflections on the First Half Century of Brown V. Board of Education*; Richard Kluger, *Simple Justice: The History of Brown v. Board of Education and Black America's Struggle for Equality*; Jack Bass, *Unlikely Heroes: The Dramatic Story of the Southern Judges of the Fifth Circuit Who Translated the Supreme Court's Brown Decision Into a Revolution for Equality*; James T. Patterson, *Brown v. Board of Education: A Civil Rights Milestone and Its Troubled Legacy*.

23. Dave Johnson, "From Court to Courts: Integration in the Schools Meant Changes in Athletics and After-School Activities as Well," http://www.dailypress.com/news/dp-brown23,0,2789860.story, accessed December 2, 2004.

24. Carole D. Bos, "Remember the Titans: A Story of School Integration," http://www.lawbuzz.com/movies/remember_the_titans/the_titans_ch1.html, accessed January 18, 2005.

25. Charles J. Ogletree, Jr. *All Deliberate Speed: Reflections on the First Half Century of Brown V. Board of Education*; Richard Kluger, *Simple Justice: The History of Brown v. Board of Education and Black America's Struggle for Equality*; Jack Bass, *Unlikely Heroes: The Dramatic Story of the Southern Judges of the Fifth Circuit Who Translated the Supreme Court's Brown Decision Into a Revolution for Equality*; James T. Patterson, *Brown v. Board of Education: A Civil Rights Milestone and Its Troubled Legacy*.

26. The most recent data from the NCAA indicates that the graduation rates for African American male athletes now stands at 49 percent which is still lower than White athletes but eleven percentage points higher than the African American males in the general student body. The same data set indicates that African American female athletes now graduate at a rate of 63 percent, which is fourteen points higher than African American females in the general student body. See http://www.ncaa.org/wps/portal/ncaahome?ncaa_global.context=/ncaa/ncaa/media+and+events/press+room/curre, accessed June 14, 2010.

27. Cited in Earl Smith and Angela Hattery, "African American Community: The Dynamics of Race, Class, Gender, and Community." In *Diversity and Social Justice in College Sports: Sport Management and the Student Athlete*, edited by Dana S. Brooks and Ronald C. Althouse, pp. 379–405, (Morgantown, WV: Fitness Information Technology, 2007).

28. Steven A. Riess," Basketball Career Still An Inner-City Dream but Only Few Achieve Star Status, Financial Rewards," http://www.america.gov/st/sports-english/200/apri/20080401/20426zjsredna0.8432886.html, accessed April 4, 2010.

29. C. Keith Harrison, "There Is More to Life Than Sports: Getting Brothers to Take the Road Less Traveled," http://diverseeducation.com/article/8143/1.php, accessed January 16, 2010.

30. Jay Coakley, *Sports in Society: Issues and Controversies*, (Dubuque, IA: McGraw Hill, 2009), p. 293.

31. Earl Smith, "The African American Student-Athlete." In *Race and Sport: The Struggle for Equality On and Off the Field*. Edited by Charles K. Ross, pp. 121–145 (Jackson: University Press of Mississippi, 2004).

32. Donna Lopiano, "Gender Equity and the Black Female in Sport." www.womensportsfoundation.org/cqi-bin/iowa/issues/disc/article.html?ecord=869, accessed April 30, 2010.

33. Sarah K. Fields, "Title IX and African American Female Athletes," In *Sports and the Racial Divide: African American and Latino Experience in an Era of Change*, edited by Michael E. Lomax, pp. 126–145, Jackson: University Press of Mississippi, 2008; Angela Hattery, Earl Smith, and Ellen Staurowsky, "They Play Like Boys: Gender, Equity, in NCAA Sports," *The Journal for the Study of Sports and Athletics in Education*, 1 (3), (2007) 249–272.

34. Michael Sokolove, *The Ticket Out: Darryl Strawberry and the Boys of Crenshaw*, (New York: Simon & Schuster, 2004).

35. Darcy Frey, *The Last Shot: City Streets, Basketball Dreams*, (New York: Houghton Mifflin Company, 1994).

36. Bell Hooks, "Dreams of Conquest" *Sight and Sound*, 5 (April, 1995), 22–23.

37. See in particular David K. Wiggins, "The Notion of Double-Consciousness and the Involvement of Black Athletes in American Sport," In *Ethnicity and Sport in North American History and Culture*, edited by George Eisen and David K. Wiggins, pp. 133–153. (Westport, CT: Greenwood Press, 1994). Reprinted in David K. Wiggins,

Glory Bound: Black Athletes in a White America (Syracuse, NY: Syracuse University Press, 1997), pp. 200–220.

38. Arthur Ashe, "Send Your Children to the Libraries" *New York Times*, February 6, 1977.

39. Anthony Leroy Fisher, "The Best Way Out of the Ghetto," *Phi Delta Kappan*, 60 (November 1978), 240.

40. Earl Graves, "The Right Kind of Excellence" *Black Enterprise*, (November 1979), 9.

41. Henry Louis Gates, Jr. "Delusions of Grandeur" *Sports Illustrated*, (August 19, 1991), 78.

42. See Pat Antonio Goldsmith, "Schools' Role in Shaping Race Relations: Evidence on Friendliness and Conflict," *Social Problems*, 51 (2004), 587–612; Idem., "Race Relations and Racial Patterns in School Sports Participation," *Sociology of Sport Journal*, 20 (2003): 147–171; Douglas Hartmann, "High School Sports Participation and Educational Attainment: Recognizing, Assessing and Utilizing the Relationship Report to the LA 84 Foundation." Los Angeles: LA 84 Foundation, 2008, 1–34; Tamela McNulty Eitle and David J. Eitle, "Race, Cultural Capital, and the Educational Effects of Participation in Sports," *Sociology of Education*, 75 (April 2002), 123–146.

43. Tamela McNulty Eitle and David J. Eitle, "Race, Cultural Capital, and the Educational Effects of Participation in Sports," 142.

44. Earl Smith to David K. Wiggins, email correspondence, April 29, 2010. Earl Smith and Angela Hattery, "African American Community: The Dynamics of Race, Class, Gender, and Community," p. 293. See also: Earl Smith, *Race, Sport and the American Dream*, 2nd edition (Durham, NC: Carolina Academic Press, 2009); Jade Norwood, "Adult Complicity in the Dis-Education of the Black Male High School Athlete & Societal Failures to Remedy His Plight" *Marshall Law Review*, 21 (2008–2009), 21–91.

45. "Outside the Lines: Unable to Read" espn.com. http://sports.espn.go.com/page2/tvlistings/show103transcript.html, accessed June 14, 2010; Dexter Manley and Tom Friend, *Educating Dexter* (Nashville, TN: Thomas Nelson, Inc., 1992).

46. "A College Sports Scam," *New York Times*, December 30, 2005; Pete Thamel, "The Quick Fix: Easy Pass, Easy Score; Schools Where the Only Real Test Is Basketball," *New York Times*, February 25, 2006; Idem., "Colleges; N.C.A.A. Schools' List Stirs More Controversy," *New York Times*, July 6, 2006; Idem., "N.C.A.A. Cracks Down on Prep Schools and Angers Some," *New York Times*, May 1, 2007.

47. Dave Leonard, "The Decline of the Black Athlete: An Interview with Harry Edwards," *Colorlines*, 30 (April 2000), 20–24. Reprinted in David K. Wiggins and Patrick B. Miller, *The Unlevel Playing Field: A Documentary History of the African American Experience in Sport*, (Urbana: University of Illinois Press, 2003), pp. 435–441.

48. Michael E. Ross, "Grim Forecast for Young Black Men: New Studies Find Them Falling Further Out of Labor Force, Mainstream Society," MSMBC.com, April 17, 2006, http://www.msnbc.msn.com/id/12154123/print/displaymode/1098/, accessed May 18, 2010; Kristin Gray, "African American Youth Face Growing Threat from

Peers," *Washington Afro*, New America Media, October 7, 2009, https://www.stlamerican.com/news/local-news/black-youth-fade-growing-threat-of-violence-from-peaks/, accessed May 9, 2010.

49. For a thoughtful critique of Edwards's notion of a "Golden Age of the Black Athlete" see Earl Smith, "There Was No Golden Age of Sport for African American Athletes," *Society*, 37, (March-April 2000), 45.

50. Douglas Hartmann, "High School Sports Participation and Educational Attainment: Recognizing, Assessing, and Utilizing the Relationship," 24.

51. William C. Rhoden, *Forty Million Dollar Slaves: The Rise, Fall, and Redemption of the Black Athlete* (New York: Crown Publishers, 2006), p. 256. For a similar type of view as that of Rhoden see: Shaun Powell, *Souled Out? How Blacks are Winning and Losing in Sports* (Champaign, IL: Human Kinetics, 2008).

52. See Kenneth L. Shropshire, *In Black and White: Race and Sports in America* (New York: New York University Press, 1996), pp. 128–141; Louis R. Harlan, *Booker T. Washington: The Making of a Black Leader, 1856–1901* (New York: Oxford University Press, 1972), p. 218; David Levering Lewis, "Martin Luther King, Jr. and the Problem of Nonviolent Populism," in *Black Leaders of the Twentieth Century*, edited by John Hope Franklin and August Meier, pp. 277–313, (Urbana: University of Illinois Press, 1982).

5

MILT CAMPBELL

Olympic Decathlon Champion
"Famous for Not Being Famous"

"One of the most famous high school athletes in the country will graduate from Plainfield (New Jersey) High very soon," wrote Margery Miller of the *Christian Science Monitor* in 1953, "and in the opinion of many sports experts it will just be a question of time before immortality claims him."[1] Miller's comments were certainly understandable and not mere hyperbole considering that just a year earlier at the Olympic games in Helsinki, Milt Campbell, a young African American with prodigious physical skills, had captured the silver medal in the decathlon and followed that up with a senior year at Plainfield High School in which *Sport* magazine named him its high school athlete of the year for his great performances in football, track and field, and swimming. He went on to an outstanding two-year athletic career at Indiana University and then captured the gold medal in the decathlon at the 1956 Olympic games in Melbourne, Australia, defeating the highly favored UCLA star Rafer Johnson with a new Olympic record of 7937 points.[2]

Unfortunately, Miller's assertion that immortality would claim Campbell never truly happened. In many ways, he would remain forgotten, the least mentioned and celebrated of all the Americans who captured the Olympic decathlon. While Johnson, Bob Mathias, Bill Toomey, Bruce Jenner, and other American Olympic decathlon champions would be showered with attention and lasting acclaim and realize fame and fortune in their post-athletic careers, Campbell struggled to be acknowledged for his great Olympic performances, essentially lost from historical memory for much of his life. He would always remain a local hero in Plainfield, but it took him years to be elected into Halls of Fame and his name simply does not resonate with the American sporting public to the extent that one would expect considering his great athletic achievements.[3]

Remarkably, while Mathias, winner of both the Olympic decathlon in 1948 and 1952, and Johnson, second to Campbell in the event in 1956 and gold medalist in 1960, were both elected in 1983 to the inaugural class of the United States Olympic Hall of Fame (USOHOF), Campbell was not even on the ballot. He was again left off the ballot in 1984 when Toomey, winner of the decathlon in 1968, was selected and yet once again in 1986 when Jenner, winner of the event in 1976, was inducted into the USOHOF. Campbell was not elected to the USOHOF until 1992, some thirty-six years after capturing gold in Melbourne. He also received other belated honors, many of them coming about through the efforts of individuals who believed Campbell had been unfairly shunned and campaigned to see that his great athletic performances were finally acknowledged.[4]

Campbell tried his best to appear he was not troubled by the decades-long lack of recognition of his Olympic decathlon titles and other sports accomplishments. His pride did not allow him to do otherwise. Inevitably, however, Campbell' irritation seemingly grew into a grudging acceptance on his part that he would never realize the national stardom he felt he deserved relative to his talented peers. The efforts of people to account for the puzzling lack of respect shown to Campbell would continue to exist over the years to the point where writer Dave D'Alessandro of the *New Jersey Star-Ledger* noted that the extraordinarily accomplished Black athlete had become "famous for not being famous."[5] What explains the relative lack of national press coverage and long-delayed honors and awards given to Campbell? What explains his anonymity and the fact his name does not resonate with even the most serious students of sport history?

Clues as to why Campbell is probably the least known of the great American decathlon champions can be gleaned from a closer look at his life and career. Campbell was the second of three children born on December 9, 1933, in Plainfield, New Jersey to Thomas Campbell, sometimes mentioned as a New York City cabdriver and at other times construction worker, and mother Edith, who has been referred to as both a homemaker and domestic worker. When Thomas and Edith's marriage broke up, Campbell and his older brother Tom moved in with their grandmother who provided a loving and supportive home for the two boys. Campbell idolized his older brother who became a star football and track and field athlete at Plainfield High School. Not unexpectedly, Campbell, who would show extraordinary athletic talent at a very early age and eventually grew to be six-foot three inches tall and approximately 215 pounds, distinguished himself in the same two sports as well as swimming when he matriculated at the school some two years later.[6]

Campbell enjoyed a sterling high school athletic career. He starred as a running back on the school's football team, amassing 140 points and was selected as an All-State player his senior season. He was described by Arthur Daley of the *New York Times* as a terror as a running back, possessing a rare combination of speed and power who "could be stopped only by gang tackling."[7] In track and field, he was an outstanding sprinter, shot putter, high jumper, and hurdler. He was the New Jersey champion in the low hurdles for four straight years and also broke state records in the high hurdles and high jump. He was, moreover, an outstanding swimmer, competing in the sport for three years at Plainfield High School. Defying the deep-seated racial stereotype that African Americans are not proficient at swimming or do not even possess the ability to float, Campbell was a member of Plainfield's state championship 200-meter freestyle relay team during his freshman and sophomore years. And if that was not indication enough of his athletic versatility, Campbell supposedly substituted for one of his sick classmates in a wrestling match and pinned in just over a minute the wrestler who would go on to win the state championship.[8]

A turning point in Campbell's career took place in February 1952 when he placed third in the high hurdles at the National Amateur Athletic Union championships in New York's Madison Square Garden. Because he placed in the top three in that event, Campbell qualified to participate for the National Amateur Athletic Union team in a meet against Great Britain that spring in London. He performed so well in London that his high school track coach Harold Bruguiere secured $1,500 from Plainfield High School's booster club to send him to both the Amateur Athletic Union Senior Track and Field championships in Los Angeles and Olympic decathlon tryouts in Tulare, California. Importantly, Bruguiere chose to enter Campbell in the Olympic tryouts even though the Plainfield High School athlete had never even competed in six of the events that make up the decathlon. After having trained him in every decathlon event the previous year, Bruguiere was convinced that Campbell had the requisite skills to be a serious contender. Bruguiere's assessment proved correct. Campbell came in second to Bob Mathias, gold medalist in the decathlon in the 1948 London Olympics, to qualify for the upcoming games in Helsinki. His chances were helped no doubt by the fact that Bob Richards, the "Vaulting Vicar," dropped out of the decathlon trials to concentrate on the pole vault.[9]

No one gave Campbell much of a chance to medal in the decathlon at Helsinki. He had lost by over 700 points to Mathias in the Olympic trials and had only been training for the event for about a year. He surpassed expectations, however, by capturing the silver medal in the event in Helsinki, losing by nearly 1,000 points to Mathias and edging out bronze medalist Floyd Simmons by almost 200 points. He did, of course, receive some press coverage for his second-place finish, commentators noting how impressive the performance was considering the fact he was just an eighteen-year-old high school student and a novice in the event. Mathias, on the other hand, received a voluminous amount of press coverage for his winning performance and because he became the first man to repeat in the event in Olympic history. Paul Zimmerman, sports editor of the *Los Angeles Times*, was effusive in his praise. "The incomparable Bob Mathias, already the greatest athlete the world has ever known," wrote Zimmerman immediately after the competition, "outdid himself again tonight under the most trying conditions as he won the XV Olympiad decathlon championship with 7887 points. This grand total shattered his own global mark of 7825, posted at Tulare less than a month ago, and placed on the Olympic record books a mark that this universe's athletes will be shooting at for years to come."[10]

Mathias and Campbell took decidedly different paths following the 1952 Olympic games. Upon his return from Helsinki, Mathias played fullback for Stanford in the 1952 Rose Bowl and then graduated from the prestigious university in 1953. The following year he starred with his first wife (Melba Mathias) in the movie, *The Bob Mathias Story* and began serving as a goodwill ambassador for the United States, visiting over 40 countries. From 1956 to 1960, he was employed by John Wayne's Batjac Productions and starred in the television show, *The Troublemakers* and the movies *China Doll* (1958), *The Minotaur, The Wild Beast of Crete* (1960) and *It Happened in Athens* (1962). In 1966 Mathias was elected to the United States House of Representatives from California's 18th District, where he served four two-year terms until losing his seat, along with many of his Republican colleagues, following the Watergate scandal. In 1977 he was appointed Director of the United States Olympic Training Center in Colorado Springs, Colorado and held that position until being appointed the Executive Director of the National Fitness Foundation in 1983. In 1998 Mathias was given a tribute dinner in Tulare, California on the fiftieth anniversary of his first Olympic gold medal. Among the 300 guests were Olympic gold medalists Bill Toomey, Sammy Lee, Dave Johnson, and Pat McCormick (Campbell was apparently not in attendance). Mathias passed away in Fresno, California from cancer in 2006 at the age of seventy-five and is interred in his hometown of Tulare.[11]

While Mathias capitalized on his fame as a two-time Olympic decathlon gold medalist and began carving out a long and successful career in public life, Campbell returned to Plainfield to finish high school, but only after a hero's welcome featuring a parade down the city's main street. He had a sterling senior year athletically and after graduation from Plainfield High School in 1953 matriculated to Indiana University on a football scholarship. For two years, he was a flanker and defensive back on the football team and member of the track and field team. His track and field career at Indiana University included many memorable performances, including 120-yard-high hurdles titles in the National Collegiate Athletic Association and Amateur Athletic Union championships.[12]

Campbell dropped out of Indiana University after two years, apparently because of grade issues, and entered the United States Navy, where he was stationed for two years in San Diego. As it turned out, it was a fortuitous turn of events for Campbell, at least in terms of his athletic career. He half-jokingly told legendary *Los Angeles Times* sportswriter Jim Murray that he served as a "watch officer on the U.S.S. Neversail. We guarded San Diego." The fact he did not have to fight "enemy amphibious landings at Mission Bay" and was freed from his academic studies as well as the need to earn a living, allowed the "able-bodied seaman [to] become a true decathlete." He spent seven and a half to eight hours a day, every day, training in the event for the upcoming Olympic games in Melbourne, Australia.[13] The irony here is that while some Americans pointed out how unfair it was that the Soviet sport system allowed athletes to train full time without being encumbered by other responsibilities, Campbell was essentially afforded the same opportunity by the United States Navy. Unfortunately, the United States fielded its Olympic teams with competitors irrespective of race in order to realize success in the most important international sporting event in the world, yet for years showed no interest in eliminating racial discrimination at home and guaranteeing African American athletes and ordinary African American citizens freedom of opportunity and equality in the intervening years between Olympic festivals.[14]

Despite his strenuous training regimen and the fact he had been runner-up to the great Bob Mathias in Helsinki, Campbell would once again be the underdog in the decathlon in Melbourne. The man projected to win the coveted event was Rafer Johnson, the outstanding African American athlete who had grown up in Kingsburg, California, just a stone's throw from Tulare, where Mathias had been born and raised. Johnson, a UCLA star who had played basketball for the legendary John Wooden in addition to competing in track and field at the well-known institution, broke the world record in the decathlon in 1954 during his freshman year and defeated Campbell by nearly 200 points in the event at the Olympic trials on July 13–14 in Crawfordsville, Indiana. Campbell, however, would turn the tables on Johnson in Melbourne, defeating him with an Olympic record of 7,937 points. His single best event was the 110-meter hurdles, amassing 1,124 points for his first-place finish of 14.0. If he had approached his previous best marks in the pole vault, Campbell could have easily broken the world record for the event.[15]

One of the most telling aspects of Campbell's decathlon victory in Melbourne is how little credit he got for it. While the press certainly acknowledged him for his great performance, almost all those who covered the event speculated whether Campbell would have been victorious if Johnson had not entered the competition with a bad knee and subsequent injury to his upper abdomen. The reality was that as the world record holder and outstanding student at a major university in star-studded and media heavy Los Angeles, Johnson had already become more celebrated, despite the fact that Campbell had garnered the silver medal in Helsinki and gold medal in Melbourne. Johnson was runner-up to diver Pat McCormick for the James E. Sullivan Award in 1956 as the outstanding amateur athlete in the United States, even though he had lost the decathlon title in Melbourne to Campbell. Campbell was not even on the list of finalists for the prestigious award, which is extraordinary in hindsight.[16]

The difference in the amount of attention garnered by Johnson relative to Campbell would become most evident in their post-Melbourne careers. Johnson returned to UCLA where he continued his athletic career and enhanced his fame, serving as the school's student body president his senior year. He continued to experience some injury problems, so much so that he was forced to sit out the 1957 track and field season. He was unable to compete in 1959 because of a car accident. But when healthy he steadily pushed the boundaries of the decathlon, breaking the world record for the event in 1958 at the first US-USSR dual track meet in Moscow that helped garner him that year's *Sports Illustrated* Sportsman of the Year Award. Johnson was pushed to his physical limits by his good friend and rival C. K. Yang, the talented Taiwanese athlete who also trained under famed UCLA coach Ducky Drake. The pinnacle of their intense competition occurred at the 1960 Olympic games in Rome. The two men battled each other during the two days of the decathlon to determine who would be considered world's greatest athlete. Televised around the world, the winner was not determined until the very last event when Johnson ran a personal best of 4:49.7 in the 1,500-meter run to give him an Olympic record and a 58-point victory over Yang.[17]

Johnson's Olympic decathlon victory in Rome garnered him the James E. Sullivan Award in 1960. He parlayed his success as an athlete and accompanying adulation and enormous media attention into a post-athletic career that included sportscasting, acting, and public service. He had roles in such movies as *The Sins of Rachel Cade* (1961), *Wild in the Country* (1961), *None but the Brave* (1965), *Roots: The Next Generation* (1979), and *License to Kill* (1989). In 1968 he worked on Senator Robert F. Kennedy's presidential campaign and, with the assistance of former football star Rosey Grier, apprehended Sirhan Sirhan after Sirhan had assassinated Kennedy. The following year, Johnson helped establish the California Special Olympics with a competition for 900 people with special needs in Los Angeles's Memorial Coliseum. In 1984, Johnson was chosen to light the Olympic flame at the opening of the summer Olympic games in Los Angeles. In addition to his Sports Illustrated Sportsman of the Year Award and James E. Sullivan Award, Johnson has been recognized many times over for his many accomplishments, including being named by the NCAA as one of the 100 Most Influential Student Athletes of the past 100 years, chosen by ESPN as one of the 100 Greatest North American Athletes of the twentieth century, and receiving the Athletes in Excellence Award from The Foundation for Global Sports Development.[18]

Milt Campbell's life since capturing the gold medal in Melbourne was decidedly different than Johnson's. The year after his gold-medal winning performance in Melbourne, Campbell competed in the 120-yard-high hurdles in several track meets, including the *Chicago Daily News* Relays, Cleveland Knights of Columbus Meet, and New York Athletic Club annual track meet. His skills in the 120-yard-high hurdles were such that he tied the world record (13.4) in the event. In 1957 Campbell was drafted in the fifth round by the Cleveland Browns for whom he played one season for the legendary coach Paul Brown. He was used sparingly, rushing just seven times for twenty-three yards. As would always seem to befall Campbell, irrespective of his performance, most of the attention was lavished on someone else, in this case his teammate Jim Brown who would become the NFL's all-time rushing leader and a Hall of Famer.[19]

Campbell was released by the Brown's at the beginning of his second season. He claimed it resulted from his marriage to Barbara Mount, a White woman, rather than due to his football skills. As Campbell related on several occasions, Paul Brown called him into his office on the eve of his second season and asked him why he had gotten married (code: to a White woman) and the following day was handed a letter by a Cleveland Brown's executive stating that his "services were no longer needed." Startled that Brown did not have the courage to deliver the bad news to him personally, Campbell was convinced that he was "blackballed out of the league." This was confirmed, he said, after the New York Giants refused to return Campbell's phone calls, despite the fact they had previously shown great interest in his services. Campbell's contention that he had been blackballed by the NFL, however, does not hold up considering his later assertion that he was offered at some point a contract by the Chicago Bears' George Halas but declined it because, in his own words, "I just agreed to sign with Canada (Canadian Football League), Mr. Halas, it's too late. I was honorable. I was also dumb."[20]

Following his release by the Browns, being rebuffed by the Giants, and declining a contract with the Bears, Campbell pursued the path taken by many African American players unable to make the rosters of NFL teams. He found his way north to the Canadian Football League (CFL). He played parts of six seasons with the Hamilton Tiger-Cats, Montreal Alouettes, and Toronto Argonauts, among other teams. His best season was with the Tiger-Cats in 1958 when he rushed for 468 yards. Perhaps the most notable part of his undistinguished career in a league where players from the United States receive scant press coverage in their home country, resulted from his 1964 trade from the Argonauts to the Edmonton Eskimos. The trade, which came about because of a rule change that allowed only three naturalized players on each team in the league, resulted in Campbell being one of three players named on a lawsuit brought against the CFL in 1965. The upshot of the lawsuit was the formation of the CFL Players Association.[21]

After some ten years of relative anonymity in Canada, Campbell returned home where he experienced more of the same. In 1967 he became involved in the local civil rights struggle in Newark, New Jersey following the riots that devastated the city. The following year he co-founded a community center and alternative school in Newark for underprivileged children that emphasized Black history and culture. After a failed business venture that left him with little money, Campbell embarked on a career as a motivational speaker. He spoke to youth groups, business executives, service organizations, and others about the importance of hard work and how to overcome failure to achieve success and live a life of meaning. It was a role that seemed ideally suited for Campbell, a man who enjoyed offering advice, philosophizing about life more generally, and serving as a mentor to young and old alike.[22]

For years following his gold-medal winning performance in Melbourne, Campbell, who was twice divorced, had four children, and lived the last years of his life with partner Linda Rusch, received scant attention and recognition relative to the other great Olympic decathlon champions from the United States. Importantly, regardless of how much Campbell was troubled by this lack of attention and recognition, he was also a staunchly private person who seemingly relished solitude and being anonymous. He once told writer Filip Bondy during his post-retirement years that he was living his life "incognito and loving it."[23] Unlike some of his more famous fellow Olympic decathlon champions, he did not write an autobiography. Doing so would certainly have allowed him to spread his personal story more widely, make a case for why he deserved more recognition, and permitted him to set the record straight regarding any inaccuracies or misconceptions that had been spread about his life and career. For reasons we will never know, he decided not to do so.

In the early 1980s individuals and various groups increasingly began to honor Campbell for his extraordinary athletic accomplishments. For example, in 1982 Campbell was elected to the University of Indiana Hall of Fame, almost thirty years after he had competed in football and track and field for the Hoosiers. Two years later, Nancy Plum, the owner of a frame shop in Plainfield worked closely with William W. Robertson, a former United States Attorney General for New Jersey, to see that a thirty-four-acre recreational park in Plainfield was named in Campbell's honor. In 1992, thirty-six years after winning gold in Melbourne, Campbell was finally elected to the United States Olympic Hall of Fame; at the time he was the last of the living United States decathlon champions to be voted in. In 1997 he was elected to the New Jersey State Interscholastic Athletic Association

Hall of Fame and two years later to the National Track and Field Hall of Fame. In 2000 the New Jersey Sportswriters Association named him the New Jersey Athlete of the Century. Finally, in 2012, just months prior to his death resulting from complications from prostate cancer and diabetes, Campbell was named to the New Jersey Hall of Fame and received a Gold Medallion from the International Swimming Hall of Fame.[24]

Campell's obituaries invariably mentioned his accomplishments, but also the belated honors and recognition that came his way. To the very end of his life, people were both puzzled and at a loss to adequately explain why Campbell never claimed the immortality Margery Miller projected in the *Christian Science Monitor* many years ago and became, in the words of Dave D'Allesandro, "Famous for not being famous." Possible explanations abound, however. As is the situation with all historical figures, in and outside of sport, the level of attention that Campbell received and how his name resonated with others had to do with timing, context, social milieu, personal choices, and pure happenstance and luck, or better still in some cases, misfortune. Some have contended that Campbell did not realize the acclaim he deserved because his medal-winning performances in the decathlon took place in foreign climes before the Olympic games were televised and at a time when other events monopolized the news and the world's attention. Larry Eldridge, writing in the *Christian Science Monitor* in 1996, shortly after Campbell had been bypassed once again by the USOHOF, noted that when Campbell won his gold medal in the Melbourne games "everything was wrong in terms of recognition." "To begin with," wrote Eldridge, "the Olympics had not yet become the TV spectacular they are today. And even by '50s standards, those particular games didn't attract much attention in the United States—held half a world away in an unusual month (November) when American interest was focused on football." In addition, "the most memorable moments involved confrontations of athletes from Hungary and the Soviet Union in the wake of the former country's abortive uprising a short time earlier."[25]

There is much truth to what Eldridge wrote regarding the Melbourne Olympic games, especially the lack of television coverage and the enormous amount of attention given over to the symbolically important and famous "Blood in the Water" polo match between Hungary and the Soviet Union. But his analysis does not seem to account fully for how Campbell was remembered or the belated honors and awards he received. Campbell himself suggested on multiple occasions that the lack of recognition he received resulted from the "fact that America was not ready for a black man to be the best athlete in the world."²⁶ This assertion certainly fits into a long historical heritage in which America holds on desperately to culturally significant titles and records and will search high and low for a "white hope" to restore order to the racial hierarchy when a Black athlete reaches the apex of his or her chosen sport. Ironically, though, those African American athletes who became the first to shatter a racial barrier in predominantly White organized sport, particularly at the highest levels of competition, have typically garnered a great deal of attention and their names have continued to resonate with the American sporting public. Since Campbell was the first Black decathlon gold medalist, one would expect this to happen to him, but this was obviously not the case.²⁷

Ultimately, there is little question that Campbell's lack of fame was impacted his entire life by the specter of Bob Mathias and Rafer Johnson. While just as handsome, well spoken, and talented, Campbell was always overshadowed by the two decathlon champions from the Central Valley of California. Jim Murray, with his usual mix of humor and cogent analysis, wrote in 1991 that Campbell was just "as magnificent an athlete as any [Jim] Thorpe or anyone who came before him or after him." Recognizing, however, Campbell's "relatively low profile in the pantheon of Olympic athletes," Murray noted that "Part of the problem is, he [Campbell] reigned between the eras of Mathias and Johnson. That's like sitting between the Pope and Gorbachev, or playing a scene with a baby and a dog."²⁸

Murray's assessment that Mathias and Johnson would always cast a shadow over Campbell was certainly true, but he offers no explanation for it. Perhaps because it defies an easy explanation. If you consider not just their Olympic triumphs but the totality of their decathlon careers, Mathias and Johnson certainly had more impressive resumes than Campbell. While Campbell apparently competed in just three decathlons in his life, albeit with great results in the most important international athletic festival of all, Mathias won all nine of the decathlons in which he competed, including four United States championships in addition to his two Olympic triumphs. He also established three world records in the event. Johnson, on top of his silver and gold medals in Olympic competition, captured the decathlon in the 1955 Pan American games and 1958 Kingsburg Invitational and broke the world record in the event in 1958 at the first US-USSR dual track and field meet in Moscow.²⁹

Of these two men, it was Johnson who probably cast the biggest shadow over Campbell. His life was like a Horatio Alger story. He became a darling of the American sporting public. He was the type of man that endeared himself to many Whites who liked their Black athletes to be humble and restrained and outwardly grateful for having the opportunity to strive for success at the highest levels of sport. Parenthetically, while many in the African American community admired his great skills and viewed him as a representative figure of the entire race, Johnson had famously incurred the wrath of Harry Edwards and younger Black athletes who led a proposed boycott of the 1968 Mexico City Olympic Games for his refusal to speak out about racial discrimination in sport and the larger society. He became persona non grata to Edwards, Tommie Smith, John Carlos, and other members of the Olympic Project for Human Rights who used the games in Mexico City to draw attention to the racial inequities in the United States and around the world.[30]

Be that as it may, Johnson's timing, as well as the decisions he made, seemed to be exactly right for drawing attention to himself and gaining notoriety. He was fortunate to have a friend and rival in C.K. Yang who pushed him to greater heights and brought him even more fame than he would have realized without stiff competition from the great Taiwanese athlete. The moment could not have been more perfect for Johnson when he beat Yang in the decathlon in dramatic fashion at the 1960 Olympic games. Captain of that year's Olympic team and chosen to carry the American flag at the opening ceremonies, Johnson and his victory over Yang in Rome effectively transformed him, for all intents and purposes, into arguably the one athlete most closely associated with the decathlon. Most importantly, while he was not the first Black athlete to win the Olympic decathlon, he was the first athlete to capture the prestigious event during the first European Olympics to be broadcast in the United States. He benefited in the same way as Wilma Rudolph, the great Black sprinter from Tennessee State who became an instant sensation among an American public that had the privilege of witnessing her famous three gold-medal winning performance in Rome through same-day television coverage.[31]

If there was any doubt about Johnson's status and lasting place in the American consciousness it was put to rest in 1984 in Los Angeles when he was asked to light the Olympic flame at that year's games. More than merely a hometown hero, Johnson was a transcendent figure. Many saw him as the perfect man to carry the torch up the long steps of the LA Coliseum to light the Olympic flame in front of some 92,500 spectators, as his entire life reflected a firm belief that sport was a uniquely impactful diplomatic tool and had the power to bring diverse groups of people together. These were especially important points that organizers certainly wanted to convey during the middle of the Cold War when the Soviet Union and several other countries boycotted the 1984 Olympics in retaliation for the withdrawal of the United States from the Moscow Olympics four years earlier. The high regard in which Johnson was held and the reason why he was considered the ideal choice to light the Olympic flame was perhaps most clearly stated by Peter Ueberroth, the man hired to organize the 1984 games in Los Angeles. About Johnson, Ueberroth noted that "He represents what the Olympics are all about—honesty, integrity, good sportsmanship, and commitment—and he brought all those ideals to our organizational efforts as a member of our board, spirit team, and speaker's bureau. There was never a time when we asked Rafer for his help that he didn't deliver."[32] Implicit in these remarks is that the Los Angeles Olympic Committee was indebted to Johnson. Ueberroth himself must have felt a deep level of gratitude toward Johnson since the great decathlon champion supposedly cast the final vote that secured his selection as "president/general manager" of the Los Angeles Olympic Committee.[33]

As one would expect, Milt Campbell was disturbed by the fact that Johnson was chosen to light the Olympic flame in Los Angeles in 1984. "Since Rafer carried that torch," noted Campbell in 1986, "he's had all sorts of speaking engagements and appearances. But why didn't the Olympic Committee pick the first black to win the decathlon instead of the guy he beat? Why the second one?"[34] These questions were certainly rhetorical in nature, meant by Campbell to express his disappointment at not being more adequately recognized while at once pricking the public's consciousness and reminding people of his Olympic accomplishments. This was characteristic of Campbell. He was a confident and racially proud Black man who spoke his mind, expressed his views on all sorts of matters, and challenged the norms of the dominant White culture. He did this by marrying a White woman, setting up an alternative school in Newark for disadvantaged youth that focused on Black history and culture, and through his piercing words as well as his deeds. One classic example of his view on race, and his belief in the limited power of sport to bring people together, was his support of the proposed boycott of the 1968 Olympic games in Mexico City. While Johnson and some past and present Olympians were adamantly opposed to a boycott on account of their belief that success in sport was advancing the race, Campbell took the opposite view. He noted in *Newsweek* that "we are simply kidding ourselves if we think winning Olympic medals is advancing our race as a whole. Remember, when you play ball you're only entertaining the White man. And Whitey isn't going to give you something unless there's something in it for him."[35]

It was this outspoken position on race, and despite his military service and notwithstanding the fact his Black nationalism had likely become far more strident than they had been during the 1950s, that perhaps partly explains why Campbell was apparently never asked to participate in State Department goodwill tours like many other outstanding African American athletes. He was not one of "The Good Negroes," the phrase used by historian Damion L. Thomas to describe those great African American athletes sent to foreign climes during the Cold War period to help convince the rest of the world that African Americans were treated fairly and did not suffer from racial oppression.[36] Campbell's outspoken position on race, along with his unwillingness to acquiesce to those in positions of power, may also partly explain why he was so slow to receive the awards and other recognition he deserved. Campbell's outspoken position on race, along with his need to be recognized and even more powerful yearning to be left alone and shun the spotlight, may also help account for why he never realized lasting national acclaim. He wanted to be acknowledged, but never wittingly sought fame and fortune. In large measure, the above-mentioned factors combined with the reality that he garnered his Olympic medals in the pre-television era and lived in relative anonymity in Canada for several years help explain why Campbell is the least known decathlon champion. In essence, Campbell's oft-repeated comment "that America was not ready for a black man to be the best athlete in the world" does not seem entirely accurate. It would have been closer to the truth if he had noted that America was not ready for a certain type of Black man to be the best athlete in the world.[37]

Tellingly, Campbell is not the only African American Olympian during the late 1940s and 1950s whose name does not resonate with the sporting public. It is also true for many others during this period.[38] Although they all had their own stories and were impacted in different ways and responded to their circumstances in a unique manner, African American Olympians during the late 1940s and 1950s are largely unknown and as a group have garnered comparatively little attention from historians based on their athletic achievements.

Great track and field stars, ranging from the better known but decidedly understudied Ohio State star Mal Whitfield and Baldwin-Wallace College's Harrison Dillard to outstanding but now very obscure individuals such as Andy Stanfield, the Seton Hall athlete who captured gold medals in the 200 meters and 4X100 relay in Helsinki, Charles Dumas, the University of Southern California athlete who captured a gold medal in the high jump in Melbourne, Leamon King, the University of California, Berkeley standout who won the gold medal in the 4X100 relay in Melbourne, and Ira Murchison, the Western Michigan University performer who garnered a gold medal in the 4X100 relay in Melbourne, were also overshadowed in the 1950s by African American athletes who were achieving greatness in those sports that mattered most to Americans.[39] Although track and field had a close following during this crucial decade and resonated more deeply with the average citizen than it does today, the visibility of the above-mentioned individuals and others paled in comparison to African American athletes who achieved success in the most popular White organized sports. For instance, outstanding African American pugilists such as Joe Louis (albeit at the very end of his career), Sugar Ray Robinson, Floyd Patterson, and Sonny Liston held legendary status in the Black community, achieving success in the bloody and popular sport where they could physically punish White men with impunity. Their careers were chronicled in detail, stories of their exploits in the ring were repeatedly told and written about as they represented a degree of Black manhood culturally significant to the African American community during a decade, as evidenced by the 1954 *Brown v. Board of Education* decision and 1956 Montgomery bus boycott, in which the civil rights movement was mounting.[40]

Equally important were the initial wave of African American athletes who integrated the predominantly White organized sports of baseball, football, and basketball during this period. Athletes such as Willie Mays, Bill Russell, and Jim Brown played an extended number of games in front of home audiences in sports that deeply resonated with Americans, captivated people, particularly those in the African American community, because it was an apparent indication that this country was finally living up to its democratic ideals and principles. They have become legendary figures, cultural icons who are forever etched in American memories. On the other hand, track and field stars during this period, no matter their accomplishments and how much honor they brought to themselves and America, were no match for these athletes regarding public acclaim and notoriety and lasting fame. Decathlon champions perhaps even less so because of their involvement in a competition antithetical to the increasing emphasis on sport specialization and adulation of those athletes who toppled records in singular high-profile events. While respected for their virtuosity, decathletes were participants in a competition that effectively guaranteed that they would achieve relatively average performances in certain events by virtue of the multiplicity and broad range of physical skills that the competition required.[41]

That being said, the fact that Milt Campbell was finally acknowledged for his Olympic achievements during the latter stages of his life did not assuage his disappointment, and, quite frankly, bewilderment, that it took him so long to be honored. He was no different than anyone else in wanting to be publicly recognized for his extraordinary achievements in a timely fashion. His loved ones shared in his disappointment. One particularly poignant statement that encapsulated both the sense of satisfaction, yet the ultimate sadness that those closest to Campbell felt about his delayed recognition was made by his partner, Linda Rusch, during the last year of his life. She told the Canadian Broadcast Company that Campbell was a "whirlwind of activity" until his cancer treatment slowed him down, "playing tennis as well as riding bikes, horses and motorcycles." The past year has been a particularly "special one," for Milt, Rusch said, because he had been "honored by the New Jersey and the International Swimming halls as well as being invited to attend the Olympic trials in Oregon . . . he didn't get the recognition in the '50s (or the '60s, 70s, or 80s). He got it all this year and [then] he died."[42]

In the final analysis, we are left with the question as to whether Campbell could have done anything differently to bring him the more immediate recognition and honors his outstanding athletic accomplishments warranted? The answer to that question can never be known with any certainty, but it seems highly unlikely. Campbell, like all human beings, could not always control his environment, influence people's decisions, and alter deep-seated stereotypes. He had no control over the fact that the two Olympic games in which he participated were on the other side of the world with no television coverage, had no control over Paul Brown's opposition to interracial marriage, and no control over Hall of Fame voters who waited so long to honor his athletic achievements. He certainly had no intention of adopting a different value scheme, not speaking his mind on racial issues and other matters, or bowing to the "powers that be" in efforts to realize the honors he so richly deserved. What Campbell could control was the manner in which he dealt with the fate that had befallen him and, in this regard, he was, like his athletic career itself, a success. While being passed over for various honors for way too long considering his accomplishments, Campbell moved forward nonetheless and carved out a productive, if not always very public, post-athletic career as a local civil rights activist, community leader, and motivational speaker.[43]

These roles, as well as his position as an Olympic champion, provided untold opportunities for Campbell to have a positive impact on those striving to make a mark for themselves in and outside of sport. His athletic successes and long years of being neglected combined with his verbal skills and worldly experiences made him the ideal person to offer advice and mentorship. Among those who received his sage counsel was Dan O'Brien, the Oregon-born athlete of African and Finnish heritage who captured the gold medal in the decathlon at the 1996 Olympic games in Atlanta. "His influence had a profound effect on my entire life" noted O'Brien in a video tribute he did on Campbell's life. "The things I learned from him weren't about throwing the javelin or going over the hurdles faster. He worked on every other area in my life, and that was preparing me to be a champion."[44] Undoubtedly, those of lesser renown than O'Brien, perhaps even those who also had patiently waited to receive the recognition they felt they deserved, could probably say the same thing about the enormously talented decathlon champion from Plainfield, New Jersey who lived proudly and unapologetically until the very end of his life.

Notes

1. Margery Miller, "High School Senior Outstanding Athlete," *The Christian Science Monitor*, 28 May 1953, 19.

2. For general information on Campbell's life and career, see Keith McClellan, "Campbell, Milton Gray ("Milt")", *Scribner Encyclopedia of American Lives, Thematic Series: Sports Figures*, https://www.encyclopedia.com/humanities/encyclopedias-almanacs-transcripts-and-maps/campbell-milton-gray-milt, accessed 20 January 2019. See also: H.L. Masin, "Campbell is Coming," *Senior Scholastic*, 62 (25 February 1953), 22; "Name Your Ticket: Milt Campbell," *Newsweek*, 61 (27 April 1953), 90; and "World's Greatest Athlete," *Ebony*, 9 (November 1953), 121–6.

3. Writers would sometimes mention that in contrast to other great athletes Campbell never appeared on the cover of a Wheaties box. A survey of the list of athletes who have appeared on the cover of the famous cereal box, however, indicates that Bob Mathias and Rafer Johnson also suffered the same fate. The American decathlon champions to appear on the cover of a Wheaties box are Bruce Jenner (1977, 2012), Dan O'Brien (1996), and Bryan Clay (2008). The first Black athlete to appear on the cover of a Wheaties box was Jesse Owens in 1936.

4. An individual cannot be considered for induction into the United States Olympic Hall of Fame until six years after their retirement from competition. Campbell, of course, exceeded that requirement many times over.

5. Dave D'Alessandro, "Somehow, despite all he accomplished, the great Milt Campbell never got his proper due," *New Jersey Star-Ledger*, 3 November 2012. https://www.nj.com/sports/index.ssf/2012/11/somehow_despite_all_he_ accompl .html, Retrieved accessed 21 January 2019.

6. McClellan, "Campbell, Milton Gray ("Milt")" and Merrell Noden, "Best Athlete You Never Knew: Milt Campbell was Dazzling as the Olympic Decathlon Champion in 1956," *Sports Illustrated*, 4 August 1996. https://www.si.com/vault/2016/08/17/best-athlete-you-never-knew-milt-campbell-was-dazzling-olympic-decathlon-champion-1956, Accessed 21 January 2019.

7. Quoted in Noden, "Best Athlete You Never Knew."

8. For Campbell's high school career, see Miller, "High School Senior Outstanding Athlete," 19.

9. Miller, "High School Senior Outstanding Athlete," 19.

10. Paul Zimmerman, "Tulare's Titan Leads American Sweep in the Event," *Los Angeles Times*, 27 July 1952, B8.

11. For information on Mathias, see Chris Terrence, *Bob Mathias: Across the Fields of Gold: Tribute to an American Hero* (New York: Taylor Publishing, 2000) and Bob Mathias and Bob Mendes, *The Bob Mathias Story* (New York: Sports Publishing, 2001).

12. Specific information about Campbell's time at Indiana University is very limited. Some details, however, can be gleaned from "IU Athletics Mourns the Passing of Hall of Famer Milt Campbell," https://iuhoosiers.com/ . . . /IU_athletics_mourns_the_passing_of_hall_of_famer_milt_ . . . accessed 17 May 2019.

13. Jim Murray, "Forgotten Decathlete Speaks Out," *Los Angeles Times*, 16 July 1991. http://articles.latimes.com/print/1991-07-16/sports/sp-2395_1_milt-campbell, accessed 13 February 2019. Campbell never explained why he chose to attend Indiana University. He did tell Russ J. Cowans of the *Chicago Defender* in 1957 that he expected to return to the university after being discharged from the Navy but decided instead to play professional football. See Russ J. Cowans, "A Visit from Milt Campbell," *Chicago Defender,* 14 March 1957, 20.

14. For American criticism of the Soviet Union's system of sport, see: Damion L. Thomas, *Globetrotting: African American Athletes and Cold War Politics* (Urbana: University of Illinois Press, 2012), esp. 87–90.

15. See United States Olympic Committee, *United States 1956 Olympic Book Quadrennial Report*, https://digital.la84.org/digital/collection/p17103coll6/id/5100/rec/10, accessed 18 January 2019.

16. No Olympic decathlon champion has captured the Sullivan Award since Bruce Jenner (now Caitlan) was bestowed with the prestigious honor in 1976.

17. For information on the Johnson and Yang rivalry, see Joseph M. Turrini, "The Purest of Rivalries: Rafer Johnson, C.K. Yang, and the 1960 Olympic Decathlon," in David K. Wiggins and R. Pierre Rodgers, eds. *Rivals: Legendary Matchups that Made Sports History* (Fayetteville, AR: The University of Arkansas Press, 2010), 5–27; and James Murray, "The Eclipse of Mr. K., by Rafer Johnson," *Sports Illustrated*, 13 (18 July 1960), 32–8.

18. For a personal account of Johnson's career, see Rafer Johnson with Philip Goldberg, *The Best that I can Be: An Autobiography*, (New York: Doubleday, 1998). See

also: "Big Man on Campus," *Ebony*, 14 (May 1959), 53–8; "New Role for Rafer," *Ebony*, 21 (December 1965), 181–84; "Sportsman of the Year: Rafer Johnson," *Sports Illustrated*, 10 (5 January 1959), 19–25; and "None but the Brave: Rafer Johnson," *Ebony*, 19 (October 1964), 110–12.

19. It is impossible, of course, to tell how Campbell's football career would have been altered if he had not been released by the Cleveland Browns. Based on his performance in the CFL, however, Campbell would have had great difficulty finding playing time in the far superior National Football League.

20. Murray, "Forgotten Decathlete Speaks Out." Campbell told the Paul Brown story on several occasions. See, for example, Norden, "Best Athlete You Never Knew: Milt Campbell was Dazzling as the Olympic Decathlon Champion in 1956;" Frank Litsky, "Milt Campbell, 78, Olympic Decathlon Champion, Dies," *The New York Times*, 4 November 2012. https://www.nytimes.com/2012/11/05/sports/milt-campbell-olympic-decathlon-champion-dies-at-78.html, accessed 21 January 2019; Filip Bondy, "Milt Campbell is the forgotten champion," New York Daily News, 18 May 2008. https://www.nydailynews.com/sports/more-sports/milt-campbell-forgotten-champion-article-1.333177, accessed 21 January 2019; Dave D'Alessandro, "Milt Campbell still a champion 55 years after he made history at the Olympics," 30 November 2011. https://www.nj.com/sports/njsports/index.ssf/2011/11/dalessandro_milt_campbell_stil.html, accessed 21 January 2019; and Keith McClellan, "Campbell, MIlton Gray ("Milt")".

21. See *Winnipeg Free Press*, 17 March 1965, 55.

22. Dave D'Alessandro, "Milt Campbell's Legacy Celebrated in Plainfield," *New Jersey Star-Ledger*, August 10, 2013, https://www.nj.com/olympics/index.ssf/2013/08/milt_cambells_legacy_celebrated_in_plainfield.html.

23. Campbell had a daughter Julee Campbell and sons Milton Campbell, Jr. (who died in 1987), Justin Campbell, and Milton Campbell III. Claire Noland, "Milt Campbell dies at 78; Olympic gold medalist in the decathlon," *Los Angeles Times*, 4 November 2012. http://articles.latimes.com/2012/nov/04/local/la-me-milt-campbell-20121105, accessed 13 February 2019; "Olympic decathlon champion, CFL player Milt Campbell dies," *The Associated Press*, November 3, 2012. https://www.cbc.ca/sports/football/cfl/olympic-decathlon-champion-cfl-player-milt-campbell-dies-1.1249270, accessed 13 February 2019; McClellan, "Campbell, Milton Gray ("Milt")"; Noden, "Best Athlete You Never Knew: Milt Campbell was Dazzling as the Olympic Decathlon Champion in 1956;" Frank Litsky, "Milt Campbell,78, Olympic Decathlon Champion Dies;" Bondy, "Milt Campbell is the forgotten champion;" Dave D'Alessandro, "Milt Campbell still a champion."

24. Campbell was elected to the New Jersey Hall of Fame along with such accomplished individuals as actor Michael Douglas, writer Joyce Carol Oates, and New York Giants owner Wellington Mara. See Associated Press, "Olympic decathlon champion, CFL player Milt Campbell dies," 3 November 2012. accessed 21 January 2019. The Gold Medallion is given each year by the International Swimming Hall

of Fame "To a former competitive swimmer for his or her national or international significant achievements in the field of science, entertainment, art, business, education, or government. There are no restrictions other than the recipient must be an outstanding adult whose life has served as an inspiration for youth." See https://ishof.org/gold-medallion.html, accessed 13 February 2019.

25. Larry Eldridge, "Decathlon star Milt Campbell bypassed again by Olympic Hall," *The Christian Science Monitor*, 29 April 1986. https://www.csmonitor.com/1986/0429/pmilt.html, accessed 18 January 2019.

26. See Noden, "Best Athlete You Never Knew" and Eldridge, "Decathlon star Milt Campbell."

27. Perhaps the most famous search for a "white hope" took place in the early part of the twentieth century when Americans tried desperately to find someone to beat Jack Johnson, the controversial Black boxer who held the heavyweight championship from 1908–1915. See, for example, Randy Roberts, *Papa Jack: Jack Johnson and the Era of White Hopes* (New York: Free Press, 1983); Geoffrey C. Ward, *Unforgiveable Blackness: The Rise and Fall of Jack Johnson* (New York: Vintage, 2004); and Theresa Runstedtler, *Jack Johnson, Rebel Sojourner: Boxing in the Shadow of the Global Color Line* (Berkeley: University of California Press, 2013).

28. Jim Murray, "Forgotten Decathlete Speaks Out."

29. See Frank Zarnowski, *The Decathlon: A Colorful History of Track and Field's Most Challenging Event* (Champaign, IL: Leisure Press, 1991).

30. See Harry Edwards, *The Revolt of the Black Athlete: 50th Anniversary Edition* (Urbana, Il: University of Illinois Press, 2018).

31. For details on the televising of the 1960 Olympic games, see Joseph Michalak, "C.B.S. Plans Same-Day Telecasts of Rome Olympic Games," *New York Times*, 21 August 1960, X 11.

32. Peter Ueberroth with Richard Levin and Amy Quinn, *Made in America: His Own Story* (New York: William Morrow and Company, 1985), 339.

33. For insightful essays on the 1984 Olympic games in Los Angeles, see: Matthew P. Llewellyn, Toby C. Rider, and John Gleaves, "The Golden Games: The 1984 Los Angeles Olympics," in Wayne Wilson and David K. Wiggins, eds. *LA Sports: Play, Games, and Community in the City of Los Angeles* (Fayetteville, AR: The University of Arkansas Press, 2018), 201–18; Stephen Wenn, "Peter Ueberroth's Legacy: How the 1984 Los Angeles Olympics Changed the Trajectory of the Olympic Movement," *The International Journal of the History of Sport*, 32.1 (2015), 157–71; Wayne Wilson, "Sports Infrastructure, Legacy and the Paradox of the 1984 Olympic Games," *The International Journal of the History of Sport*, 32.1 (2015), 144–56; and Mark Dyreson, "Global Television and the Transformation of the Olympics: The 1984 Los Angeles Games," *The International Journal of the History of Sport*, 32.1 (2015), 172–84.

34. Eldridge, "Decathlon star Milt Campbell."

35. Quoted in Louis Moore, *We Will Win the Day: The Civil Rights Movement, the Black Athlete, and the Quest for Equality* (Santa Barbara, CA.: Praeger, 2017), 177.

36. See Damion L. Thomas, "'The Good Negroes': African American Athletes and the Cultural Cold War (PhD dissertation, University of California, Los Angeles, 2002) and his subsequent *Globetrotting: African American Athletes and Cold War Politics*.

37. See Bondy, "Milt Campbell is the Forgotten Champion."

38. For a nice discussion of African American Olympians during the 1950s see: Moore, *We Will Win the Day*, 119-25.

39. Information on these athletes can be gleaned from Kevin B. Witherspoon, "'An Outstanding Representative of America;' Mal Whitfield and America's Black Sports Ambassadors," in Toby C. Rider and Kevin B. Witherspoon, eds., *Defending the American Way of Life: Sport, Culture, and the Cold War* (Fayetteville, AR: The University of Arkansas Press, 2018), pp. 129-40; Claude Reed Jr., "A History of Black Athletic Achievement," *New York Amsterdam News*, June 30, 1984, B 20; Edwin B. Henderson and the Editors of Sport Magazine, *The Black Athlete: Emergence and Arrival* (Cornwell Heights, Pa: The Publishers Agency, Inc. 1978); Arthur Ashe, *A Hard Road to Glory: A History of the African-American Athlete*, 3 vols. (New York: Warner Books, 1988); "Andy Stanfield; The World's Fastest Human," *Our World*, 6 (March 1951), 64-5; Joseph M. Turrini, *The End of Amateurism in American Track and Field* (Urbana: University of Illinois Press, 2010).

40. The decade of the 1950s is an understudied period regarding African American athletes. Far more attention has been paid to African American participation in sport during the civil rights period and the years following. In time, scholars will hopefully rectify this fact. Evidence of the importance of boxing in the African American community can be gleaned from the voluminous amount of coverage given the sport by legendary Black writers and intellectuals such as Marcus Garvey, Richard Wright, James Weldon Johnson, and Maya Angelou. For examples, see David K. Wiggins and Patrick B. Miller, *The Unlevel Playing Field: A Documentary History of the African American Experience in Sport* (Urbana: University of Illinois Press, 2003).

41. Unlike Campbell, many of these athletes wrote, sometimes with the assistance of others, their own autobiographies. Two prominent examples are: Jim Brown, *Out of Bounds* (New York: Zebra Books, 1989) and Bill Russell, with Taylor Branch, *Second Wind* (New York: Basic Books, 1976).

42. CBC Sports, "Olympic decathlon champion, CFL player Milt Campbell dies."

43. Campbell is featured in a number of YouTube videos. See, for example, "Milt Campbell Video," https://www.youtube.com/watch?v=q1utCebi7ee, accessed 13 February 2019; "Milt Campbell Advice to Youth," https://www.youtube.com/watch?v=u506xvUSqil, accessed 13 February 2019; and "Milt Campbell at the Plainfield NJ YMCA," https://www.youtube.com/watch?v=321h3y8vixa,accessed 13 February 2019.

44. Quoted in D'Alessandro, "D'Alessandro: Milt Campbell's legacy celebrated." https://www.nj.com/olympics/index.ssf/2013/08/milt_campbells_legacy_celebrated_in_plainfield.html, accessed 18 January 2019.

"STAR MAKER"

George Powles, McClymonds High School, and the Youth of West Oakland

"I have never met a finer person. I owe so much to him it's impossible to express," legendary basketball player Bill Russell told *Sports Illustrated* in 1963 about George Powles (1910–1987).[1] Vada Pinson, the outstanding outfielder who played eighteen years in Major League Baseball with five different clubs, told the *Los Angeles Times* in 1972 that George Powles was "a great man, and if everybody was like him the world would be a much better place."[2] Frank Robinson told the crowd at his 1982 Baseball Hall of Fame induction in Cooperstown, New York, that "George Powles gave me the foundation I'm still building on. I want to say to George Powles, thank you for all the youth of Oakland, because I know they appreciate it like I did and still do."[3] Curt Flood, the man who famously cleared the way for free agency by suing Major League Baseball, told those in attendance at George Powles' memorial service in 1987 how appreciative he was to Powles for "all the things he ingrained in me as a youngster. His legacy will live on. It will live on with me in my heart."[4]

The effusive praise for George Powles by four famous and influential African American athletes was certainly heartfelt. It was echoed by hundreds of lesser-known athletes who also played for the famous White man from Oakland, California, whose career as a coach of several sports spanned the years from 1946 to 1972. Referred to by one writer as a "builder of champions" and another as a "star maker," Powles established a legacy as a great developer of athletic talent and a mentor to young boys, primarily as a coach of highly successful baseball teams sponsored by the Babe Ruth, Connie Mack, and American Legion organizations, as well as equally talented baseball squads he guided at the interscholastic level of competition, first at predominantly Black McClymonds High School and then later at predominantly White Skyline High School.[5] He coached the Bill Erwin Post team of Oakland to successive national American Legion championships in 1949 and 1950, the Oakland Connie Mack team to the national championship in 1959, and both McClymonds and Skyline to several Oakland Athletic League titles.[6]

Remarkably, Powles coached seventeen players who had Major League Baseball careers (and either mentored or coached at the high school or youth-league levels and an untold number who signed professional contracts). Most of those players were African American, many of them members of families originally from the rural South who had migrated to Oakland in the first half of the twentieth century to seek a better life and find employment in the area's burgeoning economy. At McClymonds High School alone, a school prominent sportswriter Jim Murray once noted "produced more athletes than the United Kingdom," Powles coached seven players, albeit with differing levels of success, who had Major League careers.[7]

Included among this group were Robinson, Flood, and Pinson; Willie Tasby, an outfielder who began his six years of Major League Baseball in 1958 with the Baltimore Orioles; Charlie Beamon, a pitcher who had a combined 3–3 record from 1956 thru 1958 with the Baltimore Orioles; Jesse Gonder, a catcher who began his eight-year Major League career with the New York Yankees in 1960; and Aaron Pointer, an outfielder who played for the Houston Colt.45's in 1963 and Houston Astros in 1966 and 1967 before becoming a longtime official in the NFL. Although these athletes, and many others he coached, had great talent, their success resulted in no small measure to the expertise and dedication of Powles, who spent a lifetime committed to the education and development of young people.[8]

It would be inaccurate to simply categorize Powles as a kind-hearted patron of Black youth who was focused on accomplishing a sense of selfless service by uplifting people of color and helping to eradicate structural oppression. He was, more accurately, in the mold of some other White coaches at the interscholastic level of competition during this period in that he served as a mentor to many Black athletes and, as a result, became important in their lives and careers. His role in the struggle for racial equality did not mean carrying placards or protesting discriminatory practices, but instead, nurturing Black athletes and looking out for their best interests. Powles seemingly stood apart, however, from his White counterparts for the sheer depth of the relationship he established with many legendary Black athletes who realized lasting fame in their sports and, in some cases, became prominent in the civil rights struggle. The extraordinarily close connection he forged with these athletes and mutual respect that resulted from it would be evident in an assortment of different ways and continued throughout their lifetimes. They lauded Powles in their autobiographies, sang his praises in a countless number of interviews, left him complimentary tickets and visited with him when their teams were in the Bay Area for games, and paid homage to him when special tributes were given in his honor. Because of the fame and public platform of these athletes, their persistent praise of Powles added immeasurably to his own storied reputation and status.[9]

Although he left no memoir and apparently did a limited number of interviews, the expansive media coverage of him during and following his career and the testimonies of his former athletes, make clear that Powles was at heart a youth sport coach who believed in sport's power to change lives and, if organized properly, to instill important values and develop character among its participants irrespective of their race and cultural background. Unlike so many contemporary adult-directed youth sport programs, Powles' commitment to coaching was largely voluntary and a twelve-months-long affair that involved a close interconnection among community recreation programs, schools, and service organizations. Although winning was very important to him and he was proud of helping to develop famous (and not so famous) professional athletes, Powles's devotion to coaching was primarily rooted in his desire to see players reach their athletic potential and realize success in their everyday lives. Powles once noted, "I don't work with youngsters to make pro ballplayers. I'm always happy if they develop enough to make their high school teams."[10] To further establish this point, Powles' daughter Marjorie told local sport historian Paul Brekke-Miesner that perhaps her father's greatest sense of accomplishment was the fact that twenty-two of his former players had become coaches themselves.[11]

Powles, it is important to note, was merely the most famous youth sport coach in the Bay Area that had always produced many professional athletes, particularly for a time in Major League Baseball. In the early part of the century, San Francisco produced such legendary players as Lefty O'Doul, Joe Cronin, Frank Crosetti, Harry Heilmann, and Joe and Dom DiMaggio. Oakland and other Bay Area cities such as Berkeley and Richmond kept pace with such notable players as Lefty Gomez, Cookie Lavagetto, Ernie Lombardi, and Chick Hafey. By the 1950s, Oakland and neighboring Alameda were becoming an especially fertile ground for the development of Major League Baseball players. Besides those who played for Powles, the area produced such notable players as Andy Carey, Billy Martin, Elijah "Pumpsie" Green, Bill Rigney and then later Ron Hansen, Willie Stargell, Rudy May, Chris Spier, Dennis Eckersley, Dave Stewart, Gary Pettis, Ricky Henderson, Lloyd Moseby, Jimmy Rollins, and Dontrelle Willis. The reasons for the relatively large number of prominent Major Leaguers from one location has caused much speculation, ranging from the area's temperate climate and outstanding coaches to the influx of immigrants and enormous popularity of baseball at the time. Although the answer as to why the area produced so many Major League players are multilayered and cannot be explained by one factor, there seems little question that it resulted partly from the extensive and thriving after-school sports program established in the post–World War II period by the Oakland Recreation Department. In an effort to keep children out of trouble and off the streets, the department setup a program with paid coaches and competitive teams and leagues at various age levels that taught and honed the athletic skills of the participants, many of whom would take their talents to the high school level and beyond. It was a developmental program for children of different socioeconomic backgrounds that would only be supplanted by the very elite and private youth sport programs of today that have effectively eliminated some children from participating because of membership fees, travel expenses, and coaches' salaries. Powles, miraculously so considering his plethora of other duties and time commitments, was one of the leaders in the program which allowed him to mentor and coach many children who would later play for him on one of his youth sports teams or at McClymonds or for one of the other area high schools.[12]

DENIED HIS OWN DREAM SET HIM ON A NEW CAREER PATH

George Beverly Powles was born in Oakland on August 21, 1910, to Percy W. Powles and Elizabeth Howard Powles. His father Percy, born in Orillia, Ontario, Canada on March 8, 1881, immigrated to the United States in 1885 and was naturalized the following year. Based on census data, he first worked as a carpenter and then spent the remainder of his working life in the positions of switchman, brakeman, and eventually yardmaster for the Southern Pacific Railroad Company in Oakland. His mother Elizabeth was born in Illinois and spent her life in the dual role of housewife and bookkeeper.[13] The Powles' family, which also included George's older brother Gordon and younger sister Mildred, lived in predominantly White neighborhoods with no indication that they were devoutly religious or political in nature. George grew up playing baseball and basketball with future tennis great Don Budge and tagging along with Major League players Chick Hafey, Red Kress, and eventual Hall of Famer Ernie Lombardi. He was also an outstanding multi-sport athlete at University High School in North Oakland, which opened its doors in 1923 and closed in 1948. "Little George Powles was the find of the day for coach 'Mose' Lyman," noted the *Oakland Tribune* in its description of the Lowell High School and University High School opening football game of the 1927 season. "Powles got off some splendid punts and made a number of long gains on end runs and off-tackle plays. It was George's first football game and his rushing gives Lyman another good back to pair with Kenny Gibson."[14]

Like many youth baseball players, Powles had dreams of playing Major League Baseball. Unfortunately, his dreams were dashed after a very brief stint as an outfielder with the old San Francisco Seals, the outstanding baseball team which competed in the talent-rich Pacific Coast League from 1903 until their departure to Phoenix, Arizona in 1957. He ultimately chose to earn a teaching credential from San Francisco State College and in 1936 began applying for teaching positions in the Oakland Public Schools. For years, however, Powles was unsuccessful in doing so because of the very tight job market. With a family to support, which included at the time his wife Winifred and a young child (son Laurie and later daughter Marjorie), Powles initially took a position at the Pacific Brewing and Malting Company in San Jose and then later worked at an oil refinery as well as a creamery.[15] In 1943, with World War II raging, Powles was finally able to secure a teaching position, taking a job at predominantly Black Hoover Junior High School where he taught and coached for about a year before being called into military service by the US Army. He fought for two years as an infantryman, including intense fighting at the Battle of the Bulge, an experience Powles frequently recounted and one that haunted him for the rest of his life. In a story he wrote for the *Oakland Tribune* in 1985 about his time as a soldier, Powles stated, "At least once a year for the past 28 years I have had a bad dream. It is always the same." The nightmare is this: Powles is crouched, along with two other infantrymen, behind some shrubs in a monastery garden and an eleven-year-old girl is riding her bike past a house. Little did she know that within seconds mortar shells would reign down. It is always at this stage of the dream, notes Powles, that "I wake up with a strange feeling, because I know the nightmare is really a reliving of past experiences, of one that is not yet finished."[16]

When the war ended, Powles returned to Hoover Junior High School and remained there until 1947 when he took a teaching and coaching position at McClymonds High School in the heart of West Oakland. The move to McClymonds, in the same year Jackie Robinson reintegrated Major League Baseball, proved to be a life-altering experience for Powles. Founded in 1915, McClymonds had evolved over time into a predominantly Black institution, reflecting the large number of African Americans from the South who had migrated to Oakland seeking a better life and more prosperous future. Thousands of African Americans, a large percentage of them from Texas, Louisiana, Arkansas, and Oklahoma where they had increasing difficulty eking out a living and were experiencing some of the worst forms of violence, were drawn to the city by the promise of a variety of relatively high-paying jobs associated with the area's wartime economy. Part of what has been termed the second wave of migration that began in 1940, these transplanted Black southerners found an assortment of different jobs in an industrial complex boosted by a flood of federal government spending for shipbuilding and construction of the Oakland Army Base and Naval Supply Center. The census data make clear the demographic changes that took place in the city. In 1940 there were 287,936 Whites in Oakland. They made up 95.3 percent of the entire population, as opposed to 8,462 Blacks, who comprised just 2.8 percent of the total population. By 1950 there were 290,605 native Whites in Oakland who comprised 75.6 percent of the entire population, 38,192 foreign-born Whites in the city who made up 9.9 percent of the entire population, and 47,582 Blacks for an aggregate of 12.4 percent of the population. Just ten years later, there were 270,523 Whites in Oakland, who made up 73.6 percent of the population and the number of Blacks had swelled to 83,618 for a total of 22.8 percent of the city's population.[17]

The largest number of African Americans, because of restrictive racial policies established by local banks and housing authorities, were forced to move into West Oakland where they rented and bought homes, raised their families, and set up for a time a dynamic and diverse economic, social, and cultural life. Historian Aram Goudsouzian provides a vivid description of West Oakland in his biography of Bill Russell, noting that it "featured small factories and commercial districts of restaurants, bars, laundries, groceries, and barbershops catering to the black influx. The great migration had created vibrant urban spaces that illustrated the range of African American life, mixing professionals with the poor, respectable women's clubs with randy gentlemen's clubs, hot jazz with heavenly gospel, Saturday night sin with Sunday morning salvation."[18] From almost the very beginning, however, it was evident that segregated West Oakland suffered from overcrowding, squalid living conditions, and limited educational opportunities. Black children of the recently arrived immigrants in West Oakland were forced to attend McClymonds since it was the only local public high school. Not unexpectedly, with the influx of Black students into the school, White students and teachers fled McClymonds as quickly as possible. Powles was not one of them, accepting the challenge of working with students from disadvantaged backgrounds and in a school with limited resources.[19]

Powles made an immediate impact as both a teacher and coach upon his arrival at McClymonds. Decidedly older than most beginning teachers at the age of thirty-seven when he started his tenure at McClymonds, and benefiting from a wealth of experience, including his two years of combat in World War II, Powles proved very effective as a physical education teacher and coach. From the very beginning of his time at McClymonds, however, it is apparent from the sources that Powles saw himself first as a youth sport coach dedicated to curbing juvenile delinquency and teaching the values of teamwork, hard work, and sacrifice to local children both within and outside the formal educational system. This commitment proved successful and knew no racial boundaries as evidenced by many of his former athletes from various backgrounds and socioeconomic classes and decidedly different skill levels who credited him with keeping them on the right side of the law and providing guidance crucial for a meaningful and productive future. In a 1984 interview, part of the series "Black Champions" available through Washington University, Curt Flood made clear his feelings about Powles commitment to children and youth sport when asked why there were so many great athletes that came out of West Oakland. He credited it to the interest that adults in the city took in their children's welfare and especially Powles. "Here is a white guy [Powles] who, who coached the first Black manager in baseball and the first Black coach in basketball, and it, it is a tribute, really, to the interest that he really had in, in, in kids. It's one thing about being from the ghetto, I guess, we are all kind of protected there . . . and how this white guy got in and out of the ghetto night after night to, to teach, and to be a part of our lives, I just have no idea."[20]

A COACH OF "INSANELY TALENTED KIDS"

In many respects, Powles was the right person at the right time. He came along when baseball was unquestionably America's most important pastime and at the youth sport level had seen enormous growth not only resulting from the expanding post-war economy but because it was seen as the perfect antidote to what scholars have referred to as the "age of anxiety." As historian Michael H. Carriere noted in his essay on Little League Baseball that Americans in the post–World War II period, deeply impacted by the continued growth of a mass consumer culture, development of a corporate economy, and changes in the family structure (and he might have added fear about the nuclear age and atomic bomb), were confronted by an acute sense of anxiety. Nowhere was it more intense than when assessing how children would cope and find their way in this new social order. Amid this new social order, children were viewed as the hope for a better future while at once being susceptible to the same anxieties, uncertainty, and troubles encountered by adults. For Americans, this translated into a profound fear of juvenile delinquency, a topic of enormous interest to Congress, which took up the question of juvenile delinquency (and increasing crime) in a plethora of bills in the mid-1950s (What Carriere does not mention is that the normalized racism and era's segregation resulted in a disproportionate number of African Americans being charged and imprisoned for juvenile crime).[21] To many, one of the best ways to confront the scourge of juvenile delinquency was through participation in America's National Pastime, especially if adult directed and supervised.[22]

Even before taking his position at McClymonds, Powles had begun organizing baseball practices and games at Bushrod Park, an approximately ten-acre park established around 1907 and located just two blocks from his home in North Oakland. It was a wonderful facility that included an indoor gym, two ninety-foot baseball diamonds, and locker rooms. There, he would teach children the proper techniques and fundamentals of the game, throw batting practice, conduct infield and outfield drills, provide tips on base running and stealing, and arrange games that sometimes would last until nightfall. Powles and his wife also became well-known for hosting the players at their house. One observer called it "an informal clubhouse for boys" of all races and "from both sides of the track."[23] John Brodie, the future Stanford University and San Francisco 49er quarterback who played on the Bill Erwin Post American Legion baseball team, was one of those boys who took advantage of Powles' hospitality. "During vacations he'd [Brodie] turn up early each day to get George to 'hit a few,'" wrote author John Wesley Noble, "then would stay for lunch and play bridge, fan-tan, or hearts all afternoon. Perhaps he'd go home for dinner and return for more cards in the evening."[24] On the other hand, "for many Black children from working-class families," wrote Curt Flood's biographer Brad Snyder, "it was their first time inside a white person's home. Powles made them feel at ease."[25]

The sessions at Bushrod Park, almost a daily occurrence during certain times of the year, afforded Powles an opportunity to scout players for his organized youth baseball teams. These kinds of teams were popular in the United States during the 1940s and 1950s. Unlike many of his counterparts from the public schools, who could not wait for summer vacation, so they could head to the beach or mountains for relaxation, Powles for years spent that time coaching extraordinarily talented and highly successful organized youth baseball teams that garnered many titles. Engaged in strictly a voluntary experience, Powles' success as the coach of different age-group youth baseball teams brought him local fame and legendary status as both an evaluator and developer of young talent. This became abundantly clear when he led Oakland's Bill Erwin Post 337 American Legion baseball teams to successive national championships in 1949 and 1950. Among the outstanding players from those teams was Ray Herrera, the captain of the 1949 squad, who was named that season the American Legion Player of the Year, and J. W. Porter, the outstanding White catcher from Oakland Technical High School, who was named the American Legion Player of the Year in 1950. Considered one of the top prospects in the country, Porter hit .531 for the Erwin's in 1949 and .488 the following season and signed a reported $67,000 bonus with the Chicago White Sox in 1951. He ended up playing 229 Major League games with the St. Louis Browns, Detroit Tigers, Cleveland Indians, Washington Senators, and St. Louis Cardinals.[26]

Another outstanding player on the 1950 Erwin team was Frank Robinson. Referred to by local sport historian Paul Brekke-Miesner as a "man-child athlete," the future Baseball Hall of Famer and first African American to manage a Major League Baseball team when he signed in 1975 to coach the Cleveland Indians, Robinson was first discovered by Powles at Bushrod Park.[27] Powles put Robinson into one of his regular Sunday games at the park and the lanky but powerful 14-year-old launched the first pitch he saw over the centerfielder's head. From that point on, Powles watched Robinson closely, mentoring the talented ballplayer who was the youngest of ten children born in Beaumont, Texas, to a father who had abandoned the family and mother who ultimately moved Robinson and his brothers and sisters to Oakland. In many respects and akin to his relationship with so many of his athletes, Powles was like a second father to Robinson, appreciating the teenager's prodigious athletic skills and recognizing the guidance he would need as a shy and undersized boy growing up in a single-parent household in the crowded multi-ethnic tenement dwellings of West Oakland. Powles, with assistance from his wife, created a special diet to help with Robinson's persistent "nervous stomach," established an exercise regimen to improve his muscular fitness, and taught him both the physical and mental aspects of the game. At one point, when Powles inquired about Robinson following his proscribed exercise program, one of his brothers supposedly answered, "Yes, sir. When Frankie exercises, the whole house trembles."[28]

Robinson later noted that as the youngest of ten children, who was essentially fatherless after the age of eight, he was "ripe to respond to a man like George." He recalled that on weekends growing up he would begin practicing baseball at 9:00 a.m. and continue until the sun went down. Afterward, "as if we hadn't had enough baseball, George would invite us over to his house for sandwiches and baseball talk. What a student of the game he was. I learned more about baseball from George than I did from anybody in the big leagues." Perhaps even more important, continued Robinson, Powles taught us the importance of communicating and how to get along with people. "He was years ahead of his time. Just about everything I've got today—I owe it all to George."[29]

Robinson's comments about Powles being a "student of the game" were not hyperbole. Powles had a thorough understanding of the fundamentals of the game and instilled them in his players during highly organized practices characterized by endless drills and insistence on perfect execution and optimal effort. He was a disciplinarian and the result was that his teams were almost always better prepared to play than their opponents. Importantly, Powles's success guiding Robinson and other athletes also stemmed from his understanding of children and how to interact with them. Sam Bercovich, whose furniture store E. Bercovich and Sons sponsored the Erwin team and other youth clubs in the city, noted that Powles "knew kids—how they think, how to talk to them and what to do for them."[30] This was high praise coming from a man whose store was the biggest supporter of youth baseball in the city, buying uniforms and equipment every year for players and taking care of travel expenses for teams who participated in state, regional, and national tournaments. To many observers, what made Powles "stand out from other coaches" was his rapport with Black players. "A player can tell if a coach resents being around him," Powles explained to the *Oakland Tribune*. "Sometimes a player can sense you're on his side just by touch—by putting your arm around his shoulder and talking as you walk down the hall. That's part of it."[31]

Powles' very positive relationships with and mentorship of young athletes did not make him immune to some of the less positive aspects of highly organized adult-directed youth sport and interscholastic athletic programs. His more balanced approach to working with young athletes, for instance, did not belie his intense competitiveness and achievement orientation that was made apparent in his emphasis on specialization. Like many youth sport coaches of today and, despite the fact he coached a variety of sports himself, Powles encouraged his more gifted athletes to focus on those activities that were more likely to bring them career success. He found a way to get Robinson to quit football for fear he would seriously injure himself (a legitimate fear) and jeopardize his career in baseball. He did so after Robinson, playing linebacker, went down with some temporary paralysis to his left shoulder after making a tackle in his first McClymonds football game. Powles also discouraged a young Vada Pinson, in the most direct terms, from continuing to participate in music and baseball. Not especially interested in music and obviously not convinced Pinson could maintain excellence in both pursuits, Powles told the talented Black athlete he needed to choose between "the trumpet and the bat."[32] Pinson chose the latter.

Powles followed up his successive national championships with the Erwin's in 1949 and 1950 with other great youth baseball clubs. Although coming up short in the state tournament, his 1954 Oakland Babe Ruth team was loaded with talent. The best player on that team was Pinson, a very gifted player who went on to an outstanding eighteen-year Major League career with five different teams, finishing with 256 home runs, 2,757 hits, and 1,170 runs batted in. A native of Memphis, Tennessee, who moved with his family as young child to Oakland, Pinson led the 1954 Oakland Babe Ruth team with a .450 batting average and was also its best pitcher.[33] In 1955, Powles guided the Erwin's to the California State American Legion title. Leading the team on the field was the diminutive yet speedy and gifted outfielder Curt Flood. A future fifteen-year Major League player who would become famous for challenging baseball's reserve clause, Flood hit .620 with nine home runs, five triples, and twelve doubles in twenty-seven games during the run to the state title that season. In 1959, Powles' Connie Mack team captured the national championship. The stars of that team were Ernie Fazio, who played two seasons in Major League Baseball; Curt Motton, an outfielder who played six seasons with the Baltimore Orioles; and Tommy Harper, an outfielder who played fourteen years in the Major Leagues with seven different clubs and finished with career totals of 146 home runs, 567 runs batted in, and 406 stolen bases. Harper and Motton were teammates at Encinal High School in neighboring Alameda, the same school that also produced outstanding Major League players Willie Stargell, Jimmie Rollins, and Dontrelle Willis.[34]

Powles' many successes in highly organized youth baseball, which also included a fifth-place finish in the 1963 Babe Ruth League World Series, and his reputation for developing players, drew the attention of Major League Baseball officials, who for years informally sought his advice on the talents of local prospects. Powles' skills as an evaluator of baseball talent became formalized in 1958 when he signed as a bird-dog scout with the Cincinnati Reds. Powles' signing, which resulted in his resignation as coach of the Bill Erwin American Legion Post 337 baseball team, came about through the efforts of the Reds West Coast scout Bobby Mattick. An infielder with the Chicago Cubs and Cincinnati Reds from 1938 to 1942, Mattick persuaded Reds general manager Gabe Paul to sign Powles as a bird-dog scout, not simply because of his skills as an evaluator of talent but largely because of his close and trusting relationship with West Oakland's many talented Black players. Mattick, like young athletes and many others, spent a great deal of time socializing at Powles' home and became good friends with the coach, saw Powles as a crucial link between himself and Black players with whom he had difficulty identifying with and even more trouble forging connections. The relationship between the two men obviously worked, even before Powles had officially signed on as a bird-dog scout, as the Reds inked contracts with many of the city's best players. Unfortunately, the Reds signed Black players from West Oakland to contracts that only paid a few thousand dollars a year. The big bonuses, as Brad Snyder makes clear and evidenced in one notable example by J. W. Porters' $67,000 contract in 1951 (equivalent of about $753,000 today), "went almost exclusively to white prospects."[35]

"SCHOOL OF CHAMPIONS" IN WEST OAKLAND

The success Powles experienced at the youth sport level was complemented by a very impressive teaching and coaching career at McClymonds High School. The predominantly Black institution with an enrollment of barely 500 boys in a student body of just 1,200 students became a power in the six school Oakland Athletic League (OAL), which by 1961 included the larger institutions Oakland High School, Oakland Technical High School, Castlemont High School, Fremont High School, and Skyline High School. Not unexpectedly, Powles would contribute much to the athletic success of the institution that became known as the "School of Champions," although his position at McClymonds, ironically enough, did not allow him to field his best squads as coach of the Bill Erwin American Legion Post 337 baseball team.[36] Because of long-standing American Legion Baseball eligibility rules predicated on the location of a player's domicile or school they attended, the only players Powles could use for the Erwin team were those that either attended Oakland Technical High School, Emery High School, or St. Elizabeth's High School. This resulted in some creative maneuvering by prospective players and their parents, who desperately sought the expertise of Powles and undoubtedly, in some cases, also wanted to avoid attending a predominantly Black institution like McClymonds. In a 1958 *The Saturday Evening Post* article, author John Wesley Noble noted the lengths that some players and their parents would go to gain access to Powles and his Erwin team. He told the story of one boy who intentionally flunked the entrance exam at a parochial school, so his parents could enroll him at Oakland Technical High School and therefore become eligible to play for the Erwin team. Another player, an outstanding shortstop, gave up an opportunity to attend a free public school in another city and instead commuted to St. Elizabeth High School so he would qualify to play for the Erwin team. One family tried its best to sell their home in the McClymonds High School district and move to the Oakland High School district, so their son would be eligible to play for the Erwin team.[37]

Powles, as a highly competitive coach, was troubled by these eligibility rules and certainly wanted to field the best teams he possibly could for both McClymonds and the Bill Erwin American Legion Post 337 baseball team. There is limited evidence, however, as to how he dealt with the obvious conflict created by the eligibility rules other than what he did with Frank Robinson and Curt Flood. With Robinson, Powles took the precocious fourteen-year-old slugger on the Erwin team before he entered the tenth grade at McClymonds, which allowed him to compete for both the Erwin team and the school. He did the same thing with Flood, but ultimately convinced him, with the assistance of Sam Bercovich, to transfer to Oakland Technical High School by moving in with his older sister who was separated from future NFL Hall of Fame running back John Henry Johnson. Flood's transfer allowed him to continue playing for the Erwin team and to work at E. Bercovich and Sons, where he moved furniture and arranged window displays. He also flourished in his art classes and assisted in designing sets for school plays at Oakland Technical High School, an institution that was 75 percent White. Flood's transfer was certainly impacted by his close relationship with Powles. The two had a special bond, probably even stronger than the one forged between Powles and Frank Robinson. In contrast to the shy and introverted Robinson, Flood was outgoing, likable, and mature for his age, characteristics that partially accounted for why Powles was so enamored with him.[38]

Despite the restrictive eligibility rules, Powles ran a highly successful baseball program at McClymonds. Although it was difficult to consistently end up at the top of the league standings, Powles had some great teams and outstanding players in his fifteen years at the predominantly Black institution. His biggest stars were Robinson, Pinson, and Flood before the latter transferred to Oakland Technical High School after one year. Less notable but extremely gifted future Major League players that Powles also coached at McClymonds were the previously mentioned Charlie Beamon, Willie Tasby, Jesse Gonder, and Aaron Pointer. Beamon, a rarity among the Black athletes Powles coached at McClymonds in that he was born in Oakland, was an outstanding hurler who pitched for the Baltimore Orioles from 1956 to 1958. Tasby, born in Shreveport, Louisiana, played five seasons as an outfielder with the Orioles, Boston Red Sox, Washington Senators, and Cleveland Indians. His career totals included a.250 batting average, forty-six home runs, and 174 runs batted in. Gonder, born in Monticello, Arkansas, was a catcher who played from 1960 to 1967 with the New York Yankees, Cincinnati Reds, New York Mets, Milwaukee Braves, and Pittsburgh Pirates. Pointer, born in Little Rock, Arkansas, the older brother to Ruth, Anita, Bonnie, and June of the famous singing group the Pointer Sisters, and student body president at McClymonds, played briefly for the Houston Colt 45's in 1963 and again in 1967.[39]

Powles developed more than just baseball talent at McClymonds High School. For a time, he coached basketball while at McClymonds, realizing much success but by his own admission not the sport he knew best or enjoyed the most. Despite his misgivings about coaching basketball, Powles, along with Tommy Fitzpatrick, laid the foundation for an outstanding basketball program at McClymonds and as a staff member contributed to the enormous success of other sports at the school featuring Black students who, like many of their baseball-playing classmates, would have prominent post-interscholastic athletic careers. Taking the reins from Powles and Fitzpatrick in 1954, coach Paul Harless led the McClymonds basketball program to great success, leading the Warriors to a remarkable record of 110 wins and just one loss between 1958 and 1962 and by 1968 guiding the school to additional OAL titles. Included on these teams were such excellent players as Paul Silas, the rugged power forward who starred at Creighton University and enjoyed an outstanding sixteen-year career with several NBA clubs before becoming an assistant and then head coach in the league; Joe Ellis, a talented small forward who starred at the University of San Francisco before having an eight-year career with the San Francisco Warriors; and Nate Williams, another gifted athlete who had an excellent career first at Utah State University and then eight years with the Golden State Warriors.[40]

While never as dominant on the gridiron, no doubt largely a result of the school's relatively small enrollment, McClymonds produced some outstanding football players, including running back Sam Brown, who had an excellent career at UCLA, and Wendell Hayes, a basketball teammate of Silas who went on to a solid career as a running back with the NFL's Denver Broncos and Dallas Cowboys and later with the American Football League's Kansas City Chiefs. Finally, two internationally famous sprinters were McClymond's alumni. Ray Norton, who competed for the legendary coach Lloyd "Bud" Winter at San Jose State (A program famously known as "Speed City") was the world's top sprinter from 1958 thru early 1960. Equaling the world record in both the 100 and 200 meters on several occasions during this period, he captured three gold medals (100 and 200 meters and 4x100 meter relay) at the 1959 Pan American Games and that year was selected as *Track and Field News* United States Athlete of the Year. Jim Hines, who competed for Texas Southern University, captured gold medals in the 100 meters and 4x100 meter relay at the 1968 Olympic games in Mexico City and held the world record for the 100 meters for fifteen years.[41]

When Powles first arrived at McClymonds in 1947, he coached Bob Woods, who would go on to play for the Harlem Clowns, an African American exhibition team out of Chicago that existed from 1934 to 1983. He also coached Frank Robinson on the hard court. An outstanding all-around athlete who as noted previously also played football before Powles discouraged him from participating in the sport, Robinson led the McClymonds basketball team in scoring in 1953. As good as Woods and Robinson were on the hard court, Powles most famous player at McClymonds was Bill Russell, the 6′9″ center who led the University of San Francisco to successive NCAA national championships and the Boston Celtics to eleven NBA titles, captained the United States gold-medal winning basketball team in the 1956 Olympic games, became the first Black head coach in the NBA, and was selected to the Naismith Memorial Basketball Hall of Fame.[42]

There is ample evidence to indicate that Russell's enormous basketball accomplishments might not have happened without Powles' assistance and guidance. Moving with his family from Monroe, Louisiana to Oakland in 1942 at the age of eight, there was little indication initially that Russell was destined for basketball greatness. In an often-told story, when Russell first arrived at McClymonds in 1949 he was a gangly uncoordinated "Babe in the Woods" who did not project as a solid high school performer let alone a future Hall of Famer and one of the best players in the history of the game.[43] Powles, however, saw potential in the earnest Black youngster and put him on the varsity squad as the sixteenth man after he had been cut from the junior varsity team. Powles also regularly took Russell to the local playground where he worked endlessly on the youngster's game, "shooting baskets with him until their arms ached."[44] He also paid for a membership to the local Boys and Girls Club for Russell, so he could work on his game every day. If that were not enough, Powles helped secure a roster spot for Russell at the University of San Francisco by confirming with Hal De Julio, an "insurance-man scout" and former player for the school, that Russell had outstanding talent yet to be realized.[45]

All these efforts were not lost on Russell, who regularly praised Powles for what he had done for him. Russell, who once noted "If it wasn't for the kindness, support and vision of George Powles, I would not have played basketball," has provided cogent assessments of his coach that help capture the essence of the man and his core beliefs.[46] Russell paints a picture of a man who was very cognizant of racialist thinking, sensitive to the deep-seated stereotypes Whites had of Blacks, and was intent on providing every opportunity for his Black athletes to succeed on and off the playing field. How, why, and under what circumstances influenced him to adopt this stance is impossible to say, but there is no question that Powles was a visionary who tried his best as an educator and coach to overcome the debilitating effects of racism and inequitable treatment of those he taught and coached. In a 1980 interview with the *Oakland Tribune*, Russell said that most teachers at McClymonds "tried to lower our ambitions." Holding on to long-standing stereotypes, the teachers took this approach for fear they would be embarrassed by the failure of intellectually inferior Black students to complete the most basic tasks. Powles "was the exception," said Russell. He was "a compassionate man, honest in the truest sense of the word."[47] Russell also noted on several other occasions that Powles was acutely aware that every move his Black athletes made was strictly monitored and prejudged when competing against predominantly White institutions and as a result emphasized to them the importance of sportsmanship and the utmost propriety. "When we play these schools [predominantly White institutions], and if there is a fight involving us, they'll call it a riot," Russell remembers Powles saying. "But if the other teams fight, they'll call it a scuffle . . . so what we are going to do is emphasize sportsmanship."[48]

MOVING FROM MCCLYMONDS TO SKYLINE

In 1963, Powles left McClymonds and took a teaching and baseball coaching position at Skyline High School, a relatively new school in Oakland. Why Powles switched from McClymonds to Skyline is not clear. There is no indication in the written record about his reasoning for leaving the school where he had taught and coached since 1947 and taking a position at an institution that had just graduated its first class just a year before his arrival. Although it may have come about simply because Skyline was closer to Powles home, there seems little question that he had to be impacted by both the deteriorating social and economic conditions in West Oakland and its effect on McClymonds as well as the enormous potential of Skyline as an academic and athletic institution. In the 1950s and 1960s, under the pretense of urban renewal but more accurately classified as racial discrimination, some 5,000 homes in West Oakland were bulldozed and replaced with three freeways which effectively cut off the predominantly Black neighborhoods in the area from the rest of the city, the postal distribution service, and eventually a Bay Area Rapid Transit station that began in 1972. The new freeways, in turn, added to air pollution and a plethora of toxins that contributed to a variety of serious health issues, including asthma, strokes, and heart disease, which inflicted the Black citizens of West Oakland at a much higher rate than the rest of Alameda County residents. This urban displacement merely added to the economic woes of Blacks in West Oakland resulting from the loss of jobs following World War II, factors that combined to have a deleterious effect on the already limited support, economically and otherwise, of public schools in the area and this included McClymonds. At the same time, Skyline High School, initially referred to as Hill Area High School, seemed to have a great future and offered a seasoned educator and coach like Powles unlimited opportunities. Located in an affluent residential district close to Redwood Regional Park at the top of the Oakland Hills, the predominantly White institution (currently far more integrated with some 37.6 % of the students Hispanic American and 27.7 % African American) sitting on forty-five acres had state-of-the art facilities and vast resources that attracted quality teachers and coaches.[49]

With that said, Powles had some outstanding teams and players at Skyline but nothing like the prominent athletes he coached at McClymonds, some of whom would achieve great success at the collegiate and professional levels of sport and become, in some cases, household names. It would have been nearly impossible for him to duplicate at Skyline the enormous athletic success he realized at McClymonds, irrespective of the level of support and quantity and quality of resources provided him at his new institution. Importantly, Powles stepped away from his coaching duties at Skyline in 1972, retired in 1977, and died of a heart attack in 1987 at the age of seventy-seven. By the time of his untimely death, he had garnered much media attention and just about every honor and award that could be bestowed on a youth sport and high school coach. In addition to his selection to the California High School Coaches Hall of Fame in 1981, Powles was honored, for instance, in 1955 with a testimonial dinner by the 55 Club in Oakland "for his devotion to Eastbay high school athletics" and in 1967 the baseball field at Brookfield Recreation Center in Oakland was named after him.[50] In 1971, prominent author and sportswriter (and sometimes actor) Haywood Hale Broun did a special feature on the career accomplishments of Powles on CBS television, noting that the legendary coach had tutored Bill Russell, Frank Robinson, Vada Pinson, and Curt Flood. One viewer, President Richard Nixon, a longtime follower and lover of sport, was so impressed with what he had learned about Powles coaching prowess that he penned him a letter. "I know it must be a great source of pride to you and your school," wrote Nixon, "that these four fine athletes have so greatly benefited from your wisdom and teaching skills. As a Senator fan, I am pleased that now one of these stars, Curt Flood, is on 'our side.'"[51]

After Powles died, Skyline established a memorial fund in his honor and also named its baseball field the "George Powles Field."⁵² Further evidence of his lasting legacy is indicated by the fact that on January 15, 2006, nearly twenty years after his death, a special tribute for Powles titled "Safe at Home: Oaklanders Who Changed the Game" was held at the Oakland Museum of California.⁵³ Attended by many of his former athletes and their friends and family, Powles was once again feted for the "value of his teachings regarding sports and life."⁵⁴ Included among the attendees were Russell and Joe Morgan, the Castlemont High School star and future Hall of Fame second baseman who played for Powles in a high school all-star game. Russell used the occasion to reiterate how Powles "gave us [Black athletes] a sense of self-worth that it was ok to be ambitious, ok not to be afraid and really ok to find out how good you could be." Morgan, sounding a lot like Frank Robinson, noted, "He learned more in one week from George than at any other time in my entire career. He taught us how to win."⁵⁵

FROM IMPRESSIONABLE YOUNG ATHLETES TO PROUD BLACK MEN

The awards and honors aside, perhaps the most significant aspect of Powles' career was the close relationship and devotion he established with prominent Black athletes and the mutual respect and admiration they showed him. This connection was most visible with the relatively large number of great Black athletes he coached who became noteworthy not only for their outstanding performances on the field and court, but also for their social activism and involvement in the civil rights struggle. One of the distinguishing features of many of the Black athletes he coached was their participation in the civil rights movement and their willingness to speak out about racial inequality and discrimination. Bill Russell, who penned two insightful autobiographies, *Go Up for Glory* (1966) and *Second Wind: The Memoirs of an Opinionated Man* (1979), spent a lifetime fighting for racial justice.⁵⁶ In 1961, as a member of the Boston Celtics he led a protest of Black players who refused to play an exhibition game in Lexington, Kentucky, after being denied service at a local restaurant. In 1963 Russell participated in the March on Washington for Civil Rights and a few years later, along with other well-known Black athletes such as Jim Brown and Lew Alcindor (Kareem Abdul-Jabbar), came to the defense of Muhammad Ali after the great boxer refused to enter the military.⁵⁷ In 2011, while awarding him the Presidential Medal of Freedom, Barack Obama noted that Russell was "someone who stood up for the rights and dignity of all men."⁵⁸

Frank Robinson, who like his famous McClymonds High School basketball teammate was also a recipient of the Presidential Medal of Freedom spoke out vehemently about unfair housing and racially discriminatory real estate practices in Baltimore after joining the Orioles in 1966. A fierce competitor on the field who backed down from no one, Robinson was just as dogged in clamoring for head coaching positions and upper-level administrative positions in baseball and other sports.[59] Curt Flood, a three-time all-star, seven-time Gold Glove winner, and member of two World Series championship teams, sacrificed his long and lucrative career in 1969 by challenging baseball's reserve clause and refusing to be traded from the St. Louis Cardinals to the Philadelphia Phillies. He sued baseball but lost his case in the Supreme Court and by 1971 was permanently out of baseball. Four years later the reserve clause was struck down for good, in no small measure because of Flood's courageous stand against baseball, which most people, even those troubled by Flood's dismantling of baseball's status quo, would contend was the most influential legal challenge in the history of sport.[60] Tommy Harper spent a lifetime fighting racial inequality and social injustice. In a famous case in 1986, Harper filed suit against his former employer the Boston Red Sox, claiming he had been fired as a hitting instructor the previous season for speaking out against the club's policy of distributing passes to Whites only at the Elks Club in Winter Haven, Florida, where the team trained every spring. The US Equal Employment Opportunity Commission determined that the Red Sox "committed unlawful employment practices" by firing Harper and "created and perpetuated a working environment that was hostile to minorities." Ultimately, the suit was resolved out of court with Harper receiving an undisclosed settlement.[61]

Such activism begs the question: How did Powles respond to his former players becoming involved in the civil rights struggle and the fight for equality and justice? There is scant evidence to answer that question with any degree of certainty. Other than a comment he made in 1970 about Curt Flood being used by the player union's representative Marvin Miller in the case against baseball's reserve clause, there is no indication how Powles responded to the involvement of Russell, Robinson, and other Black athletes he had coached in the civil rights and Black Power movements.[62] Based, however, on his compassion, sense of fairness, awareness of racial matters, and positive relationships with and respect of those Black athletes he once coached, it is logical that Powles, while concerned about their personal safety as a result of their civil rights struggles, understood fully and appreciated their efforts to secure equal rights.

Powles himself, a humble White coach who had graciously opened his home to his players irrespective of race, provided instruction to athletes at Bushrod Park on a volunteer basis, orchestrated Curt Flood's transfer from McClymonds High School to Oakland Technical High School and helped secure a roster spot for Russell at the University of San Francisco after guiding the future Hall of Famer through his years at McClymonds, had always fought his own civil rights battles and stood up for his principles throughout his life. It was evident in 1959 when Powles brought his integrated Connie Mack team to St. Joseph, Missouri, to play for the national championship. Told by Connie Mack officials that the Black players on the team, which included Curt Motton, Tommy Harper, and Aaron Pointer, among others, would not be able to occupy the same hotel as their White teammates, Powles threatened to withdraw his team from the tournament unless all his players could stay together in the same facility. The Connie Mack officials eventually relented and all of Powles' players were allowed to stay in the same hotel during the tournament.[63] It was evident, moreover, when he came to the defense of Vada Pinson in 1962, who at the time was with the Cincinnati Reds. In June 1962, Pinson landed a punch to the chin of Earl Lawson, a sportswriter for *The Cincinnati Post* who had criticized the Reds for their lackadaisical play. Just the latest confrontation Lawson would have with Reds players over the years, *Sports Illustrated* was highly critical of Pinson's actions and Powles was not going to have any of it. In a letter published in the "19th Hole" section of the July 16 issue of the magazine, Powles took offense to *Sports Illustrated*'s portrayal of his former player. He made it very clear that Lawson should have been far more careful before heaping criticism on a player for a lack of courage or hustle, especially one like Pinson who was just coming off a three-year streak of consecutive games played. "A bad leg stopped his consecutive-game string," wrote Powles, "and, just after his return to the lineup, the people who still read Lawson were told that Vada was lackadaisical and was squandering his talent. It seems to me you all showed poor judgment in leaping to the defense of a writer who could be wrong."[64]

The support Powles showed Pinson and his other players never wavered. They all returned the favor by making clear that without Powles their lives would have been far different, some claiming they probably would have ended up on the wrong side of the law considering "the line between trouble and triumph in West Oakland was a thin one."[65] For Powles, keeping his athletes out of trouble was an important goal and probably reward enough, but the extraordinary accomplishments by many of them brought him much recognition, lasting fame, and personal satisfaction and pride.

For the youth of West Oakland, Powles' inability to realize his own dream of playing Major League Baseball would ultimately prove to be enormously beneficial to them. It provided them access to a coach who exhibited uncommon selflessness, a willingness to stay in the background, little interest in drawing attention to himself, and motivated by reasons other than fame. It gave them access to a coach with their best interests at heart, an open and inclusive approach, great communication skills, and the ability to capture championships while also teaching valuable life lessons. He was, by whatever standards are employed, a "builder of champions" a "star maker," and, as recently noted by sportswriter Howard Bryant, "became a household name as not only the beneficiary of insanely talented kids but as a white man who actually cared about them as people."[66] In the end, unlike some highly skilled athletes who become bitter and turn their back on a sport when not reaching that sport's highest pinnacle, Powles' inability to find a roster spot in Major League Baseball seemed to have just the opposite effect. He turned a personal failure into a lasting triumph by tackling a life in coaching with the same drive, energy, and determination that he exhibited in his quest to play at the highest level of America's National Pastime. He did so with the health and well-being of his athletes always uppermost in his mind. Ultimately, the middle child born to a railroader originally from Canada and bookkeeper with roots in Illinois represented the best kind of coach who inspired the youth of West Oakland and armed them with the necessary tools to realize their own dreams. He established a remarkable legacy that other coaches might do well to emulate, especially those genuinely interested in the welfare of their athletes as well as victories and championships.

Notes

The author would like to thank Paul Brekke-Miesner, Chris Elzey, Mark Dyreson, Dan Nathan, and Rob Ruck as well as the two anonymous reviewers for their cogent comments and suggestions on an earlier version of this essay.

1. Gilbert Rogin, "We Are Grown Men Playing a Child's Game," *Sports Illustrated*, November 18, 1963, accessed July 5, 2022, https://vault.si.com/vault/1963/11/18/we-are-grown-men-playing-a-childs-game.

2. John Hall, "Big A Cabaret," *Los Angeles Times*, May 18, 1972, accessed July 1, 2022, ProQuest Historical Newspapers.

3. Ryan Levi, "Remembering Frank Robinson and His Legendary West Oakland Teammates," *KQED*, February 10, 2019, accessed July 2, 2022, https://www.kqed.org

/news/11725053/remembering-frank-robinson-and-his-legendary-west-oakland-teammates.

4. Quoted in Brad Snyder, *A Well-Paid Slave: Curt Flood's Fight for Free Agency in Professional Sports* (New York: Plume, 2007), 342.

5. Art Rosenbaum, "Builder of Champions," *San Francisco Examiner*, September 29, 1968, 112; *Oakland Tribune*, May 7, 1958, 43.

6. James Schermerhorn, "George Powles," *San Francisco Examiner*, October 8, 1987, 28; Scott Strain, "Standout Coach Powles Dead at 77," *Oakland Tribune*, October 2, 1987, 65; "Powles Legacy Transcended Sports," *Eastbay Times*, January 13, 2006, accessed July 2, 2022, https://www.eastbaytimes.com/2006/01/13/powles-legacy-transcended-sports/.

7. Jim Murray, "Emperor's Waltz," *Los Angeles Times*, April 21, 1963, C1.

8. See Bill Nowlin, "Willie Tasby, Society for American Baseball Research," accessed January 11, 2023, https://sabr.org/bioproj/person/willie-tasby/; Malcolm Allen, "Charlie Beamon," Society for American Baseball Research, accessed January 11, 2023, https://sabr.org/bioproj/person/charlie-beamon/; David E. Skelton, "Jesse Gonder," Society for American Baseball Research, accessed January 11, 2023, https://sabr.org/bioproj/person/jesse-gonder/; "Aaron Pointer," Baseball Reference, accessed January 11, 2023, https://www.baseball-reference.com/players/p/pointaa01.shtml.

9. Frank Robinson dedicated his autobiography, written with Al Silverman, to his family as well as Powles. It reads "For my wife Barbara, Frank Kevin, Nichelle, and my mother, brothers, and sisters . . . and to George Powles and everyone else who helped me so much along the way." See Frank Robinson with Al Silverman, *My Life is Baseball* (New York: Doubleday & Company, 1968).

10. John Wesley Noble, "The Coach Nobody Wanted," *Saturday Evening Post*, May 10, 1958, 116.

11. Phone Interview with Paul Brekke-Miesner, January 2, 2023.

12. See Steve Treder, "Out of Oakland," *The Hardball Times*, November 21, 2006, accessed July 5, 2022, https://tht.fangraphs.com/out-of-oakland/.

13. See 1900, 1910, and 1920 US Federal Census for Percy W. Powles; 1920 US Federal Census for Elizabeth Powles; US World War I Draft Registration Cards, 1917–1918 for Percy Watts Powles; US World War II Draft Registration Cards, 1942 for Percy Walter Powles; Registration Card, US, World War II Draft Cards Young Men, 1940–1947 for George Beverly Powles; 1920 and 1930 United States Federal Census for George B. Powles. I am indebted to Chris Elzey for accessing this information for me through Ancestry. Library Edition, Library of Congress (LOC).

14. Frank Trower, "Lowell Beats University in Opening Game," *Oakland Tribune*, August 28, 1927, 32.

15. See US World War II Draft Cards Young Men, 1940–1947 for George Beverly Powles, LOC.

16. George Powles, "Flashback of Youngster Haunts Ex-Infantryman," *Oakland Tribune*, May 7, 1985, 1.

17. The census uses term Negro. I have replaced it with Black. The other listing in the 1940 census was nonwhite with a percentage of 1.9. The other listings in the 1950 census were Indian with a percentage of 0.0, Japanese with a percentage of 0.3, and Chinese with a percentage of 1.4. The other listings in the 1960 census were Indian with a percentage of 0.3, Japanese with a percentage of 0.6, Chinese with a percentage of 2.1, and Filipino with a percentage of 0.5. Bay Area Census, accessed July 8, 2022, www.bayareacensus.ca.gov/cities/oakland50.htm; Steve Treder, "Out of Oakland."

18. Aram Goudsouzian, *King of the Court: Bill Russell and the Basketball Revolution* (Berkeley: University of California Press, 2010), 11.

19. For segregation in Oakland in the post–World War II period, see Robert O. Self, *American Babylon: Race and the Struggle for Postwar Oakland* (Princeton, NJ: Princeton University Press, 2004).

20. Curt Flood Interview, November 16, 1984, Black Champions Series, Washington University Film & Media Archive, accessed August 9, 2022, repository.wustl.edu/concern/videos/k35698124.

21. The US Congress discussed in detail the possible effects that comic books, with depictions of crime and horror, were having on the juvenile delinquency of young children. See "Comic Books and Juvenile Delinquency." Interim Report. US Congress. Senate Committee on the Judiciary Pursuant to S. Res. 89 and S. Res.190, March 14. 1955, accessed August 12, 2022, https://web.archive.org/web/20091027160127/ and http://www.Geocities.com/Athens/8580/Kefauver.html. For additional works on juvenile delinquency during the 1950s, see Jason Barnosky, "The Violent Years: Responses to Juvenile Crime in the 1950s," *Polity*, 38:3 (2006), 314–344; Steven Mintz, *Huck's Raft: A History of American Childhood* (Cambridge, MA: Harvard University Press, 2004); and Herman H. Remmers and Don H. Radler, *The American Teenager* (New York: The Bobbs-Merrill Company, 1957).

22. Michael H. Carriere, "'A Diamond Is a Boys Best Friend': The Rise of Little League Baseball, 1939–1964," *Journal of Sport History*, 32:3 (2005), 351–378.

23. Noble, "The Coach Nobody Wanted," 116.

24. Noble, "The Coach Nobody Wanted," 117.

25. Snyder, *A Well-Paid Slave*, 35.

26. Noble, "The Coach Nobody Wanted," p. 118; Joe Capozzi, "J.W. Porter: 'Court Jester of Roger Dean Stadium' Mourned as 'A Sweet Soul'" October 13, 2020, accessed July 5, 2022, https://www.palmbeachpost.com/story/sports/2020/10/13/j-w-porter-former-major-league-baseball-player-dies-jupiter/3640974001/.

27. Quoted from Levi, "Remembering Frank Robinson and His Legendary West Oakland Teammates."

28. Noble, "The Coach Nobody Wanted," 116.

29. Ed Levitt, "George Powles," *Oakland Tribune*, January 19, 1981, C-12.

30. Ibid.

31. Ibid.

32. Quoted in Snyder, *A Well-Paid Slave*, 36.

33. "Local All-Stars in Ruth Playoff," *Oakland Tribune*, August 4, 1954, accessed July 9, 2022, https://www.newspapers.com/image/277359656.

34. See Treder, "Out of Oakland" and Paul Brekke-Miesner, *Home Field Advantage: Oakland, CA, The City that Changed the Face of Sports* (Oakland: Paul Brekke-Miesner, 2013).

35. Quoted in Snyder, *A Well-Paid Slave*, 39. See also, "Geo. Powles Inks Pact as Redleg Scout," *Oakland Tribune*, June 8, 1958, accessed July 9, 2022, https://www.newspapers.com/image/331933345.

36. "High School of Champions: McClymonds of Oakland, California," *Ebony*, 18 (April 1963), 25–28, 30, 32.

37. Noble, "The Coach Nobody Wanted," 116.

38. Snyder, *A Well-Paid Slave*, 37.

39. For information on these players, see: Treder, "Out of Oakland;" John Simmonds, "Big Leagues Find Stars at McClymonds," *Oakland Tribune*, June 27, 1961, 36; "Beamon, Mack Hurler, Joins Oakland Camp," *Oakland Tribune*, January 7, 1953, 30; Arthur Siegel, "Tasby Remembers Russell When Bill Stood Only 5–10," *Boston Globe*, July 13, 1960, 43; Alan McAllaster, "Pointer Aims for Big Loop Stardom," *Oakland Tribune*, September 3, 1961, 17.

40. See *Oakland Post*, "McClymonds' Warriors Were Dubbed the Original Golden Champions," *Post News Group*, August 3, 2017, accessed January 11, 2023, https://www.postnewsgroup.com/49504/; Harvey Araton, "Paul Silas, N.B.A. Defensive Star and Head Coach Dies at 79," *The New York Times*, December 11, 2022, accessed January 11, 2023, https://www.nytimes.com/2022/12/11/obituaries/paul-silas-dead.html; Eileen Mitchell, "Giving Back to the Game," *SFGate*, April 26, 2013, accessed January 11, 2023, https://www.sfgate.com/warriors/article/giving-back-to-the-game-4468366.php; Ronnie Flores, "Boys BB: All-Time Regional POYs," *CalHiSports.com*, accessed January 11, 2023, https://www.calhisports.com/2019/03/02/boys-bb-all-time-regional-poys/.

41. See "High School of Champions."

42. See, for example, Arthur Daley, "Sports of the Times: How High is Up?," *New York Times*, December 28, 1955, accessed July 6, 2022, ProQuest Historical Newspapers; "Bill Russell, Mr. Basketball," *Chicago Defender*, April 29, 1963, accessed July 6, 2022, ProQuest Historical Newspapers; Steven Lavoie, "McClymonds: 'School of Champions,'" *Oakland Tribune*, February 28, 1993, 22; Bill Russell, "We Are Nothing Without Our Mentors," *USA Today Sports*, January 21, 2016, accessed July 6, 2022, https://www.usatoday.com/story/sports/nba/2016/01/20/bill-russell-boston-celtics-mentor/79057628/; "Two MVPs Who Were Calif Teammates," *CalHiSports.com*, accessed July 6, 2022, https://www.calhisports.com/2020/12/11/two-mvps-who-were-calif-teammates/; Murray, "Emperor's Waltz;" Rogin, "We Are Grown Men Playing a Child's Game."

43. Bill Russell as told to Al Hirshberg, "I Was a 6' 9" Babe in the Woods," *Saturday Evening Post*, January 18, 1958, 66–68.

44. Noble, "The Coach Nobody Wanted," 118.
45. Russell, "We Are Nothing Without Our Mentors."
46. Ibid.
47. Strain, "Standout Coach Powles Dead at 77," 65.
48. Ibid.
49. See Katie Ferrari, "McClymonds High School Closed as Toxins and Gentrification Intersect," *Majority*, March 7, 2020, accessed August 12, 2022; https://eastbaymajority.com/mcclymonds-closure-toxins-racism-ousd-history/; "Then & Now-Oakland Public Schools-No.19," *A Bit of History*, accessed August 12, 2022, https://abitofhistory.site/2020/03/10/then-now-Oakland-public-schools-no-19/.
50. Quoted in "Capacity Crowd of 300 Looms for Dinner Honoring Powles," *Oakland Tribune*, October 21, 1955, 61. See Also: "Dinner for George Powles?" *Oakland Tribune*, September 19, 1955, 36; "George Powles Honored By 55 Club at Dinner," *Oakland Tribune*, November 1, 1955, 37; "Man to Remember: Ball Park Honors Powles," *Oakland Tribune*, September 5, 1967, 19.
51. *Oakland Tribune*, April 20, 1971, 15; "President Joins Powles Fan Club," *Oakland Tribune*, April 24, 1971, 9. Broun did a regular 5-minute segment Saturday nights on CBS featuring various stories on sport. They included more nationally known stories such as the Muhammad Ali and Joe Frazier fights and the rivalry between Bill Russell and Wilt Chamberlain as well as profiles on less prominent sports-related stories such as the national marbles championships in Wildwood, New Jersey and a rodeo clown in Cheyenne, Wyoming. In 2002 *ESPN Classic* developed a show featuring Broun's stories titled *Woodie's World*. See Broun's obituary by Richard Goldstein, "Heywood Hale Broun, 83, A Writer with Flair," *New York Times*, September 7, 2001, accessed August 12, 2022, https://nytimes.com/2001/09/07/sports/heywood-hale-broun-83-a-writer-with-flair.html.
52. "Skyline Establishes Powles Memorial Fund," *Oakland Tribune*, November 14, 1987, 36.
53. John Shea, "Teaching the Stuff of Legends/Late Oakland Coach Feted at Museum," *SFGate*, January 16, 2006, accessed July 6, 2022, https://www.sfgate.com/sports/shea/article/teaching-the-stuff-of-legends-late-oakland-2506626.php.
54. Ibid.
55. Ibid.
56. Bill Russell with William McSweeney, *Go Up for Glory* (New York: Coward-McCann, 1966); Bill Russell with Taylor Branch, *Second Wind: The Memoirs of an Opinionated Man* (New York: Random House, 1979).
57. For further insights into Russell's life and career, see Maureen M. Smith, "Pioneer and Champion of the Sixties," in *Out of the Shadows: A Biographical History of African American Athletes*, ed. David K. Wiggins (Fayetteville, Arkansas: The University of Arkansas Press, 2006), 223–239; Goudsouzian, *King of the Court*.
58. Jim Fenton, "Celtics' Russell Stands Tall Again in White House Presentation,"

Enterprise News, February 16, 2011, https://www.enterprisenews.com/story/sports/pro/2011/02/16/celtics-russell-stands-tall-again/40018631007/

59. For information on Robinson, see: Frank Robinson with Al Silverman, *My Life Is Baseball* (New York: Doubleday, 1968).

60. Snyder, *A Well-Paid Slave*; Curt Flood with Richard Carter, *The Way It Is* (New York: Trident Press, 1971).

61. Bill Newton, "Tommy Harper," Society for American Baseball Research, accessed July 9, 2022, https://sabr.org/bioproj/person/tommy-harper/; Jim Rattray, "Former Boston Red Sox Player and Coach Tommy Harper . . ." *UPI Archives*, January 30, 1986, accessed July 9, 2022, https://www.upi.com/Archives/1986/01/30/former-boston-red-sox-player-and-coach-tommy-harper/7524057230540/.

62. See Ed Levitt, "Curt Sues Savior," *Oakland Tribune*, March 8, 1970, 23.

63. "George Powles: The Coach Who Saw Through Time," *Newark Unitarian Universalism Examiner*, 26 October 2010, accessed July 9, 2022, www.thewritetrackinc.com/101026_George_Powles.pdf.

64. George Powles, "Iced Punch," *Sports Illustrated*, July 16, 1962, accessed July 9, 2022, https://vault.si.com/vault/1962/07/16/19th-hole-the-readers-take-over.

65. Quoted in Snyder, *A Well-Paid Slave*, 34.

66. Howard Bryant, *Rickey: The Life and Legend of An American Original* (New York: Mariner Books, 2022), 13.

7

VINCE MATTHEWS, WAYNE COLLETT, AND THE FORGOTTEN DISRUPTION IN MUNICH

"I knew Wayne and I were doing something out of the ordinary—from not facing the flag to not standing at attention" wrote Vince Matthews in his insightful yet little-known autobiography, *My Race Be Won*. "I knew where the flag was, but it didn't make any difference where the flag was. To me, it wasn't that I was turning my back on the American flag."[1] What Matthews referred to in the above-mentioned quotation was the controversial behavior he and his teammate Wayne Collett displayed on the victory stand following their medal-winning finishes in the 400-meters at the 1972 Summer Olympics in Munich. With Collett, the silver medalist, joining Matthews, winner of the gold medal, on the top platform of the victory stand at Matthews's request, the two African American athletes turned their backs to the American flag, chatted, and stood casually with hands on hips as the American national anthem was played. Matthews also rubbed his chin and appeared to scowl. As the two athletes stepped off the platform and made their way out of the stadium, Matthews spun the gold medal around his finger while Collett quickly flashed what seemingly was a Black Power salute. For their actions, many in the 80,000-seat Olympic Stadium met Matthews and Collett with "boos, whistles, and catcalls," and shortly thereafter they were kicked out of the Olympic games for life by the International Olympic Committee (IOC) for their violation of Olympic protocol.[2]

The Matthews and Collett display on the victory stand in Munich, while eliciting much anger from spectators in the Olympic Stadium and immediate media coverage from both the Black and White press, has received relatively little attention from scholars and others interested in Olympic history. With the notable exception of Matthews's compelling and thoughtful autobiography itself and coverage of the episode by Douglas Hartmann in his analysis of the Black athletic revolt, no extended examination has been completed on the Matthews and Collett incident and its aftermath.[3] This essay addresses that fact by focusing on four basic questions: First, what did Matthews and Collett expect to accomplish by refusing to adhere to accepted forms of behavior on the victory stand in Munich? Second, why did fans generally react so angrily? Third, why did the IOC believe it necessary to ban the two athletes from the Olympic games for life? Finally, why has the Matthews and Collett episode in Munich drawn such limited scholarly attention and not resonated more firmly in the public consciousness? Answering these questions can provide a deeper understanding of the incident and its place in Olympic history, sport more broadly, and the larger Black protest movement.

TWO ATHLETES FROM WORLDS APART

The track and field careers of Matthews and Collett were truly outstanding. Their family backgrounds, educational attainments, and personalities were, however, worlds apart in several different ways. Collett was a native of Los Angeles, starting his competitive track career at the age of fourteen and then finding his way to Gardena High School and later UCLA where he competed for the legendary coach Jim Bush. A specialist in the 400-meters but also excellent in the hurdles, sprints, and relays, Collett captured numerous PAC-8 titles and anchored three NCAA championship relay teams. His abilities were such that Bush called him the "greatest athlete he ever coached."[4] He was also an outstanding student, taking an undergraduate degree in political science and then later a master in Business Administration degree and a Juris Doctorate. Following his career in track and field, Collett practiced law and worked in real estate and mortgage finance in

Los Angeles before succumbing, after a prolonged illness, to cancer in 2010 at the age of 60.[5]

Matthews, on the other hand, was born in Queens, New York, to an African American mother and father from the West Indies. He excelled as a sprinter very early on, first at Shimer Junior High School, then later at P.S. 59 and Andrew Jackson High School, where he ran under the tutelage of coach Milton Blatt. Competing for Jackson during the regular school year and for the well-known New York Pioneer Club in the summer, Matthews became one of the nation's outstanding 400-meter runners by capturing titles in such prestigious meets as those sponsored by the New York Public School Athletic League and in the Penn Relays, the famous track carnival held at Franklin Field in Philadelphia sometimes referred to as "The Negro Olympics." Unlike Collett's academic career, Matthews's performance in the classroom did not match his accomplishments on the track. He struggled as a student, having to extend his time at Jackson to earn his high school diploma. Following high school graduation, Matthews continued his education and track career at Johnson C. Smith College, a small historically Black institution in Charlotte, North Carolina, that out recruited other HBCUs for his services, including North Carolina College, which was coached at the time by Leroy Walker, who had the distinction in 1976 of becoming the first African American Olympic head track and field coach. Matthews had an outstanding track and field career at Johnson C. Smith, one that would help prepare him for his Olympic triumphs and eventual selection into the National Track and Field Hall of Fame. His post-track and field career, while not especially well-known, would be decidedly different than Collett's, as he apparently did some coaching and worked several years for the Neighborhood Youth Corps in New York City.[6]

Although Matthews and Collett grew up nearly 3,000 miles apart and had decidedly different educational backgrounds, interests, and skills off the track, they were both impacted by the Black athletic revolt. As young African American athletes in track and field, they could not have failed to be influenced by the proposed boycott of the 1968 Summer Olympic games in Mexico City. The boycott, which was led by Harry Edwards, an instructor of sociology at San Jose College at the time, largely consisted of a group of young African American Olympic hopefuls whom Edwards had organized under the name Olympic Project for Human Rights (OPHR). Designed to publicize racial discrimination in the United States and around the world, the OPHR achieved initial success in February 1968 by throwing into disarray the one-hundredth anniversary track and field meet of the New York Athletic Club because of that organization's racist policies. The OPHR's next target was the upcoming Olympic games, to be held in Mexico City, which the group threatened to boycott unless certain demands were met. Among those demands were the restoration of Muhammad Ali's heavyweight title, which had been stripped because of his refusal to enter military service; the inclusion of more African American coaches on the US Olympic team; barring South Africa and Rhodesia from Olympic competition because of their apartheid policies; and the ouster of Avery Brundage as president of the IOC because of his alleged racist views. Ultimately, Edwards and the OPHR chose not to boycott the 1968 Summer Olympic games, electing instead to encourage athletes to protest as they saw fit.[7]

Some athletes willingly complied. Although a few African American athletes decided not to participate in the games for various reasons, perhaps most notably Lew Alcindor (now Kareem Abdul-Jabbar), several Black Olympians disrupted medal ceremonies, garnering various levels of media attention and public outcry. Easily the most famous protest was the Black Power salutes of Tommie Smith and John Carlos on the victory stand following their respective first and third-place finishes in the 200 meters. The two great sprinters from San Jose State, in an event that has been recounted many times over and still resonates with people to the present day, startled the world by bowing their heads and raising their black-gloved fists high into the sky as the "Star-Spangled Banner" was played. Angry fans booed and unleashed a torrent of catcalls as Smith and Carlos descended the platform. The United States Olympic Committee, under intense pressure from the IOC, ultimately kicked the two out of the Olympic village and sent them home.[8]

Lesser-known violations of Olympic protocol by other African American athletes also took place during medal ceremonies in Mexico City. They were, however, far more subdued and reverential than the Smith and Carlos protest as athletes had been warned by the IOC that any more disruptions during medal ceremonies would be cause for removal from the games. Unlike with Smith and Carlos, they were not punished, nor were any sent home. For instance, Bob Beamon, who shattered the world long jump record in Mexico City and set a mark that would stand for twenty-three years, stood barefoot with his pants rolled up to expose his black socks during his medal ceremony to protest racism in America and show support for his teammates. Lee Evans, Larry James, and Ron Freeman, who captured all three medals in the 400-meter run, wore black berets, which were not part of the official uniform for American Olympians, and raised their fists to the crowd as they ascended the victory platform, but removed the berets and stood upright and stared solemnly at the American flag as the national anthem was played. Finally, Evans, James, and Freeman, along with Matthews, would take a similar approach on the victory stand to receive their gold medals for the 4x400-meter relay by wearing black berets and raising their fists to the crowd but doffing the berets and staring at the American flag as they stood at attention during the playing of the national anthem.[9]

FROM CHEERS TO CATCALLS TO EXPULSION

It is likely Matthews had no idea while on the victory stand in Mexico City that he would experience another Olympic medal ceremony. Yet that is exactly what happened four years later, and it would be life-altering. After Mexico City, Matthews, who by that time was married, struggled to find employment and make ends meet. Among his many experiences was a brief tryout with the Washington Redskins football team, working for the J. C. Penny department store, serving as the payroll coordinator for Youth Corps, and being a member of the Army reserves before being discharged on account of a bleeding ulcer. He would eventually get himself in top physical condition, however, so as to compete for gold in the 400-meter run at the upcoming games in Munich, an Olympic festival in which the organizers, ironically enough, had done everything possible to avoid the politics that permeated the famous 1936 Summer Olympics in Berlin. He would be joined in the quest by a trio of men considered some of the best 400-meter runners in history. In addition to Collett, Matthews faced stiff competition from John Smith, favored by many to win the event in Munich. Smith, another quarter miler from UCLA who had been trained by Jim Bush, along with Collett, helped the Bruins capture four consecutive NCAA titles in the 4x440-yard relay. In 1971, Smith broke the world record in the 440 yards with a time of 44.5 at the Outdoor Track and Field Championships in Eugene, Oregon. Also expected to be a formidable challenger in Munich was Evans, the outstanding runner from San Jose State who won the 400-meter race in Mexico City in world record time.[10]

Based on this number of extraordinarily talented athletes, it was difficult to predict who would capture gold in the 400-meter race in Munich in 1972. With Evans finishing fourth in the Olympic trials, he did not qualify for the games in the 400-meters race (though he did qualify for the 4x400 relay team), so it was left to Smith, Matthews, and Collett to represent the United States in the event. Ultimately, it came down to Matthews and Collett competing for gold because, a few seconds into the finals, Smith was forced to stop because of a persistent hamstring injury. Matthews, running one of the best races of his life, crossed the finish line first in 44.66 seconds, followed by Collett in 44.80 seconds, and Julius Sang of Kenya in third, twelve one-hundredths of a second behind Collett. Immediately following the event, the victors received the usual cheers from the crowd of 80,000 in the Olympic Stadium.[11]

The cheers, however, would quickly turn to boos and catcalls after witnessing Matthews and Collett's victory stand debacle. The two athletes, Collett going bare foot and donning shorts and Matthews with his Olympic jacket unzipped and wearing a gray sweatshirt over his "USA" jersey, violated Olympic protocol by turning their backs on the American flag, standing with hands on hips and chatting while alternately shifting from one foot to the other during the playing of the national anthem. As previously noted, as they stepped off the platform and walked out of the stadium, Collett swung his gold medal around his finger and Collett gave a quick Black Power salute. The lackadaisical and bodily deportment shown by Collett and Matthews on the victory stand and immediately following caused not only instant condemnation from the crowd but also their own families, the press, and Olympic officials. Matthews noted that his wife Dianne and mother were both angered by his refusal to stand at attention and "had tears in their eyes" following the incident. "You should have stood at attention," Matthews's mother said. "You were on top of the world. Now you've knocked yourself down from being on top of the world." Collett's parents were also distraught over the incident, although he noted that his mother "was upset, mainly because it bothered her that eighty thousand people were booing me" and that his father respected him for "having that much courage to do something that I believed in."[12]

Soon thereafter, Jesse Owens, the famous sprinter who made history by capturing four gold medals in the 1936 Summer Olympics and had desperately attempted to keep African American athletes from protesting in Mexico City four years earlier in his role as "athlete's representative" for the United States Olympic Committee (USOC), approached Matthews and Collett and asked that they apologize for their behavior during the medal ceremony. After both athletes refused his request, Owens "tried another sales pitch" by telling Matthews and Collett if they did not show remorse they ran the risk of losing out on the increasing number of jobs being offered to African Americans by large corporations. Again, the two athletes shunned Owen's overture, with Matthews telling the hero of the 1936 Summer Olympics "That all sounds nice . . . but how come you never came to us before? None of your so-called large companies stepped forward for all the other Black athletes after other Olympic Games."[13] Shortly after their heated conversation with Owens, Matthews and Collett met with USOC committee members who read them a letter from Avery Brundage that stated in part: "The whole world saw the disgusting display of your [USOC] two athletes, when they received their gold and silver medals for the 400 m. event yesterday . . . it is the Executive Board's opinion that these two athletes have broken rule 26, paragraph 1 in respect of the traditional Olympic spirit and ethic and are, therefore, eliminated from taking part in any future Olympic competition."[14]

The Matthews and Collett episode lead to questions as to why the two African American athletes took the approach they did during the medal ceremony and why their actions elicited such vitriol. As to the first question, there was seemingly no clear strategy or carefully designed plans or explicit rationale articulated by Matthews and Collett as to why they disrupted the medal ceremony in Munich. Both men went out of their way to indicate that what they did was no protest but were not as straightforward about their intent in behaving the way they did on the victory stand. Their limited comments to the press and others following the incident were often just as murky as the body language they displayed during the medal ceremony in Munich. They did indicate that they were frustrated by the treatment of African Americans in the United States and could not in good conscience as proud Black men stand at attention and stare solemnly at the American flag during the playing of the national anthem. "It wasn't a protest," claimed Collett, the more reserved of the two men who seemingly never wavered from the comments he made to *Sports Illustrated* writer and friend Anita Verschoth that the Olympic games was never something he would talk to his children about (or few other people for that matter). "It was just me standing up there for the national anthem, and I couldn't stand there and sing the words because I don't believe they're true. I wish they were."[15] For Matthews's part, his lackadaisical attitude during the medal ceremony was not only indicative of his continued disillusionment with race relations in the United States but was perhaps emblematic of his frustration with almost everything, from unsympathetic US track and field coaches and outmoded notions of amateurism to inadequate drug testing and dishonorable shoe companies. Matthews's display on the medal stand, however ambivalent and different from Smith and Carlos's Black Power salute in 1968, was also evidently an effort to address what he believed had been a misguided decision to stand at attention during the medal ceremony for the 4x400 meter relay in Mexico City. "After 1968, I wasn't able to justify to myself everything I did on the victory stand," wrote Matthews. "I always considered what we did a token gesture. I figured that in '72, I would stand there, not at attention, just nonchalantly."[16]

DISRUPTION ON THE MEDAL STAND THE ULTIMATE SIN

Irrespective of why Matthews and Collett assumed the attitude they did during the medal ceremony, it seems remarkable now how swiftly Olympic officials meted out punishment to the two medal winners and how much hostility they experienced as a result of their actions. Perhaps one way to account for such outrage is to use the theory of ritual disruption advanced by religious studies scholar Kathryn T. McClymond in *Ritual Gone Wrong: What We Learn from Ritual Disruption* (2016). Utilizing the theory of myths espoused by Roland Barthes, David Freedberg's work on consecration, and insights from other scholars, McClymond's analyzes what she refers to as "misperformances" of Olympic ritual and uses numerous examples in support of her arguments. Although only mentioning the Matthews and Collett episode in a chapter footnote, McClymond's analysis provides a framework that perhaps helps us better understand why the two athletes were quickly banished from the games and viewed by many with contempt.[17]

In her analysis, McClymond's leans heavily on Barthes, who contends that myths are communicated in a variety of forms rather than just through language and that they consist of three key ingredients: the signifier, the signified, and the sign. The signifier, according to Barthes, is a tangible form that conveys the signified, which is typically an abstract idea. When the signifier and signified are joined it is the sign. Barthes gives as an example, according to McClymond, how a rose is typically used as a signifier to represent the signified, which, in this case, is the abstract idea of passionate love. Important in Barthes' conception of myths, the signifier "empties itself" of all elements that do not successfully convey what is being signified. Regarding the rose as a signifier, its specific identity—origins and various parts, such as petals—are "emptied" and made irrelevant as it takes on the physical representation of the abstract idea of passionate love—or, in other words, that which is being signified. Regarding the Olympics, victorious athletes during carefully crafted and choreographed medal ceremonies, which first appeared in its present form at the 1932 Winter Olympics (Lake Placid) and Summer Olympics (Los Angeles), serve as signifiers who are expected to "empty" themselves of any personal identity devoid of any historical or political constructions so as to accurately signify the great Olympic myth of universality and international cooperation and sacredness of the hallowed games. The expectation is that victorious athletes will fulfill their roles as signifiers of Olympism by conveying notions of conviction rather than ambiguity during the highly scripted ritual that is the medal ceremony. This means that for victorious athletes to successfully signify Olympism, they must follow very carefully the prescribed code of behavior expected during the medal ceremony by solemnly standing at attention with eyes on the flag during the playing of the gold medalists' national anthem. When an athlete does not cooperate and fulfill their expected ritualized role by "refusing to deploy one's body appropriately in the Olympic victory ceremony," notes McClymond, "one has, in effect, rejected Olympism." The result for not conducting oneself in the specified manner on the victory stand has typically resulted in rebukes from Olympic officials and visible scorn and disappointment from fans and other observers who feel cheated by rebellious athletes who fail to sanctify the Olympic myth. In essence, the Olympic medal ceremony is the ritual act of consecration in which athletes realize sacred status and, when they refuse to participate in or mis-perform the ritual act, audiences (fans, spectators, and other observers) feel "rejected, ignored, or dismissed."[18]

Based on McClymond's analysis, it is not surprising Matthews and Collett were removed from the Munich Olympic games and received such negative press coverage and vitriol. The two African American athletes may have contended that what they did on the medal stand was no protest, but they were, as Olympians, signifiers of an Olympic myth that was culturally yet flimsily constructed because of its fallibility and conditional nature. However, it is impossible to fully assess the Matthews and Collett incident without also viewing it through the prism of race and recognizing that throughout history Black athletes have always been permitted far less room to diverge from social norms than their White counterparts.[19] It should be remembered that the "mis-performance" on the victory stand in Munich was a bodily mis-performance by Black men, and as such underscored the negative ramifications associated with deep-seated racial stereotypes permeating American culture. In describing the incident, contemporary commentators often compared it unfavorably to the Smith and Carlos Black Power protest from 1968.

SMITH AND CARLOS: FOREVER THE BENCHMARKS

While the Black Power display of Smith and Carlos was a deliberate attempt to draw attention to the civil rights struggle in the United States, the intent of Matthews and Collett's actions during the medal ceremony was difficult to discern, and the two athletes made little attempt to explain it, other than to express the importance of making amends for previous behavior and not being able in good conscious to stand at attention during the victory stand celebration. The ambiguity of their bodily display as well as their rather limited commentary afterward angered many White and some Black journalists. They viewed Matthews and Collett's victory stand display as nothing more than a selfish and careless act by two ungrateful African American athletes with agendas known only to them. Noted sportswriter Red Smith of the *New York Times* voiced his displeasure of Matthews and Collett's actions and used the Black Power salute in 1968 as a basis of comparison when he wrote that in contrast to the "honest gesture of protest against injustice" waged by Smith and Carlos, the performance of Matthews and Collett was "simply a slovenly exhibition of bad manners." Legendary sportswriter Shirley Povich of *The Washington Post* expressed a similar view when he wrote that the display of Matthews and Collett "was, at worst, a chicken protest. The things Matthews and Collett did were not in the same league with, and lacked the boldness and grace of, the Black Power protest by Tommie Smith and John Carlos with their resolute, raised-fist show at the Mexico City Games in 1968." A. S. "Doc" Young, longtime sportswriter of the prominent Black weekly, the *Chicago Daily Defender*, and always a firm believer in the power of sport to break down racial barriers, was terribly disappointed by the behavior of Matthews and Collett. As representatives of the U.S.A.," wrote Young, "Matthews and Collett had no right whatsoever to alter the rules to which the American team was committed. If they did it unintentionally, then they should have had the class to apologize."[20]

In echoing criticism of Matthews and Collett, some observers trotted out commonly used racial tropes meant to further disparage the actions of the two African American athletes. One classic example of this was the assessment made by Erich Segal, educator, author and screenwriter who covered the Olympic marathon in 1972 and 1976 as a color commentator for ABC television. "Along with Jim Ryun's fall," wrote Segal in a 1972 edition of the *New York Times*, "Vince Matthews and Wayne Collett are the athletic sad points of the games. They were the gold and silver medalists in the 400 meters who *jived* (my italics for emphasis) disrespectfully on the victory stand as the US National (*sic*) anthem was played, and as millions watched around the world, their behavior became a major issue."[21] For other White commentators, the word of choice to describe the display of Matthews and Collett was not "jive" but "shuffling" and it was certainly not lost on Matthews. "The fact that some of the newsmen said I was shuffling represented a racial slur to me," wrote Matthews, "because the only people that shuffle in America in their minds are blacks. If I were Chinese, I don't think they would have said I was shuffling. If I were an Eskimo, I don't think I would have been shuffling."[22]

Although certainly not uniform in their assessment of Matthews and Collett's display on the victory stand, many observers, even those appalled by the actions of the two athletes, believed their expulsion from the Olympic games was unduly harsh and unwarranted. In essence, some chroniclers of the 1972 Summer Olympics, irrespective of color, contended that the punishment meted out to Matthews and Collett were not commensurate with their supposed crime. To Norman O. Unger of the *Chicago Daily Defender*, a "dual standard" had been applied. Matthews and Collett, in Unger's opinion, were unfairly ousted from the Olympic games, while Dave Wottle, a White distance runner who won the 800 meters in Munich, suffered no punishment for wearing a white baseball cap during the medal presentation ceremony. (Wottle apologized afterward. As was his usual practice, he had run the race wearing the hat and had simply forgotten to take it off for the ceremony).[23] The NAACP noted, "We decry the willingness of the Olympic officials to ignore the understandable personal ambitions and desires of our young people, both white and black, who have devoted themselves to their personal and physical development. Expulsion from competitive activity and confiscation of awards are gross impositions on fine young people for what, at most, are minor offenses, if they are offenses at all."[24]

Fellow athletes and other members of the US Olympic Team were generally silent on the matter. There were, however, exceptions. Kenny Moore, University of Oregon distance runner who finished fourth in the marathon in Munich, came to the defense of Matthews and Collett and was very pointed about his feelings toward Olympic officials who had penalized the two African American athletes. "I'm just sick over this" (Matthews and

Collett episode), noted Moore. "If I had a choice, I'd like to run in a white shirt with only my name on it. A lot of people on the American team feel that way."[25] Bill Bowerman, Moore's mentor at the University of Oregon and the 1972 Olympic track and field coach, argued that they were not fairly treated, albeit an opinion undoubtedly impacted by his frustration that the ouster of Matthews and Collett, along with John Smith's hamstrung injury, forced the United States to scratch its team from the 1,600-meter relay. "You cannot expect an Olympic squad of sixty to have everybody act like an Army private," said Bowerman in referring to Matthews and Collett. "They're great athletes. They're great individuals."[26]

With all the press coverage paid to the Matthews and Collett episode at the time it occurred, it is instructive how quickly it faded from public memory and how few scholars have taken up the topic. Could it be that it has been overshadowed by the abundance of other bizarre and horrific events that took place during the Olympic games in Munich? Although the games in 1972 witnessed such great athletic performances as Frank Shorter's triumph in the marathon, the victories of the Soviet Union's Valerie Borzov in both the 100 and 200 meters, the capturing of seven gold medals in swimming by Mark Spitz, and the three gold medals garnered by the Soviet Union's Olga Korbut in gymnastics, the Olympic games in Munich were marred by unforeseen tragedy, mistakes and controversy. Sprinters Rey Robinson and Eddie Hart of the United States, for instance, suffered one of the worst forms of humiliation when they arrived too late to run in the quarterfinal heat of the 100 meters. Working from an old schedule, assistant coach Stan Wright gave the two African American runners, among the favorites in the event, the wrong starting time for the race. The US basketball team, loaded with talent and never having lost in Olympic competition, was beaten by the Soviet Union for the gold medal in arguably the most controversial basketball game ever played at any level of competition. On three different occasions, three seconds were put back on the clock before the United States lost to the Soviet Union, 51–50. The team was so irate toward Olympic officials that they chose to boycott the victory stand ceremony honoring the top three teams. Finally, the 1972 Summer Olympics in Munich were forever tainted by the Palestinian terrorist group Black September who killed eleven Israeli Olympic officials and athletes as well as one West German police officer.[27] Often referred to as the "Munich Massacre," the murders elicited these famous words from legendary *Los Angeles Times* sportswriter Jim Murray: "Others thought the Olympic games should be sanctuaries like naves of old cathedrals or hospital ships. I mean are athletes to join Archdukes and Prime Ministers as objects of assassinations? If so, the games are doomed, to say nothing of athletics overall."[28]

THE BLACK ATHLETIC REVOLT LONG GONE

As to why the Matthews and Collett episode was overshadowed by these events, especially the "Munich Massacre" and the US and Soviet Union basketball game, considering the intense Cold War politics at the time, needs no explanation. But why it is not part of the public consciousness, and why it has received such limited scholarly attention is not quite so obvious. Perhaps the most accurate assessment of why this is the case is provided by sociologist Douglas Hartmann in his 2003 book *Race, Culture, and the Revolt of the Black Athlete.* Hartmann argues that in contrast to the attention garnered by Tommie Smith and John Carlos in Mexico City, Matthews and Collett "were mostly ignored, almost immediately and conveniently forgotten" because their victory stand display took place during a time when the Black athlete revolt led by Harry Edwards had lost much of its steam and had essentially grounded to a halt.[29] Although one may quibble with the notion that Matthews and Collett were "mostly ignored," Hartmann's claim that the attention given the two African American athletes paled in comparison to that received by Smith and Carlos on account of the demise of the Black athletic revolt seems historically accurate, as do the reasons he provides for that demise. Hartmann explains that one reason for the demise of the Black athletic revolt, and this included those on predominantly White university campuses that had diminished in number by 1972, resulted from a decline in the larger civil rights struggle and Black Power movement. It was nearly impossible for African American athletes to maintain the necessary energy and sense of purpose without the resources and support and guiding principles provided by the individuals and groups that fostered the larger movement for equal rights. This was especially true since African American athletes were so relatively new to the civil rights struggle and realized such enormous pressure from coaches and others in the sport establishment to refrain from engaging in radical displays of racial protest. Also contributing to the demise of the Black athletic revolt, in Hartmann's view, was the fact it had never been unified, lacking a clear focus and a "coherent set of goals." It was "essentially a top-down" movement led by Harry Edwards and a select number of African American athletes who were never able to establish its legitimacy or understand completely the intricacies and multifaceted nature of the institution of sport.[30] The demise of the Black athletic revolt was hastened, moreover, by the fact that some of the more blatant as well as symbolic forms of racial discrimination were gradually being eliminated from the world of sport and beyond. These included, among other things, the hiring of Black coaches, academic counseling programs established for minority athletes, and the selection of African Americans for upper-level administrative positions.[31]

Collett and certainly Matthews seemed to understand full well that their victory stand display took place after the Black athletic revolt had lost its steam and overall purpose and direction. Such a conclusion is apparent from a close reading of Matthews's autobiography as well as numerous other factors related to the status of amateur sport in the United States. Although it is difficult to assess the intentions of someone who writes a memoir, it is clear that one of Matthews's primary purposes in penning *My Race Be Won*, with the assistance of well-known sportswriter Neil Amdur, was to provide a detailed portrait of his early life and the contributions he and his teammates made to the Black athletic protest movement.[32] An important read for anyone interested in knowing more about the interconnection among race, sport, and American culture, Matthews furnishes interesting and often poignant details about his difficult childhood years, high school and collegiate track and field career, and relationships he forged with his teammates, former athletes, and coaches.

Perhaps most significant, Matthews makes clear both his disillusionment with amateur sport and the 1972 Olympic games more specifically. At the time of the publication of *My Race Be Won*, the energy that had once been expended on the Black athletic revolt had been transferred to a renewed effort to secure athlete's rights in amateur sport, most notably in track and field, that had been waged since the end of WWII. All indications from his memoir are that Matthews was part of that effort. He boldly spoke out, like an increasing number of athletes, against the hypocrisy of amateur sport and various other issues that would lead to the creation of such organizations as the Suzy Chafee and Jack Kelly-led World Sports Foundation in 1972 and six years later the passing of the Amateur Sports Act.[33] While personally finding it difficult to survive financially while competing, Matthews noted the inherent limitations of drug testing, unscrupulous dealings of shoe companies, under-the-table compensation provided elite athletes, and archaic policies of the Amateur Athletic Union (AAU), American Olympic Committee (AOC) and the IOC.[34]

Seemingly no leaders in sports-governing bodies escaped his criticism and that of Harry Edwards, the OPHR, and such notable White athletes as Harold and Olga Connolly. He was scathing in his comments about Avery Brundage, the controversial president of the IOC who held the position for twenty years, beginning with the 1952 Olympic games in Helsinki and ending in Munich in 1972. Matthews was highly critical of Brundage for numerous reasons, including how the IOC president handled the "Munich Massacre" and, not unexpectedly, how Brundage treated Collett and him because of their medal stand display. He claimed that Brundage "seemed determined to turn the deaths of the Israelis into a political forum to defend the IOC and the Olympics ... by holding a public service for the fallen in the Olympic Stadium." It would have been far more respectful, wrote Matthews, to hold the service in the "privacy of the Olympic village" so that athletes could pay their respects. Regarding the harsh punishment meted out to Collett and him, Matthews contended that Brundage and the IOC used the victory stand display as a pretense to penalize Black athletes from the United States because of their support of African nations opposed to Rhodesia's participation in the games on account of that country's racial policies. "I think Avery Brundage and the International Olympic Committee," noted Matthews, "lost face in that the black athletes from the United States united behind the athletes from Africa. There was some talk that Avery Brundage and the International Olympic Committee wouldn't have minded sacrificing the African nations as much as they would have minded sacrificing the U.S. black athletes and the Africans."[35]

Matthews's criticism of amateur sport was part and parcel of the frustration he felt regarding the mismanagement of the 1972 Olympic team. Like many Americans, he was appalled by how the team was run, frustrated by the poor showing of the United States in events it usually dominated, and embarrassed by all the miscues committed by coaches and others in leadership positions.

He was unsparing in his denunciation of head track and field coach Bill Bowerman. Other than perhaps Jesse Owens and Avery Brundage, no one incurred Matthews's wrath more than the legendary University of Oregon coach and co-founder with Phil Knight of Nike. He questioned the selection of Bowerman as head coach over Stan Wright, believed that Bowerman showed preferential treatment toward distance runners, and was angry that Bowerman did not show more public support for Eddie Hart and Rey Robinson after the two Black sprinters mistakenly missed the quarter final heat in the 100 meters. He also viewed Bowerman as old-fashioned and out of touch with contemporary athletes yet similar to other coaches who "believe it's okay to bend the rules if it serves their purposes. Any athlete who stands up for his convictions is put down for immaturity, lack of experience[,] or rudeness."[36] It was very harsh criticism, to say the least, of a man who had come to the defense of both Matthews and Collett following their dismissal from the Olympic games.

MY RACE BE WON GETS LOST AMONG OTHER MEMOIRS

Matthews's *My Race Be Won* was published importantly at a time when African American athletes and racial issues in sport more generally were receiving rapidly increasing attention from academicians and popular writers. No subject during the 1970s and immediately following seemed to escape the attention of those interested in race and its impact on sport in the United States. Essays, book chapters, and monographs were being published on topics ranging from basketball in the inner city and the experiences of African American athletes at predominantly White universities to the reasons for the underrepresentation and overrepresentation of Black athletes in certain sports to the history of Negro League Baseball.[37] The reasons for the upsurge in the writings on African American athletes are many and varied. There is little question that the Black athlete revolt, including the Olympic protests and hundreds of those on predominantly White university campuses, as well as the outspokenness of a select number of Black professional athletes, all combined to make people more aware of the racism in sport and the need to study it for the purpose of finding solutions to the problem. The increase in the number of writings on Black athletes also resulted from a growing fascination with the history of African American life and culture.[38] The significant growth in the amount of publications on Black athletes, moreover, had to do with academicians now "taking sport more seriously."[39] While scholars in various disciplinary areas had for generations viewed sport as trivial and anti-intellectual, there was now recognition that a deeper understanding of sport, including the experiences of African American athletes and race, more generally, were essential in realizing a more complete understanding of the United States and its institutions. This evolution in thinking was reflected in the founding of professional organizations devoted to studying and disseminating information on various aspects of sport and publishing companies, both university and commercial presses, showing increased interest in completing books on sport-related topics.[40]

Of all the different publications on sport that appeared during this period, memoirs by African American athletes certainly stand out as one particularly important genre. Although autobiographies by African American athletes had appeared since the early twentieth century, those published in the 1970s, typically with the assistance of professional writers, were especially interesting and thought provoking. This was certainly the case for Matthews's autobiography. Tellingly, however, the book never attracted much attention, being overshadowed by autobiographies written by other African American athletes during this period. Realizing far more attention and much longer shelf lives, for instance, were Jesse Owens's four autobiographies with Paul Neimark, *Blackthink: My Life as a Black Man and White Man*, *The Jesse Owens Story*, *I Have Changed*, and *Jesse: A Spiritual Autobiography* (1978).[41] Equally noteworthy and popular were such memoirs as Curt Flood's insightful and interesting book with Richard Carter *The Way It Is*; Jackie Robinson's frequently cited autobiography with Alfred Duckett *I Never Had it Made*; Bill Russell's candid and thoughtful autobiography with Taylor Branch, *Second Wind: The Memoirs of an Opinionated Man*; Muhammad Ali's memoir *The Greatest: My Own Story*; and finally, Joe Louis's memoir titled *Joe Louis: My Life*.[42]

The relatively little attention given to *My Race Be Won*, especially compared to the memoirs of other African American athletes during this period, is certainly understandable considering the historical figures who penned them. Matthews's memoir, however interesting and important historically, was no match for the autobiographies of legendary athletes such as Curt Flood, Jesse Owens, Jackie Robinson, Muhammad Ali, and Joe Louis. But more important, the limited coverage of the autobiography, like the Matthews and Collett disruption on the victory stand itself, was merely confirmation, in the words of Douglas Hartmann, that "African American athletic activism had become passe."[43] Interestingly, Matthews seemed to imply as much in his autobiography by noting that "When Tommie Smith and John Carlos gave the Black Power salute in '68, it was at the beginning of the Black Power era, when the consciousness of the Black community was being raised by dramatization and demonstration to further identity. Black Power salutes, Afro hairdos[,] and soul handshakes became an integral part of establishing that mood."[44] In large part, the Smith and Carlos black-gloved salute came at the height of the Black Power movement, a symbolic gesture at a historic moment that resonated and continues to resonate with an American public that is increasingly both fascinated and appreciative of the courage of the two Black athletes who risked their careers to make the racial discrimination in the United States and around the world more visible. Once viewed with absolute contempt and suffering for years from a career perspective for raising their black-gloved fists and bowing their heads on the victory stand in Mexico City, Smith and Carlos, with the passage of time and because of more progressive racial attitudes, ultimately realized a level of admiration that resulted in them receiving a number of honors and the creation of a more receptive environment in which publishers understood full well that the public's fascination with the two athletes was such that their stories needed to be told through their own memoirs.[45]

Evidence of their transformation from vilified figures to more respected and, to some, revered Black men who had courageously fought against racially discriminatory practices was perhaps first apparent in 1978 when Smith was selected to the United States National Track and Field Hall of Fame. This was followed by other honors that further confirmed the transformation of Smith and Carlos into Black men to be admired while at once making very clear that the Black athletic revolt in 1968 had become firmly embedded in the American consciousness. For example, in 1984 Carlos was hired as an adviser by the organizing committee of the 1984 Summer Olympics; in 1999 HBO produced the documentary *Fists of Freedom: The Story of the '68 Summer Games*; in 2005 Smith and Carlos were honored by their alma mater San Jose State University with a statue portraying their Black Power salute; in 2008 Smith and Carlos were recipients of the Arthur Ashe Courage Award at the ESPYS; in 2016 a statue of Smith and Carlos depicting their Black Power salute, along with second-place finisher Peter Norman of Australia, was erected in the sports gallery at the Smithsonian Institution's National Museum of African American History and Culture; and in 2019 Smith and Carlos were elected to the US Olympic and Paralympic Hall of Fame.[46]

Further indication of their newfound status and the public's captivation with their black-gloved salute and the athletic protest movement more generally, were the published memoirs of Smith and Carlos and reprinting of Harry Edwards classic summation of the Black athletic revolt. In 2007 Smith, in collaboration with David Steele, published *Silent Gesture: The Autobiography of Tommie Smith*; in 2011, Carlos, with the assistance of noted sports analyst and author Dave Zirin, published *The John Carlos*

Story: The Sports Moment that Changed the World; and in 2018 the University of Illinois Press reprinted, with the inclusion of a new introduction and dedication to Muhammad Ali, Harry Edwards's *The Revolt of the Black Athlete: 50th Anniversary* Edition. Of the three men, Carlos is the only one who writes about the Matthews and Collett medal stand display. He claims that the medal ceremony disruption by Matthews and Collett was there way of "saying to hell with the nationalism involved in these games, and sometimes I think the world would be a much better place if more people did exactly the same." Carlos was also troubled by the IOC's treatment of Matthews and Collett as compared to that of Dave Wottle. "They (IOC) made all sorts of excuses for him" (Wottle), wrote Carlos. "And I'm not saying anything about Dave because he was a nice individual as well, but I'm just talking about how they put the two together. There was this paranoia or fear of the 'angry black athlete.'"[47]

NO STATUES, NO COMMEMORATIONS, NO LEGACY

Smith's and Carlos's books appeared just prior to the beginnings of an increasing number of noteworthy African American athletes speaking out and lodging protests against racial discrimination. As a result of a combination of factors, including the deaths of several young Black men; the inception of the Black Lives Matter Movement; and the fact that, for the first time in American history, an African American occupied the White House, prominent African American athletes began voicing their disdain and protesting racial inequality in sport and the larger society. For instance, in 2014 TMZ Sports released a recording of Los Angeles Clippers owner Donald Sterling telling his mistress V. Stiviano (she went by different names) how upset he was that she posed for a photo with NBA Hall of Famer Magic Johnson—a photo that was posted on Instagram. "It bothers me a lot," Sterling is heard to say to Stiviano, "that you want to broadcast that you're associating with black people" and "you can sleep with [Black people]. You can bring them in, you can do whatever you want, but the little I ask you . . . not to bring them to my games." The response of the league's Black players, both current and former, was swift and vocal. Clippers players showed their disgust by wearing their jerseys inside out during pregame against the Golden State Warriors to hide the team logo. LeBron James and his Miami Heat teammates showed solidarity with the Clippers' players by turning their jerseys inside out prior to the game the following evening. James gave voice to players' outrage, commenting

"There's no room for Donald Sterling in the NBA." Also asking for Sterling's removal were such NBA greats as Kareem Abdul-Jabbar, Kobe Bryant, Charles Barkley, Magic Johnson, and Shaquille O'Neal. Sterling would be severely punished for his racist language. He was banned from the league for life and fined $2.5 million.[48]

Two years after the Sterling incident, LeBron James, Dwayne Wade, Carmelo Anthony, and Chris Paul garnered much attention when they pleaded with their fellow athletes at the nationally televised ESPYs to help end the recent spate of violence against Black men and to bring about social change in the United States. Coming on the heels of the recent deaths of young African American men Alton Sterling and Philando Castile, and earlier Trayvon Martin and Eric Garner, the four Black basketball greats each took turns expressing their outrage regarding the violence in America and pleading for a "call to action." Anthony, speaking first, noted, "The events of the last week have put a spotlight on the injustice, distrust, and anger that plague many of us. The system is broken." Paul followed and said the quartet was "standing together to be the change we need to see." The Clippers star then named several Black men who had been killed in controversial deaths over the last several years. Wade spoke next and proclaimed that racial profiling had to stop. "Not seeing the value in black and brown bodies," said Wade, "has to stop." James was the last of the four men to speak and he expressed how "we all feel helpless and frustrated by the violence, . . . It's time to look in the mirror and ask ourselves what are we doing to create change."[49]

One significant aspect of the Sterling incident, the episode at the 2016 ESPYs involving James and the three other NBA greats, and the increasing number of other Black athletic protests being lodged at the time, was the type of media coverage they fostered. More often than not, newspapers and other outlets covering these events often compared them to the many Black athletic protests that were lodged during the civil rights era of the 1960s, noting how once again African American athletes were speaking out about larger racial issues and inequality. Nowhere is there any mention of the intervening years when African American athletes had, with a few notable exceptions, effectively been discouraged from speaking about racial matters and social justice because, as historian Louis Moore persuasively notes, out of fear of the loss of income by those at the professional level of sport and concerns of college athletes about the loss of financial assistance resulting from the NCAA's decision in 1973 to eliminate guaranteed four-year scholarships and decisions to replace them with those that were renewed each year.⁵⁰ The Black athlete typically remembered and lionized in the recent flurry of Black athlete activism is Muhammad Ali and the event most often recalled is the Smith and Carlos Black Power salute in Mexico City. Not unexpectedly, usually as part of the written text recalling the Smith and Carlos protest, is the iconic image of the two African American athletes with their heads bowed and fists held high during the playing of the national anthem. The image, which seemingly has been reprinted in every sport sociology survey text ever published, captures perfectly the spirit of the Black athletic protest movements of both the 1960s and those most recently with Smith and Carlos defiantly disrupting Olympism while at once expressing disdain for the continued racism in the United States. Not surprisingly, the image serves as the cover for Harry Edwards's *The Revolt of the Black Athlete: 50th Anniversary Edition*.[51]

Easily the most apparent and famous connection between the Smith and Carlos salute and the contemporary Black protest movement involves Colin Kaepernick. In the same year that James and his three fellow NBA stars were expressing their concerns about the recent killings of several young Black men, Kaepernick, the talented quarterback of the San Francisco 49ers, began kneeling during the playing of the national anthem prior to each game in protest of racial discrimination and oppression in the United States. Kaepernick's "silent gesture" drew mixed reactions, some people castigating the '49ers quarterback and others heaping praise on him for his actions. One significant aspect of the Kaepernick story is the obvious link with Smith and Carlos. Seemingly every article assessing Kaepernick's controversial decision to kneel during the national anthem included a reference to Smith and Carlos's medal stand display in 1968 and typically included the famous image of them doing so. In addition, Smith and Carlos, at the time in their early seventies, and fifty years removed from their victory stand display, along with Harry Edwards, were effusive in their praise of Kaepernick, expressing their admiration and respect for the '49ers quarterback for his contentious stance against racially discriminatory practices.[52] Kaepernick returned the compliments, noting how much he respected Smith and Carlos and had been inspired by them.

In essence, one of the great legacies of Smith and Carlos was serving as an inspiration to Kaepernick and the other athletes who bravely disrupted the institution of sport to make visible the continued racism and inequality in the United States. Jere Longman of the *New York Times* perhaps summed up best the connection among the three African American athlete crusaders: "Kaepernick is a direct activist descendent of Smith and Carlos, unyielding in his conviction, fully understanding of risk and sacrifice and the power and dignity of silent gesture. And he knows something they did not a half-century ago, that history can act as sandpaper, smoothing abrasive denunciation into burnished acceptance."[53] This is not to say that the leaders in sport now welcome disruptions of their sacred institution as evidenced by the decision of the IOC in early 2020 to confirm Rule 50 of the Olympic Charter, which forbids "athletes from staging political protests on the field of play or at medal ceremonies. " In anticipation of the upcoming Summer Olympics in Tokyo, and because of the recent activism of athletes and worldwide political tensions, the IOC is acting presumptively by threatening severe disciplinary action for kneeling, politically intended hand gestures, political messages on armbands or signs, and disturbances of medal ceremonies. It is important that this ruling has received significant pushback from athletes and others who have made clear that the Olympic games by their very nature are political, as made clear by countries continually vying for international prestige through victories in sport.[54]

Be that as it may, for Wayne Collett and Vince Matthews, unlike the Black Power salutes of Smith and Carlos in Mexico City, there were no public forms of commemorations for their victory stand display in Munich. There were no statues erected of the two men depicting them conversing during the medal ceremony with jackets unzipped with no apparent regard for the American flag and national anthem. It was not an image that reflected bold and selfless protest at the height of the civil rights struggle and Black Power movement. There are apparently no plans to celebrate and honor the fiftieth anniversary in 2022 of their behavior on the victory stand in Munich through conference sessions, special symposia, media outreach, or the reprinting of *My Race Be Won*. Their impact on younger African American athletes, even prior to the untimely death of Collett in 2010, has been minimal at best, since both men and their victory stand display have largely been forgotten. They established no legacy as African American athletes who bravely confronted the sport establishment and society at large during a period of intense racial divisions and Black pride and direct confrontations. Although drawing immediate vitriol and media attention for their victory stand display, Matthews and Collett quickly faded from public consciousness almost as soon as they exited the Olympic Stadium in Munich. The world had essentially passed them by, the energy of the Black athletic protest movement now being expended on athlete's rights in amateur sport while people also confronted other serious problems such as inflation, Vietnam, unemployment, Watergate, and women's rights. The two gifted African American athletes who achieved enormous success in the most important international sporting event in the world will always be linked together, but not to the Black athlete activist movement and freedom struggle. Even if they had chosen to emulate Smith and Carlos by bowing their heads and standing erect while raising black-gloved fists high into the air during their medal ceremony, Matthews and Collett's display would probably have been viewed as nothing more than an imitative and outmoded act at a time in which protests were becoming increasingly unfashionable as a result of supposed progress that had been made on civil rights issues. Although all four African American athletes were punished for resisting the protocols of Olympism, Smith and Carlos ultimately became iconic figures for their defiant Black Power salute at the height of the freedom struggle. Matthews and Collett, on the other hand, have been viewed as inscrutable figures whose ambiguous behavior on the medal dais did little to advance the fight for civil rights and racial equality. Remarkably, only four years separated the Smith and Carlos medal ceremony from the Matthews and Collett victory stand display, an indication of how quickly and dramatically the winds of racial identity, sport, and popular culture can shift and influence who is remembered in history and who is not.

Notes

1. Vince Matthews with Neil Amdur, *My Race Be Won* (New York, 1974), 340.

2. For the Matthews and Collett episode, see ibid.; David Clay Large, *Munich 1972: Tragedy, Terror, and Triumph at the Olympic Games* (Lanham, MD, 2012); Douglas Hartmann, *Race, Culture, and the Revolt of the Black Athlete: The 1968 Olympic Protests and Their Aftermath* (Chicago, 2003); and Robert G. Weisbord, *Racism and the Olympics* (New Brunswick, NJ, 2015). For examples of the Matthews and Collett victory stand display in contemporary newspaper accounts, see: "IOC Bans Pair for 'Insulting Behavior: Incomplete Source" *Los Angeles Times*, September 9, 1972, A1; "The Olympics: Old Ideals, New Realities," *The Washington Post, Times Herald*, September 10, 1972, B6; "Incident on Victory Stand Mars U.S. Track Victories," *The Sun*, September 8, 1972, C1; Cooper Rollow, "Matthews, Collett Go Casual; Get Booed: Medal Ceremony Turns Into Farce," *Chicago Tribune*, September 8, 1972, C1; Robert Markus, "Matthews Reflects Upon His 'Golden' Activities," *Chicago Tribune*, September 8, 1972, C3; Jerry Nason, "They Got What They Asked For," *Boston Globe*, September 9, 1972, 19; Neil Amdur, "Matthews Tired of Answering That Question," *New York Times*, September 27, 1972, 55; Red Smith, "Fixing The Blame," *New York Times*, September 9, 1972, 17; William Gildea, "Athletes Condemn the Old Men," The *Washington Post, Times Herald*, September 9, 1972; Shirley Povich, "Big Boot Doesn't Fit," *The Washington Post, Times*

Herald, September 9, 1972, F1; Norman O. Unger, "'Dual Standard' in Olympics," *Chicago Daily Defender*, September 11, 1972, 24; "Treatment of Olympic Stars Riles NAACP," *New York Amsterdam News*, September 23, 1972, A1; and Erich Segal, "Munich Was The Last Olympiad-Until The Next One," *New York Times*, September 24, 1972, 42.

3. Matthews with Amdur, *My Race Be Won* and Hartmann, *Race, Culture, and the Revolt*.

4. See John Gold, "Wayne Collett, UCLA Track Star, Passes Away," *Inside UCLA*, March 17, 2010, www.insidesocial.com/ucla/2010/03/17/wayne-collett-ucla-track-star/.

5. For biographical information on Collett, see Frank Litsky, "Wayne Collett, 60, Olympian Barred Because of Protest," *New York Times*, March 18, 2010, B19; and Michael Espinoza, *The Integration of the UCLA School of Law, 1966–1978: Architects of Affirmative Action* (Lanham, MD, 2017).

6. The New York Pioneer Club, New York Public School Athletic League, and Penn Relays were all racially integrated. For African Americans, the Penn Relays resembled Negro League Baseball's East-West All-Star Games and Thanksgiving Day football games between HBCUs in that it was an annual social and athletic spectacle that drew thousands of people. See Dennis Gildea, "The Penn Relays: Celebrating the 'Black Woodstock of West Philly," in *Philly Sports: Teams, Games, and Athletes from Rocky's Town*, eds. Ryan A. Swanson and David K. Wiggins (Fayetteville, AR, 2016), 229–39. Information about Matthews post-athletic career is very limited, especially because of his reluctance to do interviews and discuss his Olympic experiences. We do know that he is an artist who specializes in burning images on wood panels and they are displayed among the group Art of the Olympians. See artoftheolympians.org.

7. Information on the Olympic Project for Human Rights and the Black athletic revolt more generally is voluminous; see, e.g., Hartmann, *Race, Culture, and the Revolt*; Harry Edwards, *The Revolt of the Black Athlete: 50th Anniversary Edition* (Urbana, IL, 2017); Amy Bass, *Not the Triumph But the Struggle: The 1968 Olympics and the Making of the Black Athlete* (Minneapolis, 2002); Kevin B. Witherspoon, *Before the Eyes of the World: Mexico and the 1968 Olympic Games* (Dekalb, IL, 2008); Louis Moore, *We Will Win the Day: The Civil Rights Movement, the Black Athlete, and the Quest for Equality* (Santa Barbara, 2017); David K. Wiggins, *"The Future of College Athletics is at Stake: Black Athletes and Racial Turmoil on Three Predominantly White University Campuses, 1968–1972, Journal of Sport History* 15 (Winter 1988), 304–33; Donald Spivey, "Black Consciousness and Olympic Protest Movements, 1964–1980," in *Sport in America: New Historical Perspectives*, ed. Donald Spivey (Westport, CT: Greenwood Press, 1985), 239–62, and Dexter L. Blackman, "'Run, Jump, or Shuffle Are All the Same When You Do It for the Man!' The OPHR, Black Power, and the Boycott of the 1968 NYAC Meet," *Souls: A Critical Journal of Black Politics, Culture, and Society* 21 (May 2019), 1–25.

8. For contemporary newspaper accounts of the Smith and Carlos Black Power salute in 1968, see "U.S. Medalists Give Black Salute," *Boston Globe*, October 17, 1968, 1; Charles Mahar, "Foreign Press Questions Protest Method Used by Smith, Carlos,"

Los Angeles Times, October 20, 1968, H11; John G. Griffin, "Black Power Bows at the Olympics," *Chicago Defender*, October 19, 1968, 1; "Smith, Carlos Leave Mexico for California," *Chicago Tribune*, October 22, 1968, C1; "Two Negro Athletes Banished: Olympic Officials Expel 2 U.S. Stars," *The Washington Post, Times Herald*, October 19, 1968, A1; and "U.S. Apologizes for Protest by Blacks: U.S. Committee 'Sorry' About Discourtesy Won't Stand for Repetition," *Chicago Tribune*, October 18, 1968, C1.

9. For contemporary newspaper accounts of these incidents, see Joseph M. Sheehan, "2 Black Power Advocates Ousted from Olympics: U.S. Team Drops Smith and Carlos for Clenched-Fist Display on Victory Stand," *New York Times*, October 19, 1968, 1; "Evans Shuns U.S. Olympic Official after Victory," *Boston Globe*, October 21, 1968, 30; "Entire U.S. Team Faced Olympic Ban," *Boston Globe*, October 19, 1968, 1; Charles Mahar, "U.S. Expels Smith, Carlos from Olympic Team: U.S. Duo Banned," *Los Angeles Times*, October 19, 1968, A1; "Long Jump Stars Stage Mild Gripe: Beamon, Boston Report Suspension of Two Negro Athletes," *The Sun*, October 19, 1968, B1; and Arthur Daley, "Sports of the time: The Incident," *New York Times*, October 20, 1968, S2.

10. This was a period of great college track and field coaches, including Jim Bush at UCLA, Bud "Tex" Winter at San Jose State, and Bill Bowerman at the University of Oregon. Of these three men, the most famous was Bowerman who coached many outstanding distance runners at Oregon, founded Nike along with former Oregon runner Phil Knight, as well as serving as the United States track and field coach in 1972. Fortunately, we know a great deal about Bowerman, partly because of the biography of his life written by Kenny Moore titled *Bowerman and the Men of Oregon* (Emmaus, PA, 2006).

11. See the following contemporary newspaper accounts: Dwight Chapin, "Matthews and Collett Booed on Victory Stand by Fans," *Los Angeles Times*, September 8, 1972; "I.O.C. Bars Matthews and Collett: Decision Appealed by U.S.," *Chicago Tribune*, September 9, 1972, A1; "Incident on Victory Stand Mars U.S. Track Victories," *The Sun*, September 8, 1972, C1; Jesse Abramson, "Milburn Wins Hurdles, Matthews Takes 400," *The Washington Post, Times Herald*, September 8, 1972, D1; and "U.S. Runners Booed: Medalist, 2nd Placer Ignore Anthem, Pair Respond with Clenched Fist Signal," *Los Angeles Times*, September 7, 1972, 1.

12. See Matthews with Amdur, *My Race Be Won*, esp. 352–54.

13. See ibid., 357–59. The story regarding Owens, Matthews, and Collett is told very well in William J. Baker's biography *Jesse Owens: An American Life* (New York, 1986), 216–17.

14. Matthews with Amdur, *My Race Be Won*, 360–61.

15. Ibid., 356, 362.

16. Ibid., 340.

17. Kathryn T. McClymond, *Ritual Gone Wrong: What We Learn from Ritual Disruption* (New York, 2016), especially, 106–38.

18. Ibid., 118–28.

19. Examples of this can be gleaned from David K. Wiggins, "The Notion of Double-Consciousness and the Involvement of Black Athletes in American Sport," in *Glory Bound: Black Athletes in a White America*, David K. Wiggins (Syracuse, 1997), 200–220.

20. Red Smith, "Fixing the Blame," *New York Times*, September 9, 1972, 17; Shirley Povich, "Big Boot Doesn't Fit," *The Washington Post, Times Herald*, September 9, 1972, F1; A. S. "Doc" Young, "The Olympic Yakiliyak," *Chicago Daily Defender*, September 18, 1972, 28.

21. Erich Segal, "Munich was the Last Olympiad-Until the Next One," *New York Times*, September 24, 1972, 42.

22. Matthews with Amdur, *My Race Be Won*, 339.

23. Unger, "'Dual Standard' in Olympics."

24. "Treatment of Olympic Stars Riles NAACP," *New York Amsterdam News*, September 23, 1972, A1.

25. Gildea, "Athletes Condemn the Old Men," *Washington Post, Times Herald*, September 9, 1972, F4.

26. Kenny Moore, *Bowerman and the Men of Oregon*, 289.

27. On the Israeli massacre, see Large, *Munich 1972*; Aaron J. Klein, *Striking Back: The 1972 Munich Olympics Massacre and Israel's Deadly Response* (New York, 2007); and Simon Reeve, *One Day in September: The Full Story of the 1972 Munich Olympics Massacre and the Israeli Revenge Operation "Wrath of God"* (New York, 2011).

28. Jim Murray, "Olympic Awards," *Los Angeles Times*, September 12, 1972, C1.

29. Hartmann, *Race, Culture, and the Revolt*, 242.

30. Ibid., 243–46.

31. Ibid., 246.

32. Amdur also cowrote biographies of Arthur Ashe and Chris Evert; see Arthur Ashe with Neil Amdur, *Arthur Ashe: Off the Court* (New York, 1981) and Chis Evert Lloyd with Neil Amdur, *Chrissie: My Own Story* (New York, 1984).

33. For an analysis of athletes' rights and amateurism, see Joseph M. Turrini, *The End of Amateurism in American Track and Field* (Urbana, Il, 2010).

34. Matthews with Amdur, *My Race Be Won*, esp. chapter 13.

35. Ibid., 376.

36. Ibid., 331.

37. One important example of an academician who immersed himself in the scholarly study of Black participation in sport was Harry Edwards; evidence of this is not only reflected in his original *The Revolt of the Black Athlete* and numerous essays, but also his classic *Sociology of Sport* (Homewood, Il, 1973).

38. For a discussion of the increasing amount of scholarly attention on the African American athlete during the 1970s and immediately following, see: David K. Wiggins, *More Than a Game: A History of the African American Experience in Sport* (Lanham, MD, 2018), chapter 6.

39. This phrase, which resonates deeply with academicians in sport studies, originated from Elliott J. Gorn and Michael Oriard's "Taking Sport Seriously," *Chronicle of Higher Education*, March 24, 1995, A52.

40. The University of Illinois Press was the first university publisher to "take sport seriously" by establishing its Sport and Society series. Many other university presses would follow its lead and establish special series on sport.

41. Books written by Jesse Owens, with Paul Neimark, include *Blackthink: My Life as a Black Man and White Man* (New York 1970), *The Jesse Owens Story* (New York 1970), *I Have Changed* (New York 1972), and *Jesse: A Spiritual Autobiography* (Plainfield, NJ, 1978).

42. See also Curt Flood with Richard Carter, *The Way It Is* (New York, 1971); Jackie Robinson with Alfred Duckett, *I Never Had It Made* (New York, 1972); Bill Russell with Taylor Branch, *Second Wind* (New York, 1974); Muhammad Ali's collaboration with Richard Durham, *The Greatest* (New York, 1975); and Joe Louis with Edna Rust and Art Rust Jr., *Joe Louis: My Life* (New York, 1978).

43. Hartmann, *Race, Culture, and the Revolt*, 242.

44. Matthews with Amdur, *My Race Be Won*, 342.

45. See Tommie Smith with David Steele, *Silent Gesture: The Autobiography of Tommie Smith* (Philadelphia, 2007) and John Carlos with Dave Zirin, *The John Carlos Story: The Sports Moment that Changed the World* (Chicago, 2011).

46. Two good articles that discuss how the Smith and Carlos Black Power salute has been portrayed are Maureen M. Smith, "Frozen Fists in Speed City: The Statue as Twenty-First Century Reparations," *Journal of Sport History* 36 (Fall, 2009), 393-414 and Gary Osmond, "Photographs, Materiality and Sport History: Peter Norman and the 1968 Mexico City Black Power Salute," *Journal of Sport History*, 37 (Spring 2010), 119-137.

47. Carlos with Zirin, *The John Carlos Story*, 147.

48. For the Donald Sterling incident, see: Renford Reese, "Donald Sterling Incident-Racism and Elitism," *Daily News*, April 28, 2014; Kent Babb, "Alleged Donald Sterling Recording is the Latest in Series of Incidents Involving Clippers Owner," *Washington Post*, April 27, 2014; Ramona Shelburne, "When the Donald Sterling Saga Rocked the NBA—and Changed it Forever," *ESPN*, August 20, 2019.

49. Melissa Chan, "Read LeBron James and Carmelo Anthony's Powerful Speech on Race at the ESPY Awards," *Time*, July 14, 2016; for a nice discussion of the recent activism of African American athletes, see Amy Bass, "Active Radicals: The Political Athlete in the Contemporary Moment," in *The Routledge History of American Sport*, eds., Linda J. Borish, David K. Wiggins, and Gerald R. Gems (New York, 2017), 401-13.

50. See Moore, *We Will Win the Day*, 190. One African American athlete during the "post-civil rights" era who suffered the consequences for speaking out about racial inequality was Craig Hodges, the longtime guard for the Chicago Bulls. For Hodges story, see his autobiography Craig Hodges with Rory Fanning, *Long Shot: The Triumphs and Struggles of an NBA Freedom Fighter* (Chicago, 2017).

51. Edwards, *The Revolt of the Black Athlete: 50th Anniversary Edition*.

52. Among the many examples, see: Greg Miller, "Raised Fists: How NFL Protests Connect to John Carlos, Tommie Smith and Jesse Owens," *Arizona Republic*, October 25, 2018; George Barlow and Barbara Trish, "How Athletes are Changing the Conversation Around Racism," *Washington Post*, October 16, 2018; John Mitchell, "From Raising a Fist to Taking a Knee," *The Philadelphia Tribune*, October 16, 2018; Jeffrey Robinson, "The Spirit of 1968 Lives on Today in Athletes Like Colin Kaepernick," October 16, 2018; Anthony Rives, "50 Years After Raised Fists at Olympics, Legacy of Protests Continues with Kaepernick," October 16, 2018; and Lindsey Sarah Krasnoff, "From the Black Power Salute to Colin Kaepernick: What's Changed?" *CNN*, October 16, 2018.

53. Longman, "Kaepernick's Knee and Olympic Fists are Linked by History," *The New York Times*, September 6, 2018.

54. See, e.g., Tariq Panja, "Olympic Protest Rules: Tweets Are Fine, Kneeling Is Not," *The New York Times,* January 9, 2020, https://nyti.ms/2t3iKm; Martin Fritz Huber, "The Absurdity of Prohibiting Protest at the Olympics," *Outside Online*, January 17, 2020, https://www.outsideonline.com/2408155/2020-olympics-protest-ban.

8

SYMBOLS OF POSSIBILITY

Arthur Ashe, Black Athletes,
and the Writing of *A Hard Road To Glory*

Arthur Ashe accomplished a great many things during his relatively short life. An outstanding tennis player from Richmond, Virginia, who fashioned a wonderful career in the sport, Ashe won a NCAA singles championship while at the UCLA, captained the US Davis Cup team for three years, and captured the singles titles at the US Open, Australian Championships, and Wimbledon. Ashe and France's Yannick Noah have been the only Black men to capture a grand slam singles title.[1]

In addition to his athletic success, Ashe's life was filled with a variety of service activities and accomplishments that benefited numerous individuals and groups in the United States and abroad. He was a strong advocate for the education of African American youth. He adamantly opposed South African apartheid, serving as co-chair with singer and actor Harry Belafonte of a group that attempted to dissuade athletes and entertainers from performing in South Africa. In 1985 Ashe was arrested for demonstrating outside the South African embassy in Washington, DC. The arrest, he believed, cost him his position as Davis Cup captain. After it was made public in 1992 that he had contracted AIDS, Ashe established his own foundation that raised money to conduct research and treat the disease. Working closely with such organizations as the International Red Cross and the World Health Organization of the United Nations, much of the money raised went to AIDS research and treatment outside the United States.[2]

Ashe complemented these activities with his own writings and publications. He authored or coauthored essays in the popular press, texts on tennis instruction, and four autobiographical works. In addition to being regularly quoted in the press, Ashe published articles on a variety of topics in popular periodicals and newspapers. Some of these were published as columns he regularly wrote for the *Washington Post* in 1981. Three of his best-known articles dealt with issues that were extraordinarily important to Ashe and that he would continue to address in various ways throughout his career. In "Don't Tell Me How to Think," in *Black Sports* (1975), he defended his right to take his own position on civil rights issues. In "Send Your Children to the Libraries," published in the *New York Times* (1977), he encouraged African American parents to emphasize to their children the importance of preparing for careers other than in sports. "Coddling Black Athletes," *New York Times* (1989), called for more rigorous academic requirements to secure athletic scholarships mandated by the new NCAA ruling known as Proposition 42.[3]

Ashe complemented these essays by writing books dealing with the acquisition of skills and techniques in tennis. Among these were (with Larry Sheehan) *Mastering Your Tennis Strokes* (1978); *Arthur Ashe's Tennis Clinic* (1981); and (with Louie Robinson) *Getting Started in Tennis* (1977). He also wrote four autobiographical works. These were (with Clifford George Gewecki Jr.) *Advantage Ashe* (1967); (with Frank Deford) *Arthur Ashe: Portrait in Motion* (1975); (with Neil Amdur) *Off the Court* (1981); and (with Arnold Rampersad) *Days of Grace: A Memoir* (1993). Ashe published, moreover, a well-known three-volume work on the participation of Black athletes in American sport titled *A Hard Road to Glory: A History of the African American Athlete* (1988). A revised edition of the book would be published shortly after Ashe's death in 1993.[4]

Ashe's accomplishments garnered him many prestigious honors and awards. He was inducted into the Intercollegiate Tennis Association Hall of Fame, the International Tennis Hall of Fame, and the Virginia Sports Hall of Fame. The United States Postal Service released an Arthur Ashe commemorative stamp; the stadium at the United States Tennis Association (USTA) National Tennis Center in Flushing Meadows, New York, is named in his honor; and his hometown of Richmond, Virginia honored him with a statue on Monument Avenue previously reserved for statues of Confederate leaders. A tennis club in Manayunk, Pennsylvania, is named in his honor and UCLA now has on its campus the Arthur Ashe Student Health and Wellness Center. *Sports Illustrated* named Ashe its Sportsman of the Year in 1992 and *USA Today* named him one of the twenty-five most inspiring people of the last quarter of the twentieth century, a list that included Nelson Mandela, Pope John Paul II, Ryan White, Mother Teresa, Oprah Winfrey, and Muhammad Ali. President Bill Clinton posthumously honored him with the Presidential Medal of Freedom.[5]

This essay, largely an effort to provide greater understanding of a little-known aspect of the great tennis champion's life, assesses the approach taken by Ashe in writing *A Hard Road to Glory*. It is, in the main, a detailed analysis of the work, explaining how Ashe arranged to have it published, how he conducted his research, and what his intentions were in writing it. In the process, the essay provides a glimpse of Ashe's writing life more generally and how it has impacted the scholarly study of African American athletes specifically, and sport history more generally. Frequently cited, the book appears in the list of sources and bibliographies of many essays, texts, and monographs that deal with African American participation in sport. Respected scholars have praised it. In *Not the Triumph But the Struggle: The 1968 Olympics and the Making of the Black Athlete* (2004), Amy Bass wrote that "Arthur Ashe took a significant step with his multiple volume work *A Hard Road to Glory*, an extensive narrative with copious bibliographic references on every aspect of African American participation in sport." Well-known sport sociologist Earl Smith said that Ashe "proved himself a highly capable scholar by writing the three-volume series, *A Hard Road to Glory*." Noted historians Elliott J. Gorn and Warren Goldstein labeled Ashe's three-volume history "a major achievement." Historian Jeffrey Sammons refers to it as the "best known and certainly most substantial" of the "popular histories of Black athletes."[6]

The idea to write a historical survey of African Americans' involvement in sport came to Ashe in 1981 while he was teaching a course on the "Black Athlete in Contemporary Society" at Florida Memorial College in Miami.[7] A lover of history and a bibliophile who would eventually accumulate a large collection of rare books on the African American experience in the United States, Ashe learned from his brief teaching experience at Florida Memorial how little his students actually knew about Black athletes of the past, and how few scholarly works had been written on them. He wrote that with the notable exception of Edwin B. Henderson's two editions of

The Negro in Sports (1939, 1949), no survey chronicling the achievements, as well as the trials and tribulations, of Black athletes in American history existed. Although not mentioning other popular works such as Henderson's *The Black Athlete: Emergence and Arrival* (1968), A. S. "Doc" Young's *Negro Firsts in Sports* (1963), Wally Jones and Jim Washington's *Black Champions Challenge American Sports* (1972), Jack Olsen's *The Black Athlete: A Shameful Story* (1968), and *Art Rust's Illustrated History of the Black Athlete* (1985) by Edna and Art Rust Jr., Ashe's contention that there was a paucity of scholarly survey texts on the African American experience in sport was essentially correct.[8]

Ashe hypothesized that the omission was partly a result of the low priority academicians placed on the study of African American athletes. "When juxtaposed alongside the more 'serious' problems of rewriting and studying the condition of Black America, a history of the Black athlete is a luxury some have reserved for their later years," he wrote in a "first draft proposal" in 1982. Ashe also argued that scholars avoided the topic because of the dearth of sources. "The compilation of names, places, facts and figures, photographs, and interviews," he noted, "is practically impossible without a grant, and a grant of sufficient size, to do justice to this body of work was found to be too much for the major publishing houses as well as our Black universities' publishing outlets." Moreover, Ashe claimed that Black sportswriters who had provided most of the information on African American athletes simply did not have the time or the inclination to put together a survey on the subject. "The problem here is that few of them [Black sportswriters] had the time to tackle such an immense subject. Such an attempt would also involve a radical change in writing style from the crisply written 200- to 750-word article written for a deadline to the tedium of research and scholarly reflection required of those that authoritatively tell us what happened 200 years ago." Finally, Ashe contended that large commercial publishers found it more profitable to produce books on individual African American athletes, but not surveys on the subject. Large "publishing houses," wrote Ashe, "have viewed a comprehensive history of the Black American athlete as a textbook . . . which are seen as attracting too small an audience."[9]

The reasons Ashe provided for the lack of surveys on the history of the African American experience in sport are open to speculation and largely personal. The reality was that many of the reasons he gave were connected to his initial inability to secure a contract from some twenty New York publishing houses, all of which apparently had serious concerns about the great tennis player's ability to complete such a project. Despite the lack of interest, Ashe remained steadfast, and on April 5, 1983, he signed a contract with Howard University Press, which included a $10,000 advance. The book contract, for what was tentatively titled "A History of the Black Athlete in America," was negotiated between Ashe's agent, Fifi Oscard, and Charles F. Harris, executive director of Howard University Press. A ceremonial signing of the book contract was held some two months later at the fashionable Palm Restaurant in Washington, DC.[10]

Ashe was cognizant of Howard's commitment to the study of African American culture. He acknowledged this fact in a news release: "I approached Howard University Press because of my long-standing knowledge of the intellectual tradition of Howard University and because of my knowledge of the development, professionalism, and the philosophy of the Howard University Press publishing program. Additionally, Howard University has the world's most comprehensive depository of information on people of African descent, the Moorland-Spingarn Research Center, which will be invaluable in accomplishing this project."[11]

University officials enthusiastically embraced the project. President James E. Cheek declared, "We are extremely honored to be the publisher of this great body of work which we are sure will find great receptivity throughout all segments of this society and throughout the world. When one considers that sports in America generates, on an annual basis, revenue in the millions of dollars, it is plain to see that a book dealing with such a major subject will take on great importance in the minds of the public."[12]

ASSEMBLING THE TEAM

The signing of the contract increased Ashe's motivation to complete the book. Working under the premise "that the psychic value of success in sports was and is higher in the Black community than among any other American subculture," Ashe wrote that he was interested in answering the following questions: How did African Americans nurture "such a favorable environment for [their] athletes?" How did so many African American athletes achieve success without adequate facilities, training, and coaching? Why did civil rights organizations not speak out more forcefully about the racial discrimination experienced by African American athletes, and why did White athletes often refuse to compete against their Black counterparts?[13] Although one can question the presumptive nature of some of these questions and whether they would be adequately answered, there is no doubt Ashe was fixed on profiling in *A Hard Road to Glory* the accomplishments of Black athletes to bring about a sense of pride in the African American community. Like many African American writers, then and now, Ashe's recounting of Black athletic success was meant to provide examples of possibility—and to demonstrate that African Americans, if given the same opportunities as others, had the requisite abilities to realize success in sport and other walks of life.

Taking the view that a project of this magnitude was too much for one individual, Ashe assembled a research team shortly after conceiving the idea for the book. He put together a group that varied in talent, aptitude, and experience. Kip Branch, who held an MA in English from Morgan State University and at the time was a professor at Wilson College in Chambersburg, Pennsylvania, was one of the first to join the team, and the one member whose specific responsibilities and payment schedule are made clear by the historical record. In a "collaboration agreement" dated June 1, 1983, Ashe was to pay Branch $275 for working two 8-hour days. Once Ashe was able to raise the $300,000 he thought necessary to complete the book, Branch would receive an annual salary of $32,500 for full-time work.[14] Another member of the research team was the better known Ocania Chalk. A former reporter for the *Washington Evening News* and employee of the US Bureau of Labor Statistics in Washington, DC, Chalk had long been interested in the history of African American athletes, as evidenced by his two books, *Pioneers of Black Sport: The Early Days of the Black Professional Athlete in Baseball, Basketball, Boxing, and Football* (1975) and *Black College Sport* (1976).[15] Rounding out the research team were Ashe's personal assistant Derilene McCloud; Charles Harris's son Francis; and librarian Sandra Jamison, who left prior to the book's completion. Rodney Howard, whom Ashe referred to as a skilled academician, replaced Jamison. Doug Smith of *USA Today* would assist with the 1993 edition of the book.[16]

Ashe and his team began much of their work in early 1983. By March of that year, just a month prior to the ceremonial contract signing, the team had already organized a bibliography of secondary sources and completed preliminary research. Ashe's home on Lexington Avenue in New York City served as a makeshift office. The appearance of a well-planned and systematic approach to the project, however, was just that—an appearance. Although enthusiastic, earnest, and well-intentioned, Ashe and his research team had no real background in historical research, a fact made clear by the way in which they collected information and searched for sources. In the days before e-journals, electronic databases, digital resources, and other assisted technologies, Ashe and his research team depended on the good will, initiative, and expertise of many others to gather much of their information on Black athletes. They conducted personal interviews and collected information from personal visits to libraries and other repositories, but Ashe and his research team amassed much of their primary source materials from whatever was sent to them by individuals and groups asked to help with the project. As Ashe noted, "We found few primary sources for all this history. Instead, we improvised."[17]

One way Ashe sought information on African American athletes was through the media and popular press. In late 1983 and early 1984, for instance, he placed announcements in the *New York Times* and ran ads on the Howard Cosell radio show requesting that readers and listeners send him material on African American athletes.[18] He also sent numerous letters of inquiry and a series of questions on the experiences of African Americans in sports to well-known Black academicians.[19] It was regular practice, moreover, for him to contact librarians, heads of manuscript divisions, and the academic leaders of major colleges and ask them to send him any materials on African American athletes at their particular institutions.[20] Playing off his fame, Ashe sent letters—some of which went to presidents and chancellors— that were seemingly far more aggressive than his approach on the tennis court. In one instance, he wrote that he was anxiously awaiting a "speedy reply" and needed the material he had requested by a specific date, *"if not sooner."*[21]

Ashe received mixed responses to his requests. One respondent, after reading the announcement in the *New York Times*, offered to send "thirty capsule biographies of Black athletes in American history."[22] Harold Shapiro, president of the University of Michigan, instructed his secretary to send Ashe a copy of John Behee's *Hail to the Victors! Black Athletes at the University of Michigan* (1974), after having been informed by his athletic department staff "that it would be very difficult, given present staffing constraints, to locate all the information" Ashe had requested.[23]

Respected scholars were also consulted. Noted historian and literary critic Henry Louis Gates Jr., forwarded an Ashe questionnaire to his brother Paul, who, according to Gates, was "an expert on sports and was quite an athlete in his day." "I never thought much about sports," wrote Gates, "except vicariously, since my dad was, and is an avid fan of just about all sports.

I was always more interested in the ritual-aspect of Black people watching sports (and me watching my family and friends watching sports), than in the event itself."[24] Historian V. P. Franklin responded to Ashe's queries by noting that Black athletes imparted a sense of "meaning in the lives of the average Afro-American because they are symbolic of some larger struggle being waged in the quest for racial advancement."

Franklin continued, "Thus if in your research on Black athletes you ground them in their particular social and cultural milieu, it is very likely that you will end up with a project that can withstand the blistering attacks of (sometimes envious) non-athletic professional historians such as myself."[25] John Hope Franklin, the famous historian who at that time was at Duke University, responded to Ashe's questions in great detail, showing an obvious understanding of, for better or worse, the role played by Black athletes in American culture. Among his many cogent comments were that "Black communities should place before their youth a variety of role models that are [as] worthy of emulation as athletes. Black parents should emphasize the total intellectual and physical development of their offspring." He concluded by suggesting, without providing a rationale for his choices, that Ashe should consult such important works on African American history as John Blassingame's *Black New Orleans* (1973) and *Slave Testimony* (1977); John Hope Franklin's *From Slavery to Freedom* (1980); Leon Litwack's *Been in the Storm Too Long* (1979); and Edwin B. Henderson's *The Negro in Sports* (1939, 1949), among others.[26]

The information Ashe collected was supplemented by material his research team retrieved. Sandra Jamison (and later Rodney Howard) arranged for interviews with athletes, coaches, and others from the world of Black sport. She also negotiated the finances necessary for the compilation of statistics and retrieval of documents and wrote letters to groups and organizations seeking information on African American athletes. On just one day— October 23, 1984— Rodney Howard solicited information from the League of American Wheelmen, the American Water Skiing Association, the US Volleyball Association, the United States Table Tennis Association, the National Skeet Shooting Association, the US Figure Skating Association, and the Professional Bowlers Association. The letters of inquiry were formulaic in nature, with Howard stating that he was writing on behalf of Ashe and seeking information on African American achievement in sport and records documenting outstanding performances and championships.[27]

THE ROAD TO PUBLICATION

Kip Branch and Ocania Chalk did the bulk of the research. Branch, who was assigned to complete research on the more recent experiences of Black athletes, conducted many interviews and traveled the country searching for information that could be included in the work. Chalk, who was assigned to uncover information on the experiences of Black athletes in early US history, conducted research and drafted reports for Ashe. Chalk was the most knowledgeable member of the research team, having already published two books on the subject, and he proved to be a particularly valuable resource, drawing upon a number of his own writings, which ended up serving as background material for various sections of the book.[28] One example was the 188-page unpublished manuscript on the life and career of famous lightweight boxer Joe Gans that Chalk sent to Ashe. Titled "The Old Master: The Joe Gans Story," Chalk informed Sandra Jamison that the manuscript "may give Arthur an insight on how boxing was for a particular Black in the 19th century—and at the turn of the century."[29] Tellingly, Ashe had to turn to others for information on African American women athletes. Chalk did not write about African American women athletes, although he was cognizant of the fact that this was a group, neglected by scholars, that needed to be studied. This is evident in the forward to Chalk's *Black College Sport* (1976) in which he stated that "the black female athlete has not been discussed in the pages that follow" and to have done so "cursorily would have compounded the sins of the past as has too often been done with the black male athlete."[30]

Ashe began writing portions of his manuscript before all the research and collection of photographs had been assembled. Like many authors, after Ashe completed a particular section of his manuscript, he would often send it to a respected academic for feedback and analysis. The responses he received were sometimes encouraging and sometimes quite critical. Henry Louis Gates wrote: "I love your manuscript and your narrative style and believe that you have in hand a book that will make a major and definitive contribution to the literature on sports and to Afro-American culture. I look forward to reading the next draft."[31] Taking a decidedly different view was Benjamin Quarles, the noted historian at Morgan State University who had written several important books on the African American experience.[32] In a letter to Jamison, Quarles expressed his belief that the manuscript lacked both cohesion and synthesis. To Quarles, there were no smooth transitions between paragraphs, and the manuscript read more like a chronicle than a cogent history. He concluded by noting, "[My] steadily negative appraisal of this manuscript really means that I am not qualified to pass judgment on it. Hence please do not consider me for any further role in the endeavor."[33]

After many drafts and at least five years of research by the author and his team, Ashe's book was finally released on November 14, 1988. The release capped a significant stretch of time that witnessed the publication of several very influential works dealing with various aspects of the African American experience in sport. The 1980s, a period characterized by great interest in African American life and culture and the discipline of sport history more generally, saw the publication of many outstanding biographies of individual African American athletes and histories of Negro League Baseball. These books, published by both influential university and commercial presses, were complemented by a special issue of the *Journal of Sport History* (Winter 1988) devoted to "The Black Athlete in American Sport" and a host of essays written on the topic during this decade.[34] In all, *A Hard Road to Glory* found itself in the company of some excellent books written by outstanding scholars committed to telling the story of African American athletes.

Most important, *A Hard Road to Glory* did not end up being published by Howard University Press. Instead, it was published by Amistad Press, a newly created publishing house that decided to distribute the book with the help of Warner Books. Amistad had originally made a deal with the publisher Dodd, Mead and Company to jointly release the book. For financial reasons, however, Dodd, Mead was not able to continue with the project. The switch was largely because of the career move by Howard University Press executive director Charles Harris. In December 1985 Harris resigned from Howard and several months later established Amistad Press with the accompanying title of "President and Publisher." The change by Harris, and the prospect of greater financial gain with Amistad (the company promised Ashe a $45,000 advance and ten shares of stock in the new enterprise), convinced Ashe to change publishers. Despite his earlier praise of Howard University Press, Ashe was always more interested in publishing with a commercial press, and the monetary gain was no small enticement since it was estimated that he had spent $300,000 of his own money on the project.[35]

Signing with Amistad Press, which would become a company devoted exclusively to publishing books on the African American experience, resulted in some initial controversy and tense moments. It took Ashe over two years to refund the $10,000 advance against royalties that Howard

University Press had provided. And had it not been for the aggressive actions taken by Howard University general counsel Daniel Bernstine, it could have taken much longer. "Please have Mr. Ashe forward a check in the amount of $10,000 payable to Howard University immediately," wrote Bernstine in August 1988 to Ashe's lawyer David Falk, the renowned sports agent who also represented basketball star Michael Jordan. "The university has been more than patient in waiting for Mr. Ashe to market his book to another publisher. Now that Mr. Ashe has done so, any further delay in repaying the advance would be grounds for legal action."[36]

PRAISE AND CRITIQUE

The publication of *A Hard Road to Glory* brought much fanfare and media attention. Amistad, in a fact sheet that included "general selling points" for the book, announced that the three-volume work deserved attention because a famous author had written it. Noting that the book was well researched and that it included "eye-witness" accounts of sporting events, the fact sheet praised the work because it illustrated the connection between sport and the history of African Americans more generally. The fact sheet also noted that the book would appeal to a wide audience. Finally, Amistad's publicity sheet pointed out that Ashe's work included rare historical information and that it was "non-traditional" in its "social and historical analysis of the effect of specific sports performances on society."[37] Major stories on the book were published in the *New York Times*, the *San Diego Union*, and the *Chicago Tribune*. Ashe himself wrote one of the stories in the *New York Times* just before the book's official release. Entitled "Views of Sport: Taking the Hard Road with Black Athletes," Ashe discussed the book's genesis and the contributions it would make to our understanding of the African American experience in sport.[38]

Although still recovering from recent brain surgery at the time, Ashe also promoted the book through interviews and public appearances and by participating in book signings and parties. One of the most publicized book signings was co-hosted by noted psychologist Kenneth B. Clark on March 12, 1989, at the Hudson Valley Tennis Club in Hastings-on-Hudson, New York. "Come and meet the author," read the flyer announcing the event. "Your copy of this historic three-volume work will be autographed by the author and available at the special price of $75.00."[39] Whether the event was successful and how many people attended is not clear from the remaining documentation.

A Hard Road to Glory was one of several books published by Amistad Press during its first year in existence. Amistad also released books on novelist Richard Wright, football player Eric Dickerson, and Black opera singers, among other topics.[40] In terms of sales, Ashe's book was not the most successful. Still, it fared well, selling 10,515 copies of volume one; 10,208 copies of volume two; and 12,881 copies of volume three by July 1990.[41] These numbers, however, fell woefully short of Amistad's projections. The publishing house had estimated that volumes one and two would sell 40,000 a piece, and volume three would sell 45,000.[42] These lower than expected numbers did not prevent Amistad from publishing a second hardcover edition in 1993, along with separate paperbacks for a number of individual sports.[43] Despite not reaching its sales projection, Amistad obviously believed strongly in the value of the book and its potential to reach a much larger audience.

There were relatively few reviews of *A Hard Road to Glory*, despite the amount of media coverage the book received. Extended reviews of the book appeared in such notable outlets as the *New York Times*, the *Washington Post*, *The Nation*, and the *Chicago Tribune*. *Library Journal*, as is its custom, published a short review of the work. Curiously, no reviews of the book appeared in Black newspapers (only a review of the 1993 edition in the July 24, 1993 issue of the *Richmond Afro-American* and *Richmond Planet*). The two known academic reviews of the book were published in *Contemporary Sociology* and the *Sociology of Sport Journal*. No reviews appeared in scholarly historical journals—not even *The Journal of Negro History*, the major academic journal devoted to the history of the African American experience. Similarly, no reviews of the book appeared in the *Journal of Sport History*, *The Canadian Journal of the History of Sport and Physical Education* (now *Sport History Review*), or *The International Journal of the History of Sport*, the most prominent sport history journals.[44]

Why there were so few reviews of *A Hard Road to Glory* in academic journals is open to speculation. A possible answer is that individuals asked to access the book simply failed to submit the reviews they had promised to complete. Or perhaps Amistad simply failed to send review copies to the appropriate academic outlets, a distinct possibility since it must have been terribly expensive to mail a heavy three-volume work. Why no reviews appeared in the major history journals may have had to do with the relatively low regard for sport as a legitimate area of scholarly study, or the fact that Ashe was a non-academician. But other books on the African American experience in sport published in the 1980s had been reviewed in these history journals. Jules Tygiel's *Baseball's Great Experiment: Jackie Robinson and His Legacy* (1983) was reviewed in the *Journal of Southern History*, the *Journal of American History*, and the *American Historical Review*, among others. William J. Baker's *Jesse Owens: An American Life* (1986) was reviewed in such journals as the *Alabama Review*, the *Journal of Southern History*, and the *American Historical Review*. Rob Ruck's *Sandlot Seasons: Sport in Black Pittsburgh* (1987) was reviewed in a plethora of disciplinary journals, including the *Journal of American History*, the *American Historical Review*, and the *Journal of Urban History*. Joseph Moore's *Pride Against Prejudice: The Biography of Larry Doby* (1988) and Andrew Ritchie's *Major Taylor: The Extraordinary Career of a Champion Bicycle Racer* (1988), both published in the same year as *A Hard Road to Glory*, were reviewed in the *Journal of Southern History* and the *Journal of American History*.[45]

The fact that no review of the book was published in The *Journal of Negro History* is difficult to understand. Did it have something to do, in the words of historian Jeffrey Sammons, with the "reluctance of most contemporary Black scholars to address seriously the athletic experiences of African Americans"?[46] That no reviews appeared in the three most prominent sport history journals is even harder to fathom. Did these three highly respected academic journals believe the book was too popular in nature to be reviewed? Did they believe the three-volume work was not academically sound enough? Did they, like several reviews from the popular press intimated, view the book as merely a compilation or reference work and therefore not suitable for a scholarly appraisal? Whatever the reasons, it is difficult in hindsight to believe that a book dealing with a topic of great interest to a good number of people and written by one of the most prominent athletes and notable citizens in the world simply slipped through the cracks. The few reviews that were published ran the gamut from high praise to harsh criticism. Milton Yinger, in a review in a 1990 issue of *Contemporary Sociology*, referred to the book as a "monumental study" and "major research project" that was "part history, part encyclopedia, part almanac, part ethical commentary, all enriched by perceptive sociological observations." In Ashe's book, noted Yinger, "rumors have been checked, long-forgotten facts remembered and placed in context, the great athletic achievements of African Americans fully documented, and the terrible record of discrimination made utterly clear."[47] Gary Sailes's 1989 review in the *Sociology of Sport Journal*, while critical of the book's organization and dry writing style, noted that *A Hard Road to Glory* was a "thorough collection of facts and information" and "a must addition to any sports historian's personal library." "Ashe's accomplishment is timely," wrote Sailes, "and it is hoped that his work will inspire other authors to research and write about America's Black sports heroes."[48]

Of the reviews that appeared in the popular press, none were more effusive than the one written by David Halberstam, the Pulitzer Prize–winning journalist who also wrote several outstanding books on sports. In his review entitled "Champions We Never Knew," published in the *New York Times*, Halberstam called *A Hard Road to Glory* "a fascinating three-volume study" that documents the "remarkable history of the Black athlete in America from 1619 to the present." "The book," wrote Halberstam, "is a compelling history of prejudice and meanness, of honor and dishonor, a book both about sports and not about sports."[49] Skip Myslenski, in a *Chicago Tribune* article titled "A Race to Succeed: The Trials and Dreams of America's Black Athletes," noted that Ashe provided an "exhaustively chronicled" account of the history of African American athletes. "Arthur Ashe—once a tennis champion, now one of sport's consciences," declared Myslenski, "recounts the closed minds, narrow thinking, and the endless prejudices encountered by Blacks as they strove to become part of America's sporting fabric."[50] David Nicholson, writing for the *Washington Post*, gave a far more critical appraisal. Although noting that Ashe deserved to be congratulated for accumulating so much information from such a wide variety of sources, Nicholson observed: "No one seems to have been able to make up his mind what sort of book—encyclopedia, reference book, coffee table book—*A Hard Road to Glory* should be. As a result, it is a little of each, and not enough of any one."[51] In an essay review in *The Nation*, which also included an analysis of Phillip Hoose's just published *Necessities: Racial Barriers in American Sports* (1989), Nicolaus Mills wrote, "Too often Ashe writes in a dreary prose that belongs in an encyclopedia, but the story he tells is nonetheless riveting. Like C. Vann Woodward's *The Strange Career of Jim Crow*, Ashe's history does not begin in a terrible past and move into an enlightened present; it records regression as well as progress."[52]

Those reviewers who criticized *A Hard Road to* Glory for its writing style, organization, and encyclopedic approach were right to do so. Ashe could have benefited from the expertise of the authors who had collaborated with him on his four autobiographical works. Although obviously a different genre, the four autobiographies are much better written, provide more thoughtful insights and interpretations, and are more sophisticated in style and presentation.[53] This stands to reason since those men who collaborated with Ashe on his autobiographies were professional writers, and in the case of Stanford University's Arnold Rampersad, an academically trained biographer with years of research experience, a thorough knowledge of the past, and wonderful skills in crafting stories that are of interest to a large readership.

Ashe was assisted in his first memoir, *Advantage Ashe* (1967), by Clifford George Gewecki, a writer who also penned the books *Day by Day in Dodgers History* (1984) and (with Bill Emmerton) *The Official Book of Running* (1978). The result is a skillfully written account of Ashe's life prior to his capturing the 1968 US Open, his first major tennis title. His next autobiographical work, *Arthur Ashe: Portrait in Motion* (1975), was written in collaboration with Frank Deford, the well-known journalist and novelist who is a member of the Sportswriters Hall of Fame. The result is a detailed and expertly crafted account of Ashe's 1973–1974 tennis season, which would prove to be one of the most successful of his career. In *Off the Court* (1981), his third autobiographical work, Ashe teamed with Neil Amdur, the former lead tennis writer as well as sports editor of the *New York Times*. The result is a very interesting and nicely fashioned account of Ashe's life and career published three years after his retirement from tennis. *Days of Grace: A Memoir* (1993), released shortly after Ashe's death, was written in collaboration with Rampersad, who wrote acclaimed biographies of Langston Hughes, Ralph Ellison, and Jackie Robinson. The result is a very reflective and poignant account of Ashe's life that discusses, among other things, the influence of his parents, his struggle with AIDS, his tennis career, his battles against South African apartheid, the inspiration for writing *A Hard Road to Glory*, his relationship with his wife and daughter, and his efforts to ensure a proper balance between education and athletics among young children. The success of *Days of Grace* is evidenced by its rise at one point to number two on the *New York Times* best sellers list.[54]

A Hard Road to Glory, while providing some good information on African American athletes—both behind segregated walls and in predominantly White-dominated areas of sport—is sprinkled with errors, as are most published works. There are several misspellings. For instance, Tom Lees is referred to as Tom Leeds (vol. 1, p. 25), Franz Alfred "Jazz" Byrd as Franz Alfred "Jazz" Bird (vol. 2, p. 100), Bob Pettit as Bob Petitt (vol. 3, p. 62), and Prentice Gautt as Prentice Gault (vol. 3, p. 110). However, it is also not sufficiently documented, and is organized in a manner that makes it difficult to assess the historical changes in sport within the context of the larger American society. Because each of the volumes is organized topically by sport, the work fails to place athletes in their proper historical contexts, and lacks sufficient details about the interconnections among race, sport, and American culture. There is no mention in the volumes of Title IX, the extraordinarily important 1972 law that contributed to a dramatic increase, albeit depending on race and socioeconomic factors among other things, in the number of women participating in sport at all levels of competition. Some of the material does not even pertain to African American athletes and there are several chapters with scant information and even fewer references. Confusingly, Ashe opens volume one with an introduction that includes sections on sport in ancient Egypt, Greece, Rome, and the Middle Ages. The chapter on cycling consists of a four-page summation of the career of Marshall "Major" Taylor, with four of the seven citations coming from Dale Somers's *The Rise of Sports in New Orleans* (1972), and the other three taken from Taylor's autobiography.[55] The chapter on tennis is just six pages, the chapter on golf is five, and the chapter on wrestling three, with the only reference curiously coming from Frederick Douglass's autobiography.

Nearly eight hundred pages of the three volumes are taken up by reference sections with listings of such disparate items as the career records of Black boxing champions, all-time rosters of professional sports franchises, African Americans on the NCAA final four All-Decade Team, Black college football players in the NFL, the evolution of world records in track and field, and African Americans receiving Associated Press Athlete of the Year awards.[56] The work would have been far more effective if it were one volume rather than three, and if Ashe had chosen—as historian Douglas Booth has noted of my own work and such scholars as Michael Oriard have done so expertly—to bring greater reflexivity to his subject. In essence, *A Hard Road to Glory* would have been that much more interesting and meaningful if Ashe had, just as he would do in collaboration with Rampersad in *Days of Grace*, depended on his unique status as both athlete and writer and imparted insights and philosophical positions based on his personal experiences in sport. Ashe had access to important individuals, events, and organizations in sport that could have complemented his use of standard archival material and published secondary sources and potentially led to a richer analysis and interpretation of the experiences of African American athletes. Who better, for example, to provide a clearer understanding of the racial realities in the world of tennis or the interconnections between sport and apartheid in South Africa? Who better to explain what it was like to be an African American athlete in a predominantly White university, or to make clear the inevitable pressure resulting from the simultaneous desire to maintain a commitment to sport while expressing one's views on larger social issues?[57]

The approach Ashe took, at least in the book's narrative portions, is very similar to the one Ocania Chalk followed in his books on the African American athlete.[58] Like Chalk, Ashe provides a litany of dates, names, events, and stories of African American athletes. The message that Ashe hoped to deliver, however, resembles more closely that conveyed by Edwin B. Henderson, his mentor Dr. Robert Johnson, and a host of other Black intellectuals throughout the twentieth century who espoused a belief in what historian Patrick B. Miller has termed "muscular assimilationism." Like the writings of such famous authors and civil rights activists as W. E. B. Du Bois, James Weldon Johnson, and Richard Wright, among others, Ashe's intent was to hold Black athletes up as symbols of possibility and thereby engender pride among African Americans based on these achievements.[59]

Showing deep emotional attachment to his subject, a profound interest in altering biases against African Americans, and a steadfast commitment to fostering equality of opportunity, *A Hard Road to Glory* is intended to demonstrate that African Americans are equally capable in realizing success in sport and, by extension other professions, and in all walks of life. Although pointing out the continuing discriminatory practices in sport, including the lack of Black managers, upper-level administrators, and owners, and perhaps not as optimistic as many others about sport's ability to break down racial barriers, Ashe believed that recounting the successes of African American athletes was crucially important for showcasing African American progress and perseverance. Essentially, Ashe believed that calling attention to African American athletic victories would uplift the entire Black community and contribute to the larger campaign for racial justice. "*A Hard Road to Glory* was an emotional experience for me," wrote Ashe in *Days of Grace*, "because it dealt so intimately, at almost every stage, with both the triumph and tragedy, the elation and suffering, of Blacks as they met not only the physical challenges of their sport, but also the gratuitous challenges of racism."[60]

Whether *A Hard Road to Glory* contributed to altering racial views is impossible to determine, but there is no question that the book has enjoyed a long shelf life and has been used by a large number of scholars who have published works on African American involvement in sport.[61] The use of the book, however, has often been accompanied by warnings to treat it judiciously because of its mistakes and limitations. One of the latest warnings came from Charles H. Martin in *Benching Jim Crow: The Rise and Fall of the*

Color Line in Southern College Sports, 1890–1980 (2010). Ashe's work "still remains a valuable resource" wrote Martin, "but it must be used carefully since it contains many factual errors."[62]

Although the claim that *A Hard Road to Glory* continues to be an important resource is probably true, it is less certain whether the book has, as Gary Sailes hoped for in his 1989 review, inspired others to write about African American participation in sport. No historical survey has been written on African American participation in sport since the publication of *A Hard Road to Glory*. Perhaps the two books that come closest to this genre are Russell T. Wigginton's *The Strange Career of the Black Athlete: African Americans and Sport* (2006) and David K. Wiggins and Patrick B. Miller's *The Unlevel Playing Field: A Documentary History of the African American Experience in Sport* (2003), but the former is far from comprehensive and the latter work traces the participation of African Americans in sport from the days of slavery through a collection of primary sources rather than through a sustained narrative.[63] Most of what we know about African American participation in sport comes from individual biographies and specialized essays, book chapters, and monographs dealing with topics ranging from the integration of predominantly White organized sport and the history of Negro League Baseball to the Olympic Games and participation in college athletics. More than anything else, each of these works resulted from the growth of sport history as an academic discipline and increased interest among scholars in examining the interconnection among race, sport, and American culture.[64]

With that said, *A Hard Road to Glory* has been the inspiration and foundation for many projects and initiatives. In 1988, a sixty-minute documentary based on the book was distributed by Wood Knapp Video and ultimately became a part of the Kodak Video Programs sports series. Hosted by Ashe, narrated by actor James Earl Jones, and including re-enactments as well as television and newsreel clips, the Emmy Award-winning documentary closely follows the same story lines as the book.[65] In 1993 Ashe approached HBO about producing a documentary on the African American athlete, but he died of AIDS two days before he was to discuss the project with HBO executives. Fortunately, HBO senior producer Rick Bernstein loved the concept and assembled a group of experts that produced the 1996 Peabody Award-winning, two-part documentary, *Journey of the African American Athlete*. Dedicated to Ashe and Gregory Hunter, a production assistant who died of cancer at age twenty-six while producing the documentary, *Journey of the African American Athlete* was written by noted *New York Times* sportswriter William Rhoden and narrated by actor Samuel L. Jackson. The documentary included as commentators, sociologist and civil rights activist Harry Edwards, historians and sports scholars Gerald Early and Randy Roberts, sportswriter Sam Lacy, and authors Dick Schaap, Frank Bolden, and Nelson George. Without intending to do so, Bernstein provided a summary of the documentary that could just as easily have been used to describe Ashe's intent in writing *A Hard Road to Glory*: "It's a wonderful history lesson. Hopefully, it will serve as an educational tool for people. That was one of our goals—to produce a show that withstands the test of time."[66]

However one judges *A Hard Road to Glory*'s quality and impact, the mere writing of the book should be viewed as an act of agency on Ashe's part and a reflection of his life, interests, and philosophical approach to racial issues. Taking on a project that many people told him he couldn't accomplish, Ashe became the very symbol of possibility and example of achievement he addressed in his book. A celebrated athlete, Ashe helped obliterate through *A Hard Road to Glory*, and his many other accomplishments, the historical image of African Americans as passive human beings who had no power over their own lives and meekly acquiesced to the whims and wishes of those in the dominant White power structure. He never allowed his commitment to sport to take away from his other interests and overshadow his intellectual pursuits and devotion to the life of the mind. Cerebral, disciplined, thoughtful, serious, and entrepreneurial, Ashe always loved history. He would become a collector of rare books on Black life, ordering "hard-to-find books from catalogs" and regularly receiving listings from "rare-book dealers in New York, Boston and Chicago." He claimed to own "every contemporary book on African-American athletes," including "seven different books about Muhammad Ali, five or six about Joe Louis, and four on Jesse Owens."[67] Ashe combined his love of reading and books with a commitment to educating Black youth and sharing information on African American life and culture, particularly from the world of sport, with different audiences through various mediums. In 1984 he organized an art exhibition on the "History of the African American Athlete" for the World's Fair in New Orleans.[68] He also proposed, along with two other partners, the selling of children's books on African American history at "kiosks in malls, department stores, toy stores, and other public places."[69] It is not surprising that Ashe wanted the statue erected of him in Richmond following his death to depict him wearing his tennis warm-ups and surrounded by children with a tennis racket and book in his hands.[70]

In 1991 the Aetna Life and Casualty Company, on whose board of directors Ashe served, published *A Hard Road to Glory* calendar that depicted Black athletic heroes such as Dave Bing, Alice Coachman, Sugar Ray Robinson, Isaac Murphy, Althea Gibson, Charles Sifford, Flo Hyman, Jesse Owens, Paul Robeson, Jackie Robinson, Nikki Franke, and Willie O'Ree. The purpose of the calendar, which included photographs from the exhibition in New Orleans and *A Hard Road to Glory*, was to present, in Ashe's words, "positive images of productive, highly disciplined and achievement-oriented role models."[71] Possessed of boundless energy, Ashe also gave lectures at many colleges and universities. For example, in a span of two months in 1982, he lectured to the sports law class at Tulane University and discussed African American history in a contemporary affairs seminar at the US Military Academy at West Point.[72] In 1983 he gave the Kiphuth Fellowship Public Lecture at Yale University, a prestigious semi-annual event in honor of legendary Yale swimming coach Robert J. J. Kiphuth.[73] Based on his résumé, Ashe gave twenty-one lectures in 1992 alone, including talks at the College of William and Mary, St. John's College of Maryland, Longwood College, University of Maryland, Ithaca College, and Kalamazoo College. Although not knowing the exact message presented in these lectures, it is safe to assume that Ashe, as he wrote in essays such as "Don't Tell Me How to Think," "Send Your Children to the Libraries," and "Coddling Black Athletes," pointed out the divergent roles of African American athletes in the civil rights struggle and warned of the dangers of devoting too much attention to sport. And as he had done in *A Hard Road to Glory*, he very likely emphasized the idea that the individual successes of African American athletes foster a sense of Black self-respect and challenge White racist beliefs and attitudes in the larger society. This was all part of, to use William Rhoden's terminology, the "burden of proof" always hanging over the heads of African Americans, both athletes and non-athletes alike, contributing to their constant "sense of longing" and "desire to measure up."[74]

Notes

1. For information on Ashe and other African Americans in tennis, see Sundiata Djata, *Blacks at the Net: Black Achievement in the History of Tennis*, 2 vols. (New York, 2006, 2008).

2. For a very poignant account of Ashe's life, see Margo Jefferson, "On the Court, In the World," *New York Times*, 13 June 1993, 7, 11, 28–29, reprinted in David K. Wiggins and Patrick B. Miller, *The Unlevel Playing Field: A Documentary History of the African American Experience in Sport* (Urbana, IL, 2003), 371–76. For insightful information on Ashe, see also Damion L. Thomas, "The Quiet Militant: Arthur Ashe and

Black Athlete Activism" in *Out of the Shadows: A Biographical History of African American Athletes*, ed. David K. Wiggins (Fayetteville, AR, 2006); and "'Don't Tell Me How to Think': Arthur Ashe and the Burden of 'Being Black,'" *The International Journal of the History of Sport* 27 (May 2010): 1313–29; Eric Allen Hall, "'I Guess I'm Becoming More Militant': Arthur Ashe and the Black Freedom Movement, 1961–1968," *The Journal of African American History* 96 (Fall 2011): 474–502; Matthew Mace Barbee, "Memory and Masculinity: Arthur Ashe in Word, Deed, and Monument" in *Southern Masculinity: Perspectives on Manhood in the South Since Reconstruction*, ed. Craig Thompson Friend (Athens, GA, 2009), 174–95; and Jaime Schultz, "Contesting the Master Narrative: The Arthur Ashe Statue and Monument Avenue in Richmond, Virginia," *The International Journal of the History of Sport* 28 (May 2011): 1235–51.

3. See Arthur Ashe, "Don't Tell Me How to Think," *Black Sports* 5 (August 1975): 35–37; Arthur Ashe, "Send Your Children to the Libraries," *New York Times*, 6 February 1977, 2; Arthur Ashe, "Coddling Black Athletes," *New York Times*, 10 February 1989, A3.

4. Arthur Ashe with Louie Robinson, *Getting Started in Tennis* (New York, 1977); Arthur Ashe with Larry Sheehad, *Mastering Your Tennis Strokes* (New York, 1978); Arthur Ashe, *Arthur Ashe's Tennis Clinic* (New York, 1981); Arthur Ashe with Clifford George Gewecke, Jr., *Advantage Ashe* (New York, 1967); Arthur Ashe with Frank Deford, *Arthur Ashe: Portrait in Motion* (New York, 1975); Arthur Ashe with Neil Amdur, *Off the Court* (New York, 1981); Arthur Ashe with Arnold Rampersad, *Days of Grace: A Memoir* (New York, 1993); and Arthur Ashe with the assistance of Kip Branch, Ocania Chalk, and Francis Harris, *A Hard Road to Glory: A History of the African American Athlete*, 3 vols. (New York, 1988, 1993).

5. The official website of Arthur Ashe lists his various honors and awards. See http://www.cmgww.com/sports/ Ashe. Scholars are fortunate that Ashe kept much of his personal correspondence and professional papers, which he donated to the Schomburg Center for Research in Black Culture in New York City (hereafter AA Papers, SCRBC).

6. Amy Bass, *Not the Triumph But the Struggle: The 1968 Olympics and the Making of the Black Athlete* (Minneapolis, MN, 2004), 15; Ronald Roach, "Keeping the Ashe Legacy Relevant," *Black Issues in Higher Education* 20, 10 April 2003, 18–19; Elliott J. Gorn and Warren Goldstein, *A Brief History of American Sports* (Urbana, IL, 2004), 270; Jeffrey T. Sammons, "'Race' and Sport: A Critical, Historical Examination," *Journal of Sport History* 21 (Fall 1994): 223.

7. Arthur Ashe and Arnold Rampersad, *Days of Grace: A Memoir* (New York, 1993), 173–75; Herbert Kupferberg, "Their Hard Road to Glory: Tennis Champ Arthur Ashe Tells the Story of Black Athletes," *Parade*, March 1989, 12, 14; Henry Briggs, Jr., "A Hard Road to Glory," 17 January 1994, box 9, AA Papers, SCRBC, 1–16.

8. Edwin B. Henderson, *The Negro in Sports* (Washington, DC, 1939, 1949); *The Black Athlete: Emergence and Arrival* (New York, 1968); A. S. "Doc" Young, *Negro Firsts in Sports* (Chicago, IL, 1963); Wally Jones and Jim Washington, *Black Champions*

Challenge American Sports (New York, 1972); Jack Olsen, *The Black Athlete: A Shameful Story* (New York, 1968); and Edna and Art Rust, Jr., *Art Rust's Illustrated History of the Black Athlete* (New York, 1985). It is especially surprising that Ashe never mentioned Henderson's *The Black Athlete: Emergence and Arrival*. The book, with a full-page photograph of Ashe, ironically enough, following his 1975 Wimbledon Championship on the inside cover, is full of good information on the African American athlete and includes an extensive 23-page bibliography of journal articles and books on the Black experience in sport.

9. Arthur Ashe, "First Draft Proposal," 8 December 1982, box 9, AA Papers, SCRBC.

10. Charles F. Harris "Publisher's Statement," in Arthur Ashe, *A Hard Road to Glory* (New York, 1993), ix; Briggs, "A Hard Road to Glory," 14.

11. "Arthur Ashe Signs Contract for Major Book with Howard University Press," *Howard University Press News,* box 9, AA Papers, SCRBC, 3.

12. Ibid.

13. Arthur Ashe, *A Hard Road to Glory*, Vol. 1, xiii.

14. "Collaboration Agreement" 1 June 1983, box 9, AA Papers, SCRBC.

15. *Pioneers of Black Sport: The Early Days of the Black Professional Athlete in Baseball, Basketball, Boxing, and Football* and *Black College Sport* were both published by Dodd, Mead and Company.

16. Charles F. Harris, "Publishers Statement," x.

17. Arthur Ashe and Arnold Rampersad, *Days of Grace: A Memoir,* 175.

18. See Robert M. Thomas Jr., "Ashe Must Turn to Scrapbooks and Letters Rather than Libraries for Facts," *The New York Times*, 27 June 1983, box 9, AA Papers, SCRBC; Arnold S. Friedman to Arthur Ashe, 11 March 1984, box 9, AA Papers, SCRBC; Joe Dance to Arthur Ashe, 14 February 1984, box 9, AA Papers, SCRBC; Donald Sturges to Arthur Ashe, 28 March 1984, box 9, AA Papers, SCRBC.

19. Most of the available evidence here is correspondence from individuals acknowledging letters of inquiry sent by Ashe. See, for example, Armstead L. Robinson to Arthur Ashe, 7 September 1983, box 9, AA Papers, SCRBC; Henry Louis Gates to Arthur Ashe, 19 October 1983, box 9, AA Papers, SCRBC; V. P. Franklin to Arthur Ashe, 7 September 1983, box 9, AA Papers, SCRBC; John Hope Franklin to Arthur Ashe, 19 September 1983, box 9, AA Papers, SCRBC; and Charles V. Hamilton to Arthur Ashe, 6 September 1985, box 9, AA Papers, SCRBC.

20. Arthur Ashe to Frederick Obear, 10 September 1984, box 9, AA Papers, SCRBC. Again, much of the available evidence here is communication from people acknowledging letters of inquiry sent by Ashe. See, for example, John Harvith to Arthur Ashe, 29 March 1985, box 9, AA Papers, SCRBC; Susan S. Lipschutz to Arthur Ashe, 6 February 1985, box 9, AA Papers, SCRBC; and Barbara M. Woods to Arthur Ashe, 8 June 1983, box 9, AA Papers, SCRBC.

21. Arthur Ashe to Frederick Obear, 10 September 1984, box 9, AA Papers, SCRBC.

22. Arnold S. Friedman to Arthur Ashe, 11 March 1984, box 9, AA Papers, SCRBC.

23. Susan S. Lipschutz to Arthur Ashe, 6 February 1985, box 9, AA Papers, SCRBC.

24. Henry Louis Gates to Arthur Ashe 19 October 1983, box 9, AA Papers, SCRBC.
25. V. P. Franklin to Arthur Ashe, 7 September 1983, box 9, AA Papers, SCRBC.
26. John Hope Franklin to Arthur Ashe, 19 September 1983, box 9, AA Papers, SCRBC. *Black New Orleans* was published by the University of Chicago Press; *Slave Testimony* was published by Louisiana State University Press; *From Slavery to Freedom* was first published by Alfred A. Knopf; *Been in the Storm Too Long* was first published by Alfred A. Knopf; both editions of *The Negro in Sports* were published by Associated Publishers. Franklin also suggested to Ashe that he read: Edwin B. Henderson with the editors of *Sport* magazine; *The Black Athlete: Emergence and Arrival*; Solomon Northup, *Twelve Years A Slave* (Buffalo, 1853); Frederick Law Olmsted, *The Cotton Kingdom* (New York, 1953); Ulrich B. Phillips, *Life and Labor in the Old South* (Boston, 1929); and Richard Wade, *Slavery in the Cities: The South 1820-1860* (New York, 1964).
27. See, for example, Rod Howard to League of American Wheelmen, 23 October 1984, box 9, AA Papers, SCRBC; Rod Howard to American Water Skiing Association, 23 October 1984, box 9, AA Papers, SCRBC; Rod Howard to US Volleyball Association, 23 October 1984, box 9, AA Papers SCRBC; Rod Howard to United States Table Tennis Association, 23 October 1984, box 9, AA Papers, SCRBC; Rod Howard to National Skeet Shooting Association, 23 October 1984, box 9, AA Papers SCRBC; Rod Howard to US Figure Skating Association, 23 October 1984, box 9, AA Papers, SCRBC; and Rod Howard to Professional Bowlers Association, 23 October 1984, box 9, AA Papers, SCRBC.
28. In an email correspondence, Kip Branch estimated that Francis Harris spent 30 percent of his time on the project and Chalk 25 to 30 percent. He also noted, "[Chalk's] book on Black college sports was invaluable for all of us." Kip Branch to David K. Wiggins, 24 June 2011.
29. Ocania Chalk to Sandra Jamison, 8 July 1983, box 9, AA Papers, SCRBC.
30. Ocania Chalk, *Black College Sport*, Foreword, n.p.
31. Henry Louis Gates to Arthur Ashe, 20 September 1984, box 9, AA Papers, SCRBC.
32. Quarles, who earned his PhD from the University of Wisconsin in 1940, was the chair of the history department at Morgan State University from 1953 to 1974. For an interesting overview of his scholarship, see August Meier, "Benjamin Quarles and the Historiography of Black America," *Civil War History* 26 (June 1980): 101–16.
33. Benjamin Quarles to Sandra Jamison, 31 May 1984, box 9, AA Papers, SCRBC.
34. Examples of these books include: Jules Tygiel, *Baseball's Great Experiment: Jackie Robinson and His Legacy* (New York, 1983); Randy Roberts, *Papa Jack: Jack Johnson and the Era of White Hopes* (New York, 1983); Chris Mead, *Champion: Joe Louis, Black Hero in White America* (New York, 1985); William J. Baker, *Jesse Owens: An American Life* (New York, 1986); Donn Rogosin, *Invisible Men: Life in Baseball's Negro Leagues* (New York, 1983); Rob Ruck, *Sport in Black Pittsburgh* (Urbana, IL, 1987); Joseph Moore, *Pride Against Prejudice: The Biography of Larry Doby* (New York, 1988); and Andrew Ritchie, *Major Taylor: The Extraordinary Career of a Champion Bicycle Racer* (San Francisco, 1988). The special issue on "The Black Athlete in American

Sport" in the Winter 1988 *Journal of Sport History* was guest edited by David K. Wiggins and includes essays by Wiggins, Thomas G. Smith, Donald Spivey, and William H. Wiggins. See the *Journal of Sport History* 15 (Winter 1988): 239–333. Another special issue on African American participation in sport recently appeared in the Fall 2011 *The Journal of African American History*. Guest edited by Scott N. Brooks and Dexter Blackman and titled "African Americans and the History of Sport," the special issue includes an introduction by Brooks and Blackman and essays by Brooks, Louis Moore, Eric Allen Hall, Tracey Owens Patton, and Sally Schedlock.

35. For information on Amistad Press and its publication of *A Hard Road to Glory*, see Charles F. Harris, "Publisher's Statement," pp. x–xi. Amistad Press, Inc. "Presidents Annual Report—1988," box 9, AA Papers, SCRBC. Amistad-Warner Authors, December 1988, box 9, AA Papers, SCRBC.

36. Daniel O. Bernstine to David B. Falk, 11 August 1988, box 9, AA Papers, SCRBC.

37. Amistad Press Fact Sheet, box 9, AA Papers, SCRBC.

38. Arthur Ashe, "Views of Sport; Taking the Hard Road with Black Athletes," *New York Times*, 13 November 1988.

39. A Book Party, "Hard Road to Glory," 12 March 1989, box 9, AA Papers, SCRBC.

40. Amistad Press, Inc., "Sales Projections—1989," box 9, AA Papers, SCRBC. Other books published by Amistad (New York) included Margaret Walker, *Richard Wright: Daemonic Genius* (1988); Robert L. Allen, *The Port Chicago Mutiny* (1989); John H. Johnson, *Succeeding Against the Odds* (1989); Erik Dickerson and Richard Walsh, *Eric Dickerson's Secrets of Pro Power* (1989); and Rosalyn Story, *And So I Sing* (1989).

41. Amistad Press, Inc., Gross Profit, Title-to-Date, box 9, AA Papers, SCRBC.

42. Amistad Press, Inc., Sales Projections—1989, box 9, AA Papers, SCRBC.

43. The 1993 version of the book is very similar to the 1988 edition. It also received relatively little attention from the academic community. For reviews of the 1993 edition, including the books on individual sports, see Leon Harris, "Critic Reviews Books for February's Black History Month," CNN, 11 February 1994, accessed 16 February 2012, http://www.lexisnexis.com/inacui2api/delivery; Laurel Graeber, "New & Noteworthy Paperbacks," *New York Times*, 23 January 1994, section 7, 24; M. L. LeCompte, *A Hard Road to Glory*, *Choice*, December 1993, 640.

44. *Journal of Sport History*, *Canadian Journal of the History of Sport and Physical Education* (now *Sport History Review*), and *The International Journal of the History of Sport* have always had a relatively long list of published book reviews. Although difficult to do so, these three journals, and the other scholarly outlets that now publish sport history related pieces, have all made efforts to continue to provide as many scholarly reviews as possible in a field that has witnessed a dramatic increase in the number of books published.

45. These reviews were completed by notable and very accomplished historians with national reputations, including the likes of Elliott J. Gorn; Joseph A. Gagliano, chair of urban history at Loyola University, Chicago; and Steven Riess, author of

multiple works on sport history from Northeastern Illinois University. For a terrific source listing book reviews, see the *Book Review Index*.

46. Jeffrey T. Sammons, "'Race' and Sport: A Critical Historical Examination," 203–78.

47. J. Milton Yinger, untitled review of *A Hard Road to Glory*, in *Contemporary Sociology* 19 (March 1990): 286.

48. Gary A. Sailes, untitled review of *A Hard Road to Glory*, in *Sociology of Sport Journal* 6 (1989): 394.

49. David Halberstam, "Champions We Never Knew," *New York Times*, 4 December 1988, section 7, 11.

50. Skip Myslenski, "A Race to Succeed: The Trials and Dreams of America's Black Athletes," *Chicago Tribune*, 27 November 1988, N3.

51. David Nicholson, "Those Championship Seasons," *The Washington Post*, 29 January 1989, X8.

52. Nicolaus Mills, "On and Off the Playing Field," *The Nation*, 8 May 1989, 634.

53. Why Ashe chose to write four autobiographies is open to speculation. Be that as it may, Ashe was bested by the great Olympic hero Jesse Owens who wrote five autobiographies in collaboration with Paul Neimark. See the jointly written Owens and Neimark books: *The Jesse Owens Story* (New York, 1970); *Blackthink: My Life as Black Man and White Man* (New York, 1970); *I Have Changed* (New York, 1972); *Jesse: The Man Who Outran Hitler* (New York, 1978); and *Jesse: A Spiritual Autobiography* (New York, 1978).

54. Neil Amdur is well-known for his many writings on sport, including coauthoring with Vince Matthews *My Race Be Won* (New York, 1974); and with Chris Evert Lloyd, *Chrissie: My Own Story* (New York, 1984). Frank Deford enjoyed a long career writing about sport, with some of his best-known books being *Big Bill Tilden: The Triumphs and the Tragedy* (New York, 1976); *Five Strides on the Banked Track: The Life and Times of the Roller Derby* (New York, 1971); and *The Old Ball Game* (New York, 2005). See Arnold Rampersad, *Ralph Ellison: A Biography* (New York, 2007); *The Life of Langston Hughes*, 2 vols. (New York, 1986, 1988); and *Jackie Robinson: A Biography* (New York, 1997).

55. Dale Somers, *The Rise of Sports in New Orleans* (Baton Rouge, LA, 1972) and Marshall W. "Major" Taylor, *The Fastest Bicycle Rider in the World* (Worcester, MA, 1928).

56. The reference section alone in volume 2 is 363 pages in length. The total number of pages in the entire volume, including sources and index, is 497 pages. See Arthur Ashe, *A Hard Road to Glory, 1919–1945*, 113–476.

57. Jeffrey T. Sammons believes the book would have been "far more appealing and accessible to a wider audience if the narrative sections of the collection appeared in one volume" rather than three. See Sammons, "Race and Sport: A Critical Historical Examination," 224. For the notion of reflexivity and methodology in sport

history more generally, see Douglas Booth, *The Field: Truth and Fiction in Sport History* (New York, 2005), particularly 218–20. Michael Oriard has taken a more deconstructionist approach and a focus on the role of language in all his books on football. See *Football: How the Popular Press Created an American Spectacle* (Chapel Hill, NC, 1993); *King Football: Sport and Spectacle in the Golden Age of Radio and Newsreels, Movies and Magazines, the Weekly and the Daily Press* (Chapel Hill, NC, 2001); *Brand Football: Making and Selling America's Favorite Sport* (Chapel Hill, NC, 2007); and *Bowled Over: Big-Time College Football from the Sixties to the BCS Era* (Chapel Hill, NC, 2009).

58. See, for example, Chalk, *Pioneers of Black Sport*.

59. See David K. Wiggins, "Edwin Bancroft Henderson, African American Athletes, and the Writing of Sport History," in *Glory Bound: Black Athletes in a White America*, David K. Wiggins (Syracuse, NY, 1997), 221–39; and Wiggins and Miller, *The Unlevel Playing Field*, esp., 3–4, 72–73, 87, 113, 155, 186, 190, 423, and 444.

60. Ashe and Rampersad, *Days of Grace*, 174.

61. Google Scholar lists 140 citations for *A Hard Road to Glory*. Ashe's memoir written with Arnold Rampersad, *Days of Grace*, follows closely behind with 92.

62. Charles H. Martin, *Benching Jim Crow: The Rise and Fall of the Color Line in Southern College Sport, 1890–1980* (Urbana, IL, 2010), 357.

63. Russell T. Wigginton, *The Strange Career of the Black Athlete: African Americans and Sports* (Westport, CT, 2006); and Wiggins and Miller, *The Unlevel Playing Field*.

64. To see a representative sample of published works on the African American athlete, consult the "Bibliographic Essay and List" in Wiggins and Miller, *The Unlevel Playing Field*, 447–77.

65. Running Movies, *A Hard Road to Glory*, 60-minute documentary, http://www.runningmovies.com/title/401.html.

66. Steve Nidetz, "HBO's 'Journey': A History Lesson in Black Success," *Chicago Tribune*, 12 February 1996, accessed 16 February 2012, http://articles.chicagotribune.com/1996-02-12/sports/9602120006_1_arthur-ashe-sports-fans-journey.

67. Daphne Hurford, "A Man of Many Words," *Sports Illustrated*, 4 November 1991, accessed 4 April 2012, http://cnnsi.printthis.clickability.com/pt/cpt?expire=&title=Arthur+Ashe+is+a+bibliophile+.

68. Sandra Jamison to Emily Dyer, 29 May 1984, box 9, AA Papers, SCRBC. Memo, n.d., box 9, AA Papers, SCRBC.

69. Memo, n.d., box 9, AA Papers, SCRBC.

70. Barbee, "Memory and Masculinity: Arthur Ashe in Word, Deed, and Monument," 190.

71. Arthur Ashe to Phyllis C. Rogers, 13 November 1985, box 9, AA Papers, SCRBC.

72. Jonathan A. Bell to Arthur Ashe, 25 January 1982, box 2, AA Papers, SCRBC; A. Lee Fentress to Arthur Ashe, 30 March 1982, box 2, AA Papers, SCRBC.

73. Ashe and Rampersad, *Days of Grace*, 169.

74. William C. Rhoden, *Forty Million Dollar Slaves: The Rise, Fall, and Redemption of the Black Athlete* (New York, 2006), 117–18.

"THE STRUGGLE THAT MUST BE"

Harry Edwards, Sport, and the Fight for Racial Equality

Harry Edwards is, by whatever definition employed, a revolutionary. Intelligent, physically imposing, highly determined, extremely confident and always courageous, Edwards has fought for almost his entire adult life to ensure that African Americans are treated fairly in sport and that the United States lives up to its democratic principles. He also has pushed, both individually and in concert with other revolutionaries, for a fundamental change in how we think about sport and what policies need to be implemented to make it better. Like many revolutionaries, Edwards has always been a lightning rod, beloved and admired by many while at the same time being loathed and disrespected by others. Like many revolutionaries, Edwards undertook different approaches in his efforts to effect change, including scholarly writings, lectures, protests and boycotts. And like many revolutionaries, Edwards, in the latter stages of his career, worked more often within the system, a result of progress and positive changes in sport rather than any fundamental alterations in his basic principles and philosophical approach to the world. Seemingly out of the realm of possibility many years ago, Edwards has recently been acknowledged for his many accomplishments. He has been invited to deliver plenary addresses and has received other tributes. Perhaps more than anything else, this recognition has come from a newfound respect people have for the man who has served for so long as the conscience of sport.[1]

EDUCATIONAL ATTAINMENTS AND LEADER OF PROTESTS

Born November 22, 1942, into squalid conditions in East St. Louis, Edwards grew up in a household that saw his mother abandon him and his seven siblings. Edwards's father worked as a laborer. Despite these circumstances, Edwards would go on to become a scholarship athlete and an outstanding student, earning a bachelor's degree from San Jose State College in 1964, a master's in 1966 and a doctorate from Cornell University in 1973. From 1967 to 1969, he was an instructor of sociology at San Jose State College, and an assistant professor, and then professor of sociology at the University of California, Berkeley, from 1970 until his retirement from the school in 2000. He complemented his academic work by serving as an assistant to the commissioner of Major League Baseball and as a consultant to both the San Francisco 49ers and Golden State Warriors.[2]

Edwards first garnered national attention in 1967 when he led a protest of Black students at San Jose State College who threatened to "physically interfere" with the school's opening football game against the University of Texas at El Paso.[3] The Black students formed a group called United Black Students for Action, put forth nine specific demands, ranging from the elimination of discrimination in housing to the mistreatment of African American athletes on campus. University administrators eventually addressed the demands, but not before racial tension became so inflamed that the football game was canceled. The cancelation of the game resulted in Edwards receiving a sharp rebuke from then California Governor Ronald Reagan, who called him "unfit to teach." Not to be outdone, Edwards responded by declaring that Reagan was "a petrified pig, unfit to govern."[4]

The confrontation at San Jose State College demonstrated the increasing involvement of African American athletes in the civil rights movement and Edwards's controversial practice of using sport to achieve racial equality. Assuming a public persona that was all fire and brimstone, Edwards confronted the White establishment head on, and the disruption of sport became one of his most powerful tools. As a former athlete, Edwards appreciated the many sporting successes of Black athletes and the symbolic importance of these achievements for the African American community. But it was precisely because of his past athletic experience that he understood widespread media attention could be gained if a sporting event was disrupted. Moreover, as a university-trained sociologist with a critical understanding of sport and race relations, he knew perhaps as well as anyone that the success of African American athletes alone would never eliminate racism in sport and American society. Far more effective, he believed, was for Black athletes, along with sympathetic White athletes, to speak out more forcefully about racial inequality and place demands on a White power structure infatuated with and financially dependent on sport. As Edwards noted regarding the San Jose State affair:

> What activity is of more relevance to a student body than the first football game of the season? What activity is of more relevance to a college town after a long and economically drought stricken summer than the first big game? And what is of more immediate importance to a college administration than the threat of stopping a game that had been contracted for under a $12,000 breach of contract clause and the cancellation of all future competition commitments if the game were not played?[5]

Encouraged by the outcome at San Jose State College, and after having many conversations with young African American athletes, Edwards organized in 1967 the Olympic Project for Human Rights (OPHR), a group that would eventually include nationally known African American athletes such as Lew Alcindor, Mike Warren, Tommie Smith, and John Carlos, and whose primary intent was to boycott the 1968 Olympic games in Mexico City. Such a proposal was not new. As Edwards has always been quick to point out, African Americans had discussed the possibility of boycotting the Olympic games years before the OPHR was founded. In 1960, for example, Black activists asked decathlete Rafer Johnson to boycott the Olympic games in Rome to protest police brutality of African Americans in the South. Johnson refused and went on to capture the gold medal in the decathlon in Rome (he was also the flag bearer and team captain). In 1964, Dick Gregory, an African American comedian and civil rights activist, advocated a boycott of the Tokyo Olympics to bring attention to racial inequality.[6] Mal Whitfield, three-time Olympic gold medalist in track and field, also urged a boycott of the 1964 Olympics. Whitfield's was an extraordinary proposal, considering his official duties as a goodwill ambassador for the United States. Yet, Whitfield argued that a boycott would call attention to the racial injustice in "a nation where the color of one's skin takes precedence over the quality of one's mind and character." Most importantly, Whitfield noted that African American athletes had "been conspicuous by their absence from the numerous Civil Rights battles around the country," and urged them to become more involved. "What prestige would the United States have if every single Negro athlete, after qualifying for the U.S. Team, simply decided to stay at home and not compete because adequate Civil Rights legislation had not been passed by Congress?" he asked in an article he wrote for *Ebony* in 1964. "For one thing, such action would seriously dampen American foreign policy during a crucial period in history."[7]

After seeking advice from prominent civil rights leaders such as Martin Luther King Jr., Floyd McKissick, and Louis Lomax, and after staging a Black youth conference in Los Angeles and another meeting at The Americana Hotel in New York City in late 1967, the OPHR issued a list of six demands. Conceived largely by Edwards, the list demanded the restoration of Muhammad Ali's heavyweight championship; the inclusion of at least two African American coaches to the men's US track and field team; the desegregation of the New York Athletic Club; the appointment of at least two African Americans to positions on the US Olympic Committee; the exclusion of White-supremacist nations South Africa and Southern Rhodesia from the 1968 Olympics; and the removal of Avery Brundage as President of the IOC because of his racist views.[8]

Edwards and the OPHR leadership soon realized, however, that there were decided philosophical differences among former and current Black athletes, the Black community more generally and the larger American public, regarding the benefits of an Olympic boycott. Part of these differences, as Jesse Owens's biographer William J. Baker notes, was generational. Former great Olympic champions such as Owens and Rafer Johnson adamantly opposed a boycott of the Mexico City games.[9] These two legendary Black Olympians could not understand the value of a boycott, rehashing the age-old argument that sport served as the great leveler in society and that athletic success would lead to racial acceptance and freedom of opportunities.[10] Importantly, some Black athletes who would most likely compete in Mexico City, as well as large segments of the Black and White communities, agreed. For instance, Ralph Boston, one of the most successful long jumpers in the history of track and field, opposed the boycott, contending that the best way to further the cause of Black Americans was through athletic success and Olympic competition, though he did say if a boycott were "strongly supported by the great majority of Negro athletes, I would have to go along with it." Still, he "believed Negroes can do more good for themselves and their race by going to the Olympics and doing well than they can by staying home."[11]

Those who opposed the boycott often incurred Edward's wrath. No one was immune, especially those legendary Black athletes whom he believed could contribute to the cause but naively maintained that sport was the great savior for African Americans and that it would eventually lead to racial understanding, and possibly even a color-blind society. Of all athletes, perhaps the one targeted most was Jesse Owens, the famous Black Olympian who symbolically shattered the Nazis belief of Aryan superiority by capturing four gold medals in the 1936 Olympic games in Berlin. Edwards spared Owens no insult, calling him "gullible," "misinformed" and an "Uncle Tom." To Edwards, Owens was naive to think that sport brought Blacks and Whites closer together, and a dupe to believe in the sanctity of the Olympic games.[12]

Edwards received as much as, or even more than, he meted out. He was castigated and called an ingrate, a radical bent on destroying the hallowed institution of sport for his own selfish purposes. Like so many other supposed Black radicals of the period, he was seen as a dangerous man whose every move needed to be watched and monitored. This task fell to the Federal Bureau of Investigation (FBI). "Considerable publicity has been given Edwards, an instructor at San Jose State College, San Jose, California, in connection with the boycotting of an athletic event by Negro athletes," wrote the Director of the FBI, in one directive to the regional headquarters in San Francisco. "Promptly review the information in your files concerning Edwards and submit a recommendation to include him on the Rabble Rouser Index if justified."[13]

The attacks on his character and the FBI surveillance only stiffened Edwards's resolve to make visible racial discrimination by disrupting the sporting world's normal way of doing things. In February 1968, the OPHR successfully boycotted the New York Athletic Club's (NYAC) indoor track meet at Madison Square Garden to protest the discriminatory policies of the club (it did not allow Blacks or Jews as members). Because of the boycott, NYAC officials were forced to cancel the meet's high school competitions and enter college teams. Even the Soviet Union national squad withdrew. In addition, Edwards and the OPHR encouraged and contributed to the protests of Black athletes on predominantly White university campuses.[14] No longer willing to accept the status quo, Black athletes, sometimes in cooperation with sympathetic White teammates, protested the discriminatory treatment from White coaches, fought for the inclusion of Black studies in university curricula and pushed for better housing and more Black administrators, among other things. These protests, which first appeared on the campuses of the University of California, Berkeley, the University of Texas at El Paso and the University of Washington, sometimes cost Black athletes their starting spots and, in the most extreme cases, their careers.[15]

On the surface, the success of the NYAC boycott and the various Black athletic revolts on predominantly White university campuses portended well for the primary goal of the OPHR, which was to boycott the 1968 Mexico City Olympic games. The boycott, however, never took place. Unable to foster unanimity of opinion among members of the OPHR, Black athletes, with Edwards's blessing, decided to compete in Mexico City but not in any victory-podium celebrations. In this way, they could maintain a semblance of unity. Asking Black athletes, particularly those from sports in which the Olympics represented the pinnacle of athletic success, to forgo the Mexico City games was asking them to commit the ultimate act of selflessness. But for other athletes, like UCLA standout Lew Alcindor, whose lifelong goal was to play in the NBA, the decision not to participate in the Olympics was less complicated. Many of these athletes, Alcindor included, never went to Mexico City.[16]

OPHR athletes ultimately decided not to boycott the medal ceremonies. They did agree, however, that individual athletes could show their own form of protest. The most famous was the Black Power salutes of Tommie Smith and John Carlos on the victory stand following their respective first and third-place finishes in the 200-meter dash. As the national anthem played, Smith and Carlos solemnly bowed their heads and raised their Black gloved fists high in the air (Smith wore his glove on his right hand, Carlos on his left). For their actions, Smith and Carlos were kicked out of the Olympic village and sent home.[17] In contrast, after capturing the gold medal in heavyweight boxing, George Foreman paraded around the ring waving a small American flag. Foreman's patriotic display and Smith and Carlos's defiant gesture illustrated the philosophical differences among Black athletes.[18]

The lasting influence of the OPHR on sport, race relations, and the larger civil rights movement has long been debated. Edwards offered his own assessment of the OPHR's influence ten years after its dissolution, claiming that the OPHR had played a valuable role in the hiring of more Black coaches and administrators at the intercollegiate and Olympic levels of competition. Most importantly, the activities of the OPHR had "shattered for all time' the 'illusion of sports inherently insular and apolitical character." The cancelation of the San Jose State-UTEP football game, the boycott of the NYAC track and field meet, the Black athletic revolts on predominantly White university campuses, and the protests lodged at the Mexico City Olympic games left no "doubt that sport was far removed from the 'toy department' of human affairs." All of these activities made clear, wrote Edwards, that not only was "sport a "serious business" (in both a figurative and a literal sense), but also an important component in this nation's domestic social control machinery and in its international political propaganda program."[19]

AN ACTIVIST SCHOLAR TAKING SPORT SERIOUSLY

In 1970, just two years after leading the OPHR, Edwards took a position as an assistant professor of sociology at the University of California, Berkeley. He seemed to settle into his new position with relative ease, teaching courses in his academic discipline, including a course on the sociology of sport, which routinely drew standing room-only crowds, and assuming the standard responsibilities of service and research expected of a tenure-track faculty member at a major university. From a quantifiable standpoint, Edwards seemingly got off to a quick start, even at an institution with such lofty scholarly responsibilities and expectations as Berkeley. He had already published his account of the OPHR in his *The Revolt of the Black Athlete* (1969).[20] Published by the Free Press, the book provides details about the inner workings of the OPHR and Edwards role in it. The same year as his appointment at the University of California, Berkeley, Edwards published *Black Students* (1970), a book examining the difficulties and experiences of Black college students.[21] In 1973, Edwards published the *Sociology of Sport*, the first monograph to seriously analyze the role of sport in America, and sports' interconnection and influence on other societal institutions.[22] In addition to these books, Edwards would later publish his memoir, *The Struggle That Must Be: An Autobiography* (1980), and numerous essays in popular magazines and academic journals such as *The Black Scholar, Society, Psychology Today, Ebony, Crisis*, and *Journal of Sport and Social Issues*.[23]

Edwards's writings were used as ammunition in the fight for racial equality in sport and American society. His words were meant to sting, to elicit responses from what he viewed as a largely naive American public unaware of the racism evident in sport. Although rather formulaic and repetitive in nature, his publications pricked the consciousness of individuals through a critical assessment of the interconnection among race, sport, and American culture. He eschewed any notion of neutrality in his publications, writing boldly and seemingly without fear about racial issues and what measures should be taken to correct them, thus creating an environment free of prejudice and discriminatory practices. Edwards's writings make clear the complexity of a man who was part academician, part radical, part activist, and part social critic.[24]

The one publication that encapsulates much of Edwards's thinking is his memoir.[25] Although *The Revolt of the Black Athlete* is perhaps his most famous work, *The Struggle That Must Be*, published when Edwards was only 38, provides detailed information about his upbringing, the people who were most influential in his life, and the forces that shaped the man he had become. In the tradition of great Black autobiographies written by such important figures as James Weldon Johnson, Maya Angelou, Langston Hughes, and Richard Wright, Edwards's memoir is honest, straightforward, smart, bittersweet, and often poignant. He traces his life from his impoverished childhood in East St. Louis to his early years at Berkeley. Among the more interesting aspects of the memoir is Edwards's disclosure of being trailed by the FBI. To the agency, Edwards was an enigma. Why a man with a PhD from Cornell would assume a life of radicalism and political protest was beyond even the FBIs vast realm of comprehension. As one G-man put it: "I don't understand why Edwards with his athletic ability, education, and background would become so angry, militant and outspoken."[26]

Whether the FBI knew it or not, Edwards's radicalism resulted in large part from the influences of Paul Robeson and Louis Lomax, two men who have individual chapters devoted to them in *The Struggle That Must Be*. In the chapter "Brother Lomax," Edwards recounts his close friendship with Lomax and the profound ways in which the well-known Black author, journalist, and television personality impacted his life. It was Lomax who suggested that Edwards discard the "suit and tie" and adopt a more radicalized persona, wholly distinct from "another middle-class Negro with something to say about Civil Rights." As Edwards notes:

> [S]lowly and quite deliberately I broke down to pseudo revolutionary rags and began to develop that separate identity Lomax thought so necessary in gaining critical access to and the attention of the media. At times it was as much as I could do to keep a straight face, standing before crowded auditoriums, under blazing television lights, delivering a lecture developed for my race relations class from a rostrum festooned with reporters microphones, or bombarding white America with rhetoric calculated to outrage.[27]

While Lomax persuaded Edwards to change his public image, Paul Robeson served as Edwards's inspiration and role model. In a chapter titled "Declaration and Disengagement: A Refuge," Edwards, who possessed a near-encyclopedic knowledge of the history of African American participation in sport, wrote that his understanding of the struggles experienced by Robeson in athletics "enhanced my understanding of the forces that had molded my own life and activities." To Edwards, Robeson, the outstanding student athlete, singer, actor and civil rights activist from Rutgers University, was the "great forerunner" whose life and numerous achievements made clear the "need for more than just protest demonstrations." "Dramatic revelation is one thing" noted Edwards:

> delineating through systematic investigation the precise dynamics of sports' relationship to society—and to the Black community in particular—is quite another. And if the sacrifices made and the insights gained were to be of any lasting consequence, the latter had to be accomplished.[28]

The call for a systematic approach to the study of sport was taken up most fully by Edwards in *Sociology of Sport*.[29] Based on his dissertation from Cornell University, "Sport in America: Its Myths and Realities," and obviously a response to his own call for the "need for more than just protest demonstrations," *Sociology of Sport* was the first textbook of its kind written in the United States, preceding the publication of several other survey texts on the sociology of sport that came out during the 1970s.[30] Edwards also wrote a large number of articles for popular periodicals and scholarly journals, gave numerous interviews, appeared frequently on television, and delivered a host of presentations and plenary addresses.[31] He was also perhaps the most-quoted man in the United States regarding issues related to race and sport. During this period, Edwards continued to be highly critical of sport, publicly declaring that despite the rhetoric about it being free from prejudice and discrimination, it was yet one more institution that reflected power relations and the systematic exploitation of Blacks in a racist America.[32]

TROUBLE WITH TENURE AT BERKELEY

Edwards's blistering assault on sport in America made him a lightning rod of sorts, a divisive force, liked by some hated by others. No one seemed to take a neutral position on the man writer Ronald Glover called a "change agent."[33] Edwards seemed to relish this fact, but at times it caused him serious problems. One famous incident occurred in 1977. In January of that year, Edwards received notice from the sociology department at the University of California, Berkeley, that he had been denied tenure by a 10–8 vote with one abstention. The reason given for the denial was that "he needed one or two more articles in established journals."[34]

Edwards received unofficial word that senior members of his department had rationalized their negative votes on the basis that sport and race relations were not worthy of sociological study. "Race Relations," wrote Edwards, "was held to be a minor subarea of stratification, and sports were regarded simply as the legitimate subject matter of physical educators-not sociologists."[35] Although impossible to confirm how much this attitude impacted the decision, there is no question that during this time the sociological study of sport had yet to realize legitimate status as a subfield in either physical education or the parent discipline of sociology. As made clear by noted sport sociologists such as John Loy and Jay Coakley, the sociological study of sport has been a low priority in departments of physical education where the sciences reign supreme and in departments of sociology where sport attracts relatively little interest to researchers and scholars.[36] This is part of a larger discussion taken up most notably by historians Elliott J. Gorn and Michael Oriard, who point out in their well-known essay, "Taking Sports Seriously," that the study of sport has always been at the "margins" of most academic disciplines, including history, sociology, philosophy, English, psychology, and anthropology.[37]

Be that as it may, Edwards was angered by the decision and, in customary fashion, announced to the world that he had been denied tenure, and went on to vehemently protest it. One of his first actions was to send a telegram to President Jimmy Carter complaining of the "rampaging racism in the institutions of higher education and other realms of minority life in this nation." Without mentioning the issue, Edwards wrote, "By deliberate intent and systematic design, the bureaucratic and administrative lynching of minorities in American higher education has emerged as a frightening but undeniable patterned reality."[38] Edwards and his followers later held a protest rally on campus in which Edwards read the aforementioned telegram to President Carter in its entirety.[39] Edwards also discussed the ordeal in an article titled, "Edwards vs The University of California," which was published in the May 1977 issue of *The Black Scholar*.[40] In the piece, Edwards cited a 1974 NAACP study that compared Berkeley to the University of Alabama and University of Mississippi in regard to the recruitment of Black students and "its hiring, retention and promotion of Black faculty and staff personnel."[41]

Why someone is denied tenure is extraordinarily difficult to assess. But Edwards was convinced that the vote to deny him a lifetime contract at Berkeley was racist and political. He claimed that Berkeley never intended for him to get tenure, and that the university did everything it could to ensure that his stay was a short one. He received a notice early in his career that his contract would not be renewed if he had not completed his dissertation by the prescribed time (customary now in academia). He suggested that he had been denied an opportunity to move from the department of sociology to the department of Afro-American studies because, as he stated, being in the latter program "would be the most difficult position from which to dislodge me." He was denied university research support to participate in a project dealing with the People's Republic of China. Moreover, he believed faculty and staff had regularly provided information to intelligence agencies regarding his campus activities and the "personal conversations" he had had "with other scholars and gentlemen."[42] In spite of these constraints, Edwards pointed out that in six years he had established an exemplary scholarly career at Berkeley, having already published three books and more than fifty articles. He also taught some of the largest and most popular courses on campus, served on committees at the departmental, university and professional levels, and had lectured at over three hundred colleges and universities worldwide.[43]

Edwards's tenure denial quickly became a cause célèbre. Thousands of Berkeley students signed a petition demanding that the tenure decision be overturned. The large majority of the sixty-three graduate students in the sociology department signed their own petition condemning the tenure decision. The Black graduate student caucus publicly denounced the decision, as did all thirteen tenured Black faculty members at Berkeley. Civil rights activists, professional groups and associations, and student organizations and faculty from universities in the United States and abroad expressed concerns about Edwards's case. Chancellor Albert Bowker received hundreds of letters and other forms of communication denouncing the decision and the negative impact it was having on the reputation of the university.[44]

Ultimately, the level of negative publicity became so great that Bowker created a "special panel" to investigate the incident.[45] After consulting with this group, Bowker reversed the decision and granted Edwards tenure.

Bowker, though, in a 1991 interview conducted by Harriett Nathan as part of the "University History Series," could not resist getting in one last jab, saying that Edwards's "scholarship was, in fact, adequate or satisfactory." In a statement that could be interpreted in a number of ways, Bowker followed up by noting, "There was a feeling of equity involved, that he [Edwards] had been hired to fill a certain role on the campus and had done that. There was never any misrepresentation about who he was." Later in the interview, Bowker was much more explicit about why he had overturned the tenure decision. Edwards, he said, "had been a useful role model for the Black athletes, and in several particular instances had been quite useful. . . . He always told them when they were off on the wrong track."[46]

Irrespective of what Bowker believed, Edwards was ecstatic about finally being granted tenure. Any thoughts, however, that the decision would soften his views or render him less outspoken or courageous, were quickly dispelled in the fall of 1978 when he confirmed a previous statement he had made to a writer for *Black Thoughts Journal*, a Black student publication on campus. "I am going to turn out the lights at Berkeley," he said. "I am going to be the last one to leave." In fact, continued Edwards:

> I was so serious about being the last one to leave UC Berkeley that I had made it a provision of my last will and testament that my ashes are to be secretly spread on the Berkeley campus so that I literally wouldn't leave until the place was bulldozed.[47]

ACADEMIC REFORM, BLACK ATHLETES, AND THE CONTINUING ALLURE OF SPORT

If anything, getting past the tenure ordeal had given Edwards a new lease on life, and he continued to publish in a prolific fashion and speak out with great fervor about the various issues regarding race, sport and American culture. Although various issues would continue to draw Edwards's attention, the two that perhaps defined him the most were the education of Black athletes and the African American community's overemphasis on sport. Always interested in the education of Black athletes, Edwards in 1983 became embroiled in the debate over the passage of the NCAA academic reform measure known as Proposition 48.[48] Intended to encourage and improve the academic performance of student athletes, Proposition 48, which did not go into effect until 1986, dictated that incoming freshmen had to demonstrate minimum academic competencies (700 on the SAT or 15 on the ACT, and a 2.0 GPA in eleven core courses in high school) before being granted eligibility. It drew much criticism from a large number of prominent African Americans, including perhaps most famously basketball coaches John Cheney of Temple and John Thompson of Georgetown who were opposed to the new legislation and to successive Propositions 42 and 16.[49] Both Cheney and Thompson believed these propositions were based on racially biased standardized tests and therefore would most negatively impact Black athletes. They were correct. Blacks did score lower than Whites on standardized tests and would be the ones most negatively affected by the academic reform measures implemented by the NCAA.[50]

Like tennis great Arthur Ashe and other influential African American leaders, Edwards initially favored the new legislation.[51] Even though the requirements were relatively low and established without the involvement of presidents from historically Black colleges and universities (HBCUs) and despite colleges being more concerned about eligibility than education, Edwards supported the new legislation "because it sent the message to young people that we did expect some semblance of academic achievement as well as their athletic proficiency. We expected them to do something intellectually as well as athletically."[52] Gradually, however, Edwards changed his opinion. In a well-known 2000 essay, titled "Crisis of Black Athletes on the Eve of the 21st Century," Edwards declared that "it is now clear that the greatest consequence of Proposition 42, and similar regulations has been to limit the opportunities—both educational and athletic—that would otherwise be available to Black youths." Although he conceded that some improvements had been made in the graduation rates of Black athletes (speculating that these improvements were perhaps more a result of improved academic support services than anything else), Edwards believed that the overall results of the NCAA's academic reform efforts had fallen woefully short because they "were neither conceived nor instituted with due consideration of Black youths' circumstances beyond the academy and the sports arena."[53]

Edwards's changing view of academic reform was intertwined with his shifting position on the role and meaning of sport for African Americans. For much of his career, he had warned African Americans of the dangers and harmful effects resulting from an overemphasis on sport. In one memorable essay, "The Single-Minded Pursuit of Sports, Fame, and Fortune Is Approaching an Institutionalized Triple Tragedy in Black Society," Edwards argued that Black youth had become so obsessed in their pursuit of athletic glory that more appropriate and realistic career choices such as education, medicine, law, economics, and politics were not even being considered. Black families, said Edwards, were partly to blame for this obsessive behavior. Imbued with the belief in innate Black athletic superiority, influenced by the media regarding sport and economic mobility, and unaware of visible and influential role models outside the world of sport, Black families had become much more aggressive than their White counterparts in encouraging their children to aspire to careers in sport.[54]

More recently, Edwards has spent far less time cautioning African Americans about their overemphasis on sport. In fact, on at least two occasions he praised African Americans for continuing to place such an inordinate amount of attention on sport. In a 2000 interview in *Colorlines*, titled "The Decline of the Black Athlete: An Interview with Harry Edwards," and in an article in *Society*, titled "Crisis of Black Athletes on the Eve of the 21st Century," Edwards pointed out that the United States was experiencing a decline in the number of outstanding African American athletes, a result of a number of societal factors and constraints.[55] Much of the Black athletic talent pool like that for Black lawyers, doctors, educators, businessmen and other professionals, was being greatly diminished, a consequence of racial discrimination, "erosion or elimination of Civil Rights gains," "exit of the Black middle-class from the traditional Black community," deterioration of the Black family and "political infrastructure," and "structural economical shifts in the broader society."[56]

Faced with this reality, Edwards softened some of his earlier arguments and contended that rather than emphasizing or abandoning sport, or simply allowing our involvement to wane, Black people must now more than ever intelligently, constructively, and proactively pursue sports involvement."[57] So now acting like an early-twentieth-century progressive reformer as much as a radical sport sociologist, Edwards stressed that Black youth must be encouraged to participate in all levels of sport so they can better learn lessons of life and the discipline required. Playing sports also put them "in contact with the clergy, mentors, health workers, counselors, government workers, with people from the economic and corporate sector."[58] In essence, sport served as the "last hook and handle," a means of keeping Black youth, particularly Black males, out of the criminal justice system or hospital emergency room or funeral parlor.[59] Importantly, Edwards's push for involvement in sport was not done naively. He fully recognized that the ultimate solution to the myriad problems faced by Black youth would require substantive changes in almost every area of American life. He was also fully aware that while he was advocating for the notion of the "last hook and handle," the privatization of children's athletic programs, cutbacks in educational funding, and the deterioration of playgrounds and other recreational sites was reducing economically disadvantaged minority groups' access to sport.[60]

THE ESTABLISHMENT TAKES NOTICE

Edwards's theoretical understanding of race and sport was put to the test in a more practical way in the 1980s when he was hired as a consultant with the Golden State Warriors of the NBA and the San Francisco 49ers of the NFL, and as a special assistant to Commissioner Peter Ueberroth of Major League Baseball.[61] These positions, when combined with his salary at Berkeley and the royalties from his various books and lectures, augmented what was already a substantial income. The new positions also brought forth a new legion of critics. His detractors questioned his commitment to reform and efforts to secure more opportunities for African American athletes, now that he was an insider employed by the White power structure he had so roundly criticized for much of his career.[62] In typical fashion, though, Edwards was seemingly unfazed. In 1988, he told the *New York Times* sportswriter Robert Lipsyte, "The establishment has changed to the extent that they decided to invite me in but I'm like a Statue of Liberty, I've been in the same position since day one."[63]

Of the three positions Edwards took in professional sport, the historical record provides far more details about his responsibilities with the 49ers and Major League Baseball. He began his consulting work with the 49ers in 1985. His responsibilities included traveling with the team, providing assessments of potential draft choices, and advising players on such issues as drug use, financial investments, and post-athletic career opportunities. Like Jack Scott, Dave Meggyesy, and many of the other radical thinkers associated with the earlier "athletic revolution," Edwards had always viewed performance-enhancing drugs and inadequate preparation for life after sport as two of the biggest concerns for professional athletes. Much of his time with the 49ers was spent talking to players about the two topics.[64]

Two years after assuming his position with the 49ers, Edwards was hired as a special assistant to baseball Commissioner Peter Ueberroth. The position was an outgrowth of the infamous remarks by Los Angeles Dodgers general manager Al Campanis that Blacks lacked the "necessities" to manage a Major League Baseball team. Edwards was tapped to help identify and prepare Blacks for managerial and upper-level administrative positions in

America's National Pastime.[65] It was a painstakingly slow process, in no small part because baseball was losing whatever appeal it had among African Americans. Nevertheless, Edwards designed strategies to increase the pool of Black candidates. His primary goal was to rid baseball of "the good old boy network of mediocre white men who keep recycling each other."[66]

Almost from the moment he took the position, Edwards was rebuked by the Frank Robinson-led Baseball Network, Inc., and other critics, for being an outsider who lacked institutional knowledge of the game. He was also criticized for acting too slowly, for effecting far too little change.[67] Recently, however, Major League Baseball has shown itself to be much more racially sensitive. The league has hired several minority candidates for managerial and upper-level administrative positions. Richard Lapchick, director of the Institute for Diversity and Ethics in Sport, gave the league an "A" for its racial hiring practices in his 2012 Major League Baseball Racial and Gender Report Card.[68] How much Edwards contributed to this grade is impossible to determine. The high mark may have had more to do with Commissioner Bud Selig's 1999 directive that requires teams to compile lists of potential minority candidates for manager, general manager and other executive positions. Still, Edwards's efforts cannot be totally disregarded.[69]

In 2000, Edwards retired from the University of California, Berkeley.[70] Upon leaving the university (he is now professor emeritus), Edwards became Director of the Oakland Department of Parks and Recreation, a position probably incongruous with his skills and temperament.[71] Therefore, it was not surprising that after three years in the position he resigned. Since then, he has continued to write and travel the country, discussing issues of race and sport in interviews, panel discussions, and plenary addresses.[72] Ironically, he has become somewhat of a media darling, the go-to man whenever reporters, journal editors, television heads, and academicians need a quote, analysis, or interpretation on matters of race and sport.[73] He is seemingly willing to talk about controversial issues in sport with anyone, anywhere. And he seldom disappoints. He is engaging, thought provoking, and serious.[74]

One interesting phenomenon is that Edwards is now occasionally offered speaking engagements that would never have been tendered earlier in his career. In 2011, for instance, Edwards was asked to deliver a plenary address by the NCAA Scholarly Colloquium at its pre-NCAA conference symposium in San Antonio, Texas.[75] Notwithstanding the fact he was extended the invitation by a group of academicians with no official ties to the NCAA, the mere fact that Edwards presented the keynote speech at a conference sponsored by an organization he had so severely criticized was a monumental and culturally significant event. In an address titled "Transformational Developments at the Interface of Race, Sport, and the Collegiate Athletic Arms Race in the Age of Globalization," Edwards revisited some of his earlier arguments, including the reasons for the slow pace of racial integration in sport and decline in number of African American athletes.[76]

PRESERVING THE LEGACY OF THE MAN

An interesting recent phenomenon is the outpouring of appreciation for Edwards's life and career, and the interest in preserving his legacy. Part of the reassessment and memorializing of the Black athletic revolt now some fifty-six years old, Edwards's many activities and accomplishments, along with the protests of Smith, Carlos, and other African American athletes, have captured the imagination of scholars from a variety of disciplinary areas. His career has gone through a reclamation project of sorts.[77] Why it has happened is open to speculation. Perhaps it has to do with the continued fascination people have with the interconnection of race, sport, and American culture. Although this is undoubtedly part of the answer, ultimately the reasons for such renewed attention now being paid to Edwards seems far more complicated. Maybe the interest stems from an effort, as Maureen Smith explains in her work on the meaning of the statue erected of Tommie Smith and John Carlos at San Jose State, to make amends for the racial transgressions "and the historical baggage of racism" so prevalent in the United States. Other plausible reasons are the ones historian Dan Nathan has used to explain the recent fascination with Negro League Baseball. To Nathan, the newfound attraction of Negro League Baseball for Whites is perhaps "a way of denoting one's liberalism and racial awareness and sensitivity." On the other hand, such interest might be "related to the yearnings for a more coherent sense of community and racial solidarity."[78] In the post–Civil Rights era, is the interest in Edwards explained by a desire among African Americans for a sense of racial solidarity that was found in the Black athletic revolts and the larger Black Power movement of the late 1960s?

All of the newfound interest in Edwards by academicians is perhaps best represented by the 2009 special issue of the *Journal for the Study of Sports and Athletes in Education*, titled "The Legacies of Harry Edwards for Sport Sociology," and the 2012 book, *Sport, Race, Activism, and Social Change: The Impact of Dr. Harry Edwards' Scholarship and Service*.[79] The special issue of the *Journal for the Study of Sports and Athletes in Education*, coedited by David J. Leonard and C. Richard King, includes essays ranging from a reevaluation of Edwards's involvement in the 1968 Olympic boycott to the Black athletic revolts on predominantly White university campuses. Although all the pieces in the special issue are nicely done and interesting, the three that seem especially insightful and thought provoking are Douglas Hartmann's essay "Activism, Organizing, and the Symbolic Power of Sport: Reassessing Harry Edwards's Contributions to the 1968 Olympic Protest Movement," Leonard and King's article "Revolting Black Athletes: Sport, New Racism, and the Politics of Dis/identification," and an interview conducted by Jay Johnson and Matthew A. Masucci with Edwards titled "No Final Victories: Forty Years on the Frontlines of Race, Sport, and Culture: An Interview with Scholar/Activist Dr. Harry Edwards."[80]

Hartmann's essay, based to a large extent on his well-known book, *Race, Culture, and the Revolt of the Black Athlete* (2003), argues persuasively that the most significant contributions made by Edwards to the 1968 Olympic protest movement were in the areas of education, organization and leadership, and media communications."[81] Edwards's rhetorical abilities, his understanding of the symbolic power of sport, organizational skills and acumen, and media savvy, helped mobilize Black athletes in the fight for racial justice and equality.[82] In their article, Leonard and King argue that Black athletes involved in the revolts of the 1960s have been memorialized and celebrated in an effort to demonize modern Black athletes while simultaneously "legitimizing national projects of meritocracy, colorblindness, and American racial progress."[83] In the interview conducted by Johnson and Masucci, Edwards's comments are reminiscent of W. E. B. Du Bois famously prescient statement in the *Souls of Black Folk* (1903) that "the problem of the Twentieth Century is the problem of the color-line."[84] Edwards, instead reminded Johnson and Masucci of one of his previously published essays from the *Civil Rights Journal* in which he wrote "that the problem of the 21st Century is going to be the problem of diversity in all its tremendous variations."[85] Edwards claimed that what he had learned from working as a consultant with professional sports teams "is that it is precisely because of the differences that we have that gives value to our diverse input." He continued:

> People are sick of the "us versus them." There is no them, there is only us, not just in this country but on this planet, and if we don't learn that lesson,

it's not going to be 'us' for very long because the situation is just that dire and dangerous.[86]

Just three years after the appearance of the special issue in the *Journal for the Study of Sports and Athletes in Education,* Fritz G. Polite and Billy Hawkins published their coedited book Sport, *Race, Activism, and Social Change: The Impact of Dr. Harry Edwards' Scholarship and Service* (2012).[87] The book includes eleven chapters, along with an introduction by Polite, a conclusion (which probably would have been better as an introduction) by Hawkins and an epilogue by Edwards. Two of the eleven chapters, Michael Lomax's "Revisiting the Revolt of the Black Athlete: Dr. Harry Edwards and the Making of (the New) African American Sport Studies" and Polite, Steven N. Waller, Stephanie Hill and Dawn Norwood's "Fostering Dr. Harry Edwards' s Legacy: Black Athletes Taking Responsibility in an Age of Sport Reform" are reprinted essays.[88] The most original chapter that deals directly with Edwards is perhaps Linda Greene's "The Impact of Dr. Harry Edward's Work on Legal Scholarship." Extraordinarily well-documented, Greene explains how legal scholars who have dealt with sport have depended on Edwards many publications.[89]

The special issue of the *Journal for the Study of Sport and Athletes in Education* and Polite and Hawkins coedited book are just two of the latest publications providing insights into the life and career of Edwards and the many contributions he has made in the struggle for racial equality. These works, combined with Edwards's own writings and many other accomplishments, make clear he is a complex man whose singleness of purpose is only matched by his energy, foresight, intelligence, and rhetorical skills. Like all revolutionaries, Edwards is extraordinarily independent. He is willing to share his ideas. He freely expresses his opinions. And he aggressively confronts injustices wherever he finds them. How he became this man is better left to psychologists to determine. But there seems to be little question that he learned a great deal from many Black intellectuals and activists who preceded him. In fact, he seems to be an amalgamation of several historically important African Americans: His writing style is reminiscent of W. E. B. Du Bois, his organizational skills recall Booker T. Washington, his courage seems hewed from that of Paul Robeson, his gift for oratory reminds many of Malcolm X, and his understanding of the media suggests Louis Lomax. Although some prefer to categorize him as a reformer, Edwards has clearly revolutionized how we conceive of sport and how it both reflects societal values and can be used to fight racial injustice. Through it all, he has never harbored any illusion that there would come a day in America where there was complete racial harmony. As he noted to me in a signed copy of his tribute issue of the *Journal for the Study of Sports and Athletes in Education*: "The challenge of achieving America is diverse and dynamic; the struggle, therefore, is multi-faceted and perpetual; and there are no final victories."[90]

Notes

1. Edwards, *The Struggle That Must Be*; Mark, Kram. "Gale Contemporary Black Biography: Harry Edwards," http://www.answers.com/topic/harry-edwards.

2. Ibid.; Robert Lipsyte, "An Outsider Joins the Team," *The New York Times*, May 22, 1988.

3. Edwards, *The Revolt of the Black Athlete*; Edwards, *The Struggle That Must Be*; and Kram, "Gale Contemporary Black Biography."

4. Ibid. Quote is taken from Kram, "Gale Contemporary Black Biography."

5. Edwards, *The Revolt of the Black Athlete*.

6. Ibid.

7. Mal Whitfield, "Let's Boycott the Olympics," *Ebony*, March 1964, 95-6, 98–100.

8. Edwards, *The Revolt of the Black Athlete*. For very nice interpretations of the 1968 Olympic boycott, see Bass, *Not the Triumph But the Struggle* and Hartmann. *Race, Culture, and the Revolt of the Black Athlete*.

9. Baker, *Jesse Owens*.

10. Edwards, *The Revolt of the Black Athlete*.

11. For Boston's views, see Wiggins and Miller, *The Unlevel Playing Field*.

12. Edwards, *The Revolt of the Black Athlete*. For a Black Olympic athlete who was highly critical of Owens, see Matthews, *My Race Be Won*.

13. Edwards, *The Revolt of the Black Athlete*. For other FBI reports, see Edwards, *The Struggle That Must Be*.

14. Edwards, *The Revolt of the Black Athlete*; *The Struggle That Must Be*.

15. Ibid.; Wiggins, "The Year of Awakening"; Wiggins, "The Future of College Athletics is at Stake," 188–208; and Brooks and Althouse, "Revolt of the Black Athlete."

16. Edwards, *The Revolt of the Black Athlete*; Edwards, *The Struggle That Must Be*; Bass, *Not the Triumph But the Struggle*; Hartmann, *Race, Culture, and the Revolt of the Black Athlete*; and Smith, "'It's Not Really My Country.'"

17. Edwards, *The Revolt of the Black Athlete*; Edwards, *The Struggle That Must Be*; Bass, *Not the Triumph But the Struggle*; Hartmann, *Race, Culture, and the Revolt of the Black Athlete*; Wiggins, "The Year of Awakening"; Smith, *Silent Gesture*; Carlos and Zirin, *The John Carlos Story*; and Brooks and Althouse, "Revolt of the Black Athlete."

18. Edwards, *The Revolt of the Black Athlete*; Hartmann, *Race, Culture, and the Revolt of the Black Athlete*; and Bass, *Not the Triumph But the Struggle*.
19. Edwards, "The Olympic Project."
20. Edwards, *The Revolt of the Black Athlete*.
21. Edwards, *Black Students*.
22. Edwards, *Sociology of Sport*.
23. Edwards, *The Struggle That Must Be*; "Change and Crisis in Modem Sport"; "Crisis of Black Athletes"; "The Black Athletes"; "The Single-Minded Pursuit," 138, 140; "The Collegiate Athletic Arms Race"; and "Beyond Symptoms."
24. Ibid.
25. Edwards, *The Struggle That Must Be*.
26. Ibid.
27. Ibid.
28. Ibid.
29. Edwards, *Sociology of Sport*.
30. Edwards, "Sport in America"; *Sociology of Sport*.
31. For a nice listing of Edwards's various publications, see Greene, "The Impact of Dr. Harry Edwards's Work."
32. Edwards first lays out most fully his conception of the relationship among race, sport and American culture, in his *Sociology of Sport*.
33. Ronald Glover, "Change Agent: Dr. Harry Edwards." *The Black Sports Network*, July 16, 2006, http://blacksportsnetwork.com/articles/features/Dr.E_071606.asp.
34. Edwards, "Edwards vs The University of California"; *The Struggle That Must Be*.
35. Edwards, *The Struggle That Must Be*.
36. Loy. "The Emergence and Development"; Coakley, "Sociology of Sport in the United States."
37. Gorn and Oriard, "Taking Sports Seriously."
38. Edwards, *The Struggle That Must Be*.
39. Ibid.
40. Edwards, "Edwards vs The University of California."
41. Ibid.
42. Edwards, *The Struggle That Must Be*.
43. Ibid.; Edwards, "Edwards vs The University of California."
44. Ibid.
45. Ibid.
46. Nathan's interview with Bowker, September 6, 1991, content.cdlib.org/view?docId=hblp3001gg&doc.view=entire_text.
47. Edwards, *The Struggle That Must Be*.
48. Edwards, "The Collegiate Athletic Arms Race"; Edwards, "The Black 'Dumb Jack'"; Edwards, "Educating Black Athletes"; Edwards, "Beyond Symptoms," 3–13; and Smith, *Pay for Play*.

49. Ibid.
50. Ibid.
51. Ibid.
52. *New Pittsburgh Courier*, December 27, 1986.
53. Edwards, "Crisis of Black Athletes."
54. Edwards, "The Single-Minded Pursuit," 138, 140.
55. Leonard, "The Decline of the Black Athlete"; Edwards, "Crisis of Black Athletes."
56. Edwards, "Crisis of Black Athletes."
57. Ibid.
58. Leonard, "The Decline of the Black Athlete."
59. Ibid.
60. Ibid.
61. Lipsyte, "An Outsider Joins the Team"; Kram, "Gale Contemporary Black Biography"; Glover, "Change Agent: Dr. Harry Edwards"; and William D. Murray, "Edwards to Assist Ueberroth in Effort to Find 'Creditable' Minorities to Fill Variety of Posts," *New Pittsburgh Courier*, June 27, 1987.
62. Eddie Jefferi "Edwards Under Fire, But He Can Handle It," *New Pittsburgh Courier*, September 19, 1987; Mary Hyman. "Some Black Players are Critical of Edwards," "*Baltimore Sun*. October 19, 1987; and "Black Group Blasts 'Failing' Edwards," *The Washington Post*, August 19, 1987.
63. Lipsyte, "An Outsider Joins the Team." See also, Mike Well, "Edwards Silent After Being Called a 'Puppet,'" *New Pittsburgh Courier*, September 5, 1987.
64. Lipsyte, "An Outsider Joins the Team"; Kram, "Gale Contemporary Black Biography." See also Scott, *The Athletic Revolution*; Meggyesy, *Out of Their League*.
65. See Hoose, *Necessities*; Peter Gammons, "The Campanis Affair," *Sports Illustrated*, April 20, 1987; Steve Springer, "April 6, 1987: The Nightline That Rocked Baseball," *Los Angeles Times*, April 6, 1997; Reggie Jackson, "We Have a Serious Problem That Isn't Going Away," *Sports Illustrated*, May 11, 1987; and Ruck, *Raceball*.
66. Quoted in Lipsyte, "An Outsider Joins the Team."
67. Ibid.
68. "Major League Baseball Earns Top Grade for Racial Hiring Practices," http://www.spokesman-recorder.com/2012/10/17/major-league-baseball-earns-top-grade-for-racial-hiringpractices.
69. Ibid.
70. Lipsyte, "An Outsider Joins the Team"; Kram, "Gale Contemporary Black Biography."
71. Janine DeFao, "Harry Edwards to Head Oakland Parks-Rec/Expert on Sports and Race is Major Jerry Brown's Pick," *San Francisco Chronicle*, May 13, 2000; Ellen Griffin, "Time Out With Harry Edwards: Oakland's New Director of Parks and Rec," *MacArthur Metro*. November 2000, http://macarthunnetro.org/pdfs/metoo-l lpdf;

and Sandra Gonzales, "Oakland Activist Takes on New Career," September 23, 2000, http://nists.village.virginia.edu/lists_archive/sixties-1/1798.html.

72. For Edwards's resignation as Director of the Oakland Department of Parks and Recreation, see J. Douglas Allen-Taylor, "The Oakland City Hall Shakeup," July 4, 2003, www.berkeleydailyplanet.com. Some of the best insights regarding &I.wards' thinking can be gleaned from his many interviews. See for example, Leonard, 'The Decline of the Black Athlete"; Johnson and Masucci, "No Final Victories."

73. Lipsyte, "An Outsider Joins the Team"; Kram. "Gale Contemporary Black Biography."

74. Ibid.

75. The NCAA Scholarly Colloquium was the brainchild of Myles Brand, former university administrator and NCAA president. In 2013, the NCAA decided to stop funding the colloquium. See Ellen Staurowsky, "NCAA's Decision to Withdraw Funding for Scholarly Colloquium is an Attack on Academic Freedom," *College Sports Business News*, June 21, 2013. http://collegesportsbusinessnews.com/issue/January-2013/article/what-does-the-ncaasdecision-to; Paul Steinbach, "Scholars React to Cancellation of NCAA Colloquium." *Athletic Business*, April 2013, http://upload.athleticbusiness.com/articles/keyword.aspx?keyword=athletics

76. See Edwards, "Transformational Developments."

77. See the *Journal for the Study of Sports and Athletes in Education* (Summer 2009) and Polite and Hawkins, *Sport, Race, Activism, and Social Change*. At the time of this writing, the Association for the Study of African American Life and History was putting together a session, "45 years since the Black power fists protest at the 1968 Olympics" at its 2013 conference. See http://www.h-net.org/announce/show.cgiID=20240l.

78. Smith, "Frozen Fists in Speed City"; Nathan, "Bearing Witness to Blackball."

79. See the *Journal for the Study of Sports and Athletes in Education* (Summer 2009) and Polite and Hawkins, *Sport, Race, Activism, and Social Change*.

80. Hartmann, "Activism, Organizing, and the Symbolic Power of Sport"; Leonard and King, "Revolting Black Athletes"; and Johnson and Masucci, "No Final Victories."

81. Hartmann. "Activism, Organizing, and the Symbolic Power of Sport."

82. Ibid.

83. Leonard and King, "Revolting Black Athletes."

84. Johnson and Masucci, "No Final Victories"; Du Bois, *The Souls of Black Folk*.

85. Edwards, "An End of The Golden Age."

86. Johnson and Masucci, "No Final Victories."

87. Polite and Hawkins, *Sport, Race, Activism, and Social Change*.

88. Lomax's essay ("Revisiting The Revolt of the Black Athlete") was previously published in the *Journal of Sport History* and Polite et al.'s essay ("Fostering Dr. Harry Edwards Legacy") was previously published in the *Journal for the Study of Sports and Athletes in Education*.

89. Greene, "The Impact of Dr. Harry Edwards's Work."
90. See *Journal for the Study of Sports and Athletes in Education.*

References

Baker, William J. *Jesse Owens: An American Life*. New York: Free Press, 1986.

Bass, Amy. *Not the Triumph But the Struggle: The 1968 Olympics and the Making of the Black Athlete*. Minneapolis: University of Minnesota Press, 2002.

Brooks, Dana D., and Ronald Althouse. "Revolt of the Black Athlete: From Global Arena to the College Campus." *Journal for the Study of Sports and Athletics in Education* 3 (Summer 2009): 195–214.

Carlos, John, and Dave Zirin. *The John Carlos Story: The Sports Moment That Changed the World*. Chicago, IL: Haymarket Books, 2011.

Coakley, Jay. "Sociology of Sport in the United States." *International Review for Sociology of Sport* 22 (1987): 63–77.

Du Bois, W. E. B. *The Souls of Black Folk*. New York: Fawcett, 1961.

Edwards, Harry. *The Revolt of the Black Athlete*. New York: Free Press, 1969.

———. *Black Students*. New York: Free Press, 1970.

———. "The Black Athletes: 20th Century Gladiators for White America." *Psychology Today* 1 (November 1973): 43–48.

———. *Sociology of Sport*. Homewood, IL: The Dorsey Press, 1973.

———. "Sport in America: Its Myths and Realities." PhD diss., Cornell University, 1973.

———. "Change and Crisis in Modem Sport." *The Black Scholar* 8 (October-November 1976): 60–65.

———. "Edwards vs The University of California." *The Black Scholar* 8 (May 1977): 32–33.

———. "The Olympic Project for Human Rights: An Assessment Ten Years Later." *The Black Scholar* 10 (Mar.–Apr. 1979): 2–8.

———. *The Struggle That Must Be: An Autobiography*. New York: Macmillan, 1980.

———. "Educating Black Athletes." *The Atlantic Monthly*, August 1983, 31–38.

———. "The Black 'Dumb Jock': An American Sports Tragedy." *The College Board Review* 131 (Spring 1984): 8–13.

———. "The Collegiate Athletic Arms Race: Origins and Implications of the 'Rule 48' Controversy." *Journal of Sport and Social Issues* 8 (Winter–Spring 1984): 4–22.

———. "Beyond Symptoms: Unethical Behavior in American Collegiate Sport and the Problem of the Color Line." *Journal of Sport and Social Issues* 9 (Summer/Fall 1985): 3–13.

———. "The Single-Minded Pursuit of Sports Fame and Fortune is Approaching an Institutionalized Triple Tragedy in Black Society." *Ebony* 43 (Aug. 1988): 138–40.

———. "An End of the Golden Age of Black Participation in Sport." *Civil Rights Journal* 3 (Fall 1998): 19–24.

———. "Crisis of Black Athletes on the Eve of the 21st Century." *Society* 37 (Mar.–Apr. 2000): 9–13.

———. "Transformational Developments at the Interface of Race, Sport. and the Collegiate Athletic Arms Race in the Age of Globalization." *Journal of Intercollegiate Sport* 4 (Jun. 2011): 18–31.

Gorn, Elliott J., and Michael Oriard. "Taking Sports Seriously." *Chronicle of Higher Education*, March 24, 1995, A52.

Greene, Linda. "The Impact of Dr. Harry Edwards's Work on Legal Scholarship." In *Sport, Race, Activism, and Social Change: The Impact of Dr. Harry Edwards' Scholarship and Service*, edited by Fritz G. Polite and Billy Hawkins, 144–66. San Diego, CA: Cognella, 2012.

Hartmann, Douglas. *Race, Culture, and the Revolt of the Black Athlete: The 1968 Olympic Protests and Their Aftermath*. Chicago, IL: University of Chicago Press, 2003.

———. "Activism. Organizing, and the Symbolic Power of Sport: Reassessing Harry Edwards Contributions to the 1968 Olympic Protest Movement." *Journal for the Study of Sports and Athletes* in Education 3 (Summer 2009): 181–94.

Hoose, Philip M. *Necessities: Racial Barriers in American Sports*. New York: Random House, 1989.

Johnson, Jay, and Matthew A. Masucci. "No Final Victories: Forty Years on the Frontlines of Race, Sport, and Culture An Interview with Scholar/Activist Dr. Harry Edwards." *Journal for the Study of Sports and Athletes in Education* 3 (Summer 2009): 233–251.

Leonard, Dave. "The Decline of the Black Athlete: An Interview with Harry Edwards." *Colorlines* 30 (Apr. 2000): 20–24.

Leonard, David J., and C. Richard King. "Revolting Black Athletes: Sport. New Racism. and the Politics of Dis/identification." *Journal for the Study of Sports and Athletes in Education* 3 (Summer 2009): 215–232.

Lomax, Michael. "Revisiting The Revolt of the Black Athlete: Harry Edwards and the Making of the New African-American Studies." *Journal of Sport History* 29 (Fall 2002): 469 479.

Loy, John. "The Emergence and Development of the Sociology of Sport as an Academic Specialty." *Research Quarterly for Exercise and Sport* 51 (1980): 91–119.

Matthews, Vincent (with Neil Amdur). *My Race Be Won*. New York: Charterhouse. 1974.

Meggyesy, Dave. *Out of Their League*. Berkeley. CA: Ramparts, 1970.

Nathan, Daniel A. "Bearing Witness to Blackball: Buck O'Neil, the Negro Leagues, and the Politics of the Past." *Journal of American Studies* 35 (2001): 453–69.

Polite, Fritz G., and Bill Hawkins. eds. *Sports, Race, Activism, and Social Change: The Impact of Dr. Harry Edwards' Scholarship and Service*. San Diego, CA: Cognella, 2012.

Polite, Fritz G., Steven N. Waller, Stephanie Hill, and Dawn Norwood. "Fostering Dr. Harry Edwards Legacy: Black Athletes Taking Responsibility in an Age of Sport Reform." *Journal for the Study of Sports and Athletes in Education* 3 (Summer 2009): 143–58.

Ruck, Rob. *Raceball: How the Major Leagues Colonized the Black and Latin Game.* Boston: Beacon Press, 2011.

Scott, Jack. *The Athletic Revolution.* New York: Free Press, 1971.

Smith, John Matthew. "'It's Not Really My Country': Lew Alcindor and the Revolt of the Black Athlete." *Journal of Sport History* 36 (Summer 2009): 223–44.

Smith, Maureen Margaret. "Frozen Fists in Speed City: The Statue as Twenty-First-Century Reparations." *Journal of Sport History* 36 (Fall 2009): 393–414.

Smith, Ronald A. *Pay for Play: A History of Big-Time College Athletic Reform.* Urbana: University of Illinois Press, 2011.

Smith, Tommie (with David Steele). *Silent Gesture: The Autobiography of Tommie Smith.* Philadelphia, PA: Temple University Press.

Wiggins, David K. "The Future of College Athletics Is At Stake: Black Athletes and Racial Turmoil on Three Predominantly White University Campuses, 1968–1972." *Journal of Sport History* 15 (Winter 1988): 304–33.

———. "Year of Awakening: Black Athletes, Racial Unrest, and the Civil Rights Movement of 1968." *The International Journal of the History of Sport* 9 (Aug. 1992): 188–208.

Wiggins, David K., and Patrick B. Miller. *The Unlevel Playing Field: A Documentary History of the African American Experience in Sport.* Urbana: University of Illinois Press, 2003.

10

KOBE BRYANT'S SECOND ACT

A Brief but Beautiful Post-Basketball Life

"Kobe was a legend on the court and just getting started in what would have been just as meaningful a second act," noted former President Barack Obama after the tragic death of Kobe Bryant, his thirteen-year-old daughter Gianna, and seven others in a helicopter crash on January 26, 2020, in Calabasas, California (Moreau 2020:1). Others expressed the same sentiment. Washington Post sportswriter Jerry Brewer (2020) wrote "We mourn Bryant and remember all that he did, but the great tragedy is what he wasn't able to finish. He was chasing more, as a media and entertainment mogul and as a man" (3). Sportswriter Steve Aschburner (2020) of NBC.com believed "This version of Kobe Bryant we had seen the past three years, though, the one we lost Sunday, was entirely original. So, we mourn for who he was, for what he did and a little extra for what he was going to do and become" (7). Writer Cynthia Littleton (2020), noted in *Variety* that Bryant's death "means that the entertainment industry will never know what the legendary basketball player might have accomplished in the second chapter of his career" (2).

While no one can argue with these sentiments and those expressed by many others regarding Bryant's inability to fulfill his vast potential because of his untimely death at the age of 41, it is also true the legendary Los Angeles Lakers guard realized a very productive and meaningful post-basketball life. It is the intent of this essay to assess what life was like for Bryant following his extraordinary basketball career and how he adjusted to not being constantly in the limelight and away from the game that had always been integral to his source of identity. How did he find fulfillment and a sense of purpose now that he was no longer engaged in the intense preparation that had been a hallmark of his career and suiting up almost every night and competing alongside his teammates against the best basketball players in the world in famous arenas across the country? Tellingly, in contrast to some athletes who have struggled to find meaning and sense of satisfaction following retirement, Bryant seemingly adjusted to his post-basketball career with great ease, fashioning a fulfilling life that mixed the right portions of family, friends, business, and service. He had the qualities, abilities, and personal characteristics that scholars who study transitioning out of sport contend athletes must possess if they are to be successful in their post-athletic careers, including the cultivation of interests beyond sport, financial independence, and early planning for retirement (Knights, et al. 2016; Martin, et al. 2014 and Park, et al. 2013). It is not an understatement to say that Bryant's retirement years, albeit far too brief, serve as a model for other athletes in that they were filled with purpose and personal satisfaction resulting from a genuine commitment to others and positively influencing individuals and groups both within and beyond the world of sport.

Bryant, to be sure, enjoyed an extraordinarily successful basketball career. The youngest of three children born in Philadelphia in 1978 to former NBA player Joe Bryant and Pamela (Pam) Cox Bryant, Bryant first started playing basketball (and soccer) in Italy where his father had moved the family so that he could continue his professional basketball career. After moving back to the United States with his family at the age of thirteen, Bryant quickly realized legendary status on the hardwood, culminating in an outstanding basketball career at Lower Merion High School outside of Philadelphia. By his senior year, he was the consensus top high school player in the country. He was selected as the Naismith High School Player of the Year and Gatorade Men's National Basketball Player of the Year and was named to both the McDonald's All-American and *USA Today* All-USA first teams. Ultimately, Bryant chose to skip college and entered the 1996

NBA draft, a decision no doubt influenced by Kevin Garnett who just a year earlier became the first high school player in twenty years to forgo college. The Minnesota Timberwolves drafted Garnett in the fifth round. Bryant, by contrast, was chosen in the first round by the Charlotte Hornets, but was traded to the Lakers by virtue of pre-draft arrangements. Bryant would spend his entire 20-year NBA career with the Lakers. He led Los Angeles to five NBA championships and was selected 18 times to the NBA All-Star Team, 15 times to the All-NBA First Team, 12 times to the NBA All-Defensive Team, 4 times as the NBA All-Star Game Most Valuable Player, and 2 times as the NBA Finals Most Valuable Player. He finished his professional career as the NBA's fourth all-time leading scorer with 33,643 points, totaled 81 points in a 2006 game against the Toronto Raptors (the second most for a single contest in league history), and tallied 60 points in his very final game against the Utah Jazz. Importantly, Bryant complemented his NBA career with membership on the gold medal winning United States Olympic basketball teams in Beijing in 2008 and London in 2012 (Bryant, 2018; Geoffreys, 2014).

EMBARKING ON A JOURNEY WITHOUT HOOPS

In 2016, Bryant retired from the Lakers after an extended farewell tour in which opposing teams showered him with video tributes, even though he had said he did not want any farewell ceremonies to be held in his honor. If there was any fear on Bryant's part as to what the future would hold for him after basketball, he never expressed it. And for good reason. It was apparent to those closest to him and others who had carefully followed his life and career, that Bryant had laid a solid foundation for life after basketball. In large measure, his transition out of the sport would be relatively easy and not filled with angst because his sense of identity was not tied solely to basketball. He also had already established a level of financial security unmatched by most professional athletes and continued to pursue initiatives he had started while still playing basketball. Following in the footsteps of Magic Johnson, Michael Jordan, and other high-profile athletes who cashed in on their celebrity status, Bryant inked lucrative endorsement deals early in his professional career with various companies to supplement his very large salary.

Even before beginning his inaugural season in the NBA in 1996, he had signed a six-year $48 million contract with Adidas. One of the first products he endorsed was his signature shoe, the Adidas Equipment KB8. He stayed with Adidas until the summer of 2002 and the following year signed a four-year contract with Nike for $40 million (The contract with Nike would end in 2021, the Bryant estate supposedly upset with the company for limiting the quantity of products, particularly kid's shoe sizes, during Kobe's retirement and following his death). Subsequent Bryant endorsements included highly profitable deals with McDonalds, Coca-Cola, Spalding, Nutella, Turkish Airlines, and BodyArmor (DePaula, 2021; Telford, 2020). It was estimated that in his final season in the league, Bryant made twenty-five million in endorsements alone, ranking him fourteenth among all athletes that year just behind such people as tennis's Roger Federer, golf's Tiger Woods, soccer's Lionel Messi, and track and field's Usain Bolt (Steinmetz, 2016). At the time of his retirement, Bryant had amassed over $280 million in endorsement deals over the course of his career (Butler, 2016). Kurt Badenhausen (2020) of *Forbes* magazine estimated that Bryant's net worth when he died totaled $600 million. Tellingly, Bryant was known to give back, generously donating large sums of money to various causes and organizations, including, for instance, one million dollars to the National Museum of African American History and Culture in Washington, DC (National Museum of African American History and Culture, 2020).

Bryant's endorsement deals were not devoid of controversy. His contract to serve as a "global brand ambassador" for Turkish Airlines sparked outrage and protests from the very large population of Armenian Americans in Los Angeles and across California. Some members of the Armenian American community threatened to boycott Bryant unless he severed ties with the airlines. This anger resulted from their long-held frustration that the United States had never fully acknowledged that the early twentieth century murders of some 1.5 million Armenians was a form of genocide committed by the Turkish government. "Many outraged fans have taken to radio and social media sites to protest the deal, and some have threatened to boycott Lakers games and Bryant merchandise," noted Casper Jivalagian, executive member of the Armenian Youth Federation's Western region. "There's a clear backlash already. People have been calling us, saying 'I hate Kobe and I won't watch the Lakers anymore'" (Li, 2010).

Far more noteworthy and crucial to understanding Bryant's subsequent decision-making process and chosen initiatives, McDonalds severed all ties, and Nike did the same for a brief time after Bryant was arrested in connection with a sexual assault charge filed against him in 2003 by an employee of the hotel in Colorado where he was staying prior to having knee surgery (Duncan, 2019). Bryant denied the sexual assault charges, contending the encounter with his accuser was consensual. Prosecutors ultimately dropped the sexual assault charges after the accuser decided not to testify and the case was finally settled out of court with Bryant agreeing to pay a very large sum of money to bring the dispute to closure. Bryant was obviously pleased that the sexual assault charge was behind him, but the incident was devastating to him and had seriously tarnished his reputation and public image and, perhaps more importantly, shamed his family (CBS, 2004; CNN, 2003; Markovitz, 2006). He was both angered and distraught by what had transpired and seemingly spent all his remaining years trying to atone for the accusations brought against him and doing his best to erase that part of his history.

In a story often told, Bryant gave his wife Vanessa a $4 million 8-carat purple diamond ring shortly after the incident in Colorado, but evidence indicates he had commissioned the ring some two months earlier. He did offer a profuse apology to Vanessa, telling her that she was his "backbone," "a blessing," a piece of his heart and the strongest person he knew. "I'm so sorry for having to put you through this," Bryant told her, "and having to put our family through this" (Silverman, 2003). Bryant's frustration over the accusations was such that he considered sitting out the 2004–05 season, but Vanessa talked him out of it, telling her disgraced husband "It's not going to take you down; it's not going to take us down" (Babb, 2018). He became estranged from friends, distanced himself from teammates, and struggled to keep his emotions in check. Eventually, Bryant found the coping mechanism he so desperately needed. One evening while at home he happened to turn on the Quentin Tarantino revenge movie *Kill Bill: Vol.2* and became mesmerized by one scene in which a character by the name of Budd suffers a horrendous death after being bitten by a mysterious and quick striking snake called the "Black Mamba." Bryant was fascinated, as noted by writer Kent Babb (2018) in a very insightful essay in the *Washington Post*, by "The length, the snake, the bite, the strike, the temperament" and it was not "lost on him that snakes can also shed their skin." He came to see himself as the snake and created an alternate persona as the "Black Mamba," a transformation he claims was the only way for him to mentally get past the humiliating events in Colorado (23–24). This newly created persona was reflected in both his attitude and actions on the court and off, including insistence he was going to do things his way and not apologize to anyone for his behavior. In short, he was going to be himself whatever the circumstances and criticism. The "Black Mamba" mentality would also initially become etched in the American consciousness by Nike which came out with a signature basketball shoe featuring a snake-like logo. The shoe's accompanying video showed Bryant vaulting over a fast-moving Aston Martin (Babb, 2018; Gaines, 2020).

As the years passed, fans, fellow players, and the sporting world in general began to embrace Bryant more positively. Undoubtedly, one of the reasons for the improved public image was his continued great performances on the basketball court, including leading the Lakers to NBA championships in 2009 and 2010, and the less frequently mentioned but important contributions he made as a member of two American gold-medal winning Olympic basketball teams. Perhaps most importantly, Bryant was much happier in his private life, which impacted everything he did. He reconciled with his estranged parents, his marriage to Vanessa was on more solid footing after she had filed for divorce in 2011, and he was enormously happy and fulfilled being the father of four daughters. While always thoughtful and empathetic, he seemed to adopt an even more caring and selfless attitude with everyone he encountered. No longer the brash and cocksure eighteen-year-old basketball prodigy from Lower Merion High School, he had matured into a man who regularly and generously contributed to charitable causes, fought to bring more attention to mental health issues, began to build a vast business empire, championed women's sports, and strove to improve the educational value of highly organized youth sports. These initiatives, some of which began prior to his retirement and others that were started and came to fruition afterward, were entered into by Bryant with the same perfectionism and drive and resolve that defined his playing career. Acting like a man who had a premonition he was not going to live much longer, Bryant moved at a breakneck speed during his last years, writing stories, setting up meetings, handling endorsements, exploring business ideas, educating himself on the intricacies of television and other forms of media, pursuing entrepreneurial ventures, visiting friends and associates, traveling the world, deciding upon humanitarian options, and being a father (Babb, 2018; Brewer, 2020; Landsverk, 2020; Lloyd, 2020; Lombardo, et al., 2020; and Telford, 2020).

GIVING BACK AND PURSUING BUSINESS VENTURES

The fact Bryant was already thinking well beyond his playing days and wanted to make an impact on the world other than just through basketball was made evident years before his retirement from the Lakers. At some point early in his career, he began granting Make-A-Wish requests, some media outlets estimating he granted over 200 during his twenty years with the Lakers (Evans, 2020; Hahn, 2020). In 2007 he became National Ambassador for After-School All-Stars, a charity that provides tutoring, academic enrichment, and athletic programs to 72,000 children. That year he also launched the Kobe and Vanessa Bryant Family Foundation which was aimed at providing young people access to sports, mentorship, and economic empowerment. In 2008 he was named a spokesperson for Aid Still Required, which assists people who suffer economic calamities after natural disasters and other crises. The next year he created the Kobe China Fund in partnership with the Soong Ching Ling Foundation and directed at the education and welfare of youth in China. In 2012 he participated in a fundraising campaign for Stand Up to Cancer which raised more than $80 million dollars for cancer research and in 2013 he founded Bryant Stibel, one of his most important business ventures (Evans, 2020; Williams, 2016).

Established in partnership with Jeff Stibel, a Tufts and Brown University graduate and lifelong entrepreneur, Bryant Stibel is a multidimensional corporation that focuses on providing capital and operational support to data and media driven companies, many of which collectively form a "Who's Who" of the business world. Since its founding, Bryant Stibel had invested in some fifteen companies, including videogame designer Scopley, sports media website The Players Tribune, legal services company Legal Zoom, Chinese e-commerce giant Alibaba, hot-sauce maker Cholula, and the home-juicing company, Juicero. One particular indication of Bryant Stibel's success and global impact was its creation in 2016 of a $100 million venture capital fund, with an undisclosed amount of that money going to VIPKID, the most important online education program for Chinese children to learn English from teachers in North America. It comes as no surprise that Bryant Stibel, which is focused on providing virtual education for children ages five to twelve, would invest in the program given Bryant's close and long-standing ties with China (Bryant Stibel, 2020; Burns, 2016). Over the years Bryant had become extraordinarily popular in China, basketball fans there purchasing his jersey in record numbers and clamoring to see him and be in his presence during his regular trips to the country. For some, he had become even more popular than native-born basketball star Yao Ming. Nike recognized Bryant's appeal in China. In 2009, for example, the shoe company produced a reality television program titled "Kobe's Disciples" which was broadcast on China's most-watched television network. The program featured twenty-four Chinese children receiving tips from Bryant while living and training in the United States (Barboza, 2008).

The enormous amount of time, passion, and energy Bryant poured into Bryant Stibel was evident in Granity Studios, a multimedia production company he launched in 2013. Originally called Kobe Studios, Bryant founded Granity Studios with the intent of developing projects which bridged his love of storytelling and sports. Fluent in four languages, a perfectionist in everything he did, highly creative and imaginative, hard-working and very disciplined, and close follower of movies and various other forms of entertainment, Bryant envisioned Granity Studios as a way to create and disseminate stories that would serve as an inspiration to young people and assist them in realizing their full potential.

The source of inspiration for Granity Studios derived from Bryant's life experiences as well as the many books he read. Like most good storytellers, he was a voracious reader who over the years made recommendations of books to teammates and via interviews and social media outlets. If it is true you can learn a great deal about someone through the books they read, then we have a better understanding of what was important to Bryant, what he valued, and what motivated him. Shortly after his death, the Los Angeles Public Library assembled a list of books Bryant had suggested over the years, titling it "Kobe's Bookshelf" (Gillette, 2020). The books on that list, both fiction and non-fiction, make clear Bryant's fascination with fantasy and his interest in stories that emphasize leadership, overcoming obstacles, the desire to learn, personal resilience, building character, and the importance of following one's dreams. These are all reflected, in varying degrees, in such works on "Kobe's Bookshelf" as Paulo Coelho's *The Alchemist* (1988); Marlon James's *Black Leopard, Red Wolf* (2019); Doris Kearns Goodwin's *Leadership in Turbulent Times* (2018); Tiffany D. Jackson's *Monday's Not Coming* (2018); and Luke Longstreet Sullivan's *30 Rooms to Hide In: Insanity, Addiction, and Rock 'n' Roll in the Shadow of the Mayo Clinic* (2012). Yet another work on "Kobe's Bookshelf" was Jason Reynold's *Track Series* (2018). Recommended to him by his daughter Gianna, the Reynold's books speak directly to Bryant's interests in that they deal with children overcoming challenges and adversity on and off the track.

Especially important to Bryant was that Granity Studios complete projects which focused on many of the themes expressed in the above-mentioned books. When asked in a CBS interview just two months prior to his death about what he wanted his legacy to be in fifty years, Bryant responded that he wanted to be known "as a person that was able to create stories that inspired children and families to bond together, and for their children to dream. But not only dream but have the initiative to wake up every morning and do all they can to help that dream become a reality" (Littleton, 2020:5). The first project completed by Granity Studios was a 2015 documentary about Bryant's life and career titled *Kobe Bryant's Muse*. Distributed by Showtime, the documentary, which is eighty-three minutes in length, provides an intimate look at who influenced Bryant's career, the mentorship he received throughout his lifetime, and relationships he forged that impacted him both on and off the court. *Kobe Bryant's Muse* was followed two years later by the celebrated animated short film *Dear Basketball*. Based on the 2015 poem of the same title written by Bryant on the eve of his retirement from the NBA to express his love for the sport, *Dear Basketball* is narrated by Bryant, directed and animated by Glen Keane, and includes a musical score provided by legendary composer John Williams. It garnered much attention and received important awards, including a Sports Emmy, Academy Award for Best Animated Short Film, and Annie Award for Best Animated Short Subject in 2018. Receiving the Academy Award was historic in that Bryant became the first professional athlete ever to win an Oscar (Breznican, 2020; Pinho, 2020; Rogers, 2018).

Unfortunately, the Academy of Motion Picture Arts and Sciences refused to offer him membership on the grounds he lacked sufficient filmmaking experience. In addition, more than 17,000 people signed a petition insisting that Bryant's nomination for an Oscar be rescinded because of his accused rape case many years earlier. Although certainly hurt by these actions and reminded once again that his subsequent good works and accomplishments would never completely erase the negative opinion some people had of him because of the Colorado incident, Bryant was also very encouraged by the success of *Dear Basketball* and continued to complete projects sponsored and financially supported by Granity Studios. These projects would be further testament to his creative writing skills, imagination, and desire to have a positive impact on athletes, children, and young adults. In 2017 Bryant developed the *Musecage Basketball Network*, and the following year *Detail*. Both television shows, consisting of episodic shorts, were intended to introduce people to the intricacies and more subtle aspects of basketball. Created, written, and hosted by Bryant, and televised on ESPN, the episodes covered topics ranging from an analysis of the NBA All-Star Weekend and examination of what the next generation of players can learn from those who preceded them to detailing the reasons for Diane Taurasi's basketball success and exploration of the Golden State Warriors effective team chemistry (Breznican, 2020; Littleton, 2020; Pinho, 2020; PR Newswire, 2018; Rogers, 2018).

A BELIEVER IN ATHLETE PROTAGONISTS

Bryant added to his Granity Studio portfolio by developing several Middle Grade and Young Adult novels in partnership with Two Rivers Distribution and an animated Podcast series titled *The Punies*. Each of the novels, developed by Bryant and written in collaboration with a well-known fiction author, revolve around athlete protagonists who overcome obstacles and realize their full potential through the utilization of their hearts and imagination. They are meant to be inspirational and intended for a diverse audience of young people who learn more about themselves through the sports they play. The first book in the series, *The Wizenard Series: Training Camp* was written by Wesley King (2019) and focuses on the West Bottom Badgers, a team made up of five players and coached by Professor Wizenard. Expected to finish last in their league, the five players, guided by their wily and committed coach, are taught to take risks and in the process learn to trust their teammates and themselves. *Training Camp* was followed by *Legacy and the Queen*, a book about a twelve-year old tennis player by the name of Legacy who lives in the magical kingdom of Nova. Written by Annie Matthew (2019), the story focuses on Legacy and how she overcame numerous obstacles to win a tennis tournament that provides her with the financial resources necessary to keep open the orphanage where she resides. The third book in the series is *Epoca: The Tree of Ecrof*. Written by Ivy Claire (2019), the book takes place against a backdrop of a world dominated by sports and centers on two children, the lower-class Rovi and crown princess Pretia, both of whom battle and overcome evil forces through a special magical power while attending an elite sports academy. *The Tree of Ecrof* was followed by *The Wizenard Series: Season One*, a book written by Wesley King (2020) that tells the story of Reggie, a basketball player who ultimately realizes success by persevering and overcoming adversity during team practices. The final book in the series is *Geese Are Never Swans*. Written by Eva Clark (2020), the book, which at the time of this writing has yet to be released, is about a character named Gus who is determined to make the Olympic swimming team but must face several challenges to do so.

The novels developed by Bryant are reminiscent in some ways to the juvenile fiction of the past which utilized sport to convey important lessons and messages about life. Among the more notable of these works are Thomas Hughes's *Tom Brown's School Days*, a novel set in the 1830s at the Rugby School in England that speaks to the development of boys and the importance of physical development, fighting spirit, and Christian morality; Gilbert Patten's stories of Frank Merriwell who excelled in several sports at Yale while leading a righteous life and committing himself to moral, intellectual, and physical development; and Clair Bee's twenty-four novels about Chip Hilton, the fictional all-around athlete and outstanding student with impeccable character who treated everyone fairly and with the upmost respect (Mangan, 1981; Anderson, 2015; Gildea, 2013). Importantly, these works were all about White males and an exclusive elite White world. This was not true, however, of the novels developed by Bryant as they are inclusive and include girls as well as boys.

Serving as a perfect companion to these novels was the animated Podcast series developed by Bryant called *The Punies*. Written by Jon Haller, produced by Granity Studios in partnership with Cadence 13 and released in 2018, the four main characters are the "loveable loser" Pete "Puny" Dawson; the "dependable but spastic" dog Scoop; the "know-it-all cheerleader" Kimberly Spice; and the "troublemaker, jokester, sportscaster'" Clark Mayhoff. The four are collectively known as "The Punies." Over two seasons, *The Punies* appeared in eight episodes with such obvious sports-inspired titles as "Righteous Rivals," "Know Your Teammates," "Visualize," and "Trust Your Skill." Accompanied by a full coloring book and discussion guide focusing on content and writing style, *The Punies* told stories of how to manage anger, effectively deal with fears of not fitting in with one's peers, and other life lessons learned from engagement in sport. One event in particular makes clear Bryant's intention and philosophy behind *The Punies*, and so many of his other creative works for that matter (Radio Link, 2018). To publicize the series and spread good will and encouragement as was his custom more frequently during his last years, in 2018 Bryant attended and did a live broadcast of an episode of *The Punies* at the Children's Hospital of Orange County. Dressed in their hospital gowns and wheeling IV carts, young patients jammed into the hospital's multimedia broadcast center to meet Bryant and watch "Trust Your Crew," an episode in the series in which Pete "Puny" Dawson enters a Soap Box Derby race in a car built by his friend Lily who unfortunately neglected to install the brakes. Following the broadcast, Bryant told Carlo Vellandi (2018) of *Sports Illustrated Kids* that "For younger kids, *The Punies* is just fun. As they get older, we hope they'll start to understand the meanings and messages, and the show will teach them things like perseverance, commitment, hard work, compassion, and empathy. Those are things that sport naturally teach" (1).

AVID SUPPORTER OF YOUTH SPORTS

Bryant's belief in the educational power of sport was possible only if conducted properly and with the best interests of children in mind, an approach that was reflected in all the projects he completed for Granity Studios. This belief was reflected even more visibly in other organizations he supported and one he founded. In 2018 he agreed to a multiyear partnership with Sports & Society: A Program of the Aspen Institute, an organization founded in 2011 and with the mission, as noted on its website, "to convene leaders, foster dialogue, and inspire solutions that help sport serve the public interest" (Aspen Institute, 2020). Bryant's initial involvement with Sports & Society was serving as a featured speaker at its 2018 Project Play Summit in the Knight Conference Center at the Newseum in Washington, DC. Appearing at the Summit along with skateboarding legend Tony Hawk, Olympic track and field champion Jackie Joyner Kersee, NBC sportscaster Mary Carillo, and a number of other well-known individuals from business, academia, and the world of sport, Bryant participated in a panel discussion with four young athletes between the ages of 11 and 13 and gave a presentation in a session devoted to the power of play and how to address the challenges in youth sports (Aspen Institute, 2018).

His second, and last, major involvement with Sports & Society took place some ten months after the Project Play Summit in Washington, DC. In early August 2019, Sports & Society, along with ESPN, Ralph C. Wilson, Jr. Foundation, US Tennis Association and several other prominent organizations, launched a public awareness campaign titled *Don't Retire, Kid*. Resulting from the realization that children were "retiring" from sport prematurely, especially team sports because of pressure from adults and the excessive cost of participation, the *Don't Retire, Kid* campaign elicited the help of many prominent sports figures in its efforts to reconnect children with one of this country's most important institutions. Among the sports figures lending a hand were Bryant, the Seattle Storm's Sue Bird, Los Angeles Dodgers Clayton Kershaw, Los Angeles Angels Albert Pujols, tennis player Sloane Stephens, basketball coach Geno Auriemma, former NHL star Wayne Gretsky, and World Cup soccer campion Julie Foudy (Aspen Institute, 2019).

Not unexpectedly, Bryant became the lead spokesman for the *Don't Retire, Kid* campaign, using his large social network, athletic credibility, and international standing to make visible what was wrong with youth sport and what steps needed to be taken to ensure all children were provided a healthy and positive sport experience. At his recommendation and that of his marketing director Molly Carter, Sports & Society chose the Boston-based agency Arnold Worldwide to spearhead the *Don't Retire, Kid* campaign. Bryant also provided a list of companion sports for the Sports & Society Sport Index that basketball players could use to improve their health and develop skills. He completed, moreover, vignettes aired by ESPN detailing what the organization refers to as its "playbook with eight strategies" to keep children involved in sport. Although not clear if it was intentional to use eight strategies to reflect Bryant's first jersey number with the Lakers or how much impact he had in selecting the strategies, there is no question that each of them reflected his personal philosophy regarding a healthy and educationally sound youth sport experience. His advice to parents and caregivers as part of the *Don't Retire, Kid* campaign is: "ask kids what they want;" "reintroduce free play;" "encourage sport sampling;" "revitalize in-town leagues;" "think small;" "think development;" "train coaches;" and "emphasize prevention." Each of the eight strategies are self-explanatory, except perhaps the fifth—"think small," which Bryant makes clear is a phrase meant to encourage children to utilize their imagination and know they can experience the positive impact of play no matter the amount of space and equipment they have available to them (Aspen Institute, 2019).

Bryant proved to be enormously valuable to the *Don't Retire, Kid* campaign specifically and Sports & Society more generally. He also greatly impacted and became a beloved figure for many of those people associated with the organization and its various youth sport initiatives. One of those people was Tom Farrey (2008), executive director of Sports & Society, former ESPN journalist, and the author of *Game On: The All-American Race to Make Champions of Our Children*. In a very poignant piece written shortly after Bryant's tragic death, Farrey (2020) movingly reflected on how he had been impacted personally by the legendary Lakers player. In a similar fashion to those who knew Bryant best, Farrey said he was struck by Bryant's inquisitiveness upon first meeting him and how passionate he was about learning, how interested he was in so many things beyond basketball, and how dedicated he was to giving "voice to the voiceless" and "sticking up for kids" (3-4). This inquisitiveness, wrote Farrey, was evident in the "sophisticated questions" Bryant posed to him about Sports & Society: "How do you approach the debate around participation trophies?" "How do you mobilize organizations to change the game?" "How do you tell your stories" (3)? Ultimately, Farrey drew a link between his childhood hero Roberto Clemente, the great Pittsburgh Pirate outfielder killed in a plane crash in 1972 at the age of thirty-eight while delivering aid to earthquake victims in Nicaragua, and Bryant, noting that Clemente's death "on a humanitarian mission left a hole in our hearts but opened up something to be filled as well by citizen-athletes, like Kobe using the modern tools of social change" (4–5).

A SPORTS ACADEMY LIKE NO OTHER

In the same year he forged a partnership with Sports & Society, it was announced Bryant had entered into a new joint business venture with Chad Faulkner, the CEO and founder of a 100,000 square-foot facility in Thousand Oaks, California known as the Sports Academy (there is now a second facility in Redondo Beach). The December 6, 2018 issue of the *Los Angeles Sentinel*, a well-known Black weekly and just one of the many outlets to announce the agreed-upon business arrangement, wrote that the Sports Academy, which Faulkner had originally opened in 2016, would be renamed the Mamba Sports Academy and now include a charitable organization referred to as the MAMBA Sports Foundation (a short time later renamed Mamba & Mambacita Sports Foundation in recognition of the nickname Bryant had given his daughter Gianna). Faulkner was obviously excited about his partnership with Bryant, perhaps even a bit awed by the great Lakers guard. "We look forward to how Kobe's involvement will move us forward in the areas of on-site training, digital cognitive training, content creation, investments and charitable endeavors," Faulkner said. "His 'Mamba Mentality' philosophy will no doubt have a major impact on the development of the next generation of athletes." Bryant, for his part, was just as enthusiastic about the new joint business venture with Faulkner. "Mamba Sports Academy is a natural expansion of my commitment to educating and empowering the next generation of kids through sports," said Bryant. "As a basketball coach to young girls, my team trained at Sports Academy, which is when I first experienced the superior level of services and attention to detail their experts delivered to our team. At Mamba Sports Academy, we will focus on offering a premium experience on proper training for young athletes, and infuse a little 'Mamba Mentality' into their programs" (Sentinel News Service, 2018:3).

As it turned out, Faulkner and Bryant both got what they wanted out of the partnership, except having additional time for the partnership to blossom even more because of Bryant's untimely death. In a little over a year in which they were in business together, Faulkner benefited from both

Bryant's celebrity status and commitment to the mission of the academy, while Bryant used the academy as his base of operations in his continued efforts to develop young athletes and insure their maximum potential. All told, the new Mamba Sports Academy would evolve from an already successful business into a flourishing one under the guidance of the two men, including a state-of-the-art athletic facility, performance coaches who taught the techniques and fundamentals of various sports, sponsorship of tournaments, clinics, and leagues, and a trained staff of physical therapists, sports nutritionists, biomechanics specialists, and sport psychologists.

Besides being reflected in the name of the organization, Bryant's influence, philosophical approach to sport and child development, and guiding principles to life more generally were visibly evident in everything the academy did. Perhaps nowhere is this observation more explicit than in the three objectives listed under what was then termed the Mamba & Mambacita Foundation portion of the academy website. To paraphrase, the goals were to: 1) Provide underserved individuals and communities opportunities in sport that lead to positive social and physical development; 2) Provide financial resources for underserved athletes; and 3) Provide the financial resources necessary to ensure women are provided equal opportunities in sport (Mamba Sports Academy, 2020).

The Mamba Sports Academy, which dropped "Mamba" from its title in "accordance with the wishes of [Kobe Bryant's] estate" a little over three months after his death and is now known simply as Sports Academy, reflected in many ways the club system Bryant must have experienced growing up in Italy in that it is highly organized and regimented (Martinez, 2020: 2). It also mirrored, however, youth sports programs in the United States which are now largely adult directed, privatized, performance oriented, and characterized by highly technical and scientific coaching. This approach has drawn much criticism from, among others, health and child development professionals, for the intense pressure exerted on children in these programs and injuries that have occurred resulting from the increasing emphasis on sport specialization. Perhaps most significantly, this approach has been admonished by some because of the enormous costs required to participate and the resulting exclusion of children from lower-income families. Although no evidence could be found indicating any criticism leveled against the Mamba Sports Academy for its "pay-to-play" approach to youth sports, it is not unreasonable to expect that its geographical locations and basic costs ($299 a month for "full-circle athlete custom program for single sport focused athletes") could mitigate the chances of children with limited financial means from participating in its programs. Interestingly, at the time Bryant partnered with Chad Faulkner in 2018, J.R. Gamble, writing in *The Shadow League,* listed what he saw as the potential "pros and cons" of the new arrangement. "Hopefully Kobe won't forget the inner-city kids and those of color who are already behind the eight ball as far as elite training and resources go," wrote Gamble in his list of "cons." Will certain sectors of society be priced out of partaking in Kobe's athletics training paradise (Gamble, 2018)?

CHAMPIONING WOMEN'S SPORTS

It is difficult to assess how successful Bryant was in not pricing children out of his "training paradise" in the short time he was involved in the Sports Academy, but every indication from the previously mentioned Mama & Mambacita Foundation (now titled the Sports Academy Foundation and led by Executive Director Angela Stanislawski) was the academy's original intent to financially support underserved athletes. It is less difficult to assess how deeply Bryant was interested in providing more opportunities for women to engage in sport at the Sports Academy and society more generally. As a father of four daughters, including a budding basketball star in Gianna, it stands to reason that Bryant would pay special attention to women's sports. There is little question he wanted his girls to have positive role models they could look up to and try to emulate. It is also plausible that being supportive of women's sports was one of the ways Bryant could make amends and recast his image in the wake of experiencing very public sexual assault accusations. It is telling, however, that the great Lakers guard had always expressed a genuine interest in women's sports and offered advice and mentored women athletes during much of his career. Such great women basketball players as Diana Taurasi, Gabby Williams, Katie Lou Samuelson, Sabrina Ionescu, and Jewell Lloyd all sang his praises, noting how Bryant had served as a mentor and "routinely gave of himself to help them improve their games." Taurasi was one of the first players Bryant mentored, becoming so impressed by her basketball skills that he dubbed her the "White Mamba." "He came to L.A. when I was a freshman in high school and we grew up together in many ways," Taurasi noted, "He worked with me and others because he wanted to see us succeed since we had similar obsessions to the game of basketball" (Associated Press, 2020:2). Bryant was also a big fan and close follower of the

United States women's national soccer team, famously inviting the 2015 World Cup champions to one of his last NBA games and attending with his family the celebration to honor the 2019 World Cup champions at the Rose Bowl in Pasadena. Importantly, Bryant had always had a passion for the sport, playing soccer as a youngster while growing up in Italy and passionately supporting the famous AC Milan professional team, his favorite soccer club (Murray, 2020).

Upon his retirement from the NBA, Bryant found more time to support women's sports and simply be a loving father. He thoroughly enjoyed coaching Gianna's basketball team, taking much satisfaction in teaching the techniques and fundamentals of the game to her and her teammates. From all indications, he practiced what he preached, always being the supportive coach who wanted his girls to have a positive experience and gain an appreciation and passion for the game. Not surprisingly, he rejoiced in sharing his love for the game and spending time with the talented Gianna who was just as enthralled with basketball. The two of them were inseparable, seen at courtside laughing and carrying-on during a basketball game or standing on the sideline watching a women's soccer match. Bryant regularly took Gianna to WNBA games, including the 2019 WNBA All-Star game in Las Vegas. For two years, the two of them took in women's college basketball games in Los Angeles, Oregon, and as far away as Connecticut. Their trips to Connecticut were especially important as Gianna had grown up to be a huge fan of the University of Connecticut's legendary women's basketball team. Connecticut coach Geno Auriemma always seemed to be in awe of her love for the program and its players. "You could just see the look in her eyes. She was so excited," Auriemma said. "The absurdity of that. Your father is Kobe Bryant and the most excited you've been is being around college women basketball players" (Associated Press, 2020:6).

In hindsight, the absurdity that Auriemma mentioned was not absurdity at all because to Gianna her father, first and foremost, was not a famous basketball player but simply dad. Bryant had obviously transitioned into fatherhood with the same ease he had in much everything else. Although having no formal education beyond high school, he was a citizen of the world. Although the primary focus for much of his life was his basketball success, he was far different than many other high caliber athletes in that early on he had also established a non-sport related identity. Although showered his entire life with constant applause and adulation for his basketball exploits, he always had empathy for the underserved and disadvantaged.

A BASKETBALL LEGEND WITH ENORMOUS RANGE

At an early point in his life, Bryant developed what author David Epstein has referred to as "range." As a young boy growing up in Italy, Bryant enjoyed different experiences and embraced broad perspectives and the complexities of life while simultaneously honing his athletic skills. He held tightly to this approach his entire life and as a result was able to adapt and expand his career beyond the confines of basketball. He was an individual who, in the words of psychologist Christopher Connolly, kept numerous "career options" open as he pursued his primary specialty as a professional basketball player. He "'traveled on an eight-lane highway' rather than down a single-lane one-way street" (Epstein, 2019:34).

How Bryant developed this approach is open to speculation, but it probably largely resulted from the influence of his mother Pam who was the glue that kept the Bryant family together. Although they would become estranged for a time later in life because of a variety of reasons, not least of which was his relationship with Vanessa, Bryant's mother doted on him as a child. From all indications, he "received the full force of her affection and attention" and "there was a close bond between mother and son" (Lazenby, 2016). She also pushed him and his sisters Sharia and Shaya to be more than just athletes, making clear to them the importance of education and the need to expand their horizons and explore all possibilities. Bryant's biographer Roland Lazenby wrote that Pam Bryant was a perfectionist herself and instilled in her children an achievement orientation that would be reflected in all their lives. "The presence of their individual athletic gifts was never allowed as any sort of excuse for her children," Lazenby wrote of Pam Bryant. "They were expected to do their school-work and to be dutiful and responsible" (Lazenby, 2016).

Bryant acknowledged his "range" in an essay written by Meagan Flynn in the *Washington Post*. He fondly recalled the trips his family took through Italy along with the family of Harvey Catchings, his father's best friend and former NBA player who was also in the country playing professional basketball. Accompany them on the trips was Catchings' daughter Tamika, who would become an All-American at the University of Tennessee, an WNBA star for fifteen seasons, member of four US Olympic gold-medal winning basketball teams, and member of both the Women's Basketball Hall of Fame and Naismith Memorial Basketball Hall of Fame. "The two dads were friends," wrote Flynn, "bringing their families together on trips to see Roman ruins like the Colosseum, which Bryant said allowed them

(Tamika and Kobe) to grow up with a 'broader perspective on life . . . thinking anything's possible'" (Flynn, 2020).

The close relationship forged between Bryant and Catchings during their time together in Italy would remain strong until the day he died. Remarkably, they would go on to become two of the greatest basketball players in the world who would both be members of gold-medal-winning Olympic teams, lead their respective clubs to NBA and WNBA championships, and garner a plethora of individual awards for their accomplishments in the sport, including being inducted into the Naismith Memorial Basketball Hall of Fame in the same year (2020). Perhaps most important, however, their friendship is a reminder of how central women were in Bryant's life, a fact that makes it difficult to reconcile the sexual assault charges brought against him and at once his apparent need to seek redress for the accusations that obviously troubled him and desperately wanted to shake. Men were important in his life, including his father and teammates, but he was always surrounded by women who provided him sustenance and he in return. As an elite athlete, he was consistently in the company of men and forever being measured against them, but much of his strength and resilience and empathy seemed to derive from the nurturing hand of his mother, close connections to his sisters, loving relationships with his wife and daughters, and myriad friendships with strong and caring women like Catchings and so many others in and outside of sport (Gentry, 2020).

THE GAME TAUGHT HIM THE ART OF STORYTELLING

With that being said, it is crucial to emphasize that Bryant's enormous success in basketball, which was punctuated by his selection posthumously (again, along with Catchings as well as outstanding people from the sport such as Kim Mulkey, Kevin Garnett, Tim Duncan and Pat Summitt) into the Naismith Memorial Basketball Hall of Fame just three months after his passing, was an essential springboard to his short, but beautiful post-basketball life. While he developed needed "range" and "traveled on an eight-lane highway," what would Bryant's life been without basketball? It is safe to say it would have been far less interesting, fulfilling, meaningful, and productive. He simply would not have been Kobe without it. The sport had provided him access to important companies, venture capitalists, entrepreneurs, and media outlets that allowed him to transition into another phase of life that proved enormously valuable to him personally as well as to others. He had a love affair with basketball that brought him immense personal pleasure, satisfied his competitive impulses, and opened a world to him that he could not have imagined as a young boy who benefited from a childhood split between Italy and Philadelphia. In his *The Mamba Mentality: How I Play*, Bryant wrote that "BASKETBALL TOOK ME EVERYWHRE," noting that hoops, both on and off the court, had taught him creativity and an understanding of human nature and how to lead. "The game, in essence," said Bryant, "taught me the art of storytelling. Without it, I would not have an Emmy, I would not have an Oscar, I would not have creative dreams and visions still to unfold" (Bryant, 2018:200). His passion for the game is also evident in his poignant and heartfelt and, some might say, melancholy poem *Dear Basketball*, especially the stanza that reads:

> And so I ran.
> I ran up and down every court
> After every loose ball for you.
> You asked for my hustle
> I gave you my heart
> Because it came with so much more (Bryant, 2015).

Not unexpectedly, upon hearing of Bryant's death and that of his beloved Gianna and seven others aboard the helicopter headed to a basketball game at his Mamba Academy, thousands of people instantaneously flocked to the Staples Center to lay wreaths, post messages, leave Laker jerseys with numbers 8 and 24 imprinted on them, and a host of other memorabilia to pay respects to those who had perished. These gestures and remembrances were followed by an assortment of memorials and special tributes, with Bryant, of course, being the central focus. Former teammates, opposing players, friends, team officials, sportswriters, and ordinary fans, crestfallen by the sudden and tragic death of Bryant, spoke admiringly and lovingly of the extraordinarily gifted athlete who had spent his entire 20-year NBA career in the "City of Angels." Those in Italy were devastated by the news of his passing, as were those in China where the great Lakers guard was idolized and a beloved figure. Luca Vecchi, the mayor of the northern Italian town of Reggio Emilia where Bryant spent part of his youth, noted on the day he died that "Kobe Bryant grew up here and he was, for all of us, a 'Reggiano.' Today, he left us. A basketball legend that all of our town will forever fondly and gratefully remember" (Flynn, 2020). In China, where Bryant had 9.2 million followers on his Weibo profile, word of his death hit particularly hard with the whole country in mourning. Among the millions of messages sent recalling Bryant was one by a user with the surname Zhang who wrote:

"He [Bryant] was the star of my student days, and no one inspired me more than him. Forever 24, Forever Black Mamba" (Brzeski, 2020).

Finally, while many recounted his greatness on the court and unmatched drive and determination to be the best who ever played the game, more often than not those who spoke of Bryant also recalled that he was a renaissance man who in the short time he had been retired from basketball had continued to make positive impacts and selflessly serve others as a coach, educator, advocate for the poor and mentally ill, businessman, entrepreneur, benefactor, fundraiser, spokesperson, author, storyteller, father, and husband. Unlike the tragic tales of athletes who garner millions of dollars during their careers only to squander it in retirement and are never able to find happiness as ordinary citizens, Bryant depended on the extraordinary work ethic and attention to detail that had marked his many years on the court to carve out a meaningful and fulfilling post-basketball life. His successful retirement years were clearly encapsulated in such aptly titled newspaper articles as: "Why Kobe's Last Chapter Was His Best," "Opinion: Kobe Bryant was One of a Kind Even in Retirement," "Investor, Author, Filmmaker: The Entrepreneurial Second Act of Kobe Bryant," and "He Was Born to Play Basketball, but for Kobe Bryant that was Never Enough." To be certain, he was not perfect. He made mistakes that would haunt him to the very end. But from his travails he emerged a much better man and likely understood he had become a beloved figure that transcended sports. In the end, Bryant fully embodied the words he scribbled on one of the posters at the 2018 Project Play Summit in Washington, DC, "Dream Big, Live Epic" (Farrey, 2020:6).

References

Anderson, R.K. 2010. *Frank Merriwell and the Fiction of All-American Boyhood*. Fayetteville, AR: The University of Arkansas Press.
Aschburner, S. 2020. "Second Career Act for Kobe Bryant Ends All Too Soon." NBA.com, https://www.nba.com/article/2020/01/27/kobe-bryant-second-career-act-ends-too-soon. Accessed April 30, 2020.
Aspen Institute. 2020. https://www.aspeninstitute.org/programs/. Accessed May 5, 2020.
———. 2018. "Kobe Bryant Partners with Aspen Institute Youth Sports Initiative," https://www.aspenprojectplay.org/kobe-bryant-news-release. Accessed May 5, 2020.
Aspen Institute. 2019. "Aspen Institute's Project Play Launches Campaign with

Industry Leaders, Pro Athletes to Keep Kids from Quitting Sports," https://www.aspeninstitute.tute.org/news/press-release/don't-retire-kid/. Accessed May 5, 2020.

Associated Press. 2020. "Kobe Bryant Leaves Lasting Impact on Women's Basketball," https://www.voanews.com/usa/kobe-bryant-leaves-lasting-impact-womens-basketball. Accessed May 6, 2020.

Babb, K. 2018. "The Revisionist: Kobe Bryant is a Storyteller in Search of Perfection, and the Most Vexing Tale is his Own," *Washington Post.* https://www.washingtonpost.com/graphics/2018/sports/kobe-bryant-hollywood-revisionist/. Accessed April 29, 2020.

Badenhausen, K. 2020. 'Kobe Bryant's $600 Million Fortune: How He Won on-and-off the court." *Forbes,* https://www.forbes.com/sites/kurtbadenhausen/2020/01. Accessed May 3, 2020.

Barboza, D. 2008. "China's Promise Excites the Sports Stars." *New York Times,* https://search-proquest-com.mutex.gmu.edu/cv_786252/pdfprintvie. Accessed May 2, 2020.

Brewer, J. 2020. "Kobe Bryant Accomplished So Much. It's Devastating to Consider What he Left Unfinished." *Washington Post,* https://www.washingtonpost.com/sports/nba/kobe-bryant-accomplished-so-much-its-devastating-to-consider-what-he-still-had-left-to-do/2020/01/26/9a8b964e-4078-11ea-b5fc-eefa848cde99_story.html. Accessed May 3, 2020.

Breznican, A. 2020. "Kobe Bryant Was Building an Entertainment Empire." *Vanity Fair,* https://www.vanityfair.com/hollywood/2020/01/kobe-btyant-oscar-hollywood-dear-basketball. Accessed May 4, 2020.

Bryant, K. 2015. "Dear Basketball." *The Players Tribune,* https://www.theplayerstribune.com/en-us/articles/dear-basketball. Accessed June 10, 2020.

———. 2018. *The Mamba Mentality: How I Play.* New York: Farrar, Straus and Giroux.

Bryant Stibel. 2020. www.bryantstibel.com. Accessed May 4, 2020.

Brzeski, P. 2020. "China Erupts in Mourning Over Kobe Bryant's Death." *The Hollywood Reporter,* https://www.hollywoodreporter.com/news/china-erupts-mourning-kobe-bryants-death-1273567. Accessed June 8, 2020.

Burns, M. J. 2016. "After $100 Million Investment Fund Announcement, Kobe Backs Chinese Education." *Sporttechie,* https://www.sporttechie.com/100-million-investment-fund-announcement-kobe-backs-chinese-education-company/. Accessed April 15, 2020.

Butler, J. 2016. "Kobe Bryant's Net Worth and Lasting Impact." *Dinks Finance,* https://www.dinksfinance.com/2016/04/kobe-bryants-net-worth-and-lasting-impact/. Accessed May 4, 2021.

CBS. 2004. "Kobe Details Alleged Rape Night." *CBS News,* https://www.cbsnews.com/news/kobe-details-alleged-rape-night/). Accessed May 4, 2020.

Cielho, P. 2019. *Black Leopard, Red Wolf.* New York: Riverhead Books.

Claire, I. 2019. *Epoca: The Tree of Ecrof.* Costa Mesa, Ca.: Granity Studios.
Clark, E. 2020. *Geese are Never Swans.* Costa Mesa, Ca.: Granity Studios.
CNN. 2003. "Kobe Bryant Charged with Sexual Assault." *CNN,* https://www.cnn.com/2003/law/07/18/kobe.bryant/). Accessed May 4, 2020.
DePaula, N. 2021. "Vanessa Bryant, Kobe Bryant Estate Elect Not to Renew Partnership with Nike." *ESPN,* https://www.espn.com/nba/story/_id/31293033/vanessa-bryant-kobe-bryant-estate-elect-not-renew-partnership. Accessed May 6, 2021
Duncan, A. 2019. "A History of Kobe Bryant's Endorsement Deals." *The Balance Careers,* https://www.thebalancecareers.com/a-history-of-kobe-bryant-s-endorsement-deals-39029. Accessed May 6, 2020.
Epstein, D. 2019. *Range: Why Generalists Triumph in a Specialized World.* New York: Riverhead Books.
Evans, K.D. 2020. "Kobe Bryant's Charitable Work Included 20 Years with the Make-A-Wish Foundation." *The Undefeated,* https://theundefeated.com/features/. Accessed May 4, 2020.
Farrey, T. 2008. *Game On: The All-American Race to Make Champions of our Children.* New York: ESPN Books.
———. 2020. "Why Kobe's Last Chapter Was His Best." Aspen Institute, https://www.aspeninstitute.org/blog-posts/why-kobes-last-chapter-was-his-best/. Accessed May 5, 2020.
Flynn, M. 2020. "My story Began in this Town: Kobe Bryant Mourned in Italy, Where He Learned to Play Basketball." *Washington Post,* https://www.washingtonpost.com/nation/2020/01/27/kobe-italy-death/. Accessed May 14, 2020.
Gaines, C. 2020. "Kobe Bryant Created his 'Black Mamba' Alter-Ego as a Way to get Through the Lowest Point of his Career." *Business Insider,* https://www.businessinsider.com/kobe-bryant-black-mamba-nickname-2015-3. Accessed May 4, 2020.
Gamble, J. R. 2018. "Pros and Cons of Kobe Bryant's Mamba Sports Academy, *TheShadowLeague,* https://theshadowleague.com/pros-cons-kobe-mamba-sports-acade . . . rOXssOveNIILhBnPgtT5F-12u1Vbj3EAD3PVFBpsOOzYOx4XPA1Y1BoBhWJYw). Accessed June 13, 2020.
Gentry, D. (2020). "Tamika Catchings on the Hall of Fame, Her Hearing and the Heart of Kobe." https://www.si.com/nba/mavericks/news/tamika-catchings-wnba-hall-of-fame-kobe-bryant. Accessed May 5, 2020.
Geoffreys, C. 2014. *Kobe Bryant: The Inspiring Story of One of Basketball's Greatest Shooting Guards.* New York: Calvintir Books.
Gildea, D. 2013. *Hoop Crazy: The Lives of Clair Bee and Chip Hilton.* Fayetteville, AR: The University of Arkansas Press.
Gillette, S. 2020. "One of Kobe Bryant's Reading Recommendations Was Inspired by Daughter Gianna: See the List Here." *People,* https://people.com/sports/kobe-bryant-reading-recommendations/. Accessed May 6, 2020.

Goodwin, D.K. 2018. *Leadership in Turbulent Times*. New York: Simon & Schuster.
Hahn, J.D. 2020. "Kobe Bryant Granted Over 200 Make-A-Wish Requests During Career: It was the 'Highlight of My Life.'" *People*, https://people.com/sports/kobe-bryant-granted-over-200-make-a-wish-requests/. Accessed June 10, 2020.
Jackson, T.D. 2018. *Monday's Not Coming*. New York: HarperCollins.
James, M. 2019. *Black Leopard, Red Wolf*. New York: Riverhead Books.
King, W. 2020. *The Wizenard Series: Season One*. Costa Mesa, Ca.: Granity Studios.
———. 2020. *The Wizenard Series: Training Camp*. Costa Mesa, Ca.: Granity Studios.
Knights, S., Sherry, E., Ruddock-Hudson, M. 2016. "Investigating Elite End-of-Athletic-Career Transition: A Systematic Review." *Journal of Applied Sport Psychology* 28 (3), 291–308 (DOI: 10.1080/10413200.2015.1128992).
Landsverk, G. 2020. "Kobe Bryant Fought the Stigma Around Anxiety by Talking About His Own Insecurities." *Insider*, https://www.insider.com/kobe-bryant-legacy-mental-health-advocacy-don't-retire-kid-2020-1). Accessed April 28, 2020.
Lazenby, R. 2016. *Showboat: The Life of Kobe Bryant*. New York: Little, Brown, and Company.
Li, S. 2010. "Kobe Bryant's Turkish Airlines Deal Outrages Armenian Americans." *Los Angeles Times*, https://www.latimes.com/archives/la-xpm-2010-dec-16-la-me-kobe-bryant-armenian-20101216-story.html. Accessed April 29, 2020.
Littleton, C. 2020. "Kobe Bryant's Death Cuts Short a Promising Second Act in Entertainment." *Variety*, https://variety.com/2020/film/features/kobe-bryant-hollywood-entertainment-granity-studios-dear-basketball-1203483095/. Accessed May 1, 2020.
Lloyd, J. 2020. "After 20 NBA Seasons, Kobe Bryant Was Building A Legacy by Sharing His Passion for Basketball." NBC, https://www.nbclosangeles.com/news/sports/Kobe-bryant-mamba-sports-academy-basketball-nba/2298967. Accessed May 4, 2020.
Lombardo, J., Lefton, T., Mullen, C., and Ourand, J. 2020. "Kobe Bryant-He Was a Creative Force." *Sports Business Journal*, https://www.sportsbusinessdaily.com/journal. Accessed May 3, 2020.
Mamba Sports Academy. 2020. https://mambasportsacademy.com/. Accessed May 6, 2020.
Mangan, J. A. 1981. *Athleticism in the Victorian and Edwardian Public School: The Emergence and Consolidation of an Educational Ideology*. Cambridge: Cambridge University Press.
Markovitz, J. 2006. "Anatomy of a Spectacle: Race, Gender, and Memory in the Kobe Bryant Rape Case," *Sociology of Sport Journal* 23(4), 396–418, DOI: https://doi.org/10.1123/ssj.23.4.396.
Martinez, P. 2020. "Sports Academy drops 'Mamba' from its name to honor wishes of Kobe Bryant's estate." *CBS News*, https://www.cbsnews.com/news/sports

-academy-drops-mamba-from-its-name-to-honor-Kobe Bryant/). Accessed May 4, 2020.

Martin, L.A., Fogerty, G.J., and Albion, M.J. 2014. "Changes in Athletic Identity and Life Satisfaction of Elite Athletes as a Function of Retirement Status," *Journal of Applied Psychology* 26 (1), 96–110 (https://doi.org/10.1080/10413200.2013.798371).

Matthew, A. 2019. *Legacy and The Queen.* Costa Mesa, Ca.: Granity Studios.

Moreau, J. 2020. "Barack Obama on Kobe Bryant's Death: 'Nothing is More Heartbreaking.'" *Variety,* https://variety.com/2020/biz/news/kobe-bryant-barack-obama-gianna-bryant-1203505268/. Accessed May 2, 2020.

Murray, C. 2020. "Kobe's Complicated Legacy as Women's Sports Supporter." *Yahoo Sports,* https://sports.yahoo.com/on-kobe-bryants-complicated-status-as-a-champion-for-womens-sports-222646611.html. Accessed May 6, 2020.

National Museum of African American History and Culture, 2020. *Museum News,* https://nmaahc.si.edu/about/news/statement-death-basketball-icon-and-museum-founding-donor-kobe-bryant. Retrieved June 14, 2020.

Park, S., Lavallee, D., and Tod, D. 2013. "Athletes Career Transition Out of Sport: A Systematic Review," *International Review of Sport and Exercise Psychology* 6(1), 22–53 (DOI: 10./080./1750984X.2012.687053).

Pinho, F.E. 2020. "Kobe Bryant Brought Sports to Page, Podcast and Film Through Costa Mesa Production Company Granity Studios." *Daily Pilot,* https://www.latimes.com/socicty/daily-pilot/news/story/2020-01-29/kobe-bryant-granity-studios). Accessed May 4, 2020.

PR Newswire. 2018. "Kobe Bryant's Granity Studios Unveils Slate of Projects." https://www.prnewswire.com/news-releases/kobe-bryants-granity-studios-unveils-slate-of-projects-300742025.html. Accessed May 3, 2020.

Radio Link. 2018. "Cadence Kobe Launches 'The Punies.'" https://radiolink.com/2018/08/23/cadence-kobe-launches-the-punies-podcast/). Accessed May 5, 2020.

Reynolds, J. 2018. *Jason Reynolds Track Series.* New York: Atheneum.

Rogers, M. 2018. "Academy Award? Business Ventures? Kobe Bryant Brings Same Level of Commitment to Post-NBA Career," *USA Today.* https://www.ustoday.com/story/sports/nba/2018/10/03/kobe-bryant-ex-lakers-guard-brings-same-commitment-post-nba-life/1509304002/. Accessed May 4, 2020.

Sentinel News Service. 2018. "NBA Legend Kobe Bryant and Sports Academy Team up to Create Mamba Sports Academy." *Los Angeles Sentinel,* https://lasentinel.net/nba-legend-kobe-bryant-and-sports-academy-team-up-to-create-mamba-sports-academy.html. Accessed May 6, 2020.

Silverman, S. 2003. "Kobe Presents Wife $4 Mil Diamond Ring." *People,* https://people.com/celebrity/kobe-presents-wife-4-mil-diamond-ring/. Accessed June 10, 2020.

Steinmetz, K. 2016. "20 Hot Athletes with the Biggest Endorsement Deals of 2016." https://www.moneytalknews.com/slideshows/20-hot-athletes-with-the-biggest-endorsement-deals-2016/. Accessed May 4, 2021.

Sullivan, L.L. 2012. *Thirty Rooms to Hide In: Insanity, Addiction, and Rock 'N' Roll in the Shadow of the Mayo Clinic*. Minneapolis: University of Minnesota Press.

Telford, T. 2020. "Investor, Author, Filmmaker: The Entrepreneurial Second Act of Kobe Bryant." *The Washington Post*, https://www.washingtonpost.com/business/2020/01/27/business-legacy-of-kobe-bryant/. Accessed April 30, 2020.

Vellandi, C. 2018. "'The Punies' Podcast to Children's Hospital of Orange County." *Sports Illustrated Kids*, https://www.sikids.com/kid-reporter/kobe-bryants-podcast-visits-childrens-hospital. Accessed May 5, 2020.

Williams, J. 2016. "What is Bryant Stibel, Venture Capitalist Fund? Kobe Unveils Investment Fund with Business Partner Jeff Stibel." *International Business Times*, https://www.ibtimes.com/what-bryant-stibel-venture-capitalist-fund-kobe-unveils-investment-fund-business-2405314. Accessed April 15, 2020.

"THE COLOR OF MY WRITING"

Reflections on Studying the Interconnection among Race, Sport, and American Culture

I am repeatedly asked, whether in my home department at George Mason University, at professional conferences, or simply in general correspondence, how and why I became involved in writing about African American athletes. When approached with such inquiries, I immediately think back to my family background and childhood experiences and question if they have in some way led me to focus on the study of African Americans in sport? How did my early personal experiences and observations shape my views about race and influence my choice of academic study? More specifically, is my interest in the African American athlete somehow connected, or perhaps even an effort to alleviate a sense of guilt, to having been raised in a family where racial stereotypes were regularly articulated and living in a segregated town where insensitivity to differences was never questioned or openly challenged?

My hometown of Fresno, a city that now has a population of over 500,000 and sits in the heart of California's Central Valley, is perhaps best known for its agriculture, close proximity to three famous national parks, and scorching heat that drives many locals over to the cool waters of the

Pacific Coast during the summer. Fresno boasts some famous people who were either born or resided in the city at one time, including actor Mike Connors, baseball's Tom Seaver, car racing's Bill Vukovich, basketball's Jerry Tarkanian, writer William Saroyan, businessman Kirk Kerkorian, and rock star Warren Zevon. Less known, or at least less written about and acknowledged or remembered, was the de facto segregation that existed in Fresno when I was growing up there in the 1950s and 1960s. I grew up in an all-White neighborhood, went to a high school that probably had no more than four African Americans in a student body of some 1,500, and had just one Black teammate during three years of playing football, basketball, and baseball. I did not have a Black teammate in baseball until playing with Dave Winfield, now a member of the National Baseball Hall of Fame, in 1971 with the Alaska Goldpanners in a well-known summer collegiate baseball league in Alaska.

In this environment I experienced numerous instances of racialist thinking, insensitive generalizations, and deep-seated stereotypical beliefs. My coaches seemed to be particularly guilty in this regard, invoking racialist thinking as part of game strategy, presumably as a way to motivate me and other team members. Not surprisingly, it was against the almost entirely Black Edison High School from the west side of town that the coaches brought out their most racially inspired material. An incident I vividly remember was the pregame speech our head football coach gave prior to our contest against Edison during my senior year. He emphasized that both teams, with the exception of Edison's tight end Charles Young, who became an All-American at the University of Southern California and an outstanding NFL player, matched up athletically. But he emphasized our squad had worked harder, were more highly disciplined, and possessed the heart and character to overcome any setbacks we would experience during the contest. The message was clear that the key to the game was to get ahead as quickly as possible because our Black opponents did not have the will and moral strength to overcome a deficit.

Unfortunately, my parents were like my coaches in that they regularly used disparaging racial and ethnic remarks. They were equal opportunity slingers of racial and ethnic epithets and slurs, with no group seemingly immune from them, whether it was the large Armenian population that had settled in Fresno or the African Americans who were forced to live in segregated neighborhoods literally on the other side of the tracks west of town or the illegal Mexican laborers who picked grapes on my grandparents' farm or the increasing number of Mongolian immigrants who were moving to the area. My parents' use of such language, interestingly enough, was intermixed with actions that now seem to be contradictory and illogical. While my mother insisted that I not jump into the swimming pool at the local YMCA until the African American children had gotten out, she was the first to volunteer to have one of the players from the all-Black Berkeley High basketball team stay in our home during a Christmas holiday tournament. Few days passed that my father did not spout off some racial stereotype, yet prominently displayed in our house was a picture of himself with his Black playmate during their first day of kindergarten, one of the few photographs he chose to take with him during his recent move to an assisted living facility.

I would like to believe my parents did not understand the implications of what they said and how hurtful their comments would have been to those groups targeted, but the fact they were careful to express their views only in the privacy of their own home or among their most trusted friends, tells me otherwise. At some level, my mother, who attended college for only a short time and spent her entire life in an assortment of blue-collar jobs, and my father, who left high school prior to graduation to enter World War II, were evidently cognizant of their racialist comments and those of their friends and my coaches. In large part, I was complicit in all of this, never openly questioning what was being said and who was being targeted. I was only awakened to the harmful effects of racialist thinking and the negative impact of racism when I left home for college. There, I went through a transformation, becoming aware of racial dynamics through classes in American history and Black studies and the more public dialogue regarding Black alienation and marginalization made evident through the civil rights and Black Power movements. It was also there that I first became aware of the role of African Americans in sport through classes taught by Lyle Olsen, the former Brooklyn Dodger minor leaguer, San Diego State University baseball coach, and eventual founder of the Sport Literature Association. Although not a prolific writer himself, Olsen was inspirational, the most voracious reader of sport I have ever known. He opened up a new world for me in which it was not just permissible but essential to study seriously the impact of sport on society.[1]

When questioned by colleagues now about my research, I usually spare them the aforementioned details, but make clear that my interest in Black athletes stemmed from a fascination with the Harry Edwards-led boycott of the 1968 Olympic games and from the fact I grew up at a time when analyzing the Black experience was in vogue and race was becoming part of the national dialogue and a central focus of American history. I also believe my interest in the African American athlete, however, is largely a result of my abhorrence of inequality in all its forms and my larger interest in and empathy for the marginalized, the downtrodden, the powerless, and the underdog. At the risk of sounding patronizing, I have always been drawn to the disadvantaged, whether it was a physically limited Little League teammate I attempted to help or a quiet and withdrawn high school classmate I befriended or an undervalued tenure-track faculty colleague I mentored. Where this approach originated I do not know, but perhaps it was actually heightened by the type of household in which I grew up. Although disgusted by my parents' racialist thinking, I would like to think that both of them, through their kind actions rather than their sometimes disparaging words, instilled in me a sense of responsibility and humanity that resulted in speaking out on behalf of those less fortunate than myself.

Irrespective, I always wonder why people are so curious about my line of research, especially knowing that the types of questions and the frequency in which they are asked are often more telling than any answers that can be provided. Is it the fact they simply do not comprehend how a White academic could be interested in uncovering the stories of African American athletes and have any empathy regarding the struggles encountered by them? Although never bothering to inquire, I often ask myself if people regularly probe historian Ron Smith regarding his research on intercollegiate athletics or historian and literary scholar Michael Oriard regarding his research on football or historian Patricia Vertinsky regarding her research on women and exercise.

The many questions regarding my line of research have been complemented by interesting personal experiences and stories told to me by colleagues over the years that furnish insights into the assumptions made about skin color, race, and identity. Three years ago, an African American colleague from a well-known southwestern university confided to me he had received a call late one night from one of his former graduate students who shouted through the phone, "Did you know that Dave Wiggins is White?" My colleague, who obviously took great delight in telling me the story, told his former student that, "yes, he knew Dave Wiggins was white and had known for some time." I found the story amusing as well as interesting, knowing that someone who had read my work assumed I was Black. Just this past year, a White colleague and friend from a university close to my own told me of being invited to guest lecture in a class on race and sport in which one of the required texts was my *Glory Bound: Black*

Athletes in a White America (1997), a book that I dedicated to my mother and father.² My colleague related that he was pleased with his lecture and the discussion that ensued afterward, but explained that one of the most telling aspects of the evening occurred at the very end of class when one of the White students stood up and announced how nice he thought it was to read the work of an African American author who could dedicate his book to two parents rather than just one.

These two stories pale in comparison to what I experienced on a job interview for an administrative position early in my academic career when department websites with pictures of individual faculty were not available. After arriving by plane from Kansas State University where I was teaching at the time, I walked into the airport waiting room and immediately approached the person holding a placard with my name on it. Before I could extend my hand to introduce myself, the person blurted out, "Oh, I thought you were Black." I was so startled I did not know what to say, but perhaps should not have been with a surname considered one of the "blackest" in the United States and a Curriculum Vita with a publication list almost entirely devoted to the history of sport among African Americans. As it turned out, this was just the beginning of an extraordinarily uncomfortable and bizarre interview that made me realize that perhaps Brenda and I and our two boys, Jordan and Spencer, could live a bit longer in Kansas. In my one meeting with the entire faculty, I was asked by one man in the front row, "How old I was," and the lone African American in the back of the room asked, "What right I had to write about black athletes?" If I could relive this event, I would have responded by asking the question posed to me by well-known historian Mark Dyreson in a recent email exchange between us: "Can you be an American historian and not be interested in race—regardless of your race?"[3]

As much as I was taken aback by these incidents, I ultimately realized I simply had the tables turned on me and had been confronted by stereotypes, assumptions and ignorance that African Americans confront on an almost daily basis. While disheartening, I had never had people pass judgment on my competence and professional abilities based on assumed age and skin color. I believe, however, that these incidents have made me a better historian and certainly given me more perspective on the complexities of racialist thinking. If nothing else, these experiences have made me cognizant of the sensitive nature of supposed "insider" and "outsider" status regarding research and scholarly work. I cannot, of course, put myself in the position of the ex-slave who noted that if "you want negro history you have to get it from someone who wore the shoe," but I have studied intently African American athletes for so long it is nearly impossible for me to think of them as "others."

Tellingly, I am no longer asked about my age and have never been publicly questioned about my right to write about Black athletes. In fact, my African American colleagues have never openly expressed any animosity toward me or shown signs of jealousy regarding my scholarship, although one of them recently asked the interesting question "if I thought my White colleagues viewed my work on the Black athlete as more creditable than that completed on Black athletes by Black academicians?" They have been complimentary of my work, sought out my advice, and shown respect for my expertise. One recent piece of evidence for this support was being asked by Lonnie Bunch, director of the National Museum of African American History and Culture, to serve as a consultant, which, in turn, has resulted in my close working relationship with noted scholar and curator Damion L. Thomas. With that said, I remain sensitive to how I come across to individuals in my writings and presentations on African American athletes. I always wondered in my classes how students would respond to a White academician lecturing and leading discussions on racial and ethnic issues in sport. My fears usually proved to be unfounded, however, as I frequently had students of every race and color approach me at the end of a semester and remark that they had their "eyes opened" regarding the historical struggles of African American athletes and were appreciative of me telling their stories.

In regard specifically to my scholarship, I have tried to tell engaging stories and never wavered from my chosen topic, passionately and unapologetically recounting the experiences of African Americans in sport. In the process of telling stories about African American athletes, I have come to realize that race, while important in bridging or widening the cultural divide, is not always the primary and consolidating factor between Blacks any more than it is between Whites. There is wide diversity in the Black experience resulting from differences such as geography, age, gender, class, political affiliation, religion, and occupation that precludes any one from being innately qualified to research and write about it. If that were not the case, we could just as easily disqualify scholars who had never been athletes from writing about sport history or scholars who had never toiled at a menial job from writing about labor history or scholars who had never been in combat from writing about military history.

This does not mean that I do not struggle with understanding the complexities of racial discourse and how African American athletes have fought to become full participants in sport. I do. It is clear to me that as I figuratively peel away each layer of the onion and dig deeper into the history of the African American experience in sport, the more I learn, the less I know. With each new project, I invariably discover athletes and sports organizations and events that are new to me. I am also reminded of the slow and incremental steps that have characterized the struggle against racial injustice in sport. Like the larger civil rights movement, the fight for equal opportunities in sport has always been distinguished by "two steps forward and one step back," with the subtitle of one of my books, *The Unlevel Playing Field*, still being a fitting description of the status of African Americans in an institution controlled by a dominant White power structure.[4]

In hindsight, I wish I had paid closer attention to African American women athletes and written even more about agency. I thought sport management scholar Jennifer Bruening was speaking directly to me when she published her insightful 2005 essay "Gender and Racial Analysis in Sport: Are all the Women White and all the Blacks Men?"[5] Bruening's point, which is a crucial one and has also been made by sport historian Sarah Fields and others, is that the literature on sport has typically ignored African American women athletes. Although some very good studies have appeared since Bruening's 2005 essay, including Jennifer Lansbury's A *Spectacular Leap* (2014) and Rita Liberti and Maureen Smith's *(Re) Presenting Wilma Rudolph* (2015), African American women athletes continue to be marginalized and hold no "complete membership in either their gender or their racial groups."[6] Much more work needs to be done on the meaning of sport for African American women athletes to offset "both the whiteness of gender analysis in sport and the maleness of racial analysis in sport."[7]

I can provide no definitive reason why I have given only limited attention to African American women athletes. I assume my minor adviser at the University of Maryland, Joan Hult, would have either claimed I did not take African American women athletes seriously or that I did not have the requisite knowledge and historical background to write about them. These are, of course, not necessarily mutually exclusive, since my lack of requisite knowledge and historical understanding could just as easily have resulted from not taking African American women athletes seriously enough to delve into the literature on the subject. This is not something easy to accept for a dyed-in-the-wool liberal who has spent his entire academic career emphasizing the importance of inclusiveness, equal opportunities, and harmful effects of inequality in all its various forms. Far easier for me to accept is the contention that I have delimited my subjects to those I feel more comfortable and confident in documenting. If that is true, then why as a White man do I feel more comfortable and confident in exploring the experiences of Black male athletes and not Black female athletes? Why has race always trumped gender for me when selecting a topic?

My regret about not spending more time on African American women athletes is matched by my disappointment in not writing more often about agency. Although having written about various forms of resistance in sport, I could have done much more on how African American athletes carved out their own space and negotiated the complex relationship with the White power structure. This includes, but is not limited to, expressive playing styles and direct confrontation with those holding power and using Black bodies for their own purposes and profit.

With that said, I assume I am similar to other academicians in desiring more immediate feedback about my impact on other researchers and quality of my scholarly contributions. The writing life, and the scholarly world more generally, is at once, at least for me, a meaningful yet ambiguous experience. Unlike my days as an athlete when performance and wins and losses decisively determined success, the publishing business is far less clear cut regarding effectiveness and irrespective of number of citations and positive reviews nothing can ever completely erase the unsettling vagueness of it all. It is no different for me in the classroom where I am never quite sure about my performance, irrespective of my teaching scores, comments from students, and the use of required rubrics and assessments that will undoubtedly be discarded by pedagogy specialists who change their methods of evaluation more often than college basketball's Larry Brown used to change coaching positions or the regularity in which historian Elliott Gorn's first name is misspelled.

This uncertainty, which I assume creeps into the minds of most academics, never stopped me from researching and writing about the African American experience in sport. Since 1979, I have made many presentations and published numerous essays, book chapters, and books on topics ranging from the play of slave children and the response of the Black press to the 1936 Olympics to Muhammad Ali's relationship with the Nation of Islam to the debate over supposed Black athletic superiority. Except for a couple of articles and book chapters, all my authored works have dealt with African American athletes and the larger issue of race. More recently, I have edited or coedited several anthologies, many of which include a large amount of information on the African American experience in sport. I find anthologies to be particularly rewarding since they allow me to work closely with colleagues, many of whom are in the early stages of their careers and looking to make their mark as academicians.[8]

What have I learned from my research over nearly four decades? Like all academics, I assume I have probably learned as much about myself through my scholarship as through the subjects I have studied. If I knew at the start of my career what I know now, I probably would have slowed down, been far more patient, and read more deeply and consulted more often with my colleagues before committing pen to paper. There are sentences I have written that I wish I could take back and interpretations and conclusions I have drawn that I would retract if I could. Now more than ever, I wonder if one of my respected former colleagues was correct when he noted that we would all be better off if everyone were limited to publishing just three pieces of work during their entire academic careers.

One important example of regret has to do with the publication of my 1989 essay "Great Speed but Limited Stamina: The Historical Debate Over Black Athletic Superiority." Five years after its publication, Jeffrey T. Sammons of New York University wrote a long essay in the *Journal of Sport History* in which he reviewed the writings on race and sport. Although very complimentary and positive about my collection of work, he criticized me for a comment I made at the very end of my essay where I noted that the "spirit of science" necessitates that researchers not be precluded from determining whether the success of black athletes was somehow the result of distinct chromosomes.[9] Sammons' criticism was deserved: looking back, I wish I had been more exact with my words and far more sophisticated in my argument. Although acknowledging then and now that genetic makeup plays a crucial role in athletic performance, I do not believe in biological determinism, recognizing that success on the playing field results from a variety of physical, social, cultural, economic, and educational factors. I will not try to skirt blame and deny responsibility for what I wrote some thirty-five years ago, but it is instructive to mention that the comments to which Sammons took offense were not included in the original draft I submitted for publication. I inserted them only after one of the external reviewers strongly suggested that it would make an already interesting essay that much more provocative and noteworthy. The lesson to be learned from all this, as far as I am concerned, is to hold tight to what you believe in and not acquiesce to external reviewers for fear you will not get published.

Regrets aside, the pace at which I have published has as much to do with my love for research and putting projects together and seeing them come to fruition as anything else. It is also partly a result of the academic home in which I have always lived and the types of universities in which I have taught. My membership in a department of kinesiology, where seemingly all that matters is quantity of publications in which the number of authors is often larger than the number of subjects, initially drove me to concentrate on articles that could be completed in a timely fashion rather than books that usually require much more time to complete. On occasion, this entailed the tactical decision not to take the additional time necessary to order through interlibrary loan yet another Black newspaper or plan for a potentially valuable interview or seek more feedback from trusted colleagues that could have made a difference in the overall quality of my publications. In essence, I did not feel time was on my side, especially when surrounded by scientists who had no understanding of how long the historical research process takes and during a period of time when there was no ProQuest, e-journals, and other digitized sources and web-based research materials.

I now spend far more time on my research projects, but it is not because I feel I have more time or am more secure in my academic position. The fact of the matter is that my expectations are now so much higher, and I do not want to disappoint myself or anybody else. Still using my number two yellow pencil, I insist that a sentence is just right before moving on to the next and that a paragraph is exactly the way I want it before making the transition to the next set of words. This all takes place after I have tried to exhaust all the primary sources necessary to answer the questions posed and the analysis and interpretations that need to be made. Once I finish my first draft, I send it to several trusted colleagues for their comments and suggestions before submitting the manuscript to an outlet for further review and hopefully eventual publication. (When all is said and done, sport history is a team game rather than a solitary activity.) This process is not one I find debilitating, but a challenging experience that satisfies my competitive nature and deep attachment to discipline and routines.

The love of challenges, as far as I am concerned, suits me quite well for studying the African American experience in sport. The topic is complex and fraught with potential mine fields because of the persistent nature of racialist thinking and discrimination in the United States. In all my work, I try to follow the advice of Carter G. Woodson, the great historian from Howard University, who noted, on the founding of Negro History Week, that "we should emphasize not Negro History, but the Negro in history."[10] I am also guided by the words of noted writer and poet Maya Angelou, who once wrote, "History, despite its wrenching pain cannot be unlived, but if faced with courage, need not be lived again."[11]

Whether I have done justice to the edicts of Woodson and Angelou is open to question, but I do believe I have contributed to a better understanding of the bifurcated nature of the African American experience in sport characterized at once by exploitation and agency, cultural expression and commodification, racial uplift and moral degradation. If there is one prominent theme that has emerged from my work, it is the utilization of sport as a means of racial uplift. Recognizing its symbolic power and how deeply it resonates with the American public, African Americans, from writers and educators and many others, have used sport to combat deep-seated notions of Black inferiority and moral decay. This approach has always been noticeable to me, but probably never more so than in my recent research on the Colored Intercollegiate Athletic Association (CIAA), the first athletic conference organized among HBCUs in 1912. The leaders of the organization, which included prominent faculty and administrators from some of the most prestigious HBCUs in the country, fashioned a sports program characterized by pristine organizational structure and adherence to strict rules that would contribute to the social advancement of African Americans and help prove their self-worth in a society that marginalized them and failed to recognize them as human beings.[12]

The quest for racial uplift, as cultural critic and African American studies scholar Gerald Early points out so clearly, has historically been accompanied by the struggles of African Americans who often face the difficult choices among "individual success, group loyalty, and integrationist ambitions."[13] These choices have been evident from at least the late-nineteenth century when a select number of African American athletes realized success in predominantly White organized sport. One classic example of this was the predicament faced by the owners in Negro League Baseball. Although undoubtedly interested in the progress of the race, seeing that African Americans could play at the highest level, and perhaps even recognizing the temporary nature of their institution, their vested interest in baseball behind the walls of segregation made it difficult for them to support the campaign by the Black press to integrate Major League Baseball (MLB). They understood that the entry of African Americans into MLB would probably mean the ultimate demise of their teams and leagues. The owners of other parallel or separate sports programs at the professional level of competition and later coaches and athletic administrators at HBCUs were faced with the same dilemma. In essence, regarding sport, integration for African Americans was a blessing and a curse, a triumph as well as a loss.

There was never unanimity of opinion among African Americans, of course, regarding sport's power to eliminate racial inequality and discrimination. Some African Americans believed that individual success in athletics, while not necessarily eliminating racial discrimination, potentially contributed to better understanding of African Americans and more appreciation of them among Whites. There were some who viewed sport as uniquely powerful in transforming racial dynamics, perhaps even more so than African Americans who had made their mark in the arts and other intellectual domains. This is certainly made true in a 1935 *Crisis* editorial under the by-line "Joe Louis and Jesse Owens." "It is not," wrote the *Crisis*, "the infinitesimal America which needs conversion on the race problem; it is the rank and file, the ones who never read a book by Du Bois, or heard a lecture by James Weldon Johnson, or scanned a poem of Countee Cullen, or heard a song by Marion Anderson, or waded through a scholarly treatise by Abram L. Harris, Carter Woodson, Charles H. Wesley or Benjamin Brawley. For these millions, who hold the solution of the race problem in their hands, the beautiful breasting of the tape by Jesse Owens and the thud of a glove on the hand of Joe Louis carry more 'interracial education' than all the erudite philosophy ever written." Striking a similar message in a 1936 issue of *Opportunity* magazine was Edwin Bancroft Henderson, the prominent teacher, civil rights activist, and historian of the African American athlete. Noting that the "mass of humanity still is motivated by feelings and emotions" and that "our keenest pleasures and most poignant pains are born of feelings rather than of intellect," Henderson argues that successful African American athletes "are emulated by thousands of growing youth of all races, and above all, they gain for themselves and the negro the respect of millions whose superiority feelings have sprung solely from identity with the white race."[14]

Always of concern to other African Americans, even those who understood the symbolic importance of Black athletic success, was that an inordinate amount of attention to sport could diminish their sense of identity and was no real solution to the problems of the race. I fall neatly into this philosophical camp, being hard pressed to see how the athletic success of an elite number of African Americans can eliminate the myriad racial problems and inequality in the United States. In fact, I take the position of sportswriter Kevin Blackistone, who makes the case that the "games we love" have not been "in the vanguard of social change" in the United

States.[15] The most famous racial advances in sport have typically followed rather than preceded major civil rights legislation and social movements. Even the historic entry of Jackie Robinson into MLB in 1947 followed on the heels of Franklin Roosevelt's 1941 executive order eliminating discrimination by federal defense contractors and Supreme Court decisions in 1944 and 1946 that made all-White primaries and segregated seating on interstate buses illegal.[16]

Tennis great Arthur Ashe and sociologist and activist Harry Edwards for years held similar views, although Edwards over a decade ago altered the course of the conversation by arguing that for many African American youth, sports may be their last opportunity to realize success and make a better life for themselves. African American youth, particularly those from impoverished backgrounds who are destined for life on the streets, crime, and imprisonment, have sport as a last resort to climb up and overcome their horrible conditions. "I still maintain," writes Edwards, "that there is a high and inordinate emphasis on sports in the black community. That emphasis has been transmuted, however, by the processes of the 'end of the golden age of black athletics' from a liability to a virtue, in a sense that it may provide us with the last hook and handle that we have on a substantial proportion of this generation of young black people."[17]

Edwards' suggestion that sport could serve as the "last hook and handle" is based on the premise that education, social welfare, and other government programs are incapable of improving the lives of poverty-stricken African American children. It is clear why he would take this view. As a society, we have all failed impoverished African American children, particularly males and their families.

Statistics from 2013 indicate that 40 percent of Black males between the ages of sixteen and sixty-four had no earnings, compared to 30 percent of all other men with no earnings in the same category. Some 6 percent of working Black males between eighteen and sixty-four years old are currently in state or federal prison, or in a municipal jail which is three times higher than all other men in the same age category. Approximately 34 percent of all working-age Black men who are not incarcerated are ex-offenders, compared to 12 percent of all other men. Black females, while generally better off than their male counterparts, fall below all other females regarding educational attainment and employment. Some 9.6 percent of Black women ages 16–64 years old were unemployed compared to 5.8 percent of all other women. Particularly troubling is that 29 percent of Black women were living below the poverty level compared to 17 percent for all other women. Black families with children under eighteen years of age headed by a single mother have the highest rate of poverty at 47.5 percent compared to 8.4 percent of Black married couples. This is compounded by the fact that 6,427,000 or 6.7 percent of all African American children come from single-family households typically headed by women.[18]

With these statistics in mind, Edwards's theory of sport as the "last hook and handle" was seemingly an acknowledgment that all possible solutions to the horrid conditions of African Americans of lower economic status have been exhausted. It was, as far as I can determine, a rare example of a fatalistic attitude on Edwards's part. It was also a clarion call for African American youth to continue to devote time honing their physical skills so that they could realize a career in professional sport. African American youth do not need much encouragement in this regard, because the research and anecdotal evidence indicates they devote an inordinate amount of time preparing for careers in sport, believing, in the words of sociologist Jay Coakley, that it is their "biological cultural destiny" to achieve greatness as athletes.[19] The pervasiveness of this view is such that White youth sometimes opt out of those sports in which African Americans are overrepresented and seen as superior. An important caveat here is that relative to many of their male counterparts, African American women athletes, as a group, especially those with strong family networks who are able to obtain scholarships, are more studious and focused more intently on post-athletic careers. I would contend this is partly a result of the very limited opportunities in professional sport for women irrespective of race and ethnicity.

Edwards's theory of sport as "the last hook and handle," moreover, was seemingly a departure from the concept of sport articulated by African American leaders prior to integration. While Edwards encouraged the individual pursuit of careers in sport by African American youth, one who famously noted that his "body was his resume," African American leaders during the interwar years, particularly those connected to schools, tied sport to larger racial issues and educational concerns.[20] For these men, basketball in particular (ironic, considering the game today), but other sports as well, were a means to help build pride, foster positive character traits, nurture race leaders, and develop model citizens who possessed the skills to be successful in all walks of life.

This conception of sport is certainly still part of the rhetoric used by coaches who work with African American youth and those in charge of such programs as Street Soccer USA, which provides guidance and life training techniques for the homeless. But it has effectively given way, in my view, to a quest for careers in sport rather than any concern in satisfying the traditional and not mutually exclusive pursuits of "individual success, group loyalty, and integrationist ambitions." It is significant that members of the growing Black middle class who have entered into prestigious and financially rewarding professions in increasing numbers now have access to the resources and educational support necessary to achieve success in sport if they so choose. This is especially true because of the growing privatization of youth sport that requires significant financial outlay for coaching, practice time, equipment, travel, and other resources necessary to compete and hone the physical skills essential to athletic success. On the other hand, many lower-class Blacks, with only minimal financial resources and social capital, view one of their only options as a career in sport that provides limited opportunities to only a select number of the most physically gifted (and fortunate).

The differences between the Black middle class and Black lower class in how they structure their sporting activities and in what attitudes they bring to pursuing sports make clear the importance of wealth, resources, and family and educational support. My assumption has always been that these differences would play out among African Americans much as they played out in the past with various ethnic groups and other minorities. It is difficult to confirm these assumptions because few scholarly studies have been completed on these groups. Based on my cursory examination of the subject, however, it is safe to say that, when compared with African Americans, White ethnic groups and other minority groups in the United States show no comparable devotion to sport. In contrast to African Americans, the athletic accomplishments of Irish, Jewish, Italian, and other European immigrant groups ultimately coincided with improvement of their economic status and social mobility. These factors have not necessarily lessened these groups' interest and enthusiasm for sport, but do not adequately explain why they show no singular devotion to it. Native Americans, Latin Americans, and Asian Americans among other ethnic groups, while embracing certain activities as participants and spectators, have shown no comparable preoccupation with sport. In fact, in some cases, these groups have shown an unwavering devotion to education in pursuit of social advancement and a better life and minimal or no interest in sport.[21]

A classic example of this involves the recent discussion of the victories garnered by Indian Americans in the Scripps Spelling Bee contest. In 2015, Gokul Venkatachalam and Vanya Shivashankar, were co-champions of the Scripps National Spelling Bee, the seventh year in a row and eleventh out of the last fifteen years in which Indian Americans won the event. The victories caused much discussion centering on why Indian Americans were dominating the contest. Especially interesting when juxtaposed with the debate over supposed Black athletic superiority, the domination of Indian Americans in the event was compared to the "way that Kenyan runners have owned the Boston Marathon" and was generally considered to be a result of hard work, years of training, and the long-standing emphasis placed on academics in their culture.[22] Very notable, in my view, were, first, the apparent lack of comments indicating that the success of Indian Americans in the event resulted from innate intellectual abilities and, second, the concerns expressed by some that there were negative outcomes associated with an overemphasis on training for spelling bees and academic achievement more generally. *Washington Post* columnist Lavanya Ramanathan, an Indian American who "was shuttled to math camp and required to explain every lost test point," is "ambivalent about the bee." In a column titled "Someday, the Spelling Bee Winners May Wish They Had Just Played Football," she contends that Indian American children would be better off if they complemented their academic work with participation in sport since it "can help teach kids healthful habits that last into adulthood." She made the point that women who had participated in sport were better able to negotiate the problems commonly associated with the workplace and life more generally. "The women who lettered in soccer, softball, and cheering," wrote Ramanathan, "respond to failures and setbacks as if they're made of Teflon. They forge alliances like it's 'Survivor.'"[23]

Notwithstanding this discussion, compared to African Americans, ethnic immigrant groups have received far less, albeit in some cases high-quality, scholarly attention regarding their connection to sport. The scholarship on sport in the United States has been more about racial ideology, about Black and White, about African Americans struggling to find their way in an extraordinarily popular and important institution. If African Americans have, in the words of scholar John Hoberman, a "sports fixation," then academicians and those in the popular press have a fixation with those with the fixation.[24]

Even with the apparent decline of the Black athlete regarding level of participation, people in the United States have continued to focus with much regularity on the history and social and economic implications of African American participation in sport. Since 2015, Google Scholar recorded 17,300 hits for studies published on sport for African Americans, as compared with 15,700 for Asian Americans, 14,300 for Native Americans,

13,800 for Italian Americans, 11,400 for Latin Americans, 7,810 for Irish Americans, and 5,840 for Jewish Americans. Although far from scientific, and not taking into consideration the tiny fraction of the population Jewish Americans and some other ethnic groups comprise and not accounting for more popular works and differentiating among recreation, exercise, and sport, the numbers do indicate a continued fascination with African American athletes. The Black body continues to garner a great deal of interest and discussion and, in some cases, controversy. While having been exploited and physically mutilated down through the years, the Black body has also held out a particular fascination for Whites, largely because of the sensory pleasure derived from the visual images and athleticism of those obviously different from themselves. At the risk of stereotyping, I believe it helps explain in part why Whites became enamored with such athletes as Jackie Robinson, Muhammad Ali, Michael Jordan, Tiger Woods, LeBron James, and Missy Copeland.

Ultimately, research on the African American experience in sport makes clear that there are still gaps in the literature that need to be filled. I am not particularly interested, however, in providing a long list of limitations regarding previously published work and making recommendations for further studies as is commonly done in quantitative research. Those do not always seem to be taken very seriously anyway. I do believe we would benefit from more studies that compare the sport experiences of African Americans with the aforementioned ethnic groups and Indigenous people around the world. I also believe it is important that academicians take seriously the lives and occupational careers of former African American athletes. If sports do indeed teach values and help develop character, a belief not uniformly held by academicians and others, then studies of the post-athletic careers of African American athletes and their White counterparts might contribute to a more thorough understanding of what is learned from the sport experience and its supposed connection to social mobility. I assume these studies would confirm the commonly held belief that African American athletes have always viewed sport as "a way out," a means to a better life, and a way to climb up the socioeconomic ladder. I also assume these studies would confirm that African Americans, like so many of us, are just as likely to participate in sport for the not easily articulated reasons of enjoyment, self-fulfillment, meaningfulness, and the desire to be somebody and show that one has arrived and is deserving of full citizenship. I would postulate that these reasons are perhaps even closer to the truth.

Future studies aside, what is particularly important for me at this point in my career is trusting that the scholarship I, and others, have conducted has contributed to a more thorough understanding of the lives of African American athletes and race relations. Finally, what interests me is a theoretical question—how closely will sport ever be tied together again with educational attainment and intellectual development and, even if the connection occurred, how effective it would be in bringing people of different backgrounds together in a truly sustained way and eliminating racial discrimination and inequality? Not unexpectedly, I have serious doubts. Now, many years removed from my childhood and having immersed myself in the complexities of race and racialist thinking, it seems clear that African Americans are still searching for asylum in a country they entered involuntarily. Although a select number of African American athletes have realized fame and fortune, a large segment of African Americans, with an immediacy and through stark physical representations made possible by the new social media, continue to confront racial injustice and face extraordinary dangers as evidenced by the recent police violence committed against them and the horrific murder of nine innocent worshippers at the historic Emanuel African Methodist Episcopal Church in Charleston, South Carolina. It is reflective, as noted by African American studies scholar Eddie S. Glaude, Jr. in his recent book *Democracy in Black: How Race Still Enslaves the American Soul* (2016), of an America that habitually values White lives over others and holds on to the belief, despite evidence to the contrary, that racial equality has been achieved.[25] Whether we can change the hearts and minds of those who hold on to these beliefs through our writings and educational efforts is difficult to determine, but if racial inequities are to be overcome we must as academicians hold out hope for a more open society while continuing to remind people, including our parents and other loved ones, about systematic forces in America that contribute to White privilege and disadvantages Blacks. To remain silent regarding racial disparities and inequities is unacceptable and ultimately harmful for all of us.

Notes

I would like to thank and express my appreciation to Mark Dyreson, Chris Elzey, Thomas Goodale, Donald Mrozek, Murray Phillips, Maureen Smith, Ryan Swanson, and David Zang for their cogent comments and suggestions on a previous version of this manuscript.

1. My academic career took a fortunate turn when I transferred from Oregon State to San Diego State. Not only did I take classes from and have endless conversations with Lyle Olsen about the study of sport, but took courses from Reet Howell, a noted sport historian who passed away at the age of forty-nine from ovarian cancer. Also at San Diego State was Reet's husband, Max, an internationally known sport historian who at the time was Dean of the College of Professional Studies.

2. David K. Wiggins, *Glory Bound: Black Athletes in a White America*, Syracuse, NY: Syracuse University Press, 1997.

3. Email correspondence with Mark Dyreson, 8/25/2015.

4. David K. Wiggins and Patrick B. Miller, *The Unlevel Playing Field: A Documentary History of the African American Experience in Sport*, Urbana, IL: University of Illinois Press, 2003.

5. Jennifer E. Bruening, "Gender and Racial Analysis in Sport: Are all the Women White and all the Blacks Men?" *Quest*, 57 (2005): 330–349.

6. Ibid., 330; Jennifer Lansbury, *A Spectacular Leap: Black Women Athletes in Twentieth-Century America*, Fayetteville, AR: The University of Arkansas Press, 2014; Rita Liberti and Maureen M. Smith, *(Re) Presenting Wilma Rudolph*, Syracuse, NY: Syracuse University Press, 2015.

7. Bruening, "Gender and Racial Analysis in Sport: Are all the Women White and all the Blacks Men?": 342.

8. I am especially excited about my new role as editor of the series on Sport, Culture, and Society with The University of Arkansas Press. It gives me the opportunity to solicit and evaluate manuscripts and to stay abreast of much of the literature being produced in sport history.

9. See Jeffrey T. Sammons, "'Race' and Sport: A Critical, Historical Examination," *Journal of Sport History*, 21 (Fall 1994): 205.

10. The Woodson quote comes from his essay "The Celebration of Negro History Week, 1927," *The Journal of Negro History* 12:2 (1927): 103–9.

11. The Angelou quote comes from her poem "On the Pulse of Morning." Which she read at Bill Clinton's first inauguration on 20 January 1993. See Mary Jane Lupton, *Maya Angelou: A Critical Companion* (Westport, CT: Greenwood Press, 1998).

12. Chris Elzey and I discuss the early years of the CIAA in "Creating Order in Black College Sport: The Lasting Legacy of the Colored Intercollegiate Athletic Association" in David K. Wiggins and Ryan A. Swanson, eds. *Separate Games: African American Sport Behind the Walls of Segregation*, Fayetteville, AR: The University of Arkansas Press, 2016.

13. Gerald Early, *A Level Playing Field: African American Athletes and the Republic of Sports*, Cambridge, MA: Harvard University Press, 2011, p. 24.

14. "Joe Louis and Jesse Owens," *The Crisis*, 42 (August 1935): 241; Edwin Bancroft Henderson, "The Negro Athlete and Race Prejudice," *Opportunity*, 14 (March 1936): 77–79.

15. Kevin B. Blackistone, "Sports could be leader in societal change; it just rarely chooses to be," *The Washington Post*, June 27, 2015, accessed August 20, 2015, https://www.washingtonpost.com/sports-could-be-leader.

16. Ibid.

17. Dave Leonard, "The Decline of the Black Athlete: An Interview with Harry Edwards," *ColorLines* 30 (April 2000), pp. 20–24.

18. blackdemographics.com.

19. Jay Coakley, *Sports in Society: Issues and Controversies*, 9th edition, New York: McGraw Hill, 2007, p.290.

20. This quote comes from *USA Today*, but after repeated attempts, I cannot locate the issue in which it appeared. I continue to look.

21. See Jay Coakley, *Sports in Society: Issues and Controversies*, pp. 298–319.

22. Joe Heim, "Indian Americans dominate the national spelling bee. Why should they continue to take abuse for it?" *The Washington Post*, March 25, 2015.

23. Lavanya Ramanathan, "Someday, the spelling bee winners may wish they had just played football," *The Washington Post*, May 27, 2015.

24. John M. Hoberman, *Darwin's Athletes: How Sport Has Damaged Black America and Preserved the Myth of Race*, Boston: Houghton Mifflin, 1997.

25. Eddie S. Glaude Jr., *Democracy in Black: How Race Still Enslaves the American Soul* (New York: Crown, 2016).

INDEX

Abbott, Cleve, 27, 45
Abbott, Robert, 17, 72
Abdul-Jabbar, Kareem (Lew Alcindor), ix, 147, 160, 216
Academic Reform, 87, 96, 222–23
"Activism, Organizing, and the Symbolic Power of Sport: Reassessing Harry Edward's Contributions to the 1968 Olympic Protest Movement" (Hartmann), 228
Adidas, and Kobe Bryant endorsement, 239–40
Advantage Ashe (Ashe with Gewecki), 186, 199
Aetna Life and Casualty Company, 203
"African American Festive Style," (Pierson), 70
After-School All-Stars, 243
Agee, Arthur, 96
Alabama Review, 197
Albritton, David, 22
Alexander, Walter, 6, 40, 66
Ali, Muhammad, 1, 173, 175, 177, 214, 270, 279
Amateur Athletic Union (AAU), 88, 109, 111, 170
Amdur, Neil, 179, 186
"American College Athletics," (Carnegie Foundation), 65
American Historical Review, 197
American League Park (Griffith Stadium), 61–62
American Tennis Association (ATA), 44, 78

American Water Skiing Association, 192
Amistad Press, 194–96
Anderson, Marion, 274
Angelou, Maya, 218, 272–73
Anthony, Carmelo, 176
Archer, Samuel H., 33–34
Armstrong, Samuel Chapman, 17, 20
Arthur Ashe Courage Award, 174
Arthur Ashe: Portrait in Motion (Ashe with Deford), 186, 197
Arthur Ashe's Tennis Clinic (Ashe), 186
Arthur Ashe Student Health and Wellness Center, 187
Art Rust's Illustrated History of the Black Athlete (Edna and Art Rust), 188
Aschburner, Steve, on Kobe Bryant's death, 237
Ashe, Arthur, ix, 97, 202–3, 223, 275; assembling the research team, 189–90; honors received, 186–87; influence of *A Hard Road to Glory*, 201–3; method for collecting research materials, 191–93; praise and critique of book, 195–202; reasons for lack of surveys on Black athletes, 188–89
Atkins, W. E., 34
Atlanta Olympic Games, 123
AT&T Nation's Football Classic, 77–78
Atwood, R. B., 46
Auriemma, Geno, 248; and Gianna Bryant, 253

Babb, Kent, and transformation of Kobe Bryant, 241

284 • INDEX

Baker, William J., 197, 214
Barco, J. W., 34
Barkley, Charles, 176
Barnett, Robert (Bob), 91
Barthes, Roland, 164
Baseball Hall of Fame, 129
Baseball's Great Experiment: Jackie Robinson and His Legacy (Tygiel), 197
Baskerville, B. S., 65
Bass, Amy, and praise for *A Hard Road to Glory*, 187
Bay Shore Resort, 26–27
Beamon, Bob, 160
Bee, Clair, 11, 45; and Chip Hilton books, 247
Been in the Storm Too Long (Litwack), 192
Behee, John, 191
Belafonte, Harry, 185
Bell, William M., 46
Benching Jim Crow: The Rise and Fall of the Color Line in Southern College Sports, 1890-1980 (Martin), 201–2
Bennington Summer School of Dance, 11
Bercovich, Sam, 138–39, 142
Berea College, 9
Berlin Olympic Games, 22, 86–88, 161, 163, 215
Bernstein, Rick, 202
Bernstine, Daniel, 195
Berwanger, Jay, 88
"Best Way Out of the Ghetto, The" (Fisher), 97
Bethune, Mary McLeod, 72
Bill Erwin Post American Legion Baseball Team, 137–42
Bing, Dave, 204
"Biological Cultural Destiny," (Coakley), 276
Bird, Sue, 248
Black Athlete: A Shameful Story, The (Olsen), 188
"Black Athlete in Contemporary Society," 187

Black Athletes, and civil rights struggle, 147–49, 157–79
Black Athletic Protests, and Colin Kaepernick, 177–78; and current players, 175–77; decline of, 169–71; participated in by George Powles athletes, 147–49; Rafer Johnson's refusal to participate in, 118; those led by Harry Edwards, 159–61, 212–19, 227–29, 265; and Vince Matthews and Wayne Collett, 161–72
Black Athletic Superiority, 271, 278
Black Autobiographies, 173
"Black Broadway," 47, 71
Black Champions Challenge American Sports (Jones and Washington), 188
Black College Sport (Chalk), 190, 193
Blackistone, Kevin, 274–75
Black Lives Matter Movement, and increased athlete activism, 175–78
"Black Mamba," persona created by Kobe Bryant, 241
Black New Orleans (Blassingame), 192
Black Power, decline of, 169–71; and Harry Edwards, 211–17; and Milt Campbell, 119–20; those athletes mentored by George Powles, 147–49; and Vince Matthews and Wayne Collett, 159–66
Black Scholar, The, 217, 220
Black September, 168
Black State High School Athletic Associations, 90–92
Black Students (Edwards), 217
Blackthink: My Life as a Black Man and a White Man (Owens with Neimark), 173
Black Thoughts Journal, 222
Blassingame, John, 192
"Blood in the Water," 116
Bob Mathias Story, The, 110
Bolden, Frank, 203
Bolt, Usain, 240

Bond, Horace Mann, 66
Bondy, Filip, 115
Booker, Jimmy, 50
Booth, Doug, 200
Borican, John, 40
Borzov, Valerie, 168
Boston Marathon, 278
Boston, Ralph, opposition to 1968 Olympic boycott, 214–15
Bowerman, Bill, reaction to Vince Matthews and Wayne Collett medal stand disruption, 168, 171–72
Bowker, Albert, 221–22
Branch, Kip, 190, 193
Brawley, Benjamin, 274
Brekke-Miesner, Paul, 131, 137
Brewer, Jerry, on Kobe Bryant's death, 237
Brodie, John, 137
Broun, Haywood Hale, and special feature on George Powles, 146
Brown, E. C., 72
Brown, Jim, 114, 121, 147
Brown, Larry, 270
Brown, Paul, 114
Brown, Sam, 143
Brown v. Board of Education of Topeka, 12; and high school sports, 85–101
Bruce, Roscoe, 90
Bruening, Jennifer, 269
Bruguiere, Harold, 109–10
Brundage, Avery, 160; response to the Vince Matthews and Wayne Collett medal stand disruption, 163, 171
Bryant, Gianna, 237, 244, 253
Bryant, Howard, 150
Bryant, Joe, 238, 254–55
Bryant, Kobe, 2–3; basketball accomplishments, 238–39; Champion of Women's sports, 252–53; charity and business ventures, 242–52; close connection with China, 243; creation of "Black Mamba" persona, 241–42; production of middle grade and young adult novels, 246–47; endorsements, 239–40; fatherhood, 253–54; exhibiting tremendous range, 254–55; as promoter of youth sport, 248–52; relationship with Venessa Bryant, 241; sexual assault charges, 240–41; snubbing by Academy of Motion Picture Arts and Sciences, 245; as storyteller, 255–57; tributes following death, 256
Bryant, Pamela Cox, 238; influence on Kobe and his sisters, 254
Bryant Stibel, 243–44
Bryant, Vanessa, 241, 254
Budge, Don, 133
Bunch, Lonnie, 268
Bunn, John, 12
Burden, Eric, 93
Burr, John, 45–46, 48–49
Bush, Jim, 158, 161
Bushrod Park, 136–37
Byrd, Franz "Jazz," 61–62, 199

Cahn, Susan, 89
California High School Coaches Hall of Fame, 146
Campanis, Al, 225
Campbell, Edith, 109
Campbell, Milt, and belated honors, 115–16; career in Canadian Football League and with Cleveland Browns, 114; comparisons with Bob Mathias and Rafer Johnson, 117–19; at Indiana University, 111; and London Olympics, 110; and Melbourne Olympics, 112; military career, 111; outspoken position on race, 120
Campbell, Thomas, 108
Camp Nelson, 8
Canadian Football League (CFL), 114
Canadian Journal of the History of Sport and Physical Education (now *Sport History Review*), 196

Cardwell, Mark, 51–52
Carey, Andy, 132
Carillo, Mary, 248
Carlesimo, P. J., 96
Carlos, John, 118; and Mexico City Olympic Protest, 160–61, 166, 173–74, 216; Reaction to the Vince Matthews and Wayne Collett medal stand disruption, 175; serving as an inspiration to Colin Kaepernick, 177–78
Carnegie Foundation for the Advancement of Teaching, 65
Carrierre, Michael, H., 136
Carroll, John, 87
Carter, Art, 46
Carter, Jimmy, 220
Castile, Philando, 176
Catchings, Harvey, 254–55
Catchings, Tamika, and friendship with Kobe Bryant, 254–55
Center for the Study of Sport in Society, 94
Chafee, Suzy, 170
Chalk, Ocania, 190, 193, 201
"Champions We Never Knew," (Halberstam), 198
Chapman, Samuel Armstrong, 7
Cheek, James, 187
Cheney, John, 223
Chicago Daily News Relays, 113
Christian Science Monitor, 107, 116
CIAA Bulletin, 16, 37–40
Civil Rights Journal, 228
Civil War, 8
Clair Bee's Long Island University Coaching School, 11
Clark, Kenneth B., 195
Clemente, Roberto, 249–50
Cleveland Knights of Columbus Meet, 113
Coachman, Alice, 204
Coakley, Jay, 220, 276
"Coddling Black Athletes," (Ashe), 186, 204

Cold War, 118, 120
Collett, Wayne, college career, 158–59; and medal stand disruption, 162–66
Colored (now Central) Intercollegiate Athletic Association (CIAA), 7–8, 15–17, 27, 273; and basketball tournament, 45–53; and *CIAA Bulletin*, 37–40; controversies, 37–40; during World War I and II, 41–42; origins of, 34–36; sports offerings, 43–45
Colorlines, 99–100, 224
Coming on Strong (Cahn), 89
Connie Mack Baseball Team, 140
Connolly, Christopher, 254
Connolly, Harold, 171
Connolly, Olga, 171
Connors, Mike, 264
Contemporary Sociology, 196–97
Cooper, Anna Julia, 20
Copeland, Missy, 279
Cosell, Howard, 171
Crisis, 217, 274
"Crisis of Black Athletes on the eve of the 21st Century," (Edwards), 223–24
Cronin, Joe, 132
Crosetti, Frank, 132
Cullen, Countee, 274
Cunningham, Glenn, 40

D'Alessandro, Dave, 108, 116
Daley, Arthur, 109
Darwin's Athletes: How Sport Has Damaged Black America and Preserved the Myth of Race (Hoberman), ix, 1–2
Davis Cup, 185
Davis, Edward P., 36, 62
Davis, Walter, 92
Day By Day in Dodgers History (Gewecki), 199
Days of Grace: A Memoir (Ashe with Rampersad), 186, 199
Dear Basketball (Bryant), 245, 256

"Decline of the Black Athlete: An Interview with Harry Edwards," 224
Deford, Frank, 186, 197
"Delusions of Grandeur," (Gates), 97
Democracy in Black: How Race Still Enslaves the American Soul (Glaude, Jr.), 280
Denishawn Dance Company, 17
Dickerson, Eric, 196
Dickey, John Miller, 68
Dillard, Harrison, 120
Dimaggio, Dom, 132
Dimaggio, Joe, 132
Dismond, Henry Binga, 72
Don't Retire Kid, and connection to Kobe Bryant, 248-49
"Don't Tell Me How to Think," (Ashe), 186, 204
Drake, Ducky, 113
Drew, Howard, 43
DuBois, W. E. B., 20, 100, 201, 228-29, 274
Dumas, Charles, 120
Dunbar, Paul Lawrence, 20
Duncan, Tim, 255
Durkee, Stanley, 64, 75

Early, Gerald, 203, 273
East-West All-Star Game, 78
E. Bercovich and Sons, 138, 142
Ebony, 217
Eckersley, Dennis, 132
Edwards, Harry, and academic reform, 222-24; birth and education, 212; and boycott of New York Athletic Club track meet, 215; changing conception of sport participation, 224-25; as commentator, 203; confrontation at San Jose State College, 212; criticism of Jesse Owens, 215; founding of Olympic Project for Human Rights, 213-14; future of Black athletic participation, 99-100; and Mexico City Olympic Games, 118, 159-61, 166, 169-72, 216-17, 265; new appreciation for his life and career, 227-30; securing positions in professional sport, 225-26; sport as "last hook and handle," 275-76; tenure struggles at University of California, Berkeley, 219-22; writing life and critical analysis of sport, 217-19
"Edwards vs. The University of California," 220
Eldridge, Larry, 116
Ellington, Duke, 47
Ellis, Joe, 143
Ellison, Ralph, 199
Emmerton, Bill, 199
Epstein, David, 254
ESPYS, 174
Evans, Lee, 160-61

Falk, David, 195
Farry, Tom, and respect for Kobe Bryant, 249-50
Faulkner, Chad, 250, 252
Fazio, Ernie, 140
Federal Bureau of Investigation (FBI), 215, 218
Federer, Roger, 240
Females, and dearth of professional sport opportunities, 95; at Hampton Institute, 11-15; lack of programs in the Colored Intercollegiate Athletic Association, 44-45; and support shown by Kobe Bryant, 252-53; status in high school sport prior to Brown v. Board of Education, 88-89; status in the Central Intercollegiate Athletic Association, 44-45
Fields, Sarah, 95, 269
Fisher, Anthony Leroy, 97
Fists of Freedom: The Story of the '68 Summer Games, 174
Fitzgerald, Ella, 47

Fitzpatrick, Tommy, 143
Flood, Curt, 140–42, 173; praise for George Powles, 129, 135–36; and civil rights struggle, 148
Flynn, Meagan, on Kobe Bryant and his family, 254–55
"Football in our Colleges," (Archer), 34
"Football in Southern Negro Colleges," (Watson), 34
Foreman, George, and anti-protest display, 216
Forty Million Dollar Slaves (Rhoden), 100
Foudy, Julie, 248
Franke, Nikki, 204
Franklin, John Hope, advice regarding Arthur Ashe's book project, 192
Franklin, V. P., 192
Franklin Field, 159
Frazier, C. R., 34
Frazier, E. Franklin, 20
Freedberg, David, 164
Freeman, Ron, 160–61
Frey, Darcy, 95
From Slavery to Freedom (Franklin), 192

Game On: The All-American Race to Make Champions of Our Children (Farry), 249
Gans, Joe, 193
Garner, Eric, 176
Garnett, Kevin, 239, 255
Gates Jr., Henry Louis, 97–98, 191–92; reaction to Ashe's book, 193
Gates, William, 96
Gatewood, Willard B., 71
Gautt, Prentice, 199
"Gender and Racial Analysis in Sport: Are All the Women White and All The Blacks Men," (Bruening), 269
George, Nelson, 203
Getting Started in Tennis (Ashe with Robinson), 186

Gewecki, Clifford George, 199
Gibbs, Theatrece, 88
Gibson, Althea, 204
Glaude Jr., Eddie S., 280
Glory Bound: Black Athletes in a White America (Wiggins), ix, 1–2, 266–67
Glover, Ronald, 219
Glover, Ruth, 45
Gold and Glory Sweepstakes, 78
Golden Gloves Boxing Tournament, 50
Goldstein, Warren, and praise for *A Hard Road to Glory*, 187
Gomez, Lefty, 132
Gonder, Jesse, 130, 142
Gorn, Elliott J., and praise for *A Hard Road to Glory*, 187
Goudsouzian, Aram, 135
Go Up for Glory (Russell), 147
Grange, Red, 62
Granity Studios, 244–47
Graves, Earl, 97
Graves Jr., Lem, 47
Great Depression, 16, 41
Greatest: My Own Story (Ali), 173
"Great Speed but Limited Stamina: The Historical Debate Over Black Athletic Superiority," (Wiggins), 271
Green, Elijah "Pumpsie," 132
Gregory, Dick, and proposed Olympic boycott, 213
Gretzky, Wayne, 248
Grier, Rosey, 113
Grimke, Frances, 74
Grundy, Pamela, 89

Hafey, Chick, 132–33
Hail to the Victors! Black Athletes at the University of Michigan (Behee), 191
Halas, George, 114
Halberstam, David, review of *A Hard Road to Glory*, 198
Hampton Institute, and creation of the

Colored Intercollegiate Athletic Association, 34–35, and intercollegiate athletics, 14–15, and physical education programs, 11–14
Hampton Institute Alumni Association, 25
Hampton Institute Creative Dance Group, 7, 15, 17–19
Hampton Singers, 17
Hansen, Ron, 132
Hard Road to Glory, A (Ashe), 186–204
Hargrave, H. P., 34
Harlem Globetrotters, 37
Harless, Paul, 143
Harper, Tommy, and civil rights struggle, 148
Harris, Abram L., 274
Harris, Charles F., 189–90, 194
Harris, Francis, 190
Hart, Eddie, 168, 171
Hartmann, Douglas, 100, 169, 173, 228
Harvard Summer School of Physical Education, 10–11
Hattery, Angela, 99
Hawk, Tony, 248
Hayes, Wendell, 143
Heilmann, Harry, 132
Hellebrandt, Frances A., 12
Helsinki Olympic Games, 107, 110, 112, 171
Henderson, Edwin Bancroft, 192, 201, 274, and founding of the Interscholastic Athletic Association and Public Schools Athletic League, 90; and Uline Arena Controversy, 50; and *The Negro in Sports*, 23, 38, 40
Henderson, Ricky, 132
Hetherington, Clark, 13
High school sports, and Brown vs Board of Education of Topeka, 85–101
Hill, Herman, 51–52
Hill, Talmadge, 45–46

Hines, Jim, 143
Historically Black Colleges and Universities (HBCUs), 3, and Colored Intercollegiate Athletic Association, 15–19, 33–53, 273; and Howard and Lincoln Thanksgiving Day football games, 59–78; and life and career of Charles H. Williams, 7–27
"History of the African American Athlete," 203
Hoberman, John, *Darwin's Athletes: How Sport Has Damaged Black America and Preserved the Myth of Race*, ix, 1–2; and "sports fixation," 278
Holloway, Lin, 49
"Hoop Dreams," 96
Hoover Junior High School, 133–34
Howard, Oliver Otis, 68
Howard, Rodney, 190, 192
Howard and Lincoln Thanksgiving Day football games, 42–43, 59–78
Howard University Press, 189, 194
"How Can Schools Co-Operate with Officials to Develop Greater Efficiency" (Henderson), 38
Hudson Valley Tennis Club, 195
Hughes, Langston, 74, 199, 218
Hult, Joan, 269
Hundley, Victor, 93
Hungary and Soviet Union Water Polo Match, 116
Hunter, Harold, 50
Hyman, Flo, 204

I Have Changed (Owens with Neimark), 173
I Never Had it Made (Robinson with Duckett), 173
Institute for Diversity and Ethics in Sport, 226
Intercollegiate Tennis Association Hall of Fame, 186

International Journal of the History of Sport, The, 2, 196
International Olympic Committee (IOC), 158, 160, 170–71, 178
International Red Cross, 186
International Swimming Hall of Fame, 116
International Tennis Hall of Fame, 186
Interscholastic Athletic Association (ISAA), 90
Interscholastic Athletic Association Basketball Tournament, 78
Ionescu, Sabrina, 252

Jackson, Nell, 45
Jackson, Samuel L., 202
Jacob's Pillow, 18
James, C. L. R., x
James E. Sullivan Award, 112–13
James, Larry, 160–61
James, LeBron, 176, 279
James, Steve, 96
Jamison, Sandra, 190, 192
Jefferson, Harry, 45–46
Jeffries, Junius L., 39–40
Jenner, Bruce, 108
Jesse Owens: An American Life (Baker), 197
Jesse Owens: A Spiritual Autobiography (Owens with Neimark), 173
Jesse Owens Story, The (Owens with Neimark), 173
Jim Crow, 26, 51, 86
Joe Gans Story, The (Chalk), 193
Joe Louis: My Life (Louis), 173
John Carlos Story: The Sports Moment that Changed the World (Carlos with Zirin), 174–75
Johnson, Corey, 95
Johnson, Cornelius, 22
Johnson, Dave, 111
Johnson, George, 34

Johnson, James Weldon, 72, 201, 218, 274
Johnson, Jay, 228
Johnson, John Henry, 142
Johnson, Magic, 176, 239
Johnson, Mordecai, 63, 68, 75
Johnson, Rafer, and connection to Milt Campbell, 107–8, 112–13, 117–19; and opposition to Olympic boycott, 213
Jones, James Earl, 212
Jones, Wally, and *Black Champions Challenge American Sports*, 188
Jones, William H., 72
Jordan, Michael, 239, 279
Journal for the Study of Sports and Athletes in Education, 227, 229–30
Journal of American History, 197
Journal of African American History, The, 2
Journal of Negro History, The, 196–97
Journal of Southern History, 197
Journal of Sport and Social Issues, 217
Journal of Sport History, 2, 194, 196, 271
Journal of Urban History, 197
Journey of the African American Athlete, 202–3
Joyner, Florence Griffith, ix
Joyner-Kersee, Jackie, ix
Juvenile Delinquency, and emphasis on rational recreation, 21; and importance of baseball, 21

Kaepernick, Colin, and link to Tommie Smith and John Carlos, 177–78
Keane, Henry Arthur, 92
Kelly, Jack, 170
Kennedy, John F., 53, 93
Kerkorian, Kirk, 264
Kersee, Jackie Joyner, 248
Kershaw, Clayton, 248
Kill Bill: Vol 2, and inspiration for Kobe Bryant persona, 241
King, Leamon, 120
King, Martin Luther, 101, 214

King, Richard C., 228
King Football (Oriard), 70
Kiphuth, Robert J. J., 204
Kiphuth Fellowship Public Lecture, 204
Knight, Phil, 171
Kobe and Vanessa Bryant Family Foundation, 243
Kobe Bryant's Muse, 245
Kobe China Fund, 243
"Kobe's Bookshelf," 244
Korbut, Olga, 168
Kress, Red, 133

Lacy, Sam, 48, 203
LA 84 Foundation, 100
Lake Placid Winter Olympics, 165
Lapchick, Richard, 226
"last hook and handle" (Edwards), 224–25, 275–76
Last Shot: City Streets, Basketball Dreams, The (Frey), 95–96
Lavagetto, Cookie, 132
Lawrence, J. H., 38
Lawson, Earl, 149
League of American Wheelman, 192
Learning How to Win (Grundy), 89
Lee, Sammy, 111
Lees, Tom, 199
"Legacies of Harry Edwards for Sport Sociology, The," 227–38
Leonard, David J., 228
Lewis, Charles A., 66
Lewis, William Henry, 72
Liberti, Rita, 269
Lincoln University, and Thanksgiving Day football games against Howard University, 59–78
Lipsyte, Robert, 225
Liston, Sonny, 121
Little League Baseball, 136
Littleton, Cynthia, on Kobe Bryant's death, 237

Litwack, Leon, 192
Lloyd, Earl, and West Coast basketball tour, 50–52
Lloyd, Jewell, 252
Logan, Rayford, 20
Lomax, Louis, as Harry Edward's inspiration, 218–19, 229
Lomax, Michael, 228
Lombardi, Ernie, 132–33
London Olympic Games, 110
Longman, Jere, 177–78
Lopiano, Donna, 95
Los Angeles Olympic Committee, 119
Los Angeles Olympic Games, 113, 118–19, 165, 174
Louis, Joe, 274
Loy, John, 220
Luffmann, Helen, 12
Lunceford, Jimmie, 47
LuValle, Jimmy, 22, 86–87

Maclean, Malcolm, 15
Madison Square Garden, 51, 109
Major League Baseball, 99, 212, 273; and hiring of Harry Edwards, 225–26; and Bay Area players, 132; and players developed by George Powles, 129–30, 134, 137–40, 142, 150
Major Taylor: The Extraordinary Career of a Champion Bicycle Racer (Ritchie), 197
Malcolm X, 101, 229
Mamba Mentality: How I Play, The (Bryant), 256
Mamba Sports Academy (Sports Academy following Bryant's death), 250–52
Mamba Sports Foundation (eventually Mamma & Mambacita Sports Foundation), 250–52
Manley, Dexter, 99
Marshall, Ernest, 34, 40

Martin, Billy, 132
Martin, Charles, 201–2
Martin, Trayvon, 176
Mastering Your Tennis Strokes (Ashe with Sheehan), 186
Masucci, Matthew A., 228
Mathias, Bob, and competition and comparisons to Milt Campbell, 108, 110–12, 117
Matthews, Clarence, 61, 64
Matthews, Ralph, 64
Matthews, Vince, disillusionment with amateur sport, 170–72; high school and college career, 159; medal stand disruption, 162–66; and *My Race Be Won*, 172–73, 178
Mattick, Bobby, 140
May, Rudy, 132
Maynor, Dorothy, 25
Mays, Willie, 121
McClane, Charles, P., 62
McCloud, Derilene, 190
McClymonds High School, 130, 134–36, 141–46, 148–49
McCormick, Pat, 111–12
McDonald's, and Kobe Bryant's sexual assault charges, 240–41
McKensie, R. Tait, 13
McKissick, Floyd, 214
McLendon, John B., and Colored Intercollegiate Athletic Association Basketball tournament, 45–47, 53
Meggyesy, Dave, 225
Melbourne Olympic Games, 107–8, 111–13, 115–16, 121, 144
Memorial Coliseum, 113, 118
Messi, Lionel, 240
Metcalfe, Ralph, 22
Metcalfe, Tristram Walker, 45
Mexico City Olympic Games, , 118–19, 143, 159–62, 166, 169, 171, 173, 177, 187, 214–17, 228, 265

Miller, Margery, 107, 116
Miller, Patrick B, 201–2
Miller, Robert, 36, 62
Mills, Nicolas, review of *A Hard Road to Glory*, 198
"misperformances," and the Vince Matthews and Wayne Collett medal stand disruption, 164–66
Moonfixer: The Basketball Journey of Earl Lloyd (Lloyd), 51
Moore, Archie, 47
Moore, Joseph, 197
Moore, Kenny, reaction to Vince Matthews and Wayne Collett medal stand disruption, 167–68
Moore, Louis, 176–77
Moorland-Spingarn Research Center, 189
Morgan, Joe, and praise for George Powles, 147
Moscow Olympic Games, 119
Moseby, Lloyd, 132
Motton, Curt, 140
M Street School, 89–90
Mulkey, Kim, 255
"Munich Massacre," 168–69
Munich Olympic Games, and the Vince Matthews and Wayne Collett medal stand disruption, 157–79
Murchison, Ira, 121
Murphy, Isaac, 214
Murray, Jim, 111, 117, 130, 168–69
"muscular assimilationism," (Miller), 201
Muscular Christianity, 10
My Race Be Won (Matthews), 156, 170, 172–73, 178
Myslenski, Skip, and review of *A Hard Road to Glory*, 198

Nathan, Dan, on Negro League Baseball, 227
Nathan, Harriett, 222

INDEX 293

Nation, The, 198
National Association for the Advancement of Colored People (NAACP), and Howard and Lincoln Thanksgiving Day football games, 72; reaction to Vince Matthews and Wayne Collett medal stand disruption, 167
National Association of College Women (NACW), 44
National Basketball Association (NBA), 50, 94, 143–44, 176, 216, 225; and Kobe Bryant, 237–57
National Collegiate Athletic Association (NCAA), 33, 36, 94, 99, 111, 113, 144, 158, 161, 176, 185, 200, 223, 226
National Fitness Foundation, 111
National Football League (NFL), 51, 114, 200, 225, 264
National High School Athletic Association (NHSAA), 92
National Interscholastic Basketball Tournament (NIBT), 15, 91–92, 100
National Invitational Intercollegiate Basketball Tournament (NIIBT), 46
National Invitation Tournament (NIT), 45
National League Park, 61, 68
National Museum of African American History and Culture, X, 174, 240, 268
National Negro Bowling Association, 78
National Skeet Shooting Association, 192
National Tennis Central, 186
National Track and Field Hall of Fame, 116, 159
National Training School for Women and Girls, 89
NCAA Scholarly Colloquium, 226
Necessities: Racial Barriers in American Sports (Hoose), 198
"Negro Athletes in the Eleventh Olympiad," (Williams), 22
Negro Firsts in Sports (Young), 188

Negro in Sports, The (Henderson), 23, 187–88, 192
Negro League Baseball, 1–2, 23, 53, 194
Negro Soldiers in WWI: The Human Side (Williams), 19–20
New Jersey Hall of Fame, 116
New Jersey Sportswriters Association, 116
New Jersey State Interscholastic Athletic Association Hall of Fame, 115–16
New Negro on Campus: Black College Rebellions of the 1920s, The (Wolters), 74
New York Athletic Club, and boycott of 50th Anniversary track meet, 113, 160, 215–17
New York Pioneer Club, 159
Nicholson, David, and review of *A Hard Road to Glory*, 198
Nike, 171; and Kobe Bryant endorsement, 240; and Kobe Bryant sexual assault charges, 240–41
Nixon, Richard, and praise for George Powles, 146
Noah, Yannick, 185
Noble, John Wesley, 137, 141
"No Final Victories: Forty Years on the Frontlines of race, sport, and culture: An Interview with Scholar/Activist Dr. Harry Edwards"(Johnson and Masucci), 228
Norman, Peter, 174
North American Society for Sport History (NASSH), X
Northern Migration, and creation of separate Black public schools, 89; and impact on social changes in the Black community, 60; and influence on sport in West Oakland, 134–35
Norton, Ray, 143
Not the Triumph but the Struggle: The 1968 Olympics and the Making of the Black Athlete (Bass), 187

Oakland Athletic League (OAL), 141, 143
Oakland Babe Ruth Baseball Team, 139
Obama, Barack, 147
Oberlin College, 9
Oberteuffer, Delbert, assessment of Jesse Owens treatment by Ohio State, 87
O'Brien, Dan, and appreciation for Milt Campbell, 123
O'Doul, Lefty, 132
Official Book of Running, The (Gewecki and Emmerton), 199
Off the Court (Ashe with Amdur), 186, 199
"Ole Master: The Joe Gans Story," (Chalk), 193
Olsen, Jack, and *The Black Athlete: A Shameful Story*, 188
Olsen, Lyle, 265
Olympic Project for Human Rights (OPHR), 118, 159–61, boycott of New York Athletic Club track meet, 215; connection to Vince Matthews and Wayne Collett medal stand disruption, 166; founding of, 213–14; lasting influence, 216–17; and protests at Mexico City Olympic Games, 216–17
Olympism, and Vince Matthews and Wayne Collett medal stand disruption, 165–66
O'Neal, Shaquille, 176
O'Ree, Willie, 204
Oriard, Michael, 200
Oscard, Fifi, 189
Outdoor Track and Field Championships, 161
Overemphasis on sport, 94–100, 223–25, 275–77
Owens, Jesse, 22, 43, 86–87, 173, 204; opposition to Mexico City Black athlete's boycott, 214–15; response to Vince Matthews and Wayne Collett medal stand disruption, 162–63

Patten, Gilbert, and Frank Merriwell Stories, 247
Patterson, Floyd, 121
Paul, Chris, 176
Paul, Gabe, 140
Pauling, Linus, 87
Penn Relays, 159
Perrin, H. C., 40
Pettis, Gary, 132
Pettit, Bob, 199
Petty, Christine, 45
Physical Education, at Hampton Institute, 9–14
Pickett, Tidye, 88
Pierce, J. W., 34
Pinson, Vada, and praise for George Powles, 129, 139
Pioneers of Black Sport: The Early Days of the Black Professional Athlete in Baseball, Basketball, Boxing, and Football (Chalk), 190
Plum, Nancy, 115
Pointer, Aaron, 130, 142
Pollard, Fritz, 61, 86–89
Pollard Jr., Fritz, 22
Porter, J. W., 137
Povich, Shirley, reaction to Vince Matthews and Wayne Collett medal stand disruption, 166
Powles, George, birth and early life, 132–33; connection to Bobby Mattick, 140; mentorship of Bill Russell, 144; mentorship of Curt Flood, 142; mentorship of Frank Robinson, 139; support of Black athletes and civil rights, 147–49; teaching and coaching career at McClymonds High School, 134–36, 141–45; teaching and coaching career at Skyline High School, 145–47; World War II experiences, 133–34; as youth sport coach, 136–40
Powles, Winifred, 133

Presidential Medal of Freedom, 147–48, 187
Pride Against Prejudice: The Biography of Larry Doby (Moore), 197
Professional Bowlers Association, 192
Project Play Conference, 248
Proposition 16, 223
Proposition 42, 223
Psychology Today, 217
Public School Athletic League (PSAL), 90, 159
Pujols, Albert, 248
Punies, The, 246–47

"rabbles," 69–71
Race, Culture, and the Revolt of the Black Athlete (Hartmann), 169, 228
"A Race to Succeed: The Trials and Dreams of America's Black Athletes" (Myslenski), 198
Racialist Thinking, 144–45, 167, 264–65
Racial Uplift, and Arthur Ashe, 201–4; and basketball, 90–91; and Colored Intercollegiate Athletic Association, 35, 39–40; espoused by Charles H. Williams, 3, 21–22; and George Powles, 131, 144–45; Gerald Early and other Black intellectuals, 273–74
Ramanathan, Lavanya, 278
Rampersad, Arnold, *Jackie Robinson: A Biography*, ix, 1–2; and *Days of Grace: A Memoir*, 199–200
Reagan, Ronald, 212
Recreation and Amusement Among Negroes in Washington, D.C.: A Sociological Analysis of the Negro in an Urban Environment (Jones), 72
"Recreation in the Lives of Young People," (Williams), 21
Remember the Titans, 93
(Re)Presenting Wilma Rudolph (Liberti and Smith), 269

"Revisiting The Revolt of the Black Athlete: Dr. Harry Edwards and the Making of (the new) African American Sport Studies: (Lomax), 229
"Revolting Black Athletes: Sport, New Racism, and the Politics of Dis/Identification," (Leonard and King), 228
Revolt of the Black Athlete, The (Edwards), 175, 177, 218
Rhoden, William (Bill), 100, 202, 204
Richards, Bob, 110
Riess, Steven, 94
"Right Kind of Excellence, The" (Graves), 97
Rigney, Bill, 132
Rise of Sports in New Orleans, The (Somers), 200
Ritual Gone Wrong: What We Learn from Ritual Disruption (McClymonds), 164–66
Rivero, Manny, 48
Robert Miller Incident, 36
Roberts, Randy, 203
Robertson, William W., 115
Robeson, Paul, 47, 61, 64, 86–87, 89, 204; as Harry Edward's inspiration, 218–19, 229
Robinson, Frank, 137–38, 141–42; and civil rights struggle,148; and praise for George Powles, 129, 138
Robinson, Jackie, ix, 86, 89, 93, 99, 173, 199, 204, 275, 279
Robinson, Mack, 22
Robinson, Rey, 168, 171
Robinson, Sugar Ray, 121, 204
Rogers, William H., 38, 40
Rollins, Jimmy, 132, 140
Rome Olympic Games, 113, 118, 213
Rose Bowl, 253
Ross, Kevin, 99
Ruck, Rob, 2, 197
Rudolph, Wilma, 118

Rule 50 of the Olympic Charter, 178
Rusch, Linda, 115, 122
Russell, Bill, 121, 135; and civil rights struggle, 147; and praise for George Powles, 129, 144–45
Rust, Edna, and *Art Rust's Illustrated History of the Black Athlete*, 188
Rust Jr., Art, and *Art Rust's Illustrated History of the Black Athlete*, 188

Sailes, Gary, reaction to *A Hard Road to Glory*, 197–99
Sammons, Jeffrey, and praise for *A Hard Road to Glory*, 187, 197, 271
Samuelson, Katie Lou, 252
Sandlot Seasons: Sport in Black Pittsburgh (Ruck), 197
Sang, Julius, 162
San Quentin State Prison, 52
Saroyan, William, 264
Schaap, Dick, 203
Schmidt, Ray, 71
"School of Champions," 141
Scott, Emmett, J., 63, 65–67
Scott, Jack, 225
Scripps National Spelling Bee, 277–78
Seaver, Tom, 264
Second Wind: The Memoirs of an Opinionated Man (Russell with Branch), 147, 173
Segal, Erich, reaction to the Vince Matthews and Wayne Collett medal stand disruption, 166–67
Selig, Bud, 226
"Send your Children to the Libraries," (Ashe), 97, 186, 204
Shadow League, The, 252
Shawn, Ted, 17–18
Shelbourne, John, 64
Shipp, Tchaka, 95–96
Shorter, Frank, 168
Sidelights on Negro Soldiers (Williams), 19
Sifford, Charles, 204
Silas, Paul, 143
Silent Gesture: The Autobiography of Tommie Smith (Smith with Steele), 174
"Single-Minded Pursuit of Sports, Fame, and Fortune Is Approaching an Institutionalized Triple Tragedy in Black Society, The" (Edwards), 223
Singleton, George C., 40, 42
Skyline High School, 130, 145–47
Slave Testimony (Blassingame), 192
Slowe, Lucy Diggs, 44
Smith, Doug, 190
Smith, Earl, 95, 99; and praise for *A Hard Road to Glory*, 187
Smith, John, 161–62
Smith, Maureen, 227, 269
Smith, Red, reaction to Vince Matthews and Wayne Collett medal stand disruption, 166
Smith, Tommie, 118; and Mexico City Olympic protest, 160–161, 166, 173–74, 216; serving as an inspiration to Kaepernick, 177–78
Smith, Wendell, 1
Snyder, Brad, 137
Sociology of Sport (Edwards), 217, 219
Sociology of Sport Journal, 196–97
Sokolove, Michael, 95
"Someday, the Spelling Bee Winners May Wish They Had Just Played Football, (Ramanathan), 278
Somers, Dale, 200
Soong Ching Ling Foundation, 243
Souls of Black Folk, The (DuBois), 228
South Africa, 160, 185, 200, 214
South Atlantic Intercollegiate Athletic Association (SAIAA), 36
Southeastern Intercollegiate Athletic Conference (SIAC), 36
Southern Athletic Conference (SAC), 43
Southern Intercollegiate Athletic Conference (SIAC), 43, 46
Southern Workman, 20–22

INDEX 297

Southwestern Athletic Conference (SAC), 36
Spectacular Leap, A (Lansbury), 269
Spier, Chris, 132
Spitz, Mark, 168
Sport Magazine, 107
Sport, Race, Activism, and Social Change: The Impact of Dr. Harry Edwards' Scholarship and Service (Polite and Hawkins), 227, 229
Sports and Society (Coakley), 94–95
"sports fixation," (Hoberman), 278
Sports Illustrated, 149, 163, 187
Sports Illustrated Sportsman of the Year Award, 113, 129, 163, 187
Sports & Society: A Program of the Aspen Institute, 248–49
Sportswriters Hall of Fame, 199
Staley, Seward C., 12
Stanfield, Andy, 120
Stargell, Willie, 132, 140
Statue of Liberty, 225
St. Denis, Ruth, 17
Steele, David, and *Silent Gesture: The Autobiography of Tommie Smith*, 174
Stephens, Sloane, 248
Sterling, Alton, 176
Sterling, Donald, 175–76
Stewart, David, 132
Stokes, Louise, 88
Strange Career of Jim Crow, The (Woodward), 198
Strange Career of the Black Athlete: African Americans and Sport, The (Wigginton), 202
Strawberry, Darryl, 95
Street Soccer USA, 276
Strode, Woody, 51, 86
Struggle That Must Be: An Autobiography, The (Edwards), 217–19
Summitt, Pat, 255
Swann vs. Charlotte-Mecklenburg Board of Education, 93

"Taking Sports Seriously," (Gorn and Oriard), 220
Tarantino, Quentin, 241
Tarkanian, Jerry, 264
Tasby, Willie, 130, 142
Taurasi, Diane, and respect for Kobe Bryant, 252
Taylor, James T., 41
Taylor, Marshall "Major," 200
Terrell, Mary Church, 44
Thomas, Damion L., 120, 268
Thomas, Russell, 96
Thomas Hughes's *Tom Brown's School Days*, 246–47
Thompson, John, 223
Thorpe, Otis E., 39
Ticket Out, The (Sokolove), 95
Title IX, 200
"To Bring the Race Along Rapidly: Sport, Student Culture, and Educational Mission at Historically Black Colleges During the Interwar Years" (Miller), 70
Tokyo Olympic Games, 178, 213
Toomey, Bill, 108, 111
tramp athletes, 35, 62
"Transformational Developments at the Interface of Race, Sport, and the Collegiate Athletic Arms Race in the Age of Globalization" (Edwards), 227
True Reformers Hall, 90
Turkish Airlines, and Kobe Bryant Controversy, 240
Turner's Arena, and Central Intercollegiate Athletic Association Basketball Tournament, 47–49
Tygiel, Jules, 197

Ueberroth, Peter, 119, 225
Uline, Michael, 49
Uline Arena, and Central Intercollegiate Athletic Association Basketball Tournament, 49–52

Unger, Norman O., reaction to Vince Matthews and Wayne Collett medal stand disruption, 167
United Black Students for Action, 212
United States National Track and Field Hall of Fame, 174
United States Navy, 111
United States Olympic Committee (IOC), 160, 162–63, 170
United States Olympic Hall of Fame (USOHOF), 108
United States Olympic Training Center, 111
United States Table Tennis Association, 192
United States Tennis Association (USTA) National Tennis Center, 186
"University History Series," 222
University of Indiana Hall of Fame, 115
Unlevel Playing Field: A Documentary History of the African American Experience in Sport, The (Wiggins and Miller), 202, 269
US Figure Skating Association, 192
US Olympic and Paralympic Hall of Fame, 174
US-USSR Track Meet, 113, 117
US Volleyball Association, 192

Vaughn, Phil, 2
Verbrugge, Martha, 12
Verschoth, Anita, 163
"views of Sport: Taking the Hard Road With Black Athletes," (Ashe), 195
Virginia Sports Hall of Fame, 27, 186
Vukovich, Bill, 264

Wade, Dwayne, 176
Walker, Leroy, T., 53, 159
Walsh, Frank, 51
War Memorial Coliseum, 52
Washington, Allen, 34
Washington, Booker T., 66, 101, 229

Washington, Jim, and *Black Champions Challenge American Sports*, 188
Washington, Kenny, 51, 86
Watson, John Brown, 34
Watson, Louis L., 38
Way It Is, The (Flood with Carter), 173
Wesley, Charles H., 274
West, Charles, 64
West Coast Basketball Tour, 50–52
West Virginia Athletic Union (WVAU), 90; and basketball tournament, 91, 100
West Virginia State, and West Coast basketball tour, 50–52
White, Walter, 72
Whitehead, J. L., 37
Whitfield, Mal, 120; and proposed Olympic boycott, 213–14
Williams, Archie, 22, 86
Williams, Charles H., 3, 7–8; and Bay Shore resort, 26–27; and Colored Intercollegiate Athletic Association, 15–17, 34, 41; early life and college career, 8–11; and Edwin Bancroft Henderson, 23; and Hampton Institute Creative Dance Group, 17–18; and National Interscholastic Basketball Tournament, 91; and physical education at Hampton Institute, 11–15; and racial uplift, 21–24; and writing life, 19–24
Williams Cup, 44
Williams, Gabby, 252
Williams, Nate, 143
Willis, Dontrelle, 132
Winfield, Dave, 264
Winter, Lloyd "Bud," 143
Wolters, Raymond, 74
Women's National Basketball Association (WNBA), 253–55
Women's Sports Foundation, 95
Wooden, John, ix
Woodruff, John, 22
Woods, Bob, 143–44
Woods, Tiger, 240, 279

Woodson, Carter G., 75, 272–74
Woodward, C. Vann, 198
Work, Monroe, 20
World Health Organization of the United Nations, 186
World Professional Basketball Tournament, 47
World War I, 8–9, 16, 19–20, 41
World War II, 8, 16, 19, 41–42; and impact on George Powles, 133–34, 136, 146, 170
Wottle, Dave, 167, 175
Wright, Richard, 196, 201, 218
Wright, Stan, 168, 171

Yang, C. K., and competition with Rafer Johnson, 113, 118

Yanger, Milton, reaction to *A Hard Road to Glory*, 197
YMCA Training School, 10–11, 18
Young, A. S. "Doc," and *Negro Firsts in Sports*, 188; reaction to the Vince Matthews and Wayne Collett medal stand disruption, 166
Young, Charles, 264
Young, Frank, 59–60, 73, 76
Youth Sport, and George Powles, 131–32, 135–40, 150; and Kobe Bryant, 248–52

Zevon, Warren, 264
Zimmerman, Paul, 110
Zirin, Dave, and *The John Carlos Story*, 174–75

The University of Tennessee Press
is a founding member of the
Association of University Presses.

Composed in 10.5/13 FreightText Pro
with FreightSans Pro display
by Kelly Gray
at the University of Tennessee Press
Designed by Kelly Gray

Freight by Joshua Darden is a collection
of intertwined typeface families
inspired by the warmth and pragmatism
of eighteenth-century Dutch typefaces.

University of Tennessee Press
1015 Volunteer Blvd
Hodges Library 323
Knoxville, TN 37996-1000
www.utpress.org

www.ingramcontent.com/pod-product-compliance
Lightning Source LLC
Chambersburg PA
CBHW070128080526
44586CB00015B/1608